Marxism and the
Call of the Future

Series: Creative Marxism
Series Editor: Bill Martin

VOLUME 1
Ethical Marxism: The Categorical Imperative of Liberation
by Bill Martin

VOLUME 2
Marxism and the Call of the Future: Conversations on Ethics, History, and Politics
by Bob Avakian and Bill Martin

SELECTED WORKS BY BOB AVAKIAN
Mao Tsetung's Immortal Contributions
Conquer the World? The International Proletariat Must and Will
For a Harvest of Dragons: On the "Crisis of Marxism" and the Power of Marxism, Now More Than Ever
Democracy: Can't We Do Better Than That?
The End of a Stage—The Beginning of a New Stage
Phony Communism Is Dead . . . Long Live Real Communism!
Preaching from a Pulpit of Bones: We Need Morality But Not Traditional Morality
Grasp Revolution, Promote Production—Questions of Outlook and Method, Some Points on the New Situation
Revolution: Why It's Necessary, Why It's Possible, What It's All About (video/DVD)
Dictatorship and Democracy, and the Socialist Transition to Communism
From Ike to Mao and Beyond: My Journey from Mainstream America to Revoluionary Communist

OTHER WORKS BY BILL MARTIN
Matrix and line: Derrida and the possibilities of postmodern social theory
Politics in the impasse: Explorations in postsecular social theory
Humanism and its aftermath: The shared fate of deconstruction and politics
The radical project: Sartrean investigations
Music of Yes: Structure and vision in progressive rock
Listening to the future: The time of progressive rock, 1968–1978
Avant rock: Experimental music from the Beatles to Bjork

Marxism and the Call of the Future

Conversations on Ethics, History, and Politics

BOB AVAKIAN *and* BILL MARTIN

Foreword by Slavoj Žižek
Preface by Raymond Lotta

*For Eleanor,
with warm feelings,
admiration, and*

love

*Billness xoxox
Salina, Kansas 4.24.05*

OPEN COURT
Chicago and La Salle, Illinois

Volume 2 in the series Creative Marxism

Front cover image: *Suprematist Composition No. 56*, 1916, by Kazimir
Malevich / State Russian Museum, St. Petersburg, Russia / Bridgeman
Art Library

**To order books from Open Court, call toll-free 1-800-815-2280,
or visit www.opencourtbooks.com**.

Open Court Publishing Company is a division of Carus Publishing
Company.

Copyright ©2005 by Carus Publishing Company

First printing 2005

Printed and bound in the United States of America

Library of Congress Cataloging-in-Publication Data

Avakian, Bob.
  Marxism and the call of the future : conversations on ethics,
history, and politics / Bob Avakian and Bill Martin ; foreword by
Slavoj Žižek; preface by Raymond Lotta.
    p. cm. — (Creative Marxism ; v. 2)
  Includes bibliographical references and index.
  ISBN-13: 978-0-8126-9579-3 (isbn 13/trade paper : alk. paper)
  ISBN-10: 0-8126-9579-8 (isbn 10/trade paper : alk. paper)
  1. Socialism. 2. Socialist ethics. 3. Revolutions. 4. History. I.
Martin, Bill, 1956- II.   Title. III. Series.
  HX73.A88 2005
  335.4—dc22

                                                  2004030777

Contents

Foreword: On Eggs and Omelets

Why is the present volume so important that it should stand on the shelf of everyone who cares about the destiny of the political Left? There are three negations of politics proper in today's Left, which follow the different modes of negation in psychoanalysis: the postpolitical pragmatic "Third Way" ("we are entering a new global society, old ideological notions of class struggle etcetera are no longer operative here"); the "principled opportunism" of the old Left (sticking to the old formulas as if nothing changed); the ludic "resistances" of the postmodern Left (the verbal radicalism with its excessive activity making it sure that nothing will really change)—three ways to avoid the Real of today's antagonisms. The present book marks the beginning of a new approach—of ruthlessly confronting these three false ways and engaging in a patient work of the theoretical and political renewal.

How are we to proceed on this path? Recall the old story about a worker suspected of stealing: every evening, when he was leaving the factory, the wheelbarrow he was rolling in front of him was carefully inspected, but the guards could not find anything, it was always empty—till, finally, they got the point: what the worker was stealing were the wheelbarrows themselves. This is the trick that those who claim today "But the world is nonetheless better off without Saddam!" try to pull on us: they forget to include in the account the effects of the very military intervention against Saddam. Yes, the world is better without Saddam—but it is not better with the military occupation of Iraq, with the new rise of the Islamic fundamentalism provoked by this occupation. The irony is thus that the U.S. themselves are paying the price for their trick. Back in 1979, in her essay "Dictators and Double Standards," published in *Commentary*, Jeanne Kirkpatrick elaborated the distinction between "authoritarian" and "totalitarian" regimes, which served as the justification of the U.S. policy of collaborating with Rightist dictators, while treating much harsher Communist regimes: authoritarian dictators are pragmatic rulers who care about their power and wealth and are indifferent towards ideological issues, even if they pay lip service to some big cause; in contrast to them, totalitarian leaders are selfless fanatics who believe in their ideology and are ready to put at stake everything for their ideals. So while one can deal with authoritarian rulers who react rationally and predictably to material and military threats, totalitarian leaders are much more dangerous and have to be directly confronted. This distinction encapsulates perfectly what went wrong with the U.S. occupation of Iraq: Saddam was a corrupted authoritarian dictator striving for power and guided by brutal pragmatic considerations (which led him to collaborate with the U.S. throughout the 1980s), and the main outcome of the U.S. intervention is that it generated a much more uncompromising "fundamentalist" opposition which precludes any pragmatic compromises.

And we should not be afraid to draw the same consequence apropos democracy itself: to look for the wheelbarrow itself which is stolen from the people when they are bombarded by the claims that "things are nonetheless better in democracy." The first thing to note here is that the certainty that democracy is "inessential," that it makes the destiny of a nation dependent on a whim of the minority which can shift the vote, and the corresponding conviction of a political agent that its mission is grounded in an insight into the true state of things, etcetera, are not false "naturalizations" which disavow the authentic democratic openness, claiming for themselves a privileged position, and thus posing a potential threat to democracy; they are rather the necessary outcome and ingredient of the democratic logic itself. That is to say, such claim to a privileged insight, dismissive of the democratic rules of the game, is only possible *within* the democratic space— they are the content which necessarily supplements the democratic *form*, they are the "stuff" of democratic procedure.

Democracy presupposes a minimum of alienation: those who exert power can only be held responsible to the people if there is a minimal distance of representation between them and the people. In "totalitarianism," this distance is cancelled, the Leader is supposed to directly present the will of the people—and the result is, of course, that the (empirical) people are even more radically alienated in their Leader: he directly *is* what they "really are," their true identity, their true wishes and interests, as opposed to their confused "empirical" wishes and interests. In contrast to the authoritarian power alienated from its subjects, the people, here the "empirical" people are alienated from themselves.

In his (unpublished) *La logique des mondes*, Alain Badiou elaborated the eternal Idea of the politics of revolutionary justice at work from the ancient Chinese "legalists" through Jacobins to Lenin and Mao, which consists of four moments: voluntarism (the belief that one can "move mountains," ignoring "objective" laws and obstacles), terror (a ruthless will to crush the enemy of the people), egalitarian justice (its immediate brutal imposition, with no understanding for the "complex circumstances" which allegedly compel us to proceed gradually), and, last but not least, trust in the people—the catch, of course, resides in the ambiguity of this supplementary term, the "trust in people": are the people who are trusted the "empirical" individuals or *the* People, on behalf of whom one can turn the terror on behalf of the people against people's enemies into the terror against the people themselves?

This, of course, in no way implies a simple plea for democracy and rejection of "totalitarianism": there *is*, on the contrary, a moment of truth in "totalitarianism." Already Hegel pointed out how political representation does not mean that people already know in advance what they want and then charge their representatives with advocating their interests—they only know it "in itself," it is their representative who formulates their interests and goals for them, making them "for-itself." The "totalitarian" logic thus makes explicit, posits "as such," a split which always-already cuts from within the represented "people." The line of separation between the "totalitarian" leader and the analyst is thus thin, imperceptible almost: both are the objects of transferential love; the difference between them is the difference between the perverse social link and the discourse of the analyst who, while occupying this place of supposed knowledge, holds it *empty*.

One should not be afraid here to draw the radical conclusion concerning the figure of the leader: democracy as a rule cannot reach beyond the pragmatic utilitarian inertia, it cannot suspend the logic of "servicing the goods"; consequently, in the same way there is no self-analysis, since the analytic change can only occur through the transferential relationship to the external figure of the analyst, a leader is necessary to trigger the enthusiasm for a Cause, to bring about the radical change in the subjective position of his followers, to "transubstantiate" their identity.

There is a precise line of separation between a nonrevolutionary and a revolutionary situation. In a nonrevolutionary one, one can solve the pressing immediate problems while postponing the big key problem ("people are dying now in Rwanda, so forget about anti-imperialist struggle, let us just prevent the slaughter"; or, "one has to fight poverty and racism here and now, not waiting for the collapse of the global capitalist order"); in a revolutionary situation, this strategy no longer works and one has to tackle the Big Problem in order even to solve the small pressing ones.

This, however, does not mean that the notion of a proper revolutionary situation concerns only the difference between short-term and long-term goal—in every authentic revolutionary explosion, there is an element of "pure" violence, i.e., an authentic political revolution cannot be measured by the standard of servicing the goods (to what extent "life got better for the majority" afterwards)—it is a goal-in-itself, an act which changes the very standards of what "good life" is, and a different (higher, eventually) standard of living is a by-product of a revolutionary process, not its goal. Usually, revolutionary violence is defended by way of evoking proverb platitudes like "you cannot make an omelet without breaking some eggs"—a "wisdom" which, of course, can easily be rendered problematic through boring "ethical" considerations about how even the noblest goals cannot justify murderous means to achieve them. Against such compromising attitudes, one should directly admit revolutionary violence as a liberating end-in-itself, so that the proverb should rather be turned around: "You cannot break the eggs (and what is revolutionary politics if not an activity in the course of which many eggs are broken), especially if you are doing it in big heat (of a revolutionary passion), without making some omelets!"*

SLAVOJ ŽIŽEK

---

* [See the postscript on Slavoj Žižek's foreword at the end of the series editor's introduction.—Ed.]

Preface

The title of this book is a provocation and invitation: Marxism and the Call of the Future.*

After all, a pervasive political and ideological message of the contemporary social order is that "communism is dead," that a Marxism of revolution is dead. The two discussants of this volume have not gotten that memo. They reject the self-justifying claim that the possibility of radical change has been foreclosed by the supposed triumph of the market (and that you might as well embrace what embraces you). No, in this world at this time, Marxism, and critical emancipatory thought that dares to envision a different future, and the struggle to build a world beyond class divisions and all relations of oppression take on ever greater relevance and urgency.

This book invites the reader to partake of a remarkable exchange. Bill Martin is a radical intellectual and a professor of philosophy who in his work engages the question of the responsibility of philosophy to society and the struggle to change the world. Bob Avakian is a visionary leader of a Maoist vanguard party, the Revolutionary Communist Party, which has its sights on the revolutionary seizure of power and the radical transformation of society in the colossus that is late imperial America—all as part of a worldwide process of revolutionary struggle whose final aim is communism, a world without exploitative and oppressive relations and the corresponding political structures, institutions, ideas, and culture. The scope and relevance of Marxism, and the nature

---

* Raymond Lotta is a Maoist political economist whose books include *America in Decline* and *Maoist Economics and the Revolutionary Road to Communism*. He has lectured widely in the United States, as well as in the Philippines, India, and Mexico.

and reach of communist revolution, are at the heart of this rich and lively dialogue. And these core themes open into, and open up, a stimulating variety of questions and concerns.

Avakian and Martin probe a wide range of issues: the place of ethics in a transformative revolutionary politics; Kant, Rousseau, and Hegel; Marx and the question of colonialism and Eurocentrism; the Maoist experience in China; sustainable agricultural development in today's world and the task of overcoming the urban-rural divide under socialism; imperialism, lopsided development in the world, and the resulting effects on social structure and revolution; animal rights; secularism and religion; the post-911 agenda of the U.S. ruling class, the political-social-cultural landscape of the U.S., and the prospects for resistance and revolution; Marxism and the question of homosexuality; the challenges confronting radical and communist intellectuals and the possibilities for engaged, creative intellectual work today.

For both Avakian and Martin, these far-reaching issues and explorations are intimately connected with the need for, and potential of, the masses to remake the world.

The conversations that make up this book touch ground in diverse places and times, whether Rome and the rise of Christianity, or the sharecropping south of the United States, and take in such figures as Heidegger, Sartre, and Derrida, making contact along the way with Tecumseh, Bob Dylan, science fiction, and "The Simpsons."

Bob Avakian and Bill Martin have known each other through their writings. This was their first opportunity for a face-to-face dialogue. Both wanted a free-flowing exchange (there had been minimal correspondence in the weeks prior in order to identify a few key issues), and part of the process that unfolds is that perspectives get clarified, dissected, and challenged. They delineate common ground and stake out differences. But wherever the dialogue takes them, and it often goes in surprising directions, there is always an intense and respectful listening and openness to critical interrogation. The give and take of the dialogue yields up rich suggestions and provocative formulations and theorizations.

A major question running through this dialogue is the relationship between materialism and ethics. Can Kant's universal ethical standards (and the idea of treating people as a means and not as an end) apply in class society? Do such standards have any real content, or are they simply "empty formalism," as was said by Hegel and echoed by Marx and Engels? In some sense, Martin comes at the question from the standpoint of wondering about the status of the ethical in materialism, while Avakian raises the issue of the material status of ethical claims. It is a lively exchange.

A few words about the principals to this dialogue.

Bob Avakian is Chairman of the Revolutionary Communist Party (RCP). A veteran of the Free Speech Movement and the revolutionary upsurges of the 1960s and early 1970s, he worked closely with the Black Panther Party. By the mid-1970s, he emerged as the foremost Maoist revolutionary in the United States. He has guided the RCP since its formation in 1975 and is a major leader of the international communist movement. Over the last 25 years, Avakian has produced a highly significant body of work, and he approaches Marxism as a living, developing science that must be constantly interrogating itself.

Avakian has written the most comprehensive account of Mao's theoretical contributions to Marxism. He has also undertaken in his writings an ongoing examination of the experience of proletarian revolution in the twentieth century—its great achievements, in particular the profound lessons of the Cultural Revolution in China, as well as its setbacks, shortcomings, and mistakes. He has addressed issues of revolutionary strategy, in the U.S. and for the international movement and analyzed why revolution is not only necessary but also possible within the U.S. itself.

Through these and other critical investigations, Avakian brings forward a vision of socialism and communism that breaks vital new ground for Marxism and the communist project. He deepens and enlarges the understanding of the tasks and contradictions bound up with the exercise of revolutionary authority and how the masses can be unleashed to rule and transform society. In recent writings, he speaks to the indispensable role of dissent in socialist society—how it contributes to deeper knowledge of socialist society, the critical spirit that must permeate it, and the continuing struggle to transform socialist society towards communism. He draws attention to the importance of the intellectual and cultural spheres in socialist society and in the revolutionary process overall, and he probes historic problems in the understanding and approach of the international communist movement. In works such as *Conquer the World: The International Proletariat Must and Will* and *Getting Over the Two Great Humps*, he conceptualizes the international dimensions of communist revolution in ways that have far-reaching implications for the world struggle.

Avakian's writings are marked by great breadth, ranging from discussions about religion and atheism and morality, to the limits of classical democracy, to basketball. It is often alleged that a vanguard party is incompatible with a searching, critical, and creative intellectual enterprise. Avakian gives the lie to this claim.

From his life experience and revolutionary perspective comes a profound sense of the struggles and sentiments among the masses of people; and he keeps his finger on the pulse of the movements of opposition in society more broadly. This is a revolutionary leader who has said about leadership: "if you don't have a poetic spirit—or at least a poetic side—it is very dangerous for you to lead a Marxist movement or be the leader of a socialist state." Avakian's unique sensibility, his revolutionary sweep and passion, and his humor are very much in evidence in these conversations.

Bill Martin has been on the philosophy faculty of DePaul University since 1990. He has written a host of books: on Jacques Derrida and social theory, Jean-Paul Sartre and political theory, political philosophy more generally, and creativity in rock music. He has emerged as an important voice on the contemporary philosophical-political scene.

In works such as *Politics in the Impasse*, Martin argues for a committed philosophy that can serve a radical politics. His is a project of engaging with the realities of postmodern capitalism—both in its brutal and in its mind-numbing incarnations: war, globalization, and marginalization, "virtual bread and cyber-circuses," and the ideological vapor of cynicism and exhaustion.

A pivotal theme in Martin's writings is what he describes as the "ethical moment in politics." More specifically, he has called for a "postsecular" approach in social theory. Such an approach takes up parts of Judaism, radical Christianity, Kant, and Mormon communitarianism. At the same time, Martin offers a reading of Mao that emphasizes an "ethics of rebellion." This, Martin believes, must be yoked more consciously to the science of history. This he calls a "redemptive Marxism": a Marxism of continuing revolution, animated not by a certainty of outcome but by a "structure of concern" for future generations, and care for those who are different or other.

In seeking to reenergize Marxism, Martin has posed the question: would it be possible to join Adorno's critical focus on the culture of contemporary capitalism, particularly the culture of commodification as it has unfolded in the West, with Lenin's understanding of imperialism? Martin believes it is absolutely essential to do so, and his work is contributing substantively to effecting such a synthesis.

As befits his philosophical perspective, Martin writes on such matters as the ideological issues raised by the Gulf War, the electoral process, and the 1992 uprisings in Los Angeles. As befits his philosophical perspective, he has also been willing to act: in 1992, for example, after the capture of the leader of the Maoist people's war in Peru, Martin traveled to Lima as part of an international delegation, braving harassment and arrest to raise world concern.

Bill Martin has played bass guitar for thirty-five years, and continues to perform and write music. He is an avid cyclist and chess player (who also writes enthusiastically of the philosophical implications of chess). In these conversations, we strongly feel his broad interests and his sense of moral and political urgency.

These conversations are testimony to the power of Marxism to engage the real world. They are testimony to that wonderfully apt description by Mao that "Marxism is a wrangling-ism." Avakian and Martin wrestle with big and difficult questions, with complex and challenging issues that truly matter, that have to do with the state of the world, the state of humanity at this stage of history, and with the possibilities and pathways of radical, revolutionary change. This dialogue gives answers and raises questions that offer new understanding. At the same time, it indicates avenues for fruitful investigation, inquiry, and debate, and opens new territories of questioning.

Towards the end of their conversation, Avakian and Martin discuss the need for broader dialogue between progressive and radical intellectuals based in the academy, who see their work in the larger context of the need for a better world, and communist intellectuals. How to bring the issues to a larger table of discussion? How to overcome obstacles and bridge gaps in understanding? How to create the conditions and vehicles for creative exchanges? And how might they all speak to broader audiences in society? Avakian and Martin puzzle over these issues with heart and mind. There is an urgent need for intellectual activity of this sort in these times of danger and opportunity.

In its content and spirit, this encounter is exemplary of the kind of exchanges needed on a much wider level in society. This volume will no doubt spur debate. Even better if it contributes to an atmosphere in which more such dialogue can take place.

RAYMOND LOTTA

Series Editor's Introduction: Finding, Forging a Road

The text you have before you is something of a *My Dinner with André* of Marxism. You may feel that you have walked in on the middle of a conversation; indeed, you have. Bob Avakian and I discuss a wide range of issues in and around Marxism, ranging from ethics, agriculture, and religion to sexuality, Kant, and the role of intellectuals and artists in social change. While I had never met Bob in person until we spent three days in the spring of 2002 taping these conversations, we share certain frames of reference that are undoubtedly more familiar to us than they will be to some readers. We certainly do not want to disinvite anyone from grappling with our own attempts to work through these difficult issues—on the contrary. Perhaps what ought to be most in the forefront is that we take up diverse topics from the perspective of believing that the basic problems of society are systemic, and that radical systemic change—a real revolution—is the way forward. Not only is it right and just to try to bring about a new society that is not based on exploitation, oppression, and domination, but such an effort and its success is indeed necessary if humanity is to have any kind of future at all.

Marxism, especially as interpreted and developed by Mao Zedong, offers a perspective on what it means to "do philosophy": philosophy (and other work of a theoretical nature) develops in the context of attempting to understand the world in order to change it. Now, such a perspective should not be construed narrowly or reductively. We have to allow for the idea that many intellectuals do not hold this perspective and yet at least some of them contribute to our understanding of the world. This is perhaps most of all the case in fields such as the natural sciences and fields involving a good deal of abstract thinking, such as mathematics or philosophy. Perhaps a defining feature of what

Sartre called "engaged" intellectual work is that, to use Kant's language, it intends not only a system (it has an orientation toward holism and integration), but also a future. Certainly, there have been more than a few swollen-headed philosophers who believed themselves to have set things down once and for all. Occasionally this attitude has infected Marxism as well. What Jacques Derrida salutes in Marx's work, however, is something different. Referring, in *Specters of Marx*, to statements made by Marx and Engels about the "aging" of their work, and the "intrinsically irreducible historicity" of the authors and their writing, Derrida asks,

> What other thinker has ever issued a similar warning in such an explicit fashion? Who has ever called for the *transformation* to come of his own theses? Not only in view of some progressive enrichment of knowledge, which would change nothing in the order of a system, but so as to take account there, another account, the effects of rupture and restructuration? And so as to incorporate in advance, beyond any possible programming, the unpredictability of new knowledge, new techniques, and new political givens? (13)

To put it bluntly, Marx even invites us to "pitch overboard" any part of his theorizing that no longer helps to explain the world and to show where we need to work to change the world. But this retheorizing of Marxism has to occur precisely in that context, in the effort to bring about a fundamentally better world. There is no shortage of people who would gladly pitch over all of Marx's theoretical work, and, even more, the revolutionary spirit that motivated that work. There are also those who would claim to hang on to the letter even while happily jettisoning the spirit. I think that Bob Avakian and I have in common that, while we both find much in the letter to keep hold of, it is the revolutionary spirit that we take first as our guide.

In that same light, I was thrilled to be asked to participate in these conversations. It is not that Bob and I agree on all of the "letters"—though we do agree on a good many of them, and where we do not agree, the differences are constructive and productive, I think—but we do agree on the spirit with which we ought to go forward. One of my roommates in college used to have a charming way of saying, "people, it's bad." Well, there are few who doubt that it is bad and that it has been bad for a long time. Perhaps I am being willfully naive in saying this, but I think that most people in their heart of hearts understand that the system is not a good one, that it is fundamentally unfair and often quite horrible. Surely many people understand, too, that we can only do so many nasty things to the planet and expect it to remain a place that sustains human life. Some of this understanding is even expressed in desperate attempts to deny these things. I am pleased to talk with anyone who believes in the necessity for systemic change, but Bob Avakian is in a special category for me, because he is not only engaged with the attempt to theorize the world and what it would take to change it, but he is also playing a special role in organizing and leading that change.

These conversations are sometimes more narrowly focused, but at other times they range rather broadly. The conversations have a certain flow to them, and there is not always a distinct point where one subject gives way to another. Our chapter titles, therefore, are more in the manner of guideposts.

One of the common assumptions in these dialogues is that Lenin enriched our understanding of both Marxism and the world. This is the case on a number of points, but two in particular that are very important to these conversations are the questions of imperialism and the revolutionary party. Lenin argued that the world changed in qualitative ways even in the decades between the death of Marx (1883) and the years leading up to the First World War. The transition was from the "classical" period of industrialization described by Marx and Engels to a world where class positions are replicated on a global scale, in the form of what we would now call "advanced" capitalist countries, which play the global role of the bourgeoisie, and the so-called "developing" countries, which are more in the position of the proletariat. The capitalists from the dominating countries, global imperialists who remain rooted in nation-states and do not form a single class (as evidenced by the conflicts between them), assimilate the colonialist enterprise to these new structures, in which capitalism becomes the dominant mode of production not only in the majority of countries (and certainly in all of the most powerful countries), taken one by one, but indeed, and profoundly, in the world as a whole. In the dialogues Bob and I discuss the extent to which this process was already advancing in Marx's day, as well as Marx's understanding of colonialism. There may have been a basis for Marx to have seen the development of imperialism if he had not been hampered by Eurocentric blinders, to some extent. However, we recognize that Lenin definitively took the measure of this qualitative development of capitalism (whether it was indeed "the highest stage of capitalism" is another question, another hundred years on) and its implications for the class struggle, such that it is right to speak of a qualitative development of Marxism, in other words, Leninism.

It is often said that Lenin's theory of the revolutionary party speaks to something called "the organizational question." I think it is less often understood that *What Is To Be Done?* is really, in some sense, even more about the question of epistemology. Marx said that "the workers have to emancipate themselves; no one else can do it for them." He was really speaking (in the vein, I would argue, of what Kant called "autonomy"—understanding that the basis of the law is within oneself—but then, "one's self" is constituted intersubjectively, in the matrix of social relations) of the only kind of emancipation there is, really, since "freedom imposed by another" would be an oxymoron. One of the steps in this emancipation is for the subjects of emancipation to know themselves, to achieve a class consciousness of the reality of their own position in the world, vis-à-vis the mode of production (broadly and structurally speaking, including legal and ownership relations, channels for disseminating the ideology of these relations, the larger culture, and so on). This truth will not by itself set people free, but it is a necessary step on the road to freedom. But the workings of capitalism obscure this understanding, and capitalism has done a fine job, since the time of Marx, of getting into the "consciousness business." People try, in various ways, to penetrate this "false consciousness," and one of Lenin's most profound and controversial arguments (such that there are many who call themselves Marxists who have a difficult time accepting it) is that the proletariat's consciousness of itself and its historic role (as Marx put it, "to liberate itself and all humankind") will mostly come to it from "outside" of itself. This is largely because most real proletarians (people at the bottom of society who really do have nothing to lose but their chains) do not have the "leisure of the theory class" (as I once heard it put, in a clever play on Thorstein Veblen's book title). Anyone from this theory class who would hope to hold a mirror up to social relations and the proletariat's situation within them, with the aim of creating critical emancipatory theory, has to become a "class traitor" to the bourgeoisie; given the milieu from which most intellectuals come, such an intellectual has to make a leap beyond her- or himself. But Marx had already shown (in a way that ought also to be controversial, because I am not sure that most Marxist activists or intellectuals have really come to grips with the point) that this is the case for proletarians as well—they also have to make a leap in consciousness.

Perhaps Lenin saw this need even more clearly in light of the development of imperialism, where the whole question of classes and the mechanisms of exploitation and domination become vastly more complicated. One of the most difficult examples of this complexity is the complicities and even institutional ties (often through labor movements and unions themselves) that imperialism creates, especially in the imperialist countries themselves, such that the working class in a given country needs to understand itself not only in relation to the capitalist ruling class of that country, but also in terms of the way the world is organized internationally and the role played in the global economy by (what Lenin called) superexploitation in the dominated ("imperialized") countries. In order to forge this understanding, and make it available as a sharpened instrument to the proletariat, there is the need for parties of revolutionary communism. These parties must, in turn, sink roots among the masses and enable the masses to turn their understanding into activism—always with an eye toward the prize, toward the overturning of the imperialist system.

All right, this is simply "Leninism 101," but a new dynamic opens up with regard to philosophy and theory. With a revolutionary party, philosophy and theory are intimately tied to the practical issues of understanding the world in order to change it. The practical issues give a certain focus, let us say, to the theoretical work. In carrying out these dialogues with Bob Avakian, I am engaging not only with him as a person and thinker who has a history and a "context," as we all do, but also with the context of a particular organization—the Revolutionary Communist Party, U.S.A.—and its history.

Herein lies a contradiction—in fact, two contradictions.

The aforementioned "focus" cuts two ways. There is a certain power to the way that theory is done in the context of an organization whose primary work is activism. There is a distinction in philosophy that goes back to Aristotle, between the *via activa* and the *via contemplativa*, the life of action and the life of contemplation, respectively. Much of the history of Western philosophy is concerned with getting thought away from the life of action, by sequestering the philosophical priesthood in monasteries or universities (symbolized in the present day by those black robes at convocation and commencement). There is an assumption at work in such sequestration, that good thinking will not come from the world, but instead comes from "the sky" or perhaps from the inner workings of especially bright minds. Now, there is something that this methodology of thought speaks to, namely that a certain amount of peace and quiet is necessary for a person to gather some thoughts and integrate them. Think of Marx in the reading room of the British Museum. This could be said to be Lenin's point about the "outside," as well.

(In this respect it is worth thinking about the passing of the "idyllic scene" in most colleges and universities—at least those that ever had such a scene to begin with. Although I do not for a moment doubt the privilege of my life as a university professor, I can also honestly say that I have never known the idyllic life, nor have my academic colleagues. The anthropologist Clifford Geertz has some interesting observations on the passing of this scene in *Available Light*.)

The question is whether the aim of such moments "outside" the buzz and hum of life is to become like the most abstract "god"—"thought thinking itself"—or to go back inside the cave in Plato's famous scenario and tell people what you saw. Interestingly, Lenin uses this image as well, and he says that the people in the cave may not be pleased to hear what the philosopher has to say, indeed, their first reaction may be to tear the philosopher limb from limb. (I have always been struck by how many of Malcolm X's speeches contain the line, "You may not want to hear this, but it is the truth.") Significantly, Lenin refers to the cave analogy in discussing what he calls "revolutionary defeatism," the idea that, in crises and wars of imperialism, the party and the people must work for the defeat of "their own" ruling class. What is perhaps more significant is that such an understanding could perhaps only come through the forging of revolutionary leadership. So perhaps the issue of an orientation toward action versus an orientation toward contemplation comes down to what counts as "knowledge," and what are the things that are worth knowing. For there has always been another tradition in philosophy, one that does not see itself as completely apart from the materiality of human life, one that understands that a human being is not simply a "mind" with a bothersome and ultimately ephemeral body attached, but that the human form of being is intrinsically a form of embodiment.

Now, this distinction between these two traditions does not play out as simply as some have supposed—I am especially thinking of Engels in his *Feuerbach and the End of Classical German Philosophy*. There it is said that there are two kinds of philosophy, idealist and materialist, and it is more or less taken for granted that the politically progressive philosophers are the materialists and vice versa. Interpreters differ, however, even over the question of whether Aristotle was ultimately oriented toward the *via contemplativa* or the *via activa*. For Marx, and this is one of a number of areas where Engels (although I resist the trend to set him aside from Marxism or to blame only him—and never Marx—for every instance of reductivism within Marxism) just did not seem to "get it," materialism is not first of all a matter of some allegiance to an ontology (a theory about what sorts of substances there are in or underlying the world), but instead the *material* of what Marx called, in the famous *Theses on Feuerbach*, sensuous human practices. We learn from practices. Our practices ultimately take place in the context of the forms in which human life is produced, perpetuated, and reproduced. These forms, at least beyond tribal societies that are not based on class division (even here, however, there is the question of a gendered division of labor), depend on divisions of labor, especially between mental and manual labor, and on a division between those who own and control the means of production and those who do not.

Marx argued that there is a structural dependency between our future as a species and the overcoming of the basic division of labor and therefore the collectivization of production. Those who are dispossessed learn about the basic injustice of a system characterized by socialized production, on the one hand, and individualized accumulation of wealth and power, on the other, through their practices—of trying to live their lives, of trying to hold body and soul together, of resisting the worst brutalities that issue from this contradiction, in "fighting the power," so to speak, and ultimately in taking the system on and overcoming it through revolution. In the midst of this practice, ideas about the sorts of things that philosophy has traditionally discussed—the true, the good, and the beautiful, and so on—are forged. For these ideas to become concentrated and integrated, and for these ideas to then become a part of the struggle to make a world that actually has a future, some things have to "get organized." There need to be ways that theoretical work can be carried out, and there needs to be organization itself, but organization that is oriented toward the idea that understanding the world and what to do about it has a great deal to do with, and to learn from, the practices of oppressed people in their struggle to overcome oppression.

Taking a "neutral" position (that in fact I do not hold), it seems to me that there is much to be said for this orientation toward practice as a methodology of philosophy; there is a prima facie case for it. For one thing, such an orientation opens philosophy to what might be called the ordinarily observed richness of human life, experience, and practice. It could also be argued that the ideal of "thought thinking itself," as indeed with some monastic and/or theological orientations, not only does not open thought to this richness, but instead denies that human experience (and the experience of being human) offers much of any significance. In Western philosophy as it is practiced in academia we see this tendency in both "continental" (for instance, Heidegger was right to critique the "chatter" of everyday life, and yet there are moments when he seems to argue that all involvement with the materiality of life, and therefore with questions of economics, politics, or even survival, is merely chatter) and "analytic" (especially of the more scientistic or what I would call—without much charity, admittedly—"microproblem" sort, the latter mainly having to do with careers, pedigrees, and cleverness) trends.

However, here we finally arrive at the first contradiction. Not only are most philosophers and social theorists (broadly speaking, working in numerous disciplines) not so cloistered these days (indeed, a propos my earlier parenthetical remark regarding the passing of the academic idyll, many of us could use just a little more of the ivory tower), but also it is the case that parties of the Leninist type can themselves become a bit insulated and insular. The trick is for those outside such organizations who are sympathetic with the aims of fighting imperialism, standing up for internationalism, taking the side of the oppressed, saving the world, and creating a new society to understand that there is a good argument for the kind of focus that such an organization has, and that much can be learned through the pursuit of philosophy and theory as "secondary" to the more basic aims of such an organization. This understanding means nothing, however, if there is not another "trick" at work, from within such organizations themselves, which is an openness to ideas and theoretical work that are generated in a social process, like all ideas and theories, but that do not come directly through the work of the party. I have the aforementioned sympathy, and Bob Avakian has the aforementioned openness, and this made our conversations not only possible, but productive.

The second contradiction that hovers behind these conversations is related to the first. I agree with the Leninist argument that there will not be a revolution without a revolutionary party. The party itself represents the contradictions in society, especially the division of labor, but there is no way around that. If there really could be a purely messianic intervention from beyond that immediately made of our planet the beautiful world that it is capable of being, I do not know how any of us could not wish for it. Lacking the basis for believing in such a thing, a road to the future must be found and forged, and revolutionary organization is an essential part of this effort. In the early 1980s, in the midst of what appeared to be a drive toward nuclear war and therefore the nuclear annihilation of humanity on the part of the two imperialist superpowers, I gravitated toward the Revolutionary Communist Party. Of course, there are many organizations out there that claim inspiration from Marx. All of them, including the RCP, are relatively small. What matters to me is not the size of the organization, however, but what it stands for. What attracted me to the RCP was their anti-imperialism and internationalism, and the fact that they did not balk at talking about and organizing for actual revolution. On the latter point, too, their aim was to build on the previous experience of revolution, especially in the Soviet Union and China (more on this in a moment). Their view, forged in the development and founding of the party in the mid-1970s (significantly, at the point when "the sixties" understood in a political sense, was turning into the anti-sixties, which continues to this day), was that Mao Zedong led the forging of a new phase of Marxism, and so they speak of "Marxism-Leninism-Maoism," or, for short, just Maoism. To be quite direct and not beat around the bush, I'm basically down with that (again, more on this in a moment). This does not mean that I agreed then or now with every position held by the party, but I think that is not really the point. There have even been some relatively sharp disagreements. To put it simply, however, I believe that the only real solution to the basic problems confronting humankind is a revolution that will take us beyond the present way that society is organized, and therefore I want to work with the people who are doing what they can about this. The contradiction is that I believe in the need for the party, and I support it, and yet I do not belong to it. That is also part of the context of these conversations, and will perhaps help the reader understand where each of us is coming from.

We might speak of three phases of the Soviet and Chinese Revolutions: the period of organization before the revolutionary seizure of power; the period of socialism, when the proletariat held power (with various contradictions and difficulties, of course—these being a substantial topic in the conversations); and the loss of proletarian power and the restoration of capitalism. Significantly, we have to speak of an additional phase in the Chinese Revolution, namely the Cultural Revolution. The reader will be able to tell from the first page of these conversations that Bob Avakian and I share the view that these experiences of revolution from the past are connected to the possibilities of the future.

Thinking on this now takes me back to when I first entered graduate school, after a period of two years after college, in which I made some somewhat feeble attempts at political activism, played music, worked at some very crummy jobs, and read a bunch of radical thinkers who had not been part of my undergraduate education—not only Marx, Lenin, and Mao, but also Proudhon, Bakunin, Trotsky, Goldman, Kollontai, Dubois, Malcolm X, Che, Fanon, Gramsci, Sartre, Beauvoir, Foucault, Dunayevskaya, the Redstockings Collective, and many more. Whoever presumed to be critiquing and banging away at the capitalist system, as well as the systems of patriarchy and white supremacy, I wanted to hear what they had to say. When I first entered graduate school, I had my first opportunity to actually take a university course on Marxism, with a professor who considered himself a Marxist. Now, please do not get me wrong, I learned a good deal from this professor and have been friends with him ever since. But it blew my mind, I have to say, to find out that there were whole trends of Marxism in the academy, especially in philosophy and sociology, that essentially had no interest in the experience of the Soviet Union or China. It is not that the folks who are exploring the thought of Sartre or Althusser or Adorno or even Habermas (yes, even Habermas) are not coming up with some good stuff—they are (and certainly Sartre and Althusser have to be set apart from a good bit of what is called "Western Marxism," because they were indeed looking at the Soviet and Chinese experiences, and at the experience of anticolonial revolution). But I still do not know how it is anything other than Eurocentric not to try to learn from these experiences and make them part of Marxism. There is a lot of good Marxist and otherwise radical thought that is done in the context of the academy, but there is also a sense in which Marxism that has become *purely academic* is not really faithful to what Marxism is really all about.

Undoubtedly there was some McCarthyism hovering over work in Marxist theory in the academy, too, resulting in at least a certain amount of self-censorship as regards thinking dangerous thoughts or at least saying anything about them, and certainly there were cases of outright repression too. Since the overturning of socialism in China (and, of course, the collapse of the Soviet Union, which is a different kind of story) we have now had almost three decades of capitalist triumphalism, one dimension of which is the continuously repeated bleat that no alternative to capitalism is possible, and that every attempt to construct an alternative, especially in the Soviet Union and China, was a dismal failure and worse. Indeed, we are under what Slavoj Žižek calls a *Denkverbot*, a prohibition on thought— do not even think for a moment that there is any alternative, and there is no need to explore any of the historical experience of the attempt to construct an alternative. This *Denkverbot* tells us that all we need to know is that socialism in the Soviet Union and China was an unending horror, and that Stalin, Lenin, and

Mao were evil monsters. If anyone asks us about these things, we will know what to say.

The Maoist view, just to be clear, is that the Bolshevik Revolution of 1917 initiated socialism in the Soviet Union, and the ascendancy of Khrushchev signaled the decisive end of socialism and the consolidation of a new, capitalist ruling class in 1956. Obviously, there is a great deal to examine in the intervening years, especially in the Stalin period. This is one of the topics of these conversations. The Maoist view is that the strategy of surrounding the cities from the countryside, and the whole strategy of "people's war," as developed by Mao, led to the countrywide seizure of power in China in 1949, and that this experience constituted a fundamental contribution to Marxism. The Chinese Revolution was decisively overturned in 1976, after ten years of struggle to create a "revolution in the revolution."

This Great Proletarian Cultural Revolution had as its primary objective to transform the superstructure of Chinese society. Mao argued that, with the achievement of a socialist economic base, class struggle does not end, but instead even intensifies in the political and cultural sectors of society (for instance, in the university system, which had remained very elitist). Mao argued that, under socialism, "capitalist roaders" will attempt to gain control of levers of power, especially within the communist party itself, because socialism is not a "settled society," it is still filled with contradictions (especially forms of the division of labor, including the difference between leaders and led). The Cultural Revolution achieved many great things (more on this in a moment), one of which was to show graphically what it means to say that capitalism can be restored from within socialist society (and not just by "external" forces, or "hirelings" of such forces, as Stalin thought). Unfortunately, this lesson was learned the hard way when capitalists seized power in China shortly after Mao's death in 1976, and today we once again have a China that is a vast sweatshop for the advanced capitalist world.

This book takes these experiences of revolution as background, but not dogmatically or uncritically. One does not have to be a Maoist or even a Marxist to appreciate the conversations we have regarding the experiences of revolution in the Soviet Union and China, as well as the wide variety of topics we consider that are less directly connected to this experience. For what it is worth, there are more than a few Maoists and other

Marxists who wonder whether I am even a "real Marxist." I am committed to the basic perspective of historical materialism, and I believe there is much to affirm and learn from in the experience of proletarian revolution in the Soviet Union and China. This is enough to make me a "Stalinist" in the view of some, and of course I think that is too simple, way too simple. For people with this formulaic view, it is not enough to say that we also need a deep critique of the Stalin period, because then the question is what perspective will guide that critique. No, really all that we need is the condemnation of that period as one of endless horrors, and as a constant reminder to never think there can be an alternative to capitalism. What we definitely do not need, from this perspective, is actual study, analysis, and critique, because that would lead to looking at particulars and contexts. One of these particulars that might be mentioned is that from 1917 until the early 1950s, the Soviet Union was either fighting wars, preparing for wars, or dealing with the aftermath of war. No other modern state has endured this kind of perpetual ordeal.

Mao was also deeply critical of Stalin—for instance, in the *Critique of Soviet Economics*, in the discussion of Stalin's book, *Economic Problems of Socialism in the U.S.S.R.*, at one point Mao writes of one of Stalin's formulations, "with friends like these, who needs enemies?" Mao gave the famous "70/30" assessment, that Stalin's leadership was seventy percent good and thirty percent bad. Some have questioned whether this kind of formula is very critical, though I do not know that Mao meant it to be—he had a knack for compressing basic ideas into simple statements, sometimes expressed quite poetically. But, just to be provocative, suppose the figure were reversed, and everything that happened in the Soviet Union during the Stalin period was seventy percent bad, and only thirty percent good. Of course, this is still too much good for the "endless horrors" perspective. I suppose that Bob Avakian and I are not really talking to those folks, because, again, to really hold that perspective you would have to avoid actually studying the period and its contexts. Surely we are hoping to talk to those who have been affected by this perspective, however, which is obviously a great many people. For my part, I would think that, even if the assessment was "30/70," I would still want to try to understand what happened with the proletarian revolution in the Soviet Union, so that some lessons could be learned. Indeed, I think that *has* to happen, because revolution is a global process, and it has a "learning curve," so to speak. And, one of the shared commitments of this book is that, regardless of the problems that socialism has encountered, none makes capitalism workable as the long-term future of humankind.

Still, the reader who does not share our perspective, and who has heard all kinds of things about these Marxist revolutions, is entitled to a bit more. We even begin with this point, and yet, reading back over the conversations, and especially the initial pages, I worry that some readers will think that we are dismissive of anyone who tells a "horror story" about the Stalin period or the Chinese Revolution. Our use of scare-quoted terms such as this may come across as callous, apart from a certain context and perspective. Our view of these experiences of revolution is not uncritical—this goes for the Stalin period especially. Since this book of conversations is obviously not a presentation of the more fully developed theoretical work of either of its authors, it is advisable to take a moment to reflect on some aspects of the Soviet and Chinese experiences.

The Soviet Union was created by an unprecedented mass uprising, led by Lenin and the Bolshevik Party. The initial military event of the October Revolution was the storming of the czar's Winter Palace in Petersburg, but the revolution spread over a very large area through two years and more of civil war. Seventeen countries, including the United States, put together an army of intervention to attempt to aid the "white" forces (the forces that were fighting for the restoration of the czar). Russia had already been devastated by the German army in the First World War. Despite this, or in large measure because of this, people rallied to the new system. "Economic growth" can be a dubious measure as presented in capitalist countries (for instance, phenomena such as home invasion and rising divorce rates contribute to "economic growth," as people buy burglar alarms and move into separate domiciles), but the Soviet economy was a great achievement, despite all of its twists and turns and contradictions. Although the perspective from which some in Russia today march in demonstrations with placards of Stalin is problematic, to say the least (generally the perspective is nationalistic, not that of an internationalist communist), still there is something to a slogan heard in recent years: "Stalin took a wrecked country and made it into a superpower; Gorbachev and Yeltsin took a superpower and made it into a wrecked country." In the first years of the revolution priority was given to the overcoming of national and ethnic inequalities and to fighting the oppression of women. On this latter point, abortion was legalized, the right to divorce was recognized, and equal rights and equal pay became public policy and law. Women in the new republics of Central Asia cast off the veil after many generations. The Soviet Union eradicated illiteracy and vastly expanded educational opportunities for people from the working class and peasantry. During the Stalin period, a modern industrial base and a collectivized system of agriculture were established.

The Stalin period was a time of intense contradictions. It has to be admitted forthrightly that many of these were not handled correctly. But this is too easy to do if one does not try to gain an appreciation for the real problems and threats that the Soviet Union faced, and the fact that the building of socialism on the scale of the U.S.S.R. was absolutely unprecedented. If you study documents from the Communist Party of the Soviet Union from the late 1920s, you will see that there is an overwhelming feeling that invasion from the west could come at any moment. Stalin thought that the Soviet Union had to accomplish an industrial and military revolution of the sort that took many decades and even centuries in countries such as Germany, England, and the United States—but in ten years. When the invasion did come, Germany threw most of its military might against the Soviet Union. Twenty-three million people were lost in the war; to gain a perspective on the scale of the destruction, the number of Soviet civilian and military deaths during the siege of Leningrad was greater than the combined losses of the British, French, and Americans for the entire war. Despite what we learn about D-day and the landing at Normandy, the real turning point of the Second World War was the Battle of Stalingrad—a battle that still bears study for the concentration of contradictions we see there, for the military strategies applied, and for one of the most important examples of an historical watershed. In large part, the United States used nuclear weapons not to defeat Japan, which was largely defeated already, but to send a message to the Soviet Union about who was top dog in the world. The message was sent in other ways, too, for instance, by American political and military leaders (most famously General George S. Patton) who called for the continuation of the Second World War, with the United States marching into the Soviet Union.

Marxism in the midst of all this increasingly became a "fortress" and "siege' mentality, a process "helped along" by Stalin's tendencies toward dogmatism and reductivism. Significantly, Mao attributed some of this to Stalin's background as a seminary student. At the same time, I again think it is too easy to simply think that Stalin was a dullard or intellectual light-weight and that this explains his tendency to be ham-fisted about the contradictions of socialist society. In reading Stalin's works, I find it remarkable that, though many of his ideas and inclinations appear wrong-headed in 20/20 hindsight, there is a certain logic to them that seems almost inescapable when understood "from the inside," from the perspective of the Soviet leadership. Many of Stalin's dogmas were simply "orthodox Marxism" for the time, and his real failure was not learning from experience and not trusting the masses. Many innocent people were victimized because of this failure, and throughout the Stalin period the political and cultural atmosphere of the Soviet Union grew increasingly rigid and oppressive. People became cynical and passive, such that, when Khrushchev and his cronies took over the CPSU in the mid-1950s and used it to restore capitalism in the Soviet Union, there was only token resistance. The legacy of this cynicism and then capitalist restoration under the cover of a reformed "socialism" remains very much with us today.

China at the time of the Bolshevik Revolution (and for a long time before that, of course) was a country divided up by foreign "interests" in the urban and coastal areas and by warlords in the interior. Politicians and capitalists in Japan, Germany, France, England, and the United States talked openly about the cheap labor and resources in China, stating their colonialist ambitions without compunction. Japan, especially, believed it had a kind of "natural right" to dominate and exploit China (and much of the rest of east and southeast Asia), a "right" that the United States hoped to take over—indeed, this is the origin of the "War in the Pacific," not Pearl Harbor. (This is why U.S. politicians and diplomats would ask "Who lost China?" after the 1949 revolution, as though it was theirs to lose.) Undoubtedly there would have been resistance to foreign domination in China apart from the October Revolution; however, as Mao said, the ideas of Marx and Lenin became known and popular in China because of the establishment of the Soviet Union.

China also had to find its own way to revolution, however. Indeed, it had to find a way to a number of revolutions: for national liberation, against colonialism, against a comprador capitalist class that facilitated the domination of China by foreign powers, for radical agrarian reform, against many centuries and even millennia of the severe subordination of women, against the subordination of minority nationalities, and even against a pervasive ideology that held that all advanced thinking came from the West. Social relations in general remained feudalistic, or at least semi-feudal. Poverty was widespread and dire. There were areas of China where people not only had no shoes, they literally had no clothes and would walk around naked. China in the first part of the twentieth century was light years away from the sort of society that Marx thought would be *ripe* for socialist revolution and socialist construction. As far away from such things as Russia was at the time of the First World War, China was even much further away—at least in the "classical" or ortho-dox Marxist conception.

Lenin had to make a leap to conceptualize the possibility of socialism in Russia. In his thesis about the weakest link in the imperialist chain, I would say that Lenin gravitated toward the view that dynamic social evolution is driven from the margins rather than the center of society. He had to break with the linear, Eurocentric view that saw socialism as emerging first of all in the most "advanced" capitalist countries (especially Germany, France, or England). At the same time, Lenin demonstrated an exemplary internationalism, seeing the class dynamics that were driving Russian society in global context and thereby develop-ing his theory of "conjuncture." Simply put, a conjuncture is a time in which the contradictions of capitalism on a global scale (what Lenin means by the imperialist system) are bound very tightly, "cast on the scales of history for resolution," as Lenin put it. It has become commonplace to say that the Bolshevik Revolution occurred "prematurely." Revolutionary situations have been rare in history, and the masses will not take advan-tage of these situations without the leadership of the party. Surely those who speak of the immaturity of Russia in 1917 would have to acknowledge the ripeness for revolution of Western Europe before and during the First World War. There were no Leninist parties there, however, to lead people through this window of opportunity; indeed, most of the socialist movement in Western Europe either threw away their internationalism the moment it might have meant something, and instead joined in with their own ruling classes for the defense of "their" countries, or, in a few cases, slogans of neutrality were raised, helping the powers that be ensure that the masses of Europe, and even more the masses of the colonized countries, were condemned to more decades of systemic (and often openly brutal) violence.

Lenin argued that our era is that of imperialism and proletarian revolution, and he saw two great streams of revolution coming together: socialism in the advanced countries, and national liberation in the dominated countries. Mao made a further leap in understanding by arguing that only socialism could save China and other countries that were dominated by foreign powers. National liberation would never occur under the leadership of a rising bourgeoisie, he argued, because it is in the nature of capitalism not to carry liberation for the popular masses (in a country such as China this would include the proletariat, the peasantry, and the relatively meager middle classes) through to actual independence, but instead to sell out to much richer and more powerful foreign capitalists at the earliest opportunity. Of course, the sorts of alliances that Mao believed were necessary to really liberate China (he even saw a role for what he called the "national bourgeoisie," that part of the capitalist class that was not beholding to foreign capital, not a comprador class or positioning itself to become such) were riddled with contradictions, as were, for that matter, the alliances necessary to create the Soviet Union. It really is an idealist fantasy, however, to think that any revolution could be made without working through contradictions. (Indeed, there are some contradictions involved in making a revolution in advanced capitalist countries, to say nothing of the imperialist hyperpower, that are, if anything, much deeper and far more difficult than those faced in Russia and China—Bob and I take up this question in the conversations.) Further, Mao argued that a socialist revolution must create a self-reliant economy; especially it must be able to feed, shelter, and clothe its people, because, in a country where these are real issues, there will otherwise be a tremendous temptation to cut deals with foreign powers. These deals can be inroads to renewed foreign domination—this is essentially the Maoist view of what happened in the case of Cuba (and it is significant, in that light, that Soviet patronage has now been replaced with a tourism economy, which not only undermines independence, but also brings with it such other Third-World problems as sex tourism).

"Food, shelter, clothing"—this is what I like to call the "trinity" of materialism. But that sounds so simple and is indeed an oversimplification. Quite possibly most people in a country such as the U.S. can hardly begin to imagine the levels of deprivation that were common in China before the revolution—I wonder if this is the reason why, for some people, the history of China under the leadership of Mao is only a history of either terrible mistakes or terrible horrors.

Here it is necessary to address the charge that the Cultural Revolution was a violent free-for-all, if not a campaign of outright physical elimination of opponents, for which Mao bears direct responsibility.

Mao's approach to waging the Cultural Revolution was one of mass debate, mass criticism, and mass political mobilization from below. The orientation was clearly set out in the Sixteen Point Decision that guided the Cultural Revolution: "Where there is debate, it should be conducted by reasoning and not by force." Many other Maoist policy statements, some with the force of law, gave further direction; for instance, Red Guards were not allowed to carry weapons or to arrest or try anyone. The Cultural Revolution was not a program of mass round-ups and summary executions.

Was there violence and personal tragedy? Yes. In an unprecedented mass movement of this scale (we're talking about 30 million young activists alone), in a country of this size (800 million at the time), and with this movement challenging entrenched neo-bourgeois elites, and meeting resistance, it would be hard to imagine conditions in which there would not be violence and excess. But does this define the essential thrust and outcome of the Cultural Revolution? The answer is no.

As for the actual number of those killed during the ten years of the Cultural Revolution (1966–1976), it has to be clearly stated that there are no reliable statistics. What we have are only estimates—ranging from tens of thousands of casualties to ideologically charged claims of one to three million deaths. Some scholars somewhat sympathetic to the aims of the Cultural Revolution, such as Maurice Meisner, cite figures of 400,000 deaths (though, as with other estimates, this is based on extrapolations). While much more investigation is needed, I think this is a plausible upper-end estimate of lives lost. I would hasten to add, however, that to leave the matter there is highly misleading.

To simply put out an aggregate number of deaths does not tell us how, by whom, and in what circumstances and contexts violence occurred. The underlying assumption, when death tolls are estimated, is that all deaths are attributable to Mao. But the violence of the Cultural Revolution did not issue from a single locus of power. Different class and social forces were involved in this complex upheaval: genuine Maoists; Red Guard organizations and worker battalions organized by capitalist roaders within the Party; conservative military forces; ultra-left groupings; criminal elements; and others. Different social interests and motivations were in play. The fervor of some sections of radical youth to "cleanse" society of bourgeois influence led to excesses and killings. On the other side, capitalist roaders within the party who were coming under political attack would often incite violence in order to deflect the struggle from them and to discredit the movement—and at certain points, they used their influence and positions in the military to brutally suppress radicals.

But the Cultural Revolution was overwhelmingly a mass political and ideological movement and struggle. It was not a plot, purge, or orgy of violence. The violence that did occur was limited and sporadic. Where harmful phenomena persisted on the people's side—for instance, Red Guard students physically attacking people, struggles escalating armed factional clashes, or people using the movement to settle personal scores and grievances—the Maoist leadership criticized, condemned, and struggled against these trends. For instance, unarmed workers dispatched to Qinghua University in Beijing put a stop to brutal factional fighting among the students. And it should be noted that in Shanghai—the hotbed of "gang of four" radicalism—the level of violence was relatively low.

The Cultural Revolution was a complicated class struggle over who would rule society: the working people or a new bourgeois class. It spawned mass organizations that divided into rebel and conservative camps. It involved seizures of political power from below. Things were not always under control; Mao did not have a totally free hand. But the Cultural Revolution was a real social revolution. Hundreds of millions were inspired by its egalitarian objectives and values. Hundreds of millions were mobilized to carry forward the revolutionary transformation of the economy, social institutions, culture, and revolutionizing the Communist Party itself. The Cultural Revolution had real, socially revolutionary results.

Undoubtedly all kinds of mistakes were made, but why is it that we hear about the sort of thing one sees in a film such as *The Red Violin* (a musician is attacked because he specializes in Western music), but we do not hear that by 1970 China had solved the problem of adequately feeding its population. Does that justify attacks on Beethoven and all who admire his music? I feel like saying, "get real!"—and I certainly admire Beethoven. We are talking about a country that had two wars fought against it by the British (at the time, 1839–1842 and 1856–1860, the predominant military power in the world) to ensure that tens of millions of people remained opium addicts (by 1949 these addicts totaled almost 90 million). Before the revolution, China had a vast criminal underground. The situation of women was especially dire—foot-binding, arranged marriages, child brides, prostitution, and the killing of female babies in the countryside were all very common. To say the least, the Chinese Revolution faced an extraordinary uphill struggle, but what, other than a revolution, could address these issues?

In the ten years after the 1949 seizure of power, land reform and cancellation of peasant debt was carried out on a scale never before seen in world history. In 1950 a new Marriage Law established marriage by mutual consent and the right of divorce. Infanticide and the sale of children were outlawed. It is true, of course, that making a law does not by itself make good things happen. There was a protracted struggle to establish gender equality in the countryside, and practices such as infanticide were largely eradicated by 1970. Significantly, this practice, as well as international "adoption," has returned since the restoration of capitalism in 1976. Indeed, what we see of China's new "freedom" and "prosperity" is almost entirely concentrated in a few urban centers—and even then we see the things that glitter and not that which is on the side streets and in the shadows. Again, let's get real—take a visit to your local discount store, which may as well add the words "Chinese Sweatshop Distribution Network" to its signs, and imagine the hardship and suffering experienced by the masses of workers who produce this stuff.

In 1949, about fifteen percent of Chinese people were literate; in one generation this figure soared to over eighty percent.

Maoist China did what the United States has never done: it established a system of universal healthcare. Unlike in the United States, the healthcare system was guided by principles of cooperation and egalitarianism, and Western and traditional practices were synthesized with the aim of treating the whole body and the whole person, in the context of the social and environmental factors that lead to health problems. One of my favorite chapters in the history of the Chinese Revolution is that of the "barefoot doctors," the 1.3 million peasants who were trained in basic medicine, who walked from village to village, not only helping other peasants with their problems, but helping the peasants to understand and treat their problems. Since 1976 this system has disappeared.

We continually hear nowadays about the supposed endemic violence of the Chinese Revolution, but how often do we hear about the fact that between 1949 and 1975 life expectancy in China went from about thirty-two years to sixty-five years? In the early 1970s, infant mortality rates in Shanghai were lower than in New York City. Does this not speak to a profound reduction in the violence of everyday life?

Perhaps a more intellectual way of saying that we should "get real" is to say that perspectives on these achievements, which are not controversial claims, and the way that people focus their attention on some things and not others, is bound up with horizons of expectation and senses of entitlement. If, in the imperialist West, we can ordinarily expect to live more than seventy years, then perhaps the doubling of lifespan in remote China will not mean very much. Maybe it is a little bit like if someone told you they finally got indoor plumbing.

"No, no, it really means a lot, now that you bring it up," I can imagine someone saying—well, I don't have to imagine it, I hear this sort of thing all the time in the intellectual milieu, which is then followed by something along the lines of, "sure, all that stuff is great, but what about . . . ?" Of course, this has to do with the Cultural Revolution, and with the intellectuals and artists in that tumultuous ten-year period. Surely these things ought to be discussed, including the way that this struggle, which was to deepen the basis of socialism and to prevent the restoration of capitalism, sometimes devolved into a certain amount of chaos, in which undoubtedly some people were treated very badly. This was a class struggle, but one where Mao and the other revolutionaries repeatedly called on people not to resort to violence or to get into a mode of "settling scores." The class of capitalist roaders, as Mao called them, especially those in the Communist Party of China who were basing themselves on the class contradictions that continue to exist in socialist society and on the possibility, as we have seen, of making deals with foreign capital, had every interest in fomenting chaos and violence, to show that socialism does not work. For instance, they had every interest in sabotaging factory committees that were breaking down the division of labor between management and workers on the shop floor—and now they have restored capitalist methods of management in the factories, and also created a new class of billionaires, one of whom is the son of Deng Xiaoping.

The Cultural Revolution as it affected universities is naturally of special interest to intellectuals. However, it is important to attempt to gain some sense of the real context in addressing this issue. Just as it is very difficult for people in the West to really understand, as a "felt reality," the levels of deprivation that were common in China before 1949, it may be difficult for intellectuals in the West to grasp to what extent the few universities that existed in China by 1949 were the provinces of the elite. This goes back somewhat to the kinds of alliances that made the revolution of 1949 possible in the first place, and also to the way that, for at least the first ten years or more of the revolution, reforming the university system was not a major priority. In the United States, the university and college system is on the whole quite plebeian, not only compared to a place such as China before the Cultural Revolution, but even compared to countries such as Germany, France, and England before the 1960s and '70s. A large percentage of people in the U.S., even from the working class, attend some sort of college. In China at the time of the revolution, teaching basic literacy and providing grammar school for most people were the priorities. Some of the academic elite in China figured that, since their fields had not been touched very much by the revolution from 1949 until the mid-1960s, life would go on more or less in the same way. Some of them took their elite status for granted, and when their privileges and autocratic teaching methods were criticized, they reacted with a sense of entitlement about the lifestyle to which they had become accustomed. This makes me think of a similar situation in the early years of the Soviet Union. There, some aristocratic and bourgeois families that had lived in large houses with many rooms were told that they had to move into one half of the house, so that a working-class family that had previously lived in a hovel or had been homeless could move into the other half. (By the way, this happened to the family of Ayn Rand.) This is the sort of situation where we see the class basis of a sense of entitlement. Could those aristocratic families not have said, "You know, we have lived in luxury for many years, we were very lucky to have had that experience, and to be able to acquire some of the things that go with great wealth, such as a sense of culture. But, after all, the basis of the wealth of any society is the actual work that people do, and these people have done that work, and we haven't, so they could at least have half of this house, which is ridiculously large for a single family in any case"? But, gee, rich people rarely seem to say anything like that! No, they are outraged, about what has been stolen from them and how their lives have been shattered.

Surely, though, there are particularities to the intellectual milieu that are not accounted for by this analogy. And, let it be said, any revolutionary movement on any kind of scale, but especially a very large scale, is going to lose track of some particularities, *period*. When I say about this, "Let's get real," I do not mean to take recourse to a mere utilitarianism. Rather, a legitimate struggle will sometimes have aspects that fall short of or even go against the ideal. Some of us know the old discussion about "after the revolution . . . ," where it is very tempting to wonder what we would do if we encountered a certain previous landlord or employer or even college professor. Of course it would be wrong to use the revolution to simply settle scores. Imagine what the temptation would be if you never had the old professor, because the old professor's idea about you is that you should be out in the countryside your whole life growing rice and other crops for food, and you do not need even basic literacy for that, much less advanced study in the humanities or sciences. So, as Frasier and Niles Crane often say, when dismissing their social inferiors, "Off you go!"

The temptation to settle scores is related to what might be called the problematic side of egalitarianism, *leveling*, which was severely criticized by Marx. Surely there were some, perhaps driven by resentment (though often understandable resentment), who took egalitarianism to the point of mere leveling, especially when it came to the elite university system. Intellectuals generally have grand plans for writing projects for many years to come and need to be very protective of how their time gets organized. To really carry through with intellectual work, one has to pursue it as a calling, a vocation, a life project. To have that life project disrupted can be traumatic, perhaps in a way that would be very difficult to comprehend for someone who has never conceived of a life project in that way. There is a class dimension to who gets to even consider having life projects, and who is brought up to think he or she is entitled to have a vocation, and the assumption of an elite educational system (which, again, is somewhat different, for the most part, from much of what is done in most colleges and universities in the United States—though not without significant exceptions) is that the masses of workers and peasants are not the sorts of people who should or ever could have life projects. "Trauma" comes from the Greek word for "cut" or "break" (as in a break in the skin); the traumatization of the cloistered scene of elite academic work could actually have a salutary *intellectual* effect.

Now, having said all this, the fact is that the decade of the Cultural Revolution was one in which the educational system was broadened considerably. For instance, in the countryside, middle school enrollment went from fifteen million to fifty-eight million. For this to happen, teachers were needed in the countryside; some professors did not want to go there, but many embraced the idea of breaking down the divisions between city and countryside, schooled and unschooled, privileged and dispossessed. Many found that the peasants had a thing or two to teach them.

Well, what I have said here barely scratches the surface, but let us keep some things clearly in focus. The participants in the conversations presented here believe that the solution to the basic problems and contradictions of the imperialist world order is revolution by the proletariat and oppressed and marginalized people more generally. The flaws in the system are fundamental, not incidental or superficial. Therefore it behooves us to grapple with the previous experiences of proletarian revolution—and with the unfolding of history in general and in broad perspective.

One could argue, instead, that whether these experiences were predominantly good or bad, they are a closed chapter, and it is not immediately clear anymore what they have to do with the present and future. This is indeed a difficult problem, for at least two reasons. Bob Avakian wrote some time ago of "The End of a Stage—The Beginning of a New Stage." The stage that had ended was one in which there were socialist countries in the world, the period from 1917 to 1976, with a brief period in the middle when there was even a "socialist camp," albeit riddled with contradictions. (Avakian argues that, apart from the U.S.S.R. itself, the Warsaw Pact countries were never socialist, as there were never proletarian revolutions in those countries. This goes as well for those "socialist" countries that emerged as Soviet client states in the period after capitalism was restored: including Cuba, North Korea, Ethiopia, South Yemen.) We are now in a stage where our "models," so to speak, are in the past, even as the goal is not to go back to the past (we cannot do that even if we wanted to) but to create a different future.

The second factor that we have to struggle over concerns the new things in the world that have developed in the most recent thirty years or so. (It is interesting that this coincides with the end of the first wave of proletarian revolutions, and my guess is that this is not a mere coincidence.) There are new factors of production (developments in cybernetics, transport, materials science), new levels of concentration and dissemination of the culture industry, new configurations of class, and the general acceleration of life (one author calls it "turbo-capitalism"). Of course, because of the end of the earlier stage of socialism, and the collapse of the Soviet bloc, there is an immense grab for power and resources underway, which is an important dynamic that is driving U.S. aggression in the present period. Even if the argument is that the basic outline of the imperialist world system still underlies all of this new stuff, there are developments that are not simply quantitative add-ons to what already existed—there are transformations going on in the world that are real, even if certain underlying contradictions remain essentially the same (again, socialized production and individualized accumulation, the division of labor, the division between imperialist and dominated countries). A "Marxist orthodoxy" that blithely ignores these developments will ossify into a mere "belief system" that has little to do with changing the world.

There is yet a third reason why we might ask what the past experience of revolution has to do with the future, one that has to do with the basic idea of proletarian revolution as conceived by Marx. A moment ago I referred to the "unfolding" of history. It might be argued that however much credence Marx would invest in this idea depends on the depth of his commitment to Hegel. There is no need for a heavy and thick, somewhat theological, sense of capital-H "History" if the mechanism of social change in our period can better be described in terms taken from political economy rather than philosophy. In such terms, what matters most is that the contradictions of capitalism call forth the "gravediggers" of the system, as Marx put it, and that this process is an integral part of the workings of capitalism. Other ways of coming at this question, of something "law-like" at work in society, range from what might be called Aristotle's teleological humanism (that there is a sense of what it would mean to flourish inherent in the human species—and every other species or even thing, for that matter—and people strive toward that possibility of flourishing) to Mao's view that, "where there is oppression, there is resistance." Marx, who was influenced at least a little by Aristotle (Scott Meikle and others claim that Marx actually owes a large debt to Aristotle), held that the specific form of capitalist exploitation increasingly brings forward the agents of its ultimate overturning—a class that eventually is global in scope, as capital increasingly is, but that is also, unlike the different capitalist classes that are rooted in different nation-states, a *single, international* class. This is, of course, the international proletariat.

Past revolutions were undertaken by the proletariat as part of a global process, not necessarily a continuous one. The process contains advances as well as setbacks. Mao said that "the road is tortuous" (though the outlook is bright); to use a more recent metaphor, we might say that the "learning curve" for revolution is very steep. But why, now, believe that there is a "process" (or

"road") any more, if there ever was one? Why believe this especially now, when there are no socialist countries in the world,
when capitalism is exulting in triumphalism (indeed, when we
live in a strange time of monopolarism, with the United States
as the "hyperpower"), when new factors of production and culture are reshaping society in ways that seem unprecedented and
quite foreign to at least some of the economic and social phenomena that Marx analyzed?

To say the least, all of these factors militate against the re-cre-
ation of or retreat to a Marxist orthodoxy. This goes as well for
any call to return to "classical Marxism," an easy way out in the
face of the twists and turns of the twentieth century. Instead,
these factors call both for recognition of what is actually unfolding in the world, and for creative thought and theorizing. One
achievement of these dialogues, in my view, is that we brought
a number of questions to the table, for example (what I call) the
"animal question," issues of secularism (and even the old philosophical question of "the meaning of life"), and issues involved
in sexuality. Indeed, on this last score, I was especially pleased
that Bob and I were able to explore some problems in the way
that the Revolutionary Communist Party had previously understood homosexuality, an issue that had been problematic for
many people who are generally supportive of the organization.
Beyond the particularities of this specific question, the party's
previous stand (which has been definitively overturned in recent
years) was a good example of the kind of cul-de-sac thinking in
which Marxists sometimes find themselves stuck. On some level,
such thinking can be a testimony to a style of inquiry that wants
primarily to do something about the awful state of the world.
And yet, a thinking that erects barricades will soon enough not
be engaged, other than with mental ossification. The give and
take of these conversations shows, I hope, the opposite of such
ossification—we do raise questions and attempt to arrive at
some answers, or at least some terms, but more than that we
want to open things up and grapple with the real difficulties of
finding and forging the road to another world.

*   *   *   *   *

I have undertaken to write this introduction as the series editor
for the Creative Marxism series. This seemed an appropriate way

to create a little distance from the book, or to insert something of a "gap," in that there are characterizations in this introduction that express aspects of my views with which Bob Avakian is not in complete agreement, and there are formulations that are undoubtedly different from the way Bob would express things, and yet there could easily be an assumption or inference made by the reader that the views and approaches discussed in this introduction are all held in common. In reading the conversations, the reader will see that this is not the case. Of course, the authors each have their own works where their individual positions are developed more systematically. What is significant about the present work, I think, is the way that two perspectives, close in some ways and quite different in others, generate what we hope are radical and creative sparks (and you probably remember what Mao said about sparks).

It is more than a bit presumptuous to name the series, "Creative Marxism." For sure, there is plenty of creative Marxism out there—in this book Bob and I mention a number of authors, from Theodor Adorno and Jean-Paul Sartre to Fredric Jameson, who have certainly been creative Marxists. While the Creative Marxism series will not be exclusively "Maoist," by any means, the aim is to find a resistance to orthodoxy that retains an orientation toward radical social transformation, a Marxism that is theoretically lively and adventurous and not merely academic.

In another book appearing in the series, I develop many of the questions discussed here from my own perspective—which is also the title of the book—"Ethical Marxism." One chapter of the book is titled "Maoism as Ethical Marxism," and this contains a section of reflections on the conversations presented here. Bob Avakian has had an especially productive period lately, and many of the questions we discuss here are also developed further from his perspective, for instance in the talk, "Dictatorship and Democracy, and the Socialist Transition to Communism" (this can be found at the website for the *Revolutionary Worker* newspaper, at rwor.org). There Bob poses sharply and speaks to the question and contradiction of whether, and how, it is possible to be part of a communist vanguard and pursue critical and creative work in the arts, sciences, and other fields of intellectual endeavor.

*   *   *   *   *

In past revolutionary experience, the contradictions of society have tended to manifest themselves indirectly, or at least such that the "last straw" that brings people into the streets, that is exemplary of a general crisis where people cannot live in the old way anymore and the existing system is constrained from providing any new answers, may appear to be something relatively small. The 1905 revolution in Russia (which failed, ultimately, but from which Lenin and others took many lessons) was called forth by a million oppressions, but its immediate spark was a moment in a strike by the people who set type for printing presses. Previously, they had been paid for setting letters, but not punctuation marks, and now they wanted to be paid for this. Government repression of the strike led to many other workers coming into the streets, and a general uprising spiraled from there. A revolution for the apostrophe! The fire next time may come from some equally "far-fetched" source that gets framed as a "clash of civilizations"—quite possibly from the effects of capitalism's war on our very planet, which is manifesting itself in rising rates of skin cancer, "dead zones" in oceans and seas, soil erosion, a preponderance of excrement and junk, the severity of the obesity/starvation contradiction, the pandemic of HIV/AIDS, the (related) writing-off of much of sub-Saharan Africa from the supposed advance of "global prosperity," and wars of aggression to control energy resources.

I am sure the reader knows the list (which is far longer than the one just given) of horrors as well as I do. In the final analysis, the main assumption lying behind these conversations, apart from interpretations of past experience, is that the horrors are systemic and therefore must be dealt with on that level. People, it is bad. People, we need a new society. In that light, it was a rare privilege to engage in direct dialogue with a committed revolutionary whose dynamic and creative thinking I respect tremendously.

Bill Martin

Postscript: Beyond Eggs and Omelets— A Note on Slavoj Žižek's Foreword

The authors are deeply grateful to Prof. Slavoj Žižek for agreeing to provide the foreword to this book, especially on short notice and after only having seen a lengthy excerpt. We understand the foreword to be in the spirit of the provocation, humor, and intensity with which it is clearly intended—the particular combination of these qualities being unique to Prof. Žižek's inimitable style. In addition, we appreciate Prof. Žižek's commitment to the "Big Problem," revolution, as he has expressed this especially in recent works. For my own part, I feel that Prof. Žižek has done a good deal to urge intellectuals to go beyond just fooling around with ostensibly radical rhetoric. In recent years, too, Prof. Žižek has played an important role in bringing forward again, and rethematizing, the revolutionary legacy of Lenin. In his discussions of totalitarianism, he has also made it clear that the way "beyond Stalin" is not created by simply engaging in condemnatory rhetoric, but instead by engaging with the full scope of the historical period. In this, and on some other crucial points, Prof. Žižek reminds me of Sartre, especially the Sartre of the anticolonialism writings and the *Critique of Dialectical Reason*. I will mention one of these other crucial points in a moment. Significantly, Prof. Žižek does not really engage with Mao or the Chinese Revolution. As I recall, one of the few places where Prof. Žižek does mention Mao is in *The Ticklish Subject: The Absent Centre of Political Ontology*, where he chides (not unjustly, I think) "Maoist students preaching and practicing the 'sexual revolution'," even while "the China of the Maoist Cultural Revolution involved an extremely 'repressive' attitude towards sexuality." For my part, I would like to study this issue more (one source I have reconsidered in the last little while is *The Spiral Path*, the 1981 book by David Fernbach, which attempts to combine Maoism and gay liberation). In the present book, and in our own separate works, Bob Avakian and I have argued that "Mao's revolution" forged a new, better, and different understanding on a number of fronts, and among these are three important issues raised by Prof. Žižek: leadership, ethics, and violence.

We take Prof. Žižek's arguments on these three points (and others, of course) as both provocation and challenge. It is very common in many parts of the political left (and the right, for that matter) to simply assimilate Mao to "Stalinism." We don't agree with that move, and yet at the same time we don't think it is simply a matter of "disavowing Stalin"—because, with this all too simple and easy move, nothing is understood and nothing is transcended. Furthermore, in this book and elsewhere, there is an attempt to reach a new synthesis on these questions (and many others). To be fair, Prof. Žižek was kind enough to write his foreword without seeing the whole book, so what will be interesting and valuable to us is to see what he thinks about this attempt at a synthesis that aims to get beyond Stalin, and even beyond Mao in some respects, and yet still takes the "Big Problem" very, very seriously. So, we take Lenin's concept of the party very seriously, as we do Mao's refinements of this concept, and in attempting to go "beyond" here, we do not want to cancel or negate. It is true, we are not fond of the notion, associated with Stalin, that it is the leader who "knows," while "the masses" are some solid, unitary, inert receptacle. But perhaps Prof. Žižek's comment here might also be read as a provocation on the difficult Leninist epistemological issue, that working class consciousness comes to the working class "from the outside," and in particular through the mediation of the party. Readers will undoubtedly find it worthwhile to study Prof. Žižek's more nuanced and developed analysis of "perverse logic" in works such as *The Puppet and the Dwarf: The Perverse Core of Christianity*. It would be interesting to have a deeper discussion of the relationship between perversive and subversive logics.

We take the question of "the ethical" seriously—what I prefer to call "the ethical moment in politics"—but our aim is certainly not to lower "ethics" to what it typically is reduced to in academic discourse, a code of personal behavior that is somehow unrelated to larger social structures. At one point in our book we even say that the problem of "ethics" is that it does not have what it takes to be ethical. For my part I explore the interconnections among Kant's three formulations of the categorical imperative, and the connection of these with Marx's famous reference to "the categorical imperative to overturn all of those social relations in which people are debased." But again, I take Prof. Žižek's comment to be provocative, since there certainly are plenty of "boring ethical considerations" that get so caught up in the "small things" (as Žižek puts it) that not only is the "big thing" not addressed (or two "big things," the existing social system and an alternative way of organizing life), and it is more than a shame when Marxism gets involved in being a "small ethics" in this sense, indeed it is a betrayal. This is a major theme of the present book.

On the question of violence, perhaps I can simply speak in my own voice as someone who has done a good deal of work on the philosophy of Jean-Paul Sartre and who is in some sense a "Sartrean" (among seven or nine other things!). Prof. Žižek's claim about "revolutionary violence as a liberating end-in-itself" recapitulates an argument from Sartre, seen perhaps in its most acute form in his (famous) preface to Franz Fanon's *The Wretched of the Earth*. This is where Sartre says that, when a colonial subject kills a colonizer, he kills two birds with one stone—essentially, he both gets rid of an enemy, and he forms himself as a subject. While I do not entirely disagree with what Sartre said, especially in the particular case, I cannot go all the way with the idea that this violence is somehow "glorious" because it is liberatory. There are things that need to be done, and without doing them, no good will come about, and the bad system will be allowed to continue. But we need not make the next step and, shall we say, completely valorize every thing, or every aspect of the thing, that needs to be done. Perhaps it is a distinction between justification and legitimation (which of course would need further argumentation). As Bob Avakian notes (in this book and elsewhere, especially his book, *For a Harvest of Dragons*), quoting Marx, one of the ways that capitalism gets its revenge is in what it forces the revolutionaries to become in carrying forward the overthrow of capitalism. It seems to me that this is precisely where "the ethical" has a substantial and real role to play: what is it that "is to be done," and how do we go about doing this without in fact replicating and reinforcing the essential violence of the capitalist system. Stalin's "eggs and omelets" is too much within the capitalist logic of means and ends. On the other hand, and here again I take Prof. Žižek's remarks as provocative, just as it would be the easiest thing in the world to "disavow" Stalin, it would certainly be easy, and make life far easier for some of us, to disavow revolutionary violence and to be one of those nice pacifists whom some people find far more likable. The problem is that capitalism and its system of violence (a system with no moral limits—

and I'll just say this one thing, because it was formative for me when I was much younger and became aware of this against the background of the Vietnam War: any system that creates and uses a substance such as napalm has no moral limit to what it will do to people) has never given the least indication that it will exit the stage of history without a protracted struggle.

Lastly, Prof. Žižek's brief discussion of Alain Badiou is a provocation on all three of these points, and also a provocation to Prof. Badiou himself. To use the latter's term, the "fidelity to an event" (for example, to the Bolshevik Revolution, or to the Cultural Revolution), which in Badiou's philosophy is the place where truth might be found (in one of four event-domains, science, politics, art, and love), is also a place of great danger. Perhaps Prof. Žižek's most profound provocation is to have thematized the way that nothing revolutionary can happen without the risk of this danger. I hope that the present book in its entirety takes risks that are worthy of Prof. Žižek's provocations.

BILL MARTIN

The
Conversations

1
History and Responsibility

AVAKIAN: In the material that you prepared in anticipation of our conversations you raised the issue of *The Black Book of Communism* (setting forth the alleged crimes of communism in the twentieth century),* which is just one particular book, but there are obviously bigger implications. I agree: I think we do need a detailed response to these kinds of things; we have to go into the actual history of these things, examine them and bring the essence of it to light, actually confront what has happened and try to understand it as best we can and explain it as best we can. It is difficult, because we have to put this in the context of a lot of other things that need to be done. It's also the case, as Lenin said, that "one sentence of falsehood requires ten pages of truth to explain it"—or I heard something by Mark Twain the other day about how "falsehood travels halfway around the world before truth has put on its shoes." [*laughs*]

MARTIN: Right.

AVAKIAN: You have that sort of problem. These people can churn out this stuff, and they have the power of the status quo and the state and all that behind them, but that doesn't relieve us—in fact in a certain way that makes the responsibility greater to answer that. But one of the things that has to be figured out is *how* to do it and who can take this up; who can be brought forward. A lot of different people should actually be brought forward to go at this, even if they go at it from somewhat different angles or somewhat different perspectives.

----

* *The Black Book* is an 800-page compendium of articles and studies purporting to "catalog and analyze the crimes of communism over the last seventy years." Intermixed with its many lies and slanders is some discussion of actual shortcomings and mistakes in the Bolshevik and Chinese revolutions.

MARTIN: Uh-huh.

AVAKIAN: I think one of the things is finding the ways to identify, mutually identify, the people who would want to take up the challenge of answering the attacks on socialism and digging into the actual history of socialist countries, and then finding out the ways that, in some overall sense, their efforts can be coordinated to do it.

MARTIN: Uh-huh. I'm partly thinking it's almost the *feel* of how one would come at this. I saw the other day in the *Chronicle of Higher Education* that some woman from China is now launching on some project to tell the horror stories of the Cultural Revolution in detail and . . . not that that hasn't been done already, but for some reason now they want to keep doing it and keep doing it and keep . . . It's a little bit like that . . . you know the second Alien movie . . . [*Aliens*], where that one guy said, "They're going to keep coming in here and coming in here and coming in here" and he's freaked out and it's clearly meant to . . . it's that pounding, insistent beat . . . And how do you go against that without assuming a merely defensive sort of posture? And I think some of that goes back to the whole "Hitler/Stalin" equation that we get pounded with constantly. On the one hand, how do we say, "Yes, that's part of our story"; while, on the other hand, "That's not everything we want to spend our time on—that is only talking about what's gone on in the past of the movement," so to speak. It's a little bit like *spurious* lawsuits or spurious arrests where they'll just arrest people for no reason but it takes up their time, resources, etcetera. And there's a lot of this where it's out there purely just to take up all of your time.

AVAKIAN: I remember that even happening to Lenny Bruce. His comedy became totally focused around, and he became totally absorbed in, defending himself when he was continually arrested for obscenity. But anyway . . .

MARTIN: Right, right. So, it's a hard nut to crack and I guess I think the larger question is, how do we relate to our history? What does it mean that we have this history? I tend to look at this in a kind of narrative framework. What does it mean that these are chapters in our book, so to speak; that we have more chapters to write; the story's got a long way to go yet. I read this interesting article by Fredric Jameson just the other day, called "Actually Existing Marxism" that was in this book of "rethinking Marxism"–type essays [The book is *Marxism Beyond Marxism*] and it's interesting. He's one who is generally sympathetic to the Soviet experience under Stalin and he thinks it is part of our story. He's even much more sympathetic to Mao and Maoism but at the same time it was interesting because he was sort of casting it in the light of, these historical experiences are our early steps that we need to go beyond in such a way where we can say, "Well, yes, those were the first big steps but on the other hand, we have a lot bigger steps to make and we also have to make them in very different conditions and in a very different time." And actually it goes a little bit to what you wrote . . . when was this? This is going back to maybe 1991 or 1992 about "The End of a Stage and a Beginning of a New Stage," which I thought was fascinating and I always wanted to get into it more in the sense of a time when there were no socialist countries, a time for what—about seventy years when a large part of the world was socialist and now a time when we don't have that, and how to define the character of this time. Because to me, part of what's interesting about our society, and why I call it an "impasse," is that society has come to be defined in some deep structural way—it's not the totality of it but it is a part of the deep structure that not only do we not have socialist countries in the world right now, but, "Don't even think of the possibility of that anymore because that didn't work," as they say. That whole sort of thing.

AVAKIAN: That's the "history of the twentieth century."

MARTIN: Yeah. "Don't even think there could be something different from this basic system." The way that continual bleat structures a lot of things, a lot of the way that horizons are formed. So, how to bring that history, how to grapple with that history and that whole . . .

AVAKIAN: Yeah, I think that is a big question. Part of it is that you do have to answer particular things without getting completely bogged down in them. Some of these things, like this *Black Book*, are more an attempt to "systematize" the "crimes" of communism. Then there is the other thing you were referring to—there's this whole spate of basically anecdotal attacks where these particularities are raised above the essence of what it was really about. It's like Mao said when he was talking about the peasant rebellion in Hunan Province way back in the 1920s. He made the point that some people were saying that the peasants were going too far, and he replied, "Yes there are excesses but if excesses are not committed in righting a wrong, then the wrong cannot be righted." Which doesn't justify the "excesses," but you have to understand that that's part of the process, and then you have to sum them up and learn from them and try not to repeat the errors. But it doesn't obliterate the essence. That was Mao's point: Is the essence of this that the peasants are going too far? Or is the essence of it that the peasants have risen up, righteously? So, I think we have to sift through and bring to the fore the essence. Sure, there were lots of things that weren't handled correctly and lots of ways in which people's personal careerism and other things got into the picture. I remember Mao said at one point that you could buy a Party Branch Secretary for a pack of cigarettes. [*both laugh*] So this is obviously a problem that he was . . .

MARTIN: Another reason to give up smoking, really. [*more laughter*]

AVAKIAN: Well put. That's a real thing. That same thing happens in prison. Cigarettes become a big commodity and medium of exchange. But the point Mao was making was obviously that we're still at the stage where a lot of this bourgeois ideology and people's narrow self interests get asserted above the larger things. But is that the essence of what happened with the Cultural Revolution? Or, as I have pointed out about Jared Diamond who wrote the book *Guns, Germs, and Steel*: that book has a lot of interesting and valuable things, but then I saw a tape of him speaking—he says something like, "Well, this is why you can't have a powerful centralized state, because it enables things to happen like happened in China, where in the Cultural Revolution some idiots decided to close down education." And this becomes a verdict on what the Cultural Revolution . . .

MARTIN: Right.

AVAKIAN: That, and all these anecdotes. So I think part of what we have to do is bring out the essence of it. For example, in your book on Sartre, *The Radical Project*, you were actually doing, I think, a good part of what we have to do, which is to situate this in its context. In other words, both historically, but also in a particular context, if we're going to criticize Stalin—which we should and have, and we need to deepen our understanding of that—you first have to situate this in what the necessity was. What were they actually dealing with, and then how well did they do in dealing with that? What errors were owing to the circumstances and would have been very difficult if not impossible to avoid? Or what things that were done wrong were largely owing to the circumstances, and which ones were more owing to methodology and outlook?

I think if we do that, then we can point toward the future in a certain sense. We can examine the past to point to the future, rather than getting completely bogged down in every anecdotal horror that's recounted. As you pointed out, you can get into defending yourself against every charge. That's happened to every revolutionary group, every political opposition group of any significance, in this country, for example: one of the big strategies of the powers-that-be is that they keep coming at you with legal charges and bogging you down. You have to raise money for that. You have to mount legal defenses. And what you were setting out to do is entirely diverted into that. So we have to find some way to answer these charges but make them serve the future in a sense.

MARTIN: Yes. I forget what it was specifically you just mentioned but, for example, especially right in the period after Deng Xiaoping came to power and when you started having rehabilitated Chinese intellectuals and people from the academic milieu coming over to the United States, and I guess they were going to Europe, too, and were telling their horror stories, which sort of amounted to they weren't able to pursue this or that academic project and instead had to go work on a farm for awhile. It's the sort of thing I would hear repeatedly. Things like, "Production stopped for ten years" and my point about that is that clearly on one level that's just so easily refutable it's hardly even worth refuting.

I would be in meetings where somehow these people would show up and they would say these things and I would feel compelled to say, "Now wait a minute, this was a society of close to a billion people; surely production could not stop for ten years." And so then, of course, what was interesting was what they meant was something called "economic growth" in some of those years was not very high or maybe for one or two years it was zero or not much more than zero and of course we know in the West that this whole idea of economic growth is kind of a dubious concept anyway. But my real point is that on another level what is it in the structure of our society where somebody can actually say, "Yeah, production stopped for ten years"? In a certain sense, what's the cognitive or the epistemological structure where there's a receptivity towards someone saying, "Yeah, we have this society of a billion people and they had no production for ten years"? [*chuckles*] "Yeah, man, that was terrible. Aw man, they must have really been hurtin'!"

So it becomes part of our project to kind of kick-start some critical consciousness here and some ability to just think about even very basic *inferential* sorts of things. So in a certain sense going back into that history divides into two. Part of it is the part of the history that we have to accept the criticisms of, and we have to work through the criticisms of, and in a certain sense that divides into two as well, where we have to say on the one hand, "Yeah, they just screwed up; Stalin just in some ways screwed up out of dogmatism and narrowness" and on other levels we have to say, "They were trying to do something for the first time, without a road map, without knowing where to go with it and they did the best they could, and it wasn't all just one horror after another, but in fact they did achieve some very important things in the world." But then the other side of that thing that splits into two is we have to get into this sort of basic question of what is the state of consciousness in our world, what are we up against in terms of kind of getting people to sink their teeth into some difficult questions?

AVAKIAN: Well, that last point let's hold in abeyance just for a second; I think it's an important question, but just to go back a step first. I think that even these slanders and the anecdotal stuff and everything, the more systematic slander like the *Black Book* as well as the anecdotal stories or "personal account" books and whatever—even there we have to divide that into two and sift through and see what we can learn from it, even where it's raised from a completely reactionary standpoint, a completely bourgeois, individualistic standpoint, or whatever. We still have to see what insights we can gain—and that's one thing I have tried to do, and I'm still trying to do, even with these statements that came out in that period right after the coup and when Deng Xiaoping was coming back and they had this whole campaign to repudiate the Gang of Four—they had all these quotes, which were alleged to be from Mao, criticizing the Gang of Four. My view is that, whether there was any truth to them, or authenticity to them, they were totally out of context; but I've still been trying to look at them this way: Okay, let's assume he did say these things—what could we learn from that? So, I think that's part of what we have to do but, once again, the other side of it is we do have to answer these things and answer them in the larger sense of pointing to the essence of what was going on and also, as I said, trying to point to the future.

In other words, not ignoring the past or just "covering up the past" but actually analyzing and synthesizing from the past to point to the future. I think that's something that will always be a task for us as long as the bourgeoisie and reactionaries are around. They're going to have their "objections," and we're going to have to sift through them and try to use this as material for our cause actually. Partly we have to refute this, but also we should use this as a way of educating people about what this process is actually about—what you do actually have to confront and transform in the course of it, and where we've done well and made real breakthroughs and where we've kind of fallen on our face or stumbled in terms of doing it. And, exactly as you said, putting this in historical perspective too: these were unprecedented—the Soviet Union was an unprecedented development. It was the first real breakthrough. There was the Paris Commune, but that never really got consolidated as a state. It never really had to take on the challenge: okay, now you're in the midst of all this imperialist encirclement and now . . . They never really dealt with the peasant question, for example, in France.*

MARTIN: Right.

AVAKIAN: If they'd had to deal with the peasant question, the Paris Commune would have been a lot different. They wouldn't have been able to maintain it in the form that they did. That was one of Mao's points. It's one thing if you have an historic breakthrough but it lasts only two months. It isn't really confronting questions like what do you do about the whole economy? What do you do about the peasant economy and the peasant culture, and how do you integrate that into an overall socialist society?

MARTIN: That's right.

---

* The Paris Commune of 1871 was the first successful seizure of power by the working class. For seventy-six days, between March 26 and May 30, the revolutionary workers held the city of Paris.

AVAKIAN: All those kinds of things were never confronted by the Paris Commune but were confronted for the first time by the Soviet Union, so it's necessary to keep going back to that even while we're answering some of these things.

2
Agriculture and Sense of "Place"

MARTIN: Right. Anarchists quite often appeal to the Paris Commune as the authentic experience, and as somebody who tends to be critical of the urban-centric orientation, that's kind of interesting, right, because in a certain sense that's all they had to deal with. And like you say, they didn't have to deal with the peasant question and how would they have done that on the basis of their ideology. I don't know how urban-centric they were but that was the context in which they were trying to do this thing. Clearly it would have been a very, very different problem for them to have to go out to that.

AVAKIAN: Even Lenin didn't really confront the "peasant question" until October, 1917. He did write things, important things, about agriculture and its transformation in different countries, including the U.S. and Russia, but to really confront it programmatically and in its deepest dimensions when you actually have responsibility for it—okay, now you've swept aside the old ruling class; now how are you going to mobilize masses of people to deal with these contradictions, of the countryside, the peasants, and their interconnection with the workers in the city? This was a proletarian revolution, which by definition is centered in the cities, but it was in a society different than China, for example, in important ways, yet similar in that the vast masses of the population were in the countryside and basically in feudal or semifeudal conditions. When October came and then the civil war, this was the first time they really had to confront this. In other words, they didn't work, like Mao, "from the countryside in." They worked, in a certain sense, "from the city out." So they didn't have that accumulation of experience over decades of working through some of these contradictions.

In any case, as the Chinese experience shows, the peasant question is different when you have swept aside the old system and now you're trying to go on and take the socialist road—that was different than during that entire long period of the revolutionary war in China, when they were carrying out a new-democratic revolution based in the countryside. So even there, there was a lot still to be learned. Could you go on to collectivization or did you have to stop at individual ownership? All those kinds of questions had never been confronted before, and they weren't really—I guess the point I'm trying to make is that they weren't really in the ken, so to speak, of the Marxist leaders in Russia up until October. They weren't really high on the agenda. Not that they were unaware of them or didn't pay attention, but they weren't prominent on the agenda, so to speak.

MARTIN: Do you think, though, that's from a kind of urban-centric orientation of Marxism all along up to that point, up until the point when that actually became a problem that had to be confronted? Because it's hard to think of Marx and Engels as being other than very urban oriented. Of course, they have all these statements about, going way back, about the idiocy of rural life and there's not a lot to learn out there. It's almost as if once the more scientific methods of industrial production developed, "Oh, agriculture will just be this relatively simple problem within that because after all the society is sorting out industry and you just need idiots to do the agriculture," so to speak. I think some of that approach was carried forward with Marxism, and that actually then became a problem when agriculture became a pressing question—where is the food going to come from?

AVAKIAN: I think when they were talking about the idiocy of rural life, they didn't literally mean that everybody is an idiot [*laughs*] in the countryside; but I do think, yes, there was a certain orientation because this was focused, and rightly so, on the proletariat. But then the question is: okay, that's the leading force of your revolution, but then what are other main forces of the revolution and how do you integrate and get the right synthesis of the city and the countryside? While in China they had to solve that on a certain level even in order to win power. And then in both cases, although from different angles, so to speak, in the Soviet Union and China, they had to confront it on a different level when they had power (throughout the country).

When power is seized, then what do you do? That was the point about the Paris Commune I was trying to make. A lot of times these anarchists will say, "Well, the good thing about the Paris Commune was that it had no vanguard; it was just pure work- ers' democracy." The answer that I've always given to that is, "Yeah, that's one of the reasons why it was defeated so quickly." And that's not to say, "Oh, well, having a vanguard solves all the problems"; but what I am trying to say by that (the same point I was making earlier about "they only lasted two months") is that they didn't really confront all the complexity of what it takes to go from capitalism to communism, and a big part of that was they didn't really confront the contradictions that make a van- guard necessary in the first place but that also, on the other side of that, hold the potential for the vanguard to turn into its oppo- site. Those questions were never really put on the agenda in the Paris Commune. If they'd gone on longer, they would have had to either transform what they had into something that had a van- guard—and then face all the contradictions that this involves— or they would have been defeated a little farther down the line.

MARTIN: Uh-huh. I want to come to two things there. The vanguard's a funny question. In the intellectual milieu, there are a lot of even progressive or radical people who will use "van- guard" as a kind of swear word. [*Avakian laughs*] To me what's interesting about that is there was a vanguard in the Paris Commune. There were leaders; there were people who, in the midst of mass activity, said, "Hey, we've got to get this going in a certain direction." Obviously they got it going in a certain direction. They couldn't have had the commune in the first place if they hadn't had that and the point would be sort of, "Gee, and they could have had it better if they'd done that better, if they'd gotten more organized."

But the other thing is that the very intellectuals who will often criticize the vanguard idea, at the very same time they don't have any problem with understanding themselves as being a certain kind of vanguard, playing a certain function of trying to centralize some thinking and taking it forward. So there's a kind of irony to me in terms of the way some people will address this. Maybe we should save this for another part of the discussion, but for me, what Lenin's about in *What Is to Be Done* is really a kind of epistemology. It's really about, "How does it come together so that we know what we're thinking about? And then we can sort ourselves out a bit and then go to the next step with it." As opposed to—what you often hear is that "this is Lenin's book on the organizational question," which just makes it sound very bureaucratic. I know for example when Trotskyists write about this, it's always the organizational question; we accept him on the organizational question and, interestingly, in some sense where they come down is they accept him on that but they reject him, I would say, on the imperialism question. So what are they left with? Well, we know how to start an organization. Well, yeah, they know how to start a lot of organizations because most any one they started breaks into about thirty others within ten minutes. I once heard a story that the Spartacists group started an organization in (I think) Poland after the breakup of the Eastern bloc with five members and within a few days it had actually split into three and two. [*laughter*]

Do you want to keep up with that a little bit, because I want to go back to the agriculture question a little bit, too.

AVAKIAN: Sure, go ahead.

MARTIN: I do think there's a little more to it than the proletariat being the leading force. I think part of what Marx was getting at with that idiocy remark was the disconnectedness of rural life, the entrenchment of lifeways and the seemingly unreflective way you do it because this is how it's been done. I mean, there are a number of things to be said about that. For example, when it comes down to things like how to grow plants, there is something to be said for doing it because that's how it's been done. There's not something to be said about doing it on an unreflective level, but there's also (maybe this connects with the other point) a tendency from the urban perspective to think that's all they're doing out there and that they don't really have knowledge, they just do it because that's how it's been done. Whereas I think the point is (and I think Mao actually brought this forward), "No, they do it that way because they have knowledge of the land, because they live on the land even if they may not be able to write a textbook about it." But to me one of the fantastical things that came out of the Cultural Revolution was how some of these people who taught agronomy and related subjects at Beijing University—they would go out to the countryside and they didn't have the first idea of how to actually grow anything because they didn't know, and their textbook knowledge wasn't really getting them very far out there.

But I think there's also this thing where Marx on this question still reflects something very deep in Western culture and it even goes back to Plato. Plato has the theory of the forms, but some things are so base that they're beneath the forms, for example, dirt and excrement. But without dirt and excrement this world couldn't turn around. Dirt and excrement are what makes this world turn around. There's this sensibility taken up in Western thought generally and I think Marx reflects it, that, "Well you don't really have to know anything about dirt." And I love what Wendell Berry says about this in his book *Home Economics*, which I think is a really fine book, where he says, "Well, I'll tell you one thing we know about topsoil. We know how to destroy it and we don't know how to make more of it. When it's gone we don't know how to make more of it."

So, people who are real farmers and people who engage in sustainable farms, farming— they know how to take care of soil so that it'll be there in the future and that's a *knowledge*—and if society loses that knowledge on the basis of shifting everything to where we can just do it industrially. . . . Some of my intellectual urban-centric friends will just say the most bizarre things, like, "Well they can grow hydroponic tomatoes in skyscrapers or something" or, "They can put gardens on top of Cabrini Green" and that's great. That's great if people put gardens on top of Cabrini Green but that's not going to feed . . . that's not agriculture. You know what I mean? That whole thing has to get addressed on a better level than it has been.

AVAKIAN: I think in any specific sphere of life, or any endeavor, the people who are directly engaged in the practice of it do have a lot of knowledge, not simply raw empirical knowledge but also some summed up and even synthesized experience. Obviously it's necessary to learn from that while there is also the question of integrating and synthesizing that with theories developed more abstractly, drawn from lots of experience about agriculture in different places and also drawing from advanced science that has to be concretely applied. And then some aspects of it are going to be shown to be not applicable, and that's the process that they also went through in China.

But the way I interpret the "idiocy of rural life" thing has more to do with, say, what you could call the "cultural" dimension, or being steeped in tradition, being weighed down by tradition, sort of. The pace of bourgeois life has its . . . particularly in the early phases—this whole thing they say in the *Manifesto* about all that's holy is profaned, everything solid becomes broken apart. All that kind of thing, I think, has its positive side. In other words, people don't get stuck in. It's one thing to say, like you were saying, okay, there's some reason why farming is done the way it is and you can't just come in and say, "Never mind that, let's just throw that all out" and impose something from the outside that really doesn't have any "organic" basis or relation to what they're doing, if you'll pardon a certain pun. [*Avakian laughs*]

MARTIN: Right, right.

AVAKIAN: On the other hand, there is something about that constant shaking up of things that doesn't go on as much in the countryside and among people more steeped in tradition. That is a problem actually, and I think we have to . . . Obviously you don't just one-sidedly negate all tradition, but the tradition especially of class-divided society, the traditions that have been carried forward are mainly negative, socially and politically and even culturally, but there's also the additional dimension of things being sort of staid. The constant motion and change of things and the complexity of things and wrangling with that complexity doesn't get spontaneously generated or whatever by rural life as much as it does when you're in a society or a social setting that's more cosmopolitan. You don't, for example, in the rural areas have as much—although that's changing in the U.S.—but you don't historically have as much connection with people from other countries, other places. I mean, in the U.S. now, from what I understand, you have people in the rural areas who are coming from many different countries and working in small towns as well as on farms, so that's a little different and that's a positive thing. In other words, there is a thing of rural . . . I guess I'd say two points—rural isolation and the weight of tradition. That, to me when I think of the "idiocy of rural life"—which is a phrase that for many reasons I have focused on a lot—when I think of that, I think more of those two things.

MARTIN: Uh-huh.

AVAKIAN: It's true, Marx and Engels didn't have the experience with the peasantry, nor did Lenin, that Mao did. And there are a lot of things that have come out of the Chinese revolution that are positive as a result of that experience, but I do think there are those two things—the isolation and being sort of tradition-steeped and weighed down by it—that are more valid points, whether you want to use the phrase "idiocy" or whatever—that's deliberately provocative.

MARTIN: I think I disagree with you on this. I mean, look at it this way. Just to go back to where you were starting, part of where you were starting, the famous "everything solid melts into air." I know in my own intellectual, whatever, trajectory, there was a point where I was admittedly somewhat bedazzled by postmodernism, you might say, and so then when there was a bit of a, I wouldn't call it a conservative reaction, but there was a bit of a concerned reaction along the lines of, "Well, what you're really valorizing there is a certain fragmentation of life." There was a point where I would sort of say "Hey, fragment away; it's a ridiculous form of life to begin with."

And it's not that I completely forgot some basic Marxism there, but it was more that I was looking at the idea that great disorder can lead to great order—that it's got to fragment before it can come back together, in another way. I think I was more sanguine about that in some ways than I am now. Part of that has to do with thinking that agriculture is where everything really, pardon my pun, comes to ground in the sense that there are some thresholds that, if humanity crosses them, we may not make it back, and that's where I take Wendell Berry's point about topsoil to be very important. There are some thresholds where you can't just keep coming at it and coming at it. There are only so many holes that you can have in the ozone layer. There is only so much crap that you can dump in the rivers and the oceans, and then there comes a point where a critical mass of this stuff has been reached and the fish can't live and you can only cut down so many trees, that sort of thing. To my mind the real idiots out there are the sort of people who'll say, "There's plenty more trees out there," or "They'll grow back." The extreme version of it is, "God will decide when this world will end; we can't do anything to end it." [*Avakian chuckles*] I tend to think, "No, we probably can," we human beings. And obviously the blame for that goes to those who are at the top of these structures.

But, to come to this whole thing about living in towns, I live in a smaller town half of the year, so I have this split thing where

I live in a big city half the year, a very big city, and a small town half the year, and yeah, it's great. There are people in that small town from all over the place and especially coming up from Mexico, but lots of Asians now, etcetera. And that's great, that's good. It broadens everyone's perspective and all of that, but without getting into any sort of essentialistic "these people belong here or these other people belong there" kind of thinking, there's also the question of—that people live in places and if they don't live in places, then those places tend to get destroyed because they're not valued as places and the city is something that becomes less and less of a place. And it spreads out from there so these small towns become less and less of a place because they become McDonaldized, they become Wal-Martized, etcetera and there's nothing about them as places or as regions and then people don't know anymore how to live in them and even in these smaller towns get more and more the idea that "You know where food comes from? It comes from the grocery store." "I'm eating this? What is this? I don't even recognize what's in this." Okay, but they become more and more accustomed to that sort of thing. It's this point about the general and the particular that it's great that we have these general principles about summing up what has been learned but there's also a sense in which it's got to be with the perspective that if we're going to live in this world it's going to have to be a world of places. Unless we are really looking at this kind of idea that ultimately we'll pave it all over and we'll take it from there. Part of what's great about agriculture is that it gives us a model of decentralization and it gives us a model of where everything isn't yet so fully commodified and where money enters into every exchange.

One problem I have with Marx is that I think he thought that what would really happen is that all the forms in which we've known place, which is a question he doesn't really address as such, all the forms in which humanity has known community, all the forms in which humanity has known all those things that he and Engels say in the *Manifesto*, that relationship between priest and parishioner, and basically lover and beloved, all these things will break down and be replaced by the cash nexus. But then somehow on the other side of that we'll reinvent those human relationships in a noncommodified way. And what I worry is that what will happen instead is that if there aren't certain forms of things, and you can call them "tradition" or you can call them whatever, but if they're not carried forward in some way, even if a transformed way, it's not that they'll be reinvented, it's just that they'll be lost because we'll have no idea what they were to begin with. We'll have no memory of them. We'll have no sense of what it would mean to have a relation, a human relation with another person.

AVAKIAN: Well, when I'm talking about tradition I'm not talking—again it has to be divided into two, it does divide into two, but I'm talking more about patriarchy, religious obscurantism, a lot of these things that are reinforced by rural isolation, or tend to be. Look, the point you're making about capitalism, the way I look at it, it does divide into two. In other words, all these things they mentioned in the *Manifesto*—if the *Manifesto* were some sort of paean to capitalism then that would be a problem. In other words, they're not saying all these are great things in and of themselves. What they're saying is that these things lead to, or point in the direction of and provide an important basis for (as they would put it), being negated by something better. In other words, it's not that capitalism has solved these problems. Capitalism breaks apart certain things and then solidifies things on a certain level and in other forms, other forms of oppression, other forms of exploitation, alienation, if you will, and we have to go beyond it. So, commodity production and commodity relations will be increasingly introduced into agriculture, regardless of what we do or regardless of what we want, as long as capitalism is running the world; and it won't do it in the way it was done in the U.S. For most of the world, it won't happen the way it's happened in countries like the U.S. It will happen in a way that reintegrates forms, precapitalist forms—feudal forms, whatever, even some forms of slavery outright—but it will happen on a certain level. The question is, how do we go forward beyond that? Not how do we celebrate what capitalism has done or, on the other hand, try to go back before it?

MARTIN: Uh-huh.

AVAKIAN: But how do you go forward and integrate things that are positive from history, and even from tradition, but recast them—resynthesize them so that you get something radically different which bursts apart and uproots the relations of oppression and exploitation and the alienation, but achieves a new synthesis through that? So, this point you're making about place—maybe you could explain that a little more, because the way I look at it—and I think this was the experience of China—it's not that we want to have bigger and bigger megacities, obviously not in the form in which they exist now, surrounded by all these favelas or shantytowns or whatever. That's obviously something that's a creation of imperialism, and they were trying to move away from that in China, toward a different synthesis where they spread some of the more advanced understanding and culture that came from the cities to the countryside. But also some of the ways of doing things that had evolved in the countryside were integrated into that synthesis, even in terms of how they tried to do things in the cities. In other words, sometimes they'd form neighborhood cooperative things which, on the one hand, reflected where the economy was at but also were a way of getting people together in groups to do certain things, a form of collectivity, both economically and socially.

MARTIN: Uh-huh.

AVAKIAN: And I think there's a lot to learn more about—and sift through and draw further lessons from—in that experience. But I think it's true we don't want the capitalist model of the way the countryside and the city are. We don't want either of those. I could also make the point by looking at it on an international level—just to try to shed a little more light on what I'm trying to say. Obviously, a lot of the culture that comes from the imperialist countries is a lot of crap and worse. It gets imposed on these other countries, and there is a real point to the whole cultural imperialism indictment. On the other hand, not everything that comes out of these imperialist countries is just crap and should be rejected. In fact, that was one criticism we have of the Chinese: they condemned everything—rock-'n'-roll, jazz—and our feeling is that there was an element of . . .

MARTIN: Beethoven.

AVAKIAN: Yeah, they did try to be more dialectical there, but still they weren't even dialectical with jazz and rock-'n'-roll [*laughs*]; it was just bourgeois or imperialist junk.

MARTIN: Western decadence.

AVAKIAN: Right, exactly. And obviously there is a lot of that, particularly in rock-'n'-roll, but there's something else too. There is a lot of that in rap, especially the rap that gets promoted now, but there's something else too. How the Chinese dealt with this was one of the things we felt reflected a certain nationalism as well as being a little undialectical; and I think there's some kind of synthesis that needs to be worked toward—which will never be achieved under this system. Some of the ways in which the culture in different countries, say in the Third World, has been influenced by some of the negative but also some of the positive in culture from the imperialist countries, but in turn has influenced it. Not that we should have a "homogenization"—that's not my point—but a continual interplay between these things, on a certain level, internationally. And that's kind of like the city and the countryside, too, understood metaphorically.

MARTIN: Uh-huh.

AVAKIAN: I'm trying to make sort of the same point about the city and countryside within a particular country. In other words, I think they're both going to need to be transformed. But maybe, if you think it's a line you want to pursue, you could explain more about what you meant by this point about place. Or if you want to go somewhere else.

MARTIN: Yeah, no, because it's funny too, the "rock-'n'-roll question," because in a way it does address this larger historical question — what is our history but also what is our future with it?—in the sense that every now and then I have to say to a young student, an undergraduate student who is having trouble with this or that professor and they're somebody in the older generation from me and every now and then the explanation seems clear and the student will generally understand it, though they won't understand it the way those of us who grew up in the sixties and not so long after that, understand it, but I'll say, "In a way there's such a thing as 'before and after rock-'n'-roll' and this person you're talking about is before rock-'n'-roll and you're after rock-'n'-roll." And they'll understand it and we're sort of after rock-'n'-roll. There's something funny about that "we're after rock-'n'-roll," but we'll have a conversation about the Stalin question. In most "after rock-'n'-roll" circles that will not be a question people are going to talk about a lot.

It's a little bit like we need to deal with the old things but we need to deal with the new things, and what does it mean to put the new things on the front burner and yet take responsibility for the old things as well and carry them forward and make what we can out of them, and that's a difficult issue. In a way I guess it's good that people keep bringing up the old things because there would be a tendency to say, "Well, those are the old things and we're going to go on" and then of course you'll hear, "Yeah, but aren't you those guys who 'did Stalin?' Aren't you part of that?" And we have to say, "Yes" and we take responsibility for that. We *want* to be a part of that. We think that's something that started to unfold and we want to continue to unfold that but now we want to take it further and we want to go to a higher level with it. But to come back to the "place question" . . .

AVAKIAN: Could I just say one thing about that point before we leave it? I do want to hear what you have to say about place, but I was just thinking that partly on this Stalin thing and the whole "history of the twentieth century"—in other words the history of socialism, so to speak—in a certain way there's an aspect in which we have to make this a question rather than an accusation. Right now it's an accusation, and yet we have to make it a question. Even on the level where it is a "settled" question, in the negative sense, we have to reopen the question on a different level. I think that's also part of what we have to do.

MARTIN: How the heck do you think we can do that?

AVAKIAN: I didn't want to take this entirely . . .

MARTIN: Maybe we'll come back to it because that is a wall you can just bang your head on.

AVAKIAN: I'd like to hear and learn from some of your experience, because I think there is a whole sphere of work and struggle and engagement with intellectuals—particularly ones who are interested in the idea of a better world but who have been basically convinced that this road is closed off, that history has passed its verdict on this: everything from a failed experiment to a disaster and worse. I think we have to find the ways to reengage people around that question. I would actually like to hear a lot of what your thinking is on that, because these are circles that you're more able to be involved in.

MARTIN: Right, right.

AVAKIAN: Certainly more than I am directly, although the party is trying to get more into these circles to become more familiar with them and engage them more.

MARTIN: Let's come back to it, but one interesting experience to go to around that is, for example, how this plays out, within intellectuals, among people who work on Sartre.

AVAKIAN: But do you think we should go back to this whole thing later?

MARTIN: We should definitely go back to it. Let me just say one very quick thing about it, because this is always raised if you work on Sartre. "Wasn't he a Stalinist? Didn't he defend that?" And, of course, the thing you hear over and over again, in fact apparently in France this is like, they practically set it to a beat. You know, "The Thousand Mistakes of Sartre" and in fact I heard a wonderful talk by Michel Rybalka, who is French, taught in the U.S. for many years, a Sartre scholar, but who knew Sartre personally—some of those last interviews that are in books of Sartre's stuff that have come out, he did those interviews and he was with Sartre in the early seventies. But he's older; he was part of the older generation rather than the younger, Benny Levy and that generation. He said, "I want to affirm the thousand mistakes of Sartre." I'm glad. It's a little bit like what Mao said to W. E. Dubois about the "mistake you didn't make was quitting." But how that question plays out in the circles is an interesting model for maybe a larger sense of "how do you come at that?"—but it's mainly a model for the difficulties of it. It's mainly a model for how difficult this is, but I'm sure we'll come back to that.

The "place" thing, one way this kind of came home to me and that concentrated some things for me, was reading Wendell Berry, which really did open up a lot of questions for me, and especially the book *Home Economics*. It opened up a lot of questions for me, and stuff where, when I was first reading it, I thought, "This guy's insane; this guy's a cave man," but a lot of it really then started to take effect. But I have a student who I get together with regularly and she said, "You know, my daughter has gotten sort of hooked on eating kiwi and I don't know if that's such a great thing because it has to come from New Zealand." So why does somebody living in Chicago in January think they're entitled to eat something that's grown in New Zealand and that couldn't grow anywhere near here and has to be brought over on a ship and a lot of not only resources or just money or whatever is tied up in that, but basically you have to have a whole international system of relations to get this kiwi here and it's inseparable from a lot of other international relations that allow that to happen. And it seems to me there are two broad points that can come out of that. There is something to be said for, if kiwi doesn't grow here then that tells us something about our bio-region, as ecologists put it, and about whether we should then make something happen by reconfiguring the earth in ways that are not easily unconfigured once they're configured that way.

I think the outstanding example, Wendell Berry comes back to this quite often, is a city like Phoenix, Arizona, that has no local ecological basis for existing whatsoever and you have to, as they say, "divert mighty rivers" in order to have air conditioning in the desert for that thing to exist. And there's a kind of, and I don't mean to wax new-agey on you, but it seems to me there's a kind of wisdom of the land that would tell human beings who are not utterly wrapped up in commodity relations that you don't just come at the earth that way—that you have a respect for it and you let it teach you something. And I don't know if that's very much a part of Marx's outlook. In fact, I think Marx's outlook was more, "No, actually what capitalism is going to give us is this great, great, great concentration and development of industry and dirt isn't much worth thinking about." Why do you need to think about dirt? Which is sort of what Plato was saying too. Dirt? That's *beneath thought*. There's no form, there's no *idea* of dirt. You don't need to think about dirt. Dirt takes care of itself, doesn't it? Well, it takes care of itself until humans start reconfiguring it in radical ways.

So, I think there's something that place tells us and there's something to the idea that, if you don't live in a place, then after a while you live in no place, and after a while what you are is one of these fragments that melts into air and you're "available." It is that postmodern giddiness— everything is up for, not for grabs, after a while it's not everything is up for grabs or how we're going to re-create society on a noncommodified basis. It's up for grabs just in the sense that you're going to be whipped around by this or that thing flowing in the commodity stream and I guess I think there's something there, I hope, in rural life mainly outside of imperialist countries, that could still be a resistance to that, even with all of the elements of it that are highly problematic that need to be transformed, especially the patriarchal stuff.

Yeah, when you say religious obscurantism of the sort of Eastern European peasant life where it's highly developed Eastern Catholic Orthodoxy, maybe that's a problem. I think if it's

more of a, just as I feel when I ride my bicycle out into the countryside and it's a beautiful day and I just feel "the earth is good"—
I mean there's something that's being given here that I know I
sure as hell didn't have anything to do with bringing about.
When I'm out and I can see stars, when I can see the Milky Way
which is something I don't think Marx saw from the city, that you
can't see from the city, I mean there's something about that, and
even about the idea that this is a common world that I and my
fellow humans should share with one another, and I didn't put it
here. Where we go with that is a whole other question.

I don't think one has to go to a god with a long, white beard
sitting on a throne, saying, "Let there be light." I don't, but on
the other hand there's a kind of gift about it that to me is an
inspiration toward communism, because it's the common inher-
itance of humankind and of all the other creatures on this planet
that we ought to find some way to share rather than carve out
and commodify and put a price tag on, or, as Rousseau said—I
think these are some of the greatest words ever written, in the
Discourse on Inequality, about how the first time somebody put
a fence around a piece of land and convinced everybody else
that there was this thing called ownership and that they owned
it, this was like the greatest . . . I don't know what he said in
French, but the greatest bamboozle perpetrated on humankind.
To me there's inspiration in all of that; it's not religious obscurantism. It might be a kind of vaguely religious point of view,
but not in a way that I find at all problematic.

AVAKIAN: Well, I . . .

MARTIN: So, I take a lot of inspiration from that.

AVAKIAN: I share a lot of the concerns and even the sensibilities that you're expressing on a certain level. I think it is wrong
to endow them or imbue them with a magical—or certainly a
religious—content or meaning, or surround them with a certain
aura of religion or magic or whatever.

MARTIN: Why is it wrong, necessarily? For example, "magical"—what does that mean?

AVAKIAN: It depends on what you mean. If you mean metaphysical, if you mean something that isn't reality—isn't material
reality and has to be explained by some other means, or is inexplicable—then that's what I mean. I see a problem with that.

MARTIN: What if I just meant by magical, like I say, I'm out
on a beautiful day, the sun is shining and I just say, "Man, it's

so beautiful." I mean, I can see why ancient peoples worshipped the sun, because it just gives and gives and gives. There's not a damn thing you can give back to it. [*Avakian laughs*] There's nothing you can do to help it. It's not asking for your help. Just gives. I see that as an inspiration. I see that as like, "Why don't we all share it?" So why don't we have a beautiful world where we all share in this beauty instead of carving it up and saying, "Oh, but I own . . ." I don't know if you ever get to watch *The Simpsons*, which I think is our greatest popular sort of social satire in the U.S. now, but there's this great episode. I don't know if you know the characters in *The Simpsons* but there's this guy [Montgomery Burns] who is the owner of the nuclear power plant in the town of Springfield and he comes up with this scheme. It's just so brilliant. He has one of these things like out of James Bond where the conference table, the surface sort of pulls back and this whole model rises up. It's the model of the city [of Springfield] for his grand scheme. And the way he's introducing it to the executives who are part of the nuke plant, he says, "Since the beginning of time man has had but one dream—to destroy the sun!" [*laughs*] and what it is is a scheme to erect a shield over the whole city such that the people in the city have to pay in order to get sunlight. And I love that because it just shows . . . and that's happening, that's what's incredible.

We are now at the point where, because you think about it, how is it that people can *own* land? On some level, that's just bizarre. That is just an absurd idea—that people, that individuals and a handful of individuals among all of humankind could own the land when the land is absolutely necessary; it's not optional to have land in order for people to be able to live, so how the hell is it that just a few people own it? And then you think, gee, if they can own the land, why can't they own the atmosphere? Why don't I just jump out and say, "I have this deed. I own the atmosphere now, you're going to have to pay me to breathe!" I think that movie where Arnold Schwarzenegger goes to Mars [*Total Recall*], that's based on the Philip K. Dick story, and on Mars they just live in these enclosed habitats where the air is produced and if you don't pay your tax, you don't breathe. So they've got that down. Well, why can't I own the sunlight; why can't I . . . ? Well, because it's absurd. It's just absurd. I mean, I just take inspiration from that and if somebody wants to think, and yeah, there's just a wonderment to that, there's a wonderment to this even existing and that we're here in the midst of this. And even if they make some sort of theology out of it, I mean I wouldn't do that necessarily, but I don't see it as a very big problem, in fact I don't see any impediment.

I think we ought to save some of this, because I know we're going to go at religion to some extent. I think for Marx, like you said, that is also part of his sense of the idiocy of rural life, whereas I just don't see it as a big problem and in fact I would see it more as the problem when that just gets broken down to where a person is thought of as a fool for looking at it that way but they're not thought of as a fool to look at it as, "What's needed instead is a centralized system of production that gets us kiwis in January in Chicago."

AVAKIAN: Well . . .

MARTIN: To me that way is insanity, and . . . wasn't there this whole episode where Stalin, the famous thing—Mao wrote about it, right?—where Stalin wanted pineapple from China or something.

AVAKIAN: That I don't remember, I know he was critical of them for making the people in historically Muslim areas grow pigs, which may have something to do with what you're raising. But just to clarify my . . .

MARTIN: I'm sorry, I know I blasted a lot in your direction.

AVAKIAN: No, no, that's fine. But just to explain what I meant about magic, I'm perfectly enthusiastic about magic in the poetic sense, or the lyrical sense, if you will, but not when things are mystified and when it's presented—when reality is presented as other than it is—or something that is not reality is presented as reality, or as even the essential reality. Again, we'll talk more about religion, but to me that's the essence of religion: to present things that are not reality as if they're not only reality but the essential and defining character of reality. And I do think that's a problem. But lyrically, metaphorically, poetically, sure, anybody that doesn't feel moved in a certain way by being able to stand out and look at the stars is losing something. So I certainly agree with that, and I certainly agree with your point about the earth. But just to be fair to Marx, this is a point that Marx did make, as I'm sure you're aware: he did make this point that individuals are not owners of the earth, they're only its guardians and have to pass it on from generation to generation.

So on that level, and even on the level of agriculture, I don't think the comment about the idiocy of rural life is the sum total, or the sum and substance, of what Marx and Engels thought about agriculture. It's true they didn't understand it, and didn't really wrestle with a lot of the questions involved in it, in the same way they had to in the Soviet Union—that's why they did, because they had to—or the way Mao did as part of the basic orientation of revolution there after a very short period of a city-based revolutionary effort which, as we know, was crushed mercilessly. So, on that level, on the level of, yes, we are care-takers of the earth, I agree.

The problem with . . . well, just take your point about the sun. To me, the sun is the sun, and it's why we're here on one level but it also does have (if you want to get into that), it has its negative side.

MARTIN: No, no! [*laughing*]

AVAKIAN: It makes certain areas inhospitable.

MARTIN: Yeah.

AVAKIAN: People can't live, they can't grow anything in cer-tain areas. On the other hand, there is lots of wildlife that's extremely interesting in places like the desert, so all these things present their different aspects, but . . .

MARTIN: What do you mean they can't live?

AVAKIAN: Well, there are certain areas where the sun is just too much, so to speak.

MARTIN: Right.

AVAKIAN: It's very difficult to live there. That's what I meant.

MARTIN: But shouldn't that tell us something? I mean this doesn't even go to the magic question, but like with Phoenix, Arizona, or maybe I have a bit of a puritanical streak on this, but like Las Vegas where they basically are using the Colorado River to light up a million light bulbs twenty-four hours a day. To me it's like, gee, the sun is telling us, and the sand and where the water is, is telling us, that shouldn't even be there. It shouldn't even be there if they were doing something other than what they're doing there, but it's especially an insult that it's being done for the sake of a mob-administered casino city and all that.

AVAKIAN: Yeah, there are a lot of things we could look at in the world and say, "We would not, should not, and will not do things that way." I once saw this story about Saudi Arabia where they're pumping and desalinating billions of gallons of water for golf courses for the elite there and for imperialist businessmen. That's obviously an obscenity on many different levels, so there are a lot of things that are done under the anarchy of capitalism which are not the way we would do things. But, on the other hand, I do think a word has to be said for not just appreciating but also for transforming nature. In our party's *Draft Programme* we talk about a socialist economy that would be economically productive, ecologically rational, and socially just, and would provide sustainable development. I think those things all go into it, and that's something that capitalism cannot even approach. On any of those things, including being ecologically rational and sustainable, it's not something that can even be on the capitalist agenda, so a lot of the stuff they do we would want to undo and create a whole different way of going about things.

MARTIN: Just going at that point very narrowly too, to me that's something that ought to work in our behalf. I'm not a political economist and maybe there are dimensions of this that I'm just speaking very naively on, but obviously I haven't lived in the Third World and I'm sure it's a very different question there. I think we have reached the point where we can say on some questions, "How much more production do we really need?" For example, I think the *Programme*, the *Draft Programme*, addresses this very well in the case of transportation. We don't need more and more cars or more and more generations of cars or whatever. We don't need to keep cranking this stuff out forever. And that's a very significant sector of production.

AVAKIAN: I don't think it's a question of *how much* do we need but *what kind* do we need. Because people have to keep producing and reproducing in order to live.

MARTIN: Yeah, but for example, how much more, when you just think of, what I think of as the "trinity" of materialism—food, shelter, clothing. For example, we know that homelessness is not caused by there being a lack of places for people to live. In other words, how many more, how much more land do we need to fill up with places for people to live? We've got, if anything, we probably have an overabundance in some parts of the world.

AVAKIAN: Yeah, I think a lot of that has to do with the lopsidedness in the world, and there's a certain lopsidedness within even the "advanced" capitalist—in other words, imperialist—countries: there's lopsidedness there, too, in all different kinds of ways. There are some people who have a tremendous amount of consumer goods as well as capital and who engage in all kinds of self-indulgent consumption, and then there are other people who are homeless, not because there are not the raw materials to build them homes or whatever—who are unemployed and homeless when they could be working and building homes or doing other things and could contribute to everybody having decent shelter. There will always be—for example, even under communism, decisions will have to be made about how much time people want to put into producing x, y, or z for basic needs and also to progressively diminish the time that has to be spent by individuals in just producing the basic needs of life, so that all kinds of other avenues can be opened up for all kinds of people, including the 90-plus percent of the world that's completely blocked from those avenues now.

How much do you want to do that versus how much do you want to leave things undeveloped? And how do you go about developing things so that you can still see the stars at night? All these will be real questions; but the thing is, I still think that there will always be a question of production, in one form or another, and there will always be a question of transforming nature in order to carry out production. The question is not whether, but how? According to what principles. To me, that's the question—what kind of needs, both material and nonmaterial, if you want to put it that way, in the sense of not immediate sustenance for people, but having more to do with culture and, broadly speaking, ideas, art, all that sort of thing. How much do you want to devote to that, versus how much do you want to build this or that, that might meet people's basic needs? One of the things I was thinking about in relation to our *Draft Programme*, for example, is we talk about—this is a little bit off this immediate subject, but we talk about valuing dissent in socialist society. Well, decisions have to be made. Somebody comes to whomever, or whatever institutions are funding things, for example, and says, "I want to be funded to write a newspaper that criticizes what you're doing." How much value do you put on that versus building a hospital for people who don't have health care? Well, it's not an answer to just say, "You can't do that, because we have to build a hospital."

MARTIN: No, or what resources do you want to devote to me putting out an album of avant-garde cello improvisations? [*laughter*]

AVAKIAN: We have to figure out: how do you, as you say, valorize those things? How much importance do you attach to one thing versus another? You can't be narrow and economist about it and instrumentalist about it. On the other hand, you also can't ignore real needs that people have—and production will always have to be carried out in some form to meet those needs.

I did want to say one thing about Rousseau. The thing with Rousseau is, on one level, that's true, but it's not exactly . . . it's also ahistorical. It's not exactly the way things evolved or how they have evolved, that somebody just put up a fence. In one sense it is—there was a certain point at which early communal societies broke apart and other forms which began to have class differentiation and private property did emerge. But it isn't just that somebody said, "I'm going to put up a fence"; because if that had been the only problem, then other people would have said, "No you're not"—and that would have been the end of it. So something historically evolved that was going on. This is another point I am just throwing out there because I want to come back to it: I was thinking of the point you were making, in something you have written, that people can't do good if they're not setting out to do good. That's something I'd like to explore. On one level, I think people can do good "by accident." In other words, on a certain level, here or there they can do something that, whatever their intent is, has a good effect for humanity or whatever. But in the sense in which you were raising it—that you have to be conscious of trying to create a better society in order to actually do it—I think there's a lot of truth to that, but here's my problem also with mystification and religion. I don't think you can set out to transform society in the way it needs to be transformed, both in the material conditions and relations and in people's thinking and everything, without having—and I know this is a much maligned phrase [*laughs*] but I still think there's something to it, if understood correctly—without having a scientific approach to that.

3
Ethics and the Question of Truth

AVAKIAN: I don't think you can do it [transform society] spontaneously, and I don't think you can do it if you think there are mystical forces that are out there that are going to either influence this or have to be relied upon to do it. If that's what's guiding you, you're going to fall short at some point, because it doesn't actually conform to the way the world really is, the way existence is, so you're going to get led astray. That's the analogy I'm trying to make with what you're saying about how you can't do good if you're not setting out to do good. I think you can't transform everything that needs to be transformed if you have a fundamentally erroneous idea about what it is you're trying to transform and what are the motive forces of it.

MARTIN: Okay, but . . . so are you aligning what I said about "you can't do good if you don't set out to do good" with this sort of scientific standpoint of understanding the motive forces? Because on some level that's the alignment I would make, but I think you're making a distinction between those two sides, right?

AVAKIAN: Well, let me put it this way. You can correct me if I'm wrong or if I'm vulgarizing, but from what I've read of what you've written and what I'm trying to understand of it, maybe we could put it this way, which might sharpen things up in a good way: I think you are very concerned about a materialism that isn't in a certain sense, as you say, "grounded in the ethical."

MARTIN: Right.

AVAKIAN: I'm concerned, on the other hand, about an ethical that's not grounded in materialism and in the historical. In other words, I don't say, "Oh, there's no role for the ethical."

MARTIN: Yeah, I think that's great. I think that sharpens it up nicely.

AVAKIAN: And you don't say there's no role for materialism. So I think maybe at some point to join those questions might be very helpful.

MARTIN: Yeah, beautiful. I think that does sharpen it up nicely. But I mean, okay, and this gets into something pretty deep philosophically because in some ways it's like saying, "Okay, you've allowed a role for there to be something magical in the 'poetic sense of wonderment' at seeing the stars or the sun" and you might ask, "What is the status of that as regards truth?" So I think there's a sense in which I'd want to say—it's a powerful truth and it's just as powerful as the other kind of truth that I also value, which is the sun is also a gigantic nuclear reaction, there are forms of matter at work, there are forms of matter at work that are not found on earth or that can be approached directly. It's a magnificent human achievement that scientists have come to some understanding of the processes involved. It's a magnificent human achievement that we've understood that the sun is in some sense not special but is one of, as Carl Sagan liked to say, "billions and billions, and billions" [*both laugh*] and that it's a funny thing for me to say (and in fact it sort of brings that poetic thing together) because as suns go, it isn't particularly remarkable, it's a medium-sized star, it's out on one arm of the Milky Way, it's not really in the core— although apparently there is a big-ass black hole in the core. In fact they now think a lot of galaxies have black holes, especially spiral galaxies and that's why they have the shape they do, but it's maybe not so good to be in there anyway; it's probably better to be out in our neighborhood, out on the edge and all that. And that's great. I mean, that is a magnificent human achievement and it has its poetic qualities too. It's creative. Science is not merely descriptive but it is also creative. It's beautiful. It's a wonderful human achievement.

But then there is that other "poetic proper" side. It's our sun and those other suns out there are great; I'm all for them, but man, I *love* this sun. This sun is, this sun is *doing it* for us. Maybe I'm just waxing sentimental; I'm a bit of a sentimentalist, but if you say, "Yeah, that's great and that's a poetic thing and people have written poems and hymns and songs and dances and, banjo solos or something to the sun forever since they've done anything, more or less," and I want to say, "That's right" and there's a status to that that is the truth, as well, and it's just as powerful a truth. Well, I don't know if it's just as powerful but it's true, it's true, and what I mean by that is there is a tendency to say, "Well, yes, that's a poetic thing and, yes, I accept it as a poetic truth" but often that's said to sort of assign it this far lesser status and when you really get into that status. This is what I find fascinating about the logical-positivist philosophers like Carnap. I give him credit because he actually comes to terms with it and says, "Well, look, there's scientific truth and if we're going to call that truth, we just can't call this other stuff true." We just have to say that's beauty, that's the good, that's the ethical, but don't call it "truth" because what's the common model to say we examined this and we have done investigation and we see that that's true? The form of investigation doesn't seem to correlate and therefore let's just set it aside from truth. And another form of that is to say, "Yeah, yeah, that's powerful and I guess I think, yeah it's real powerful, it's real powerful" and it doesn't bother me that people have thought that it's powerful and then maybe given it all sorts of theological window dressing.

And yeah, some of that's completely "whack." Whenever people talk about, "Well, why can't creationism be taught in schools as a theory?," there's a better response to that, which is that creationism is not a theory. It doesn't meet the scientific criteria of being a theory. Another response that has some validity is to say, "Yeah, and why don't we teach that the earth is on the back of a giant turtle and the turtle's legs are on the backs of four elephants and the elephants are on the back of whatever," but then at a certain point, as Bertrand Russell says, "It's turtles all the way down." Actually, someone said that to Russell, the famous story where this very old woman who was present at a lecture Russell had given. Russell himself was old at this point, and this woman was even much older, ancient. And she said that bit about the world being on the back of a giant turtle, and then came the elephants, and so on. So Russell played along and said, "Then what is holding up the elephants?" The woman responded, "Oh, very clever young man, but it's turtles all the way down." You know, the moon is made of green cheese, or whatever; aren't those theories too? Yeah, great, but on some level in terms of the poetic expressions or to call them poetic, well the poetic expression, it just doesn't worry me and I don't see it as a problem. I see it as a problem when obviously it's used to reinforce social relations that are oppressive.

But one thing I find interesting, and again this goes into a whole area that we have to open up, I almost always find in those same, if I could call them, poetic traditions, countervailing elements, that are against using that to found social hierarchies. And it's a little bit like the way that Marx started talking early about the foundation of all criticisms is the criticism of religion and later he didn't talk that way much any more, and I guess I think, man, there's nothing religion could do to oppress people the way capitalism has so secularized society. It integrates religions in various ways and uses it but it can't begin to touch what capitalism can do.

AVAKIAN: I think if you examine what characterizes some of these feudal societies and what it does to people, particularly women, I'm not sure I would agree with that. It's not just capitalism, and religion is not—it's a superstructural expression—it doesn't oppress all on its own, but certainly in the ideological sphere and what it reinforces, it's a tremendous weight on people all over the world. My problem is, what do we mean? In other words, when I say something is poetic, I don't mean that in a pejorative sense.

MARTIN: Right, I thought you were valorizing the term, but I wondered if in some sense it's a kind of "formal" valorization. If that is the case, well, you may even be right; I mean, there's a point to be argued here. There's a way of valorizing the poetic dimension that's ultimately damning with faint praise—"Yeah, that's great too"—but ultimately there's nothing substantial to poetic truth.

AVAKIAN: Well, here's the problem I have. In other words, I don't intend it that way. But let me pose the question: when you say it's truth, as opposed to beauty, then we have to examine what we mean by truth because, without falling into logical positivism, I do think there is a point that truth is something that, in essence and in short, is a correct, or essentially correct, reflection of objective reality. That's what I think truth is, in simple terms. And I think there's a difference between that and values that are assigned to various things which, if we're not careful, if you call that truth, then you can say anything that anybody holds dear is truth and who are we to say that something is not true if at least a significant number of people hold it to be true because it's important to them? And then you open the door to all kinds of things, including all kinds of horrors. And even all these apologists for capitalism, they think that they're upholding the just, and the good, and the true—and even, some of them, the beautiful. [*both laugh*] However many lies they tell on one level, on another level at least some of them believe they are championing freedom against tyranny in the world, and so on and so forth. So, if we don't have an objective standard—to me the objective standard is "Does this essentially reflect objective reality or not?" If we don't have that standard, for truth, then anything can get admitted under the signboard of truth, can't it?

MARTIN: All right, but then I worry about the problem of, in a certain sense, overloading the question by using the term "objective" in speaking of objective truth, not because I want to flip it over and somehow say it's all subjective, but just that I think there is something in the scientific tradition where objective truth becomes something like the world as objective, as instrumentalized, as manipulated and . . .

AVAKIAN: But does it have to mean that?

MARTIN: Well, here's the thing. It's going to mean that if you don't fill out what's meant by that. So, for example, if I say, if I make some claim, like, there's a person standing on the other side of that door right now, I can specify for you criteria, under which we could answer that question, and we could probably quickly reach agreement on how we're going to answer that, which is to open the door or look through the peephole or something.

We could agree on criteria for that, but on the poetic side . . . this was what these positivists were on about. What kind of criteria? It certainly doesn't seem to be the same kind of, and this is a question for me. Don't get me wrong; it's not something I feel like I have any very good answers to and I, while on the whole I think it's good to resist a kind of monomaniacal monism, on the whole I'd like to think actually that truth and beauty and the good and all of that are bound up in some way, because we live in a world and we are people and there should be some basis for understanding our commonality. And actually, though, on some level I think that's, to use that word, all the "objectivity" that you need. I think that's about enough to keep you from sort of just thinking, "Oh, anything goes then," if you don't make a mantra out of objective truth because then everything else from there is the actual investigation, the actual getting your hands into it, living in it, experiencing it.

I was rereading William Blake's poem *Jerusalem* recently and it's amazing how powerful that poem is. I mean, I remember Terry Eagleton once said that, on some level, almost everything you need of the critique of this emerging industrial capitalism and commodity form, it's already there, and I think the point about some poetic works that demonstrate things powerfully . . ., well, for instance, I know you've discussed, and it's a book that's very dear to my heart, Ursula LeGuin's novel, *The Dispossessed*. I mean, there's a sense of course in which that can't do what *Capital* does. It can't do what other systematic works of political theory, of Marxist theory, political economy can do. It can't do that, nor should it. It wouldn't even be any good as a novel, as you've said, if it tried to do that. There's another level in which it can do things that those other theoretical works could never do, and it can do them more powerfully even. On some level, it could do them more powerfully. Its truth speaks more powerfully, and to me that's, if you want to call something poetic truth, or the power of that experience of the world, and how does that square then with sort of more "discrete," analytical truth, that's part of the question too. I mean, science tends to take elements of the world in more discrete packets and to break them down and see what goes into making them up. What's the meeting place? I think that's hard. I guess you could say there's something like, well, science can tell you there are neutrinos in the sun, and what are neutrinos? You've never going to get there through poetry and that's why I always think it's funny these books on "Buddhism and quantum mechanics," that sort of thing. You're just not going to discover the properties of subatomic particles through Buddhism or Christianity, or whatever. You're just not going to get there. The mode of coming at it, is it proper to what you're trying to find there? At the other end, just the gloriousness of the sun and the giving of it. Again, you're not going to get there through the neutrino, and is there some meeting place there? I don't know. I'd like to think there is but I don't know how to conceptualize it.

AVAKIAN: Well, I do think . . .

MARTIN: But I find both sources of inspiration. That's the thing.

AVAKIAN: I do think—this is one thing I have written about and it's also a point that has been touched on in various ways in things that have been written by Ardea Skybreak—but I feel like there is a very important dimension of humanity, the awe and wonder and even mystery on a certain level, that life would be greatly impoverished without. And to the degree that people are thwarted in that, their lives are impoverished. So, I agree with that thrust of it. But, on the other hand, to say, like you say, "The sun is giving" in other than a poetic sense, doesn't, to me, have any meaning. In other words, the sun's just . . .

MARTIN: What meaning does it have in the "poetic" sense? See, that's the problem.

AVAKIAN: Well, in other words . . .

MARTIN: Because it doesn't bother, for me it doesn't bother me to say it has a meaning in something you're calling a poetic sense, the root of which is "giving," because it means creativity, *poiesis* is creation. That's great to me, but I still think there's a sense in which it's kind of being relegated . . .

AVAKIAN: Well I just mean this: The sun isn't really doing anything consciously. It's not giving, [*laughter*] it's not withholding, it's just doing what it does, on one level. But what I mean by poetic is that if someone chooses to present reality that way in order to express an idea, I think (a) that could be valuable in its own right, and (b) it may actually help us to get an insight into the actuality of what the sun is and what it does, indirectly anyway. So, on both those levels, not just one or the other, that's what I mean by poetically valuable. Here's another way to get at it—I was thinking of this dispute that's going on now, in a kind of follow-up to the negative side of Kansas, the evolution thing [*laughs*], it's now focusing in Ohio, right?* I'm sure you're following this whole thing.

MARTIN: Yeah, yeah.

AVAKIAN: One of the things one of these scientists on the right side of the thing, speaking against creationism, said was that science means accepting the world the way it is, whether we like it or not. Now I don't think he meant we can't change things. I think he meant the world is the way it is and you have to accept that on a basic level, whether it makes you feel good or bad, or whatever. That's what it means to be scientific. To me, truth on the one hand, and beauty and justice, for example, on

---

* This refers to the role of creationist agendas within school boards in these states.

the other, are in qualitatively different categories in this sense: Truth is not socially or historically determined. Now, that's not to say that what's held to be truth at a given time is not socially or historically determined, and it's not to deny that social and historical factors influence people in the pursuit of the truth. Both things are in fact true, but truth is not a socially or historically determined thing. Truth is, as I said before, an essentially correct reflection of reality. Beauty and justice, things like that, are socially and historically defined.

MARTIN: Uh-huh.

AVAKIAN: Different societies, different classes within different societies, different groups in different parts of the world, have different views of what's beautiful and what's just, and often these things are in antagonistic opposition. We don't think the same thing is beautiful as George Bush or William Bennett does, or even Bill Clinton . . . I don't know why I said "even" Bill Clinton. [*laughter*]

MARTIN: Didn't he say recently that one of his favorable musicians is Peter Brotzmann? [*laughter*]

AVAKIAN: But, anyway, to me that's an important distinction. In other words, what is the good, the ethical, the beautiful is socially and historically determined. They're not viewed as the same by everybody and probably—not only probably—never will be viewed the same by everybody. Even though you remove social fetters, like classes, still different people will have different views of that, and that's "as it should be" in the sense that that's the way it will be.

MARTIN: Okay, but why on a certain level? Why not say, "Someday we will understand the dialectical laws of beauty and the good as well, and we will truthfully go forward and . . ."?

AVAKIAN: Because things are always changing and people are always trying to—they're living in the world and trying to deal with the world as it is and as it's changing, and people will not always see things the same way, nor would we want that kind of a society where people would see all those things all the same way.

MARTIN: Yeah, but see, that gets at the quandary here because, and I don't think this is just kind of a First World or privileged perspective. I don't want to live in a world that's just a world of "truth." I've got to have beauty in the world. I've got to have something in the world that I can look up to as good and I imagine that that's part of what's distinguished, that's something about our species and maybe others, for that matter, but that's something about our species that goes all the way back. I mean those cave paintings were not just, "This is what a deer looks like, so you'll know this when you go out with your spear to try to catch one." I mean, they had their aesthetic quality too.

AVAKIAN: Yeah, that was one of the points in that series of Skybreak articles on the social role of art.

MARTIN: Right.

AVAKIAN: And I agree with you.

MARTIN: So, but once we say that, because I agree with you, of course, I mean I hope someday when people do live in a future society not based on exploitation and domination that there still will be many conceptions of the beautiful, or at least that there won't be something like some reigning monolithic formula because that runs contrary to the idea of creativity to begin with. But, if we say then that human beings are not going to make it in this world and never have made it in this world without some sense of truth, I always like to say to people who argue about creationism and evolution, and I think Sagan had it right by just saying, "Look, evolution happened; it's not a theory." The theory is natural selection. The theory is punctuated equilibrium or the theory is some way of explaining how it happened and what mechanisms were at work.

Creationists like to say, or people of that kind of mindset like to say, that there are these gaps, and yes it does follow this sort of typical pattern that Lenin looked at, that there are some who want to insert God in those gaps, rather than just saying, "Yeah, this is a complex phenomena and we need to study it more; someday we'll understand the gap; even if we don't, even if there's some gap where we never find a fossil record or, we're still going to be somewhat uncertain as to how it happened." That's no warrant to say therefore God created the earth in six days and rested on the seventh. That's just a leap of logic and it's a category shift.

I like to say there are big gaps in the understanding of gravity. How are you going to live your life now that you can't be too sure about gravity? Are you going to jump off the Sears Tower and say, "Gravity—that's just a *theory*; I don't accept it." [*laughter*] It sort of goes to your point. You're going to find yourself accepting it, on the way down. [*laughter*] So, we can't live in this world without truth, but I guess I don't think we can live in this world without beauty or the good either, and I mean, just using these terms in very broad ways, and so, okay, you and I, we're material beings living in a material world, but we can't live without these things that don't seem to be just sort of unifiable on this subatomic level or on the atomic or on the molecular or even much further into the larger forms of matter. Conceptually it seems very difficult, and I guess on some level, to be slightly narrow and academic about it, professionally. I function in a profession that's sort of divided among different ways of doing philosophy and the larger split is between "analytic" philosophy and "continental" philosophy and sometimes analytic philosophy is characterized as, in the best of cases, wanting to model itself on scientific inquiry, and continental philosophy, in some broad sense, models itself on historical and literary inquiry. Well, I think all those things are good. How I ultimately am able to put them all together, I don't quite know, but I do know they're all good. I do know that it'd be hard to make it without science and it'd be hard to make it without literature, and the vision that's given to me on either side, to me, seems to speak a certain truth, and is it one truth or two truths, I mean that's a problem as old as Plato, or older.

AVAKIAN: Well, see, I agree on one level. I think that we don't just need scientifically arrived at truths to have a full life, if you want to put it that way. We need beauty. We need other considerations. I also believe that there will always be ethical considerations. I just think they are socially and historically grounded—that's a whole discussion we could get into, but we need those things. What I'm saying, I guess to put it in sort of Maoist terms, is that we shouldn't combine them, two into one, and call them all truths. In other words, that's why I was trying to distinguish them. I think there are scientifically established truths, if you will, and there are other things that aren't of the same quality—like Mao said in *On Contradiction*, qualitatively different contradictions are resolved by qualitatively different means. There's the particularity of contradiction. Science is a particular sphere of human endeavor, if you want to put it that way—that may sound academic but anyway, you know what I'm saying . . .

MARTIN: Uh-huh.

AVAKIAN: . . . whereas art and other things are different. And they have different internal dynamics, a different essence to them. They're trying to do something different, and they fulfill a different need, in the broad sense of need—not necessarily narrow utilitarian, but a little different need—and I just don't want to call them all truths when one of them is trying to arrive at what I think is truth, the way I've tried to define it, and others of them are trying to do something different . . .

MARTIN: Uh-huh, Uh-huh . . .

AVAKIAN: and should be doing something different. Like you say, to go back to the cave paintings, some of them may have had a very utilitarian function, but I agree with you, and with what was being said in that Skybreak article . . .

MARTIN: I'm sure they had that function but not . . .

AVAKIAN: Right, what I think she was pointing out in that article is that to reduce them to that is to miss something important about what art is in general and even what that art was more specifically. Like she said, maybe it was just somebody's idea of fun on a raining day, but even that's important. Even play is important. Human beings, and even some other species, need to engage in and need play. So all those things are important. It's just that to me they're different and shouldn't all be lumped under the category of truth. That's what I'm trying to get at.

MARTIN: Right. So, for example, would there ever be a poetic truth or a poetic whatever-it-is that could in some sense trump a scientific truth? For example, would there ever be something poetic that would tell us one thing, or seem to tell us one thing, and something scientific that would tell us another thing, and where the poetic could win out?

AVAKIAN: Trump truth in what sense, or win out in what sense?

MARTIN: Well, for example, the sorts of things that might give us the basis for social bonds to rise, for society to rise to a higher level, like fellow feeling, love, affection, sweetness, pleasure, desire. I mean I think all of these have elements where maybe we could give some chemical description of what's going on in affection or physical attractiveness or something, pheromones exchanging, or something, but it sounds absurd, right? I mean, we sure haven't described the totality of what's going on there, and indeed some of the greatest things that we in fact, after the fact, would affirm quote/unquote scientifically, have occurred out of that sort of inspiration.

I mean, this actually will go, I think, to a larger question that we'll need to have a whole other conversation about, but the whole question of interests and materiality and what drives us, what allows us to make a leap over certain gaps, or for example of where we have to think about just doing the right thing and where then those ethical questions actually become quite acute. I think, for example, Lenin's whole approach to revolution in Russia, and for that matter what he was saying about Europe in general, there's an element that's very underdetermined by anything you could study scientifically, or at least not before the fact. Maybe after the fact, yeah, we can in retrospect say, you see how those elements came together in that way.

But I think if you go too far with that, all you're going to get is a kind of determinism, that, yeah, those elements were there, it had to go that way, whereas it didn't have to go that way. I mean, as you know, people were looking for Lenin, in the days before the insurrection. Certainly there's a lot of contingency there where some very small elements, the famous moment where the insurrection began with a phone call from Moscow to Petersburg, where a single word was spoken, "Yes." Well, what if the phone line was down? All sorts of historical contingencies. After the fact you can sort of put all the connections together, but before the fact, there has to be vision that drives it forward. I think this is a fascinating phenomena. I think in fact William James gives a very good sense of it in *The Will to Believe*. Some things are true because they *could be* true, but their truth actually involves us getting going and getting to work on it, and we get to work on it because we're inspired by the possibilities. But it's all very underdetermined scientifically and I think there are a lot of things that are maybe in that poetic category that are a bit like that because they have to do with creativity.

AVAKIAN: When you say "underdetermined scientifically" what do you mean exactly by underdetermined? Do you mean not fully explained?

MARTIN: Well, those things where after the fact you can see how the elements fit together but there was no way to have seen them. Like necessary for them to happen, but not necessarily going to happen. Even though some of them in the aftermath sort of assume, and I don't mean this in the bad sense, but then they sort of take on that force of necessity. Like how they say in sports, sometimes they'll say "this is a team of destiny" but then, of course, the team's sense of their destiny is part of what makes them the team of destiny. That's what allows them to surge forward in that way, but it's not something that you could really . . .

AVAKIAN: Unless it's a case where David Stern anoints them as the team that's gonna win. [*laughs*] But I don't want to detract from your . . .

MARTIN: Right, well, why not make a pill that would give people the [inspiration], and they do. Of course, they give people the pill, the Prozac, or the whatever, that gives them the feeling that they can do the thing. It's still something other than just . . . It's that inspiring thing that I think it isn't just . . .

AVAKIAN: But isn't there always, in every necessity, isn't there also always contingency, and accident—and vice versa. In other words, another example from Lenin is—if you want a true "existential moment"—when he was in hiding, right before the insurrection, and he had to go across the ice . . .

MARTIN: Right.

AVAKIAN: . . . and there was a point where he thought . . .

MARTIN: It started breaking up.

AVAKIAN: . . . he was going to die and he said, "What a stupid way to die!" And of course if he had died, I think it's probably safe to say, given everything we know, that there would have been no Soviet Union. There would have been no October Revolution. There would have been no socialist society there, and the history of the world would have been vastly different. But, on the other hand, there were real reasons why the Russian empire became ripe for revolution at that time. This is, I think, one of the better aspects of Stalin, in *Foundations of Leninism*, where even if it's sometimes a little mechanical, there's still something there that's other than just mechanical materialism where he's analyzing the interconnections of the imperialist system and why things did come to a head in Russia at that time. And in that sense there is necessity. There's materiality beneath that. And it's true, if Lenin hadn't gone—never mind about slipping on the ice or falling through—if he hadn't gone and read Hegel at that time there probably would also have not been a Russian revolution, because that was important in sort of "loosening up" his thinking to be able to see the possibilities. So that's kind of an irony.

MARTIN: That to me, just as a side thing, that's a fascinating question because, as you know, of course, there's this whole trend that kind of builds everything around that. And in some sense it's not only that the Bolshevik revolution could have occurred because Lenin read Hegel, but that it degenerated because Stalin didn't. [*Avakian laughs*] Well, if Stalin had just read Hegel, so that was the pressing question in 1927 or . . .

AVAKIAN: But then you could go back another level and there were probably reasons why Lenin read Hegel and Stalin didn't.

MARTIN: Right, right.

AVAKIAN: In other words, what I'm trying to say is that there's contingency, or accident, and necessity, at one and the same time. There are reasons why Lenin didn't fall through the ice, if you examine it on one level, but on another level it's an accident, viewed against the backdrop of the Russian revolution. It isn't literally miraculous that he didn't fall through the ice. There are reasons. We could examine them scientifically with physics and whatever, and just where he happened to put his feet, etcetera. In turn, you can find reasons for where he put his feet, but then on another level that's an accident. I mean, to me, there's always contingency. Nothing is ever pure necessity. And least of all is revolution ever going to happen without a great deal of conscious initiative on the part of individuals but at another level broader masses of people.

MARTIN: But also, here's where broadly speaking the poetic dimension comes in. It's also going to require a lot of sacrifice and it's going to require some people to lose their lives and to give up their lives.

AVAKIAN: Right.

MARTIN: And it's going to require people who live to in some sense give up their lives in the sense that they can't live a quote/unquote normal bourgeois life, even if they come from circumstances of privilege, but where they give their life to try and bring about this new world, as opposed to just sort of having fun with their privileges and their quote/unquote entitlements. And, that's uncertain. I mean, I wrote about this at the end of that Sartre book. I think Sartre was truly dedicated to the radical transformation of society. And I point out that he lived seventy-five years and that this also happened to be a number that Marx had cited as, in that famous passage about how the proletariat will need seventy-five years or more of civil wars and reversals and struggles to make itself ready to wield power. So Sartre lived another seventy-five years and he didn't see it. I mean, he saw some great days...

AVAKIAN: Yeah.

MARTIN: . . . some really great days, but what keeps you in it? What keeps you in it? I think it's not just "truth"; it has to be a vision of not only the society of truth that, doggone it, I mean, this species could be beautiful, and we're not beautiful right now. We have some beauty but we're not beautiful. We could be a beautiful species. I think this is an old vision. This species could make something of itself. Humanity could make something wonderful of itself and why do you throw yourself into that machinery and possibly get torn apart and possibly killed? There is a point at which that's not just because there's a scientific analysis that the laws of history or how capital works will ultimately lead to its dissolution and the formation of the new society. It's a higher vision than that in some way, that, if you didn't have that, then society could not be transformed. For one thing, if you didn't have that, since those seventy-five years have passed twice over by now, and where, yes, there's great possibility in the world, but as you point in the "Challenges" document ["The New Situation and the Great Challenges," written by Bob Avakian in the aftermath of September 11, 2001] there's great possibility, there's also the great possibility of setbacks that could be very, very deep, and not to sort of stretch that in a pessimistic way, but in other words, how do you keep yourself looking toward the wonderful day that probably, the promised land that most of us living now are not actually going to see? I don't think it's ultimately science that gets you there. I mean, you can't get there without science, don't get me wrong. I'm not trying to denigrate science, investigating things materially and trying to understand their laws of motion, but even at a certain point, the reason I want to keep with that investigation is because I'm hopeful that one day our species will make something beautiful of itself.

AVAKIAN: I agree with you; you need vision that's much broader than what exists today and sees beyond these horizons as much as you possibly can, even though it's going to be limited because you're always going to be limited by your circumstances—you have to try to surpass them even while you're living in them and limited by them.

MARTIN: And like with utopian visions in general, it will be structured by the system of exploitation and domination that you live with at the present.

AVAKIAN: I think that's true, you do need that, and without that you wouldn't get very far, or where you would get wouldn't be very good. But to me that's not in contradiction to science, in the sense that I think that it is scientifically based that you see the possibility for that. It's by examining the actual nature and contradictions of society and human historical development and the way nature is and by seeing the possibilities out of all that, and then on that basis you develop a vision toward the future. But even this point about our species making something out of itself is also historically conditioned, in the sense that Mao once said: "ten thousand years from now, we'll all look very foolish".

MARTIN: Right.

AVAKIAN: Assuming we even get to the future, that we get to communism, in a thousand years let's say, or five hundred years—well, five thousand years from then people will look back on whatever the stage was then and say, "There were a lot of really ugly things about what they were doing back then; even though they surpassed capitalism and had gotten beyond the horizon of bourgeois right, there was a lot of what they were doing that was pretty ugly, viewed from today."

MARTIN: Right, right.

AVAKIAN: It seems to me that will always be true. The new will still come into being and what has been will give way—not without a struggle, but it will give way—and then people will look at the old and say, "That's old." They won't see it as beautiful in the same way we would now. Not because they want to go back to capitalism . . .

MARTIN: Right.

AVAKIAN: They're not viewing it from that vantage point. But because they've gone to a different place and new things have come into being and they view what we're doing . . . I think they'll have a dialectical approach so they won't say it's all ugly, but they'll say there are aspects of that which should be left behind in the dustbin of history, just the way we say—in a qualitatively different sense on one level, but on a another level similarly to what we say about the society we're in now, even though that future one will be much better than this one . . .

MARTIN: Right.

AVAKIAN: I guess I'm saying our species will *keep* making something out of itself.

MARTIN: Right, yes. I mean, I think art does pose certain problems for that. Maybe that's just my limitation. So, a thousand years from now there'll be something better than John Coltrane?

AVAKIAN: [*laughs*] You find that hard to envision?

MARTIN: I sort of hope it's not true on some level, and obviously I don't even know what it would mean, but that's because I live now, I live in the time of John Coltrane, or a little after. I'm sort of sorry I lived after the time of John Coltrane.

AVAKIAN: It would be better for people then, is my point.

MARTIN: Yes, yes, yes.

AVAKIAN: Not necessarily.

MARTIN: But on that thousand years point, too, did you read this novel, it's called *Lenin, the Novel?* This British writer, Alan Brien.

AVAKIAN: No, I haven't.

MARTIN: Have you ever heard of this?

AVAKIAN: I don't think so.

MARTIN: I love it. I think it's a revolutionary book. It's written from the perspective of, as if Lenin had kept a diary from the time he was about seven years old until about two weeks before he died. To me it is uncanny, and it would be interesting—because I've read Lenin's works pretty thoroughly; I feel pretty connected to them; I'm sure you're even much more connected to them—but it'd be interesting if you had this feeling about it because it's basically like, if Lenin had kept a diary, *this* would be the diary. If we ever found Lenin's diaries, this would . . . it's already there. It just seems so much that this guy did just inhabit Lenin's mind and part of what's touching, but also sort of hard to take about it, is that there's a diary entry toward the end where he says, "I realize I'm losing my faculties; I'm dying and losing it and I'm going to ask that these diaries be put away for seventy-five years"—(I don't know why this number keeps coming up)—"sealed away, but when they come into the light of the new day, whatever we've accomplished here, it's going to look so backward, people will look at what we've done here and just think man, they were really operating on a low level, because humanity will have passed so far beyond." I have to admit it made me cry to read that and it made me sick to read that because it was true. Yes, I'm not wanting to set aside that there was a whole other period and whole other great movement and leader that did in fact go beyond, but that doesn't entirely connect up to this point, but that book makes a powerful statement, I think.

AVAKIAN: On the Coltrane point, I think the fact that people in the future society would find other art more beautiful to them, doesn't mean—I'm not an expert, by any means, on jazz or art in general for that matter—but it doesn't mean it's not beautiful now, or important now, or whatever. That's not the point. I just think that people will be encountering new contradictions, new circumstances that their art will reflect, in different ways than art of our era. Even the really advanced art that we really appreciate, addresses—it sounds kind of cold, but anyway you know what I mean.

MARTIN: I know, yeah.

AVAKIAN: It's art that speaks to different things than what people will be speaking to at that time. So you won't really be able to put them one against the other and say, "This one's good and this one's not" or "This one's better than that one." Also, I think people in the future will still have an appreciation for things that are past, even as we do and we should now. Even if we put them in their historical context. You put Shakespeare in his historical context. You analyze the social content of it, but you also can appreciate the use of language, and not just in some "linguistic sense." In the artistic sense you can appreciate the use of language—and not just the use of language but the way different things are dramatically set up and brought into play and brought into conflict, and all that kind of thing. You can appreciate that, even with historical perspective and even seeing what the social and historical context of it is at the time, I think.

MARTIN: Uh-huh.

AVAKIAN: I just mean that people will look back on us now and say there were aspects of what they were doing that deserve to be left behind, just as we say right now that there are things that we have to strain to get beyond. If I understand you correctly, that's the pathos of the end of that novel, that we should be to the point where we're looking back on what they did. But, see, here's where it gets tricky. I heard this story about how this delegation from Germany went to the Soviet Union in the thirties, and they went to the countryside where they still had outhouses and things like that, and so one of these (they were supposed to be communists from Germany) says, "Socialism is wasted on these people." [*laughter*] Which kind of captured a lot of contradictions all in one statement. Now that kind of view of things that are backward is wrong. Or, to put it the other way around—positively: I remember when we organized these delegations to China in the early seventies, and we had one where workers from the U.S. went there. And when they came back, one of the people I knew had a little informal get together with other people they knew, other workers, to talk about their experience. And one of the people said, "Well, what was it like going to China?" And the person who had been on the delegation said it was like going through a time machine. And the person who asked the question, who was very influenced by the way things are here, was saying, "Well, you mean kind of like going backward." And the response was: "No, *forward*." That kind of gets it from the positive side.

In other words, the production relations and the superstructure, if you want to put it that way—the whole nature of the society and the culture and everything—was much more advanced, even though they had outhouses in the Soviet Union or even not such formal structures as outhouses in China in some places. So, that's not what I mean by what's advanced or what's "backward"—the level of technology.

4
Agriculture and Ethics

MARTIN: That's really interesting because it sort of brings us back around to the agriculture question. When I read Wendell Berry, one thing just blew my mind. I just thought, "This guy's just crazy; he wants us to go back to living in caves or something." He has a chapter in that book *Home Economics* where he says that it's better to farm with horses rather than tractors and he gives a whole argument about that that I think broadly speaking I want to accept, and it's an argument about basically things that you can take out of the earth without having any idea of how you would ever put them back in again, and keep an ecosystem going on that basis—extractive economy basically, which is in a sense what an industrial economy is all about, and for that matter conditioning world historical events in our time. It's not just oil, but oil clearly is a big thing here. Okay, so that's a little bit like this China example in the sense that, okay, so go forward from the tractor to the horse, you know what I mean? It takes a certain imagination to be able to see that something like that could be, whether you accept that example or not, but that something like that could be going forward.

AVAKIAN: Yeah, you have to examine that concretely. They were trying to correctly utilize more tractors in China, but they were trying to do it without all of the problems and the relations that come with capitalization of tractors, if you want to put it that way. Because you do have to feed the people. They had nearly a billion people in China. By the time we would get to communism, we'd probably have, who knows, ten, fifteen billion people. Partly that's going to be as a result of the anarchy of capitalism, too, so what are we going to do about those ten or fifteen billion—what are we going to do about it? What is humanity collectively going to do about feeding and clothing itself?

By saying that I'm not saying that there's nothing to the idea that sometimes you go backward in order to go forward. There are a lot of instances in which, on different levels—like even the point of going through the phase of "land to the tiller" in a lot of these countries where some people are saying that's now *dépassé*—you don't do that anymore because the technology has created the basis for going right away from capitalist agriculture to highly socialized agriculture; but, in fact, by doing that you leave out most of the masses and you don't overcome that lopsidedness.

MARTIN: Uh-huh.

AVAKIAN: And you end up reproducing, in the form of state capitalism, what you basically had in agriculture to begin with. So there are ways in which you go backward in order to go forward, and I'm not frankly knowledgeable enough to say whether certain things, particularly in agriculture, have validity to them or not, and certainly at the time at which different revolutions would come into power, they're going to have to examine, concretely, what are steps backward (or to the side, maybe) they have to make in order to bring everybody forward, even if it's wave after wave, and what are leaps that they can make in a more "linear" way. In other words, capitalism has prepared the way for—in some aspects, it's actually presented obstacles, and you can't just go ahead linearly from capitalism, but you also can't fail to build on some things that it's done.

MARTIN: Uh-huh.

AVAKIAN: And to get the right synthesis, in my view—what I'm wrestling with, both in the political/economic realm but also what we're talking about, which is more the philosophic realm, if you will, is how do you go about getting the right synthesis of those kinds of things?

MARTIN: Yeah, I really agree with that. I really think that it's an accomplishment if the revolution creates new problems and with some of those new problems you are in something like a field of difference. It's not clear what to do and probably just the best thing that can be done is to talk with people and struggle with people over the question of how do we know how to do it now and are there elements that are oppressive, and that are rooted in systems of oppression that have to be broken with? But there's no royal road to it. There's no *a priori* other than our hope that we can find ways to overcome those forms that . . . I mean, yeah, we know that it's not that we're coming from nowhere and we don't know anything about how this has been dealt with, of course, and good and bad examples and all of that.

AVAKIAN: But agriculture in the U.S. is very different than in China, for example. Here's another one. What do you do with the fact that the development of capitalism within the U.S. itself has led to a tremendous diminution of the actual . . .

MARTIN: Labor intensive agriculture . . .

AVAKIAN: Yeah, or just the farm population as a whole—it's just shrunk to a couple of million, a few million—probably less than a million farmers, farm owners, or farming-owning families. So there's an example. Do you want to go forward from that, in a linear way? Or, in other words, obviously the way in which that's happened under capitalism is not what you want to perpetuate.

MARTIN: Right.

AVAKIAN: And everything that's going to tend to go into that is not what you want to perpetuate, including the lopsidedness—it goes back to what we were discussing earlier—the differences between the city and the countryside. But how do you get the right synthesis between what are "strong points of the city" and what are things from the rural life, including even some aspects of the past rural life, that you'd want to preserve? The way I would see it is "preserve but transform" as part of the new synthesis.

MARTIN: Uh-huh, uh-huh.

AVAKIAN: In other words, not just preserve as such, but how do you sort of break them in two and discard the parts that point backward—and I'm talking in terms of social relations— point backward, not essentially technologically but socially, like around the woman question, for example.

MARTIN: Yeah.

AVAKIAN: But now here's something to preview (because I don't want to divert us into this now, but before I forget about it), when you were talking about farming with horses instead of tractors, I was thinking, off of what you wrote about the question of ethics as applied to animals, wouldn't you run into that?

MARTIN: Yeah.

AVAKIAN: You've got some contradictions. I mean, "horses were meant to run free and run wild."

MARTIN: Yeah, I agree.

AVAKIAN: I don't agree with some of the things you're saying there about animal rights, but I do think you're raising important questions, and I'm not trying to be facetious or belittle it, but to me it's like, okay, horses evolved in a certain way and had a certain existence, and since they've interacted with human society—or since human society has interacted with them—their existence has become different. They don't exist—and to a significant degree can't even exist—in the wild in the same way they did before. Even though there are some of these programs where they reintroduce or rerelease them into the wild, they can't really do it on a big scale because of human society. And there is the history of different animals, including oxen and horses and other things, being harnessed by human beings to meet human needs. So to me—I guess I'm taking this off in a way I said I didn't want to right now, so let's just come back to that, because I think it's a question worth pursuing.

MARTIN: But I think that . . .

AVAKIAN: I don't want to be dismissive of it, because I think there are some real questions there.

MARTIN: I think without even making it the horse versus tractor question, and I think there is a problem in Berry's view about that too, but I think his larger view, which itself gives rise to a contradiction that I think you were addressing with the whole question of down the road if we're in a world with ten, fifteen billion people, how are people going to feed themselves? I think, on the one hand, Berry's strength is as a critic of the forms of economy and extractive economy that put us in a place where it's not just . . . it's bad enough in a certain sense that you've taken a lot of stuff out of the earth that you can't put back into it. Of course, he's looking at it in terms of not only sustainability but also some sort of cultural critique standpoint: a lot of it's just made into pure junk anyway that nobody ever needed in the first place and it's just all beer cans and candy wrappers floating down rivers or whatever, in landfills. It's a concatenation of issues. Berry makes some good arguments against what you might call big social structures (and this is also a whole other field of the "complexity problem" that people have had to come behind Marx to try to figure out), that there is a problem of complex, big social structures being alienating even when their aim is to be socialist. I think Berry is a good

critic of those sorts of things and the way that they can have logics that spin out of control and you can have vast systems to get
the kiwi from New Zealand to Chicago or whatever. But Berry's
weakness is that he doesn't recognize sometimes that you have
to deal with structures on the large level *in order to* deal with
them on the small level. You have to. You have to look at how
the whole grid is arrayed in order to talk about how this or that
situation is placed within the grid. So, to go back to where I
introduced something earlier . . .

AVAKIAN: I just want to say . . .

MARTIN: . . . that to address the question of a particular
place, you have to then look at the things that structure where
every place is and be able to move from there to . . .

AVAKIAN: I think that's a very important point.

MARTIN: Well, I think it is where a more dialectical view
becomes really important.

AVAKIAN: On your kiwi example, just to trip out for a second,
I think this is another dimension—and it goes to your point
about the big and the small, if you will—I think the society that
we're struggling to envision and to bring into being is one in
which it's going to be a combination of the big and the small,
and the centralized and the decentralized, and not all one or all
the other. In other words, a society that makes use of "high technology" but a lot of other technology too. I think it's going to
have to be some continually evolving or transforming synthesis
of those things. Not one synthesis for all time but a continually
reforged synthesis of those things.

For example, yes, a lot of the anarchy of capitalism and the
parasitism of imperialism and the way things are—the coffee
example, or the kiwi example, or other things in which things
are just totally out of whack, they reflect the lopsidedness and
they're totally out of alignment with the best use of and the best
interaction with nature and so on, and they have negative
repercussions for humanity's ability to correctly interact with
nature. I can see, on a trippy side, though, when you get to the
future, where first of all there would be a need and a role and
a value for international trade—but what would be "international" because there would be no nations?—or rather for
global trade, and even some things that are "exotic" in one part
of the world being introduced to another, but not in the way
it's done now. Not in a way that reinforces lopsidedness and

distorts and disarticulates things and causes humanity to inter-act badly with nature, but—I don't even have a clear vision of it, I'm just trying to trip out here—I was thinking of that Dr. Sharma statement that I quoted in something I wrote, his com-ment that "if you made revolution in the United States, 90 per-cent of the problems of the world would be solved right away," which is something of an exaggeration but nevertheless a good one . . .

MARTIN: Something to it.

AVAKIAN: . . . a good one to be motivated by, even if it's exaggerated. But he also made some point about how in certain parts of the world you can't grow bananas. And I guess it's a question: "Does everybody in the world need bananas?" I can see that there's a role for the regional, for the local, and for some articulation and "rational interaction" with nature, but I can also see some dimension in which people in Iceland (where I presume they don't grow bananas) would have bananas—just using bananas as a metaphor here, or mangos or whatever—without its having the whole meaning that it has now. Like pineapples in Saskatchewan without it doing what it does now, where people starve and pineapples (production of pineapples) are moving from Hawaii to the Philippines to wherever, and people are brutally exploited so that people can have pineap-ples in a few enclaves of wealth . . .

MARTIN: Luxury, yeah.

AVAKIAN: . . . something vastly different than that, and some-thing that doesn't distort the whole character of human society and the world and our relation with nature in the way that hap-pens now.

MARTIN: Right. I grew up with a mango tree in the yard, actually, so mangos are sort of close to my heart, but on another level maybe it would be better to have international or world exchange of some goods that are more local or regional in char-acter. Hopefully we could find ways that show good sustain-ability and care for the earth, then sure, great. And, of course, without creating unequal social relations in the process, or dependencies and that sort of thing. Something that might even be better is what if people can go around and see each other in different parts of the world and see how people live and occupy spaces and experience the world differently in different parts of the globe?

Not to keep banging on the kiwi, but I think one thing interesting and actually fascinating and something that our side ought to start making a lot more of—and it comes around to this whole question of socialism being a planned economy and I think it'd be great if people who do political economy would dive into this (hint, hint)—that is, the world has actually reached the point where socialism would actually require less planning. I mean you would have to address the *character* of the planning, of course, but just the shear quantity of planning; it may actually require a hell of a lot less planning than imperialism.

I mean, one thing that's sometimes said about the Soviet Union is, "Well, one problem with the plan was they were only planning for about five thousand different products, and modern gleaming capitalist economy has many, many, many, many, many magnitudes of products." Yeah, we've got many, many, many, many, many more types of toothpaste or brands I should say, not types. We've got many, many, many, yeah, of all this junk. We have to come at the spiritual dimension of the junkiness of this kind of culture and the way that even though, yes, it may mean that there are some forms of industry and some forms of things like using tractors and agriculture that may have to be expanded in some parts of the world. Some of it even goes to the whole question of, if China were to industrialize on the level of a First World country, we may as well kiss this earth good-bye. I mean, it can just pretty much be shown empirically that the earth cannot sustain that level of pumping junk into the ecosystem, but I think that ought to be something that we could actually say very much on our behalf that, yes, it's planned economy but, for example, we're not going to be planning to build an aircraft carrier and all the tender ships that have to go with it and all the F-16s that are parked on it, and all the computer systems, that advanced technology that has to be developed to run all that. That's the whole sort of strata, there are whole huge strata that we just don't envision as part of this future and so in many ways and again, not to wax new-agey about it, but there would be a certain simplification. It's not that this planning would be a burden but it would actually not only release a great burden from humankind in terms of us focusing on an economy that's already vastly collectivized, that's already thoroughly collectivized but *for* something else.

In orienting it away from that, and giving a different character to it, we can eliminate a great deal of planning that's oppressive and that creates these gigantic structures that people have to find some way to fit in, and they only fit as just some cog in it, and they're expendable. It doesn't even matter how well they're functioning, but if it's just not a profitable enterprise anymore, that sort of thing. So, I mean, I actually think that it's conceivable that socialist society could involve, just on a quantitative level, less planning than imperialism does, because this is a massively planned economy now. I mean that's also a useful answer to our critics who say, "Oh, you want planned economy." You guys have planning on a level that just, Marx couldn't have even, nobody could have foreseen.

AVAKIAN: Well, this economy is both planned and anarchic—that's something that Engels pointed out. Both plan and anarchy exist in a very concentrated way and they reinforce each other under capitalism. That's one of the ironies, I guess.

MARTIN: Right, right, right.

AVAKIAN: But do you see . . . ?

MARTIN: I agree, absolutely.

AVAKIAN: . . . that it's the size of the structures that's the problem? Or the nature of the structures or . . .

MARTIN: Well, I do think there's a problem with complexity, and with size. I do think that manifests itself as a problem, in and of itself, and the Soviet Union under Stalin manifested a lot of those problems—and in China they actually addressed a lot of those problems. It has to do with commandism, top-downism, but also just getting lost in the structure.

AVAKIAN: Well that's . . .

MARTIN: Just things that are so big that even no matter how the decisions are being made and with what intention, they take on a logic of their own and a life of their own.

AVAKIAN: I remember back in the Free Speech Movement that was one of the big things—the anonymity—I guess what Sartre would call the serialization. Yeah, you were just sort of a number. In fact, a lot of the culture that was produced around the Free Speech Movement was like that, those early IBM cards . . .

MARTIN: Keypunch cards . . .

AVAKIAN: . . . had the words "Do not fold, spindle, or mutilate." There was this whole thing where there were these parodies of Christmas carols that were done up as part of the Free Speech Movement. One of the choruses was "Do not fold, spindle or mutilate." [*laughter*] So there is something to that. On the other hand, I think you're right; I think China was addressing this. As Mao pointed out, planning and initiative are also a unity of opposites. In other words, there's also a question—everything doesn't have to be planned centrally and at the "highest level of concentration." What I mean by "planning and initiative are a unity of opposites" is that you can have plans that are made in broad strokes on a certain centralized level, because it goes back to your point—you do have to look at the whole grid, as you were saying, in order to deal with the parts, in order to know how to approach the parts. I think it's the same with everything. If you try to do more with something than you can do at a given point, you fall into all kinds of problems and errors. Like if you try to draw conclusions in science when you don't have the basis for the conclusion, you create all kinds of problems. This is something we're wrestling with a lot.

MARTIN: One problem is very typical, as you've pointed out as well or better as anybody, of the Stalin period, where you cut the toes to fit the shoe.

AVAKIAN: Yeah.

MARTIN: And you, often out of just frustration, declare the problem solved because it's solved to the extent that it can be understood through the apparatus that you're using to look at it, instead of thinking, "Okay, well, we've seen something here, but to see further we're going to have to come up with something better."

AVAKIAN: Yeah, well, I mean . . .

MARTIN: But those things are, I don't want to say the perennial human problems or anything like that, but I mean those kinds of things do come in with these big structures and where you have general principles, and I'm all for general principles, but where you have general principles that in some sense don't really subsume the particularities or don't really work out of the particularities but really start to obliterate a lot of the particularities and so it's just going to be this way. Sartre's great example in *Search for a Method* is saying that it was hard to dig through the ground under Moscow to build the subway because the ground itself wasn't sufficiently Marxist. [*laughter*] That was the problem. The problem wasn't they hadn't studied it closely enough to say, "Well, should we really build the subway here or not?"—it's the ground. The dirt wouldn't get with the program.

AVAKIAN: [*laughs*] Yeah, there was that approach to science also in the Soviet Union, and a mixing up of different contradictions. The way I understand it . . .

MARTIN: Like with Lysenko.

AVAKIAN: Lysenko, or also just setting out to refute Einstein— this is my understanding—basically because Einstein "had" to be wrong because of his political views or whatever.

MARTIN: Right, right.

AVAKIAN: Or mixing those two things up. In other words, there is a particularity to science, and specific fields of science, which isn't the same thing as what your political and ideological line is, or your outlook. I mean, in my view ultimately, if you're using something other than dialectical materialism, you're going to run into shortcomings. We always run into shortcomings, but without dialectical materialism you're going to run up against more pronounced and more significant shortcomings, sooner or later; but that doesn't mean you can't discover a lot of truth. People who have been politically reactionary have led to a lot of advances in the sciences that have actually even benefitted humanity—various medicines and so on.

MARTIN: To me, the profound and difficult example is, I don't know if you ever talk with mathematicians, but almost to a one, they have a Platonic and a validly Platonic metaphysics, and they'll say that "the numbers are the real; we take the numbers to be the deepest reality." And yet they're able to do mathematics. They're able to do it.

AVAKIAN: Yeah.

MARTIN: I mean, I found the whole story where this guy at Princeton, Andrew Wiles, solved this 300-year-old problem, Fermat's last theorem—I don't know if you saw this *Nova* episode about that.* It's fascinating. As if there's this cloud of numbers over here and there's this cloud of numbers over there and somehow he got those clouds to interact, but as a materialist, I have to think it can't just be the clouds interacting, but there's something in the ground that's . . .

AVAKIAN: Underneath all that.

---

* The episode was called "The Proof." The producer of the episode, Simon Singh, is also the author of a book on the subject entitled *Fermat's Enigma*.

MARTIN: Yeah, and it's letting that interaction happen, but I sure as hell don't understand that and I sure as hell don't at this moment understand exactly why it's harmful for Wiles and the whole rest of them to be Platonists. Yeah, I don't understand the relationship. I suppose you could say, "Well, look, if they're able to do that, then in actuality, no matter what they think about what they're doing, they're doing materialism." If it really works it must be because there's something material that allows it to work . . .

AVAKIAN: On a certain level.

MARTIN: . . . even though they'll say, "Well, I have this ideal notion of what the number is."

AVAKIAN: Right, I think the world is "materialist," so that it asserts itself even when people don't—when in their philosophical views they may be inconsistently materialist or even in important spheres nonmaterialist or against materialism.

But getting back to this thing . . . I think we got off of the thing about tendencies of Stalin's in particular to overcentralize, and I do think there's obviously truth to that. I think you're right, in China they were trying to deal with that. Knowing what's appropriate to what level is part of it. You do have to have some central planning, but then what should you leave to another level, and what in turn should they leave to another level, and how do these different levels interact? How do you keep a certain sense of mass line going with the experience from these decentralized basic levels? Both there's a lot of initiative left to that—and initiative taken on that level—and then it's also fed back up so you can be learning from it and centralizing without overcentralizing, I guess. You don't want just all initiative with no centralization, or you get the anarchy in another form. On the other hand, you don't want just centralism without a lot of initiative, because even big things are made up of small things. Even big structures—not on their own, but they can be broken down into smaller components, and in so doing you qualitatively change them too. In other words, if everything is a cog in a machine, that's one thing. If everything, on the other hand, is made up of different levels in which there is relative autonomy and initiative, that's another thing. Then it's not so "impersonal" as it is when basically everything is directed from the top and it's all just cogs in a machine, and there's nothing coming from the bottom up, but also there's no room for any initiative to be taken.

In other words, to me, planning—whether you're planning a demonstration or planning an economy, or whatever else you might plan—it is a unity of opposites of centralization and decentralization. There are certain things you want to scope out or sketch out in broad strokes, but if you try to plan beyond a certain point, it's going to turn into its opposite and there is no role for any initiative of individuals or people on a different level or for the parts to be other than just cogs. In other words, how do you get it so the whole is greater than the sum of the parts, and the parts are not just cogs? Put it that way—that's another way to look at it.

MARTIN: So let me just say two things back on that, that then will connect to things I'm sure we'll take up later but I'll just try to say it in a brief form. I think sustainable agriculture, it's obviously important for itself—if we ultimately can't grow our food in a way that's sustainable, then obviously that has dire consequences, but it's also a nice, somewhat generalizable model on this very question. Or maybe by coming at it the other way, that forms of, you can't even hardly call them agriculture, but industrialized, chemical-intensive, etcetera, "food production," and I would think long-term and not even, for the much greater short-term, are not sustainable. Part of what makes them not sustainable is, I suppose the most extreme example would be this sort of ideology of making the desert bloom, which is basically saying the desert doesn't want to bloom, but damn it, we're going to go in there and make it bloom. Well, how do you do that? Well, you import into it, you pump into it, all kinds of stuff. It's true, you can bend it to human will that way, well the will of some humans anyway, as opposed to in a certain sense, rising up through it. I don't have any basis for saying that it will always be a bad idea to get a desert to bloom but just as our hopes that people will bloom, we have to find the ways to, as you've taught me and many others, to unleash them. And so I think that actually says something about centralization and planning and initiative and local and the larger structures and whatnot. If all the larger structure can do, and I'm not saying anything you haven't taught me, if all it can do is send down the order, then this goes to the Stalin thing.

This is the second thing, this bigger question of ethics and normativity that we can come back to. When we talk about people being unleashed in some sense *as people* and not just to be a cog in a machine, I guess I think no matter what you or some others in the Marxist tradition think of Kant, I don't think we can talk that way without having some feel for the idea of autonomy, the idea that human freedom and human liberation is bound up with this idea of people coming to give the law to themselves, so to speak, and not having it imposed upon them by an external force. And I think that sets the terms in a certain way for the kind of conversation we have to have around that. What's interesting is that you can set that aside by saying, "Well, that particular figure in the history of philosophy or that particular language is part of bourgeois society or some epoch other than that we feel we're working toward," but then the language comes back in other forms and I guess I feel like, as it should, because in some sense if that's not a key part of what we're after, well heck I don't know what we're after, because it's not about just creating, even on a sustainable basis, a big massive, centralized, planned economy where everybody can eat. Not that that wouldn't be a fantastic accomplishment; don't get me wrong. I think these people who talk about "wasn't the Chinese revolution violent and didn't they kill X number of people" and all that—apparently it's meaningless to them, to deal with such mundane questions. Does it ever enter the orbit of their consideration that the average life span of people in China from 1949 to 1964 *doubled?* I mean, given the size of that population, that's the greatest reduction in violence in human history. Why isn't there any credit for that? So I certainly don't mean to run down food, eating, or that side of things, but ultimately we're not aiming toward just making a big machine that happens to work in one way or another, but instead a society where people are *free.*

In some sense the human problem is to solve the problem of production so that we can then make it a far lesser part of what we're all about. Let's get that taken care of so we can do these other things, we can play, we can be creative, and also we can transform the nature of that work itself into something that's creative, that's fulfilling, that's good work. To me, this is the connection to the other issues. There's a point where with Stalin you just have to say, "God, what was that guy thinking?" He really did seem to have the mindset that it would just flow out of his orders and even at a certain point, I know I read this in one of the biographies. It may not be true, and obviously the biography was written with a certain standpoint. I think it was that one by Volkogonov, was that his name? The one who was a general in the Soviet Union and had access to archives. *Triumph and Tragedy*, was the subtitle—where Stalin more or less said, if he wasn't running it, it wasn't socialism as far as he was concerned. And I mean he might have said that in a certain context where, I don't know, it might even have been true on some level, but there's another level in which you almost did wish that, as all of us have, don't we wish we could have gone back in time and sort of shaken the guy a little bit and said, "Man, get your bearings, maybe it's worthwhile just thinking about some general principles, like if you send an order down that this population needs to be moved, what are you getting into there and isn't there some normativity that can be appealed to here?" So, that's the point where a lot of these issues kind of come, they get bound up and things get really complicated.

AVAKIAN: Well, I think that's at the heart of a lot of what we want to take up and get into. I have a few other things I want to raise, too, but I think that's a good place to stop.

5
Ethics:
Imperialism and Interests

MARTIN: Lenin had this argument that if in an imperialist country we engage in revolutionary defeatism and anti-imperialist activism, that the initial reaction of the masses would be to try to tear us limb from limb. One thing I think is funny about that is people tend to not want to recognize that Lenin was actually quoting Plato on that point, that's something that comes from the "Myth of the Cave," from the *Republic*; and I still accept Lenin's argument and I still accept his whole argument about revolutionary defeatism. I more than accept it. I think it's profound. But I wonder if we need to take in the particularities of the culture of imperialism, insomuch as you can call it a culture, and especially American imperialism and especially the way that moral rot sets in very deeply and that the outright, I would just call it stupidity, that goes with this, isn't just a surface phenomenon and that this rot and stupidity isn't really addressed, I think, by appealing to something called the "real interests" of the masses in imperialist countries and again especially in a country like the United States. I'm not making some sort of exceptionalist argument, but there might be some real sense in which there has never been a country "like" the United States in the sense of a superpower in the kind of position that the United States is in now, and it just seems to me that this social form has made a very significant number of people very stupid and mean, just to be straight up about it. [*Avakian laughs*]

And that this part of postmodern capitalism, as I like to call it, gives you a kind of, I call it a "postinferential" and a "postlegitimation" society and what I mean is that whatever forms of exposure might expose what the bad guys are really doing, what the system's really up to, there's a tendency for that to just go into a kind of cultural mush where it doesn't penetrate very far. We're in a "say anything" sort of culture, where people in a certain sense are expected to swallow contradictions. People are expected to accept the idea that "Yeah, gee, no one was really dying in Palestine until these Palestinians started blowing themselves up," or that people somehow come around to accepting or maybe even think that it was really Israel that was there first and the Palestinians must have come from somewhere else to make the trouble, and apparently it's very hard for people to see through this thing.

Or on the legitimation question, there used to be this term in social theory, "legitimation crisis," and I'm not saying it's completely gone away, but on the other hand there's so much stuff that could almost transparently be shown to not be legitimate but it doesn't penetrate very far to point that out. In the current situation, for instance, I even heard on NPR someone saying, "Well, the Pakistanis, we have to ("we" meaning the U.S.) be very careful there because they [meaning the government of Pakistan] have their own problem with the Pashtun population." That's a good example of a typical statement, where you can't even go to the next step with that before it unravels. Well, of course they have a problem, because borders were drawn through the middle of the region where people live and the borders were drawn by other people.

So that's just an example, but it's an example of something where you can't even push that an inch before it unravels and yet it's hard to push it that inch, it's hard to get people to make basic inferences. It's hard to raise questions of legitimacy, and so it is as if exposure of the bourgeoisie, it's necessary, it's not that it is no longer necessary, but there is a way in which it is not sufficient because there's some gap there in terms of the critical apparatus as regards a lot of folks.

This is a side point but it seems to me there's evidence for it, and I think some sort of psychology needs to be done on this or something, but there is this whole wave in the U.S. post-9/11, where there are a lot of people, and I realize they are probably mostly white, middle-class, suburban people but, there are a lot of people just walking around feeling like, "we're just so doggone good," and you've got to think on some level they just know, "Well, wait a minute, why are you so much of a better person today than you were yesterday? Oh, because evil has shown itself in the world, and we're just so doggone good." And

I just wonder what kind of cultural mindset is out there where that kind of thing can kick up and I know that some of it is basic insecurity, and that under certain circumstances that can crumble and whatever.

What I really want to connect that to, so this is finally coming around to something, is that I think there are problems with the question of whether Marx and, certainly, classical Marxism really have the conceptual resources to respond to imperialism. I know that's why we have Lenin and Mao and other things we've done for that matter, but I think it's further complicated by the fact that you can't understand imperialism apart from colonialism. And I think that's where there's something of a problem in Marx, that the material underpinnings of the imperialist system were generated through colonialism. There was no shortage of colonialism in Marx's day, but I don't think that he really necessarily grappled with that on the deepest level or took account of all of the implications for that. And that's where I think the concept of interest, or "basic interest," or "real, true interest," or however you want to shape that—it just doesn't bridge the gap.

It just seems to me that there's what I call a kind of "ethical gap" there, that to talk about interests won't get you from one side of that to the other, especially in an imperialist country. And part of what I think the problem on a more theoretical level is— I wonder if *political economy*, if you take that as the sort of foundational discipline, so to speak, into theoretical inquiry about the world we live in and what to do about it—if you take that as the core of it, it seems to me it's in some sense conceptually predisposed toward a notion like interest, and away from something like the question of the ethical. So that, and this is part of a larger conversation, but when I want to bring ethics into it, it's not in this narrow sense of interpersonal ethics or "am I being good," or something like that, but more in the sense, for example, that if we could create a society that's beyond this society, that's not only the most ethical thing we could do, it is our ethical obligation to do everything to create such a society.

And, it just seems to me that's why this whole business about taking political economy and interests as the core and in some sense shying away from the question of ethics, it seems to me that's the real reason why subsequent Marxists, whether it's Lenin or Mao or Gramsci or Lukacs, Adorno, Sartre, or somebody who is sympathetic to Marx but isn't a Marxist per se like Derrida, that they've attempted to supplement Marx ever since the time of Marx. There's something going on there; there's something that makes us queasy there that we find we have to smuggle in in various ways even though maybe we're a bit embarrassed about it—as I think Marx was a bit embarrassed about it. And, to me this is what I, I call it kind of parallel structure or, to use Dubois's term, there is a kind of doubleness or a "two-ness" to this. It needs to be made more explicit where on the one hand there is the scientific analysis of capitalism and its laws of motion and what potentials may come of that, but then there's the other level on which we talk about the ethics of what exists and what *could* exist. And that it comes out in things such as when people talk about imperialist wars. On the one hand, yes, of course we need the political economy of why it's happening, what we hope will happen in terms of it backfiring on the imperialists and what openings that may create, but we also need to just say that they're just wrong, it's just wrong, it's wrong for the United States to invade other countries and I don't mean that in an ahistorical way although I can't really think of a historical way that would ever justify it. But, it's just wrong. It's unethical. It's immoral. And an analysis that couldn't say that, I think, would be very, very seriously lacking.

I think I'll just stop with that but to me that's where space opens up, where if you don't fill that space with something like the ethical, what are you going to fill it with? What you find instead is that you're filling it with interests, but then you find that interests are not quite cutting it, so then we find ourselves saying, well, but the "real interests" or the "true interests" or the "deeper interests" or the "long-term interests"—and I don't really know how you address the structures of an imperialist society out of those categories.

AVAKIAN: Wow.

MARTIN: So that's a lot of stuff.

AVAKIAN: [*chuckles*] I'm saying wow because there are about four or five big questions wrapped up in there, which is fine but I think we have to figure out how to come at them separately as well as in their interconnectedness. There is the initial thing that you started out with: the cultural, the superstructural and particularly cultural dimensions of the way in which people are influenced—we could put it sort of like you did, people are stupid and mean. I think there is a real aspect of that—or at least, ignorant and mean, but also stupid in the sense that people are trained in a bad methodology. And they are trained to be mean. It's sort of like the "dumbing down." Believe it or not, the things that I get sent to me include supermarket tabloids, because I like to look and see what they're doing with that stuff.

MARTIN: Uh-huh.

AVAKIAN: And what has struck me about them is not only the thing that everybody comments on—the whole scandal aspect of it, and the tabloidization of the news—but it's really striking that the ones that are most that way, in terms of scandal, are also the most openly reactionary politically. It's not like they have an evenhanded use of their scandals. There's definitely a really hard-core reactionary political agenda driving those things, which I think gets at something you're speaking to. The "dumbing down" is real, but it also goes hand in hand with the promotion of—it's the creating of a certain mentality to make people not only accept, but to become actively passionate for a certain mean-spirited ethic if you will, which is also obviously applied internationally. So, that's one whole set of questions.

Another one is the question of interests, sort of in its own right, but then also interests versus ethics. And, then another question which encompasses all of this in a certain sense but is separate also: to put it simply, is there something lacking in Marxism, as it's developed? (What I mean by "as it's developed" is that today we say Marxism-Leninism-Maoism. At some point, we're just going to have to go back and say communism, because I don't know how many . . . [*both laughing*] over centuries I don't know how many names they can add on until it gets to be impossible to say it, without its being totally cumbersome.) But, in any case, in looking at that as an ongoing thing—and not just Marx and that's the end of it.

MARTIN: That's right.

AVAKIAN: I know that's the way you meant it too. But is there something, some inherent or essential flaw in Marxism which requires it to be supplemented by something else, which is different than asking: are there, have there been, weaknesses or shortcomings in how Marxism has been applied or even how it's been understood as well as applied? Is there something that Marxism is incapable of encompassing, to really deal fully with what we need to be dealing with, and does it need to be supplemented with or informed by something else, or modified by something else? There are about three or four . . . from listening to what you were saying . . .

MARTIN: . . . and that frames that question very well. I mean I do think those are two separate questions although I guess I would also—and this goes back to your earlier formulation, the emphasis on the ethical or on the materialist and having the ethical within it—I guess I would like to think, though, that even if there is this shortcoming or if there is this something missing, that there could be a Marxism that could grow toward that . . .

AVAKIAN: Well yeah, that's . . .

MARTIN: . . . and the question, if when we frame it around materialism and ethics, I suppose the question is could you grow toward a certain sense of what the ethical would be without jumping into philosophical idealism?

AVAKIAN: Yeah, that, I think, is one of the big questions you're raising, not only here but in general and in what you've been grappling with and writing about, and so on. And here as well. So, I think we should definitely not only come back to that but get into that in as thorough a way as we're able to under the circumstances.

But on the first point you raised, about the cultural rot—and the moral rot along with it, as I was just indicating by talking about the "dumbing down" with the tabloids and everything—I do think there is a definite point to that, and there are a lot of apt analogies with the Roman empire, their bread and circuses, including the cruelty that was deliberately incorporated into that to condition people in a certain way. And they always say, "Well, this is what people want." They have ratings—just like they have polls to tell people what they're supposed to think politically, they have ratings to tell them what they like culturally and so on. But these desires are socially conditioned and also consciously created by a ruling class that wants the population to be conditioned in a certain way, so I do think there is some reality to that, and it's not a minor aspect of the situation.

MARTIN: Well, can I add two very quick things to that?

AVAKIAN: Sure, sure.

MARTIN: One is, I think part of that conditioning, and this probably does apply to the Roman example as well, part of the conditioning is to accept cruelty as ordinary and as just the lot in life that some people are going to get and maybe we'll have a few crocodile tears over it or whatever, or we'll say yeah, gee, that's a shame, isn't it? But, there's nothing you can do about it, and indeed your own stake depends on going along with it and perhaps even joining in with it enthusiastically.

But, then the second thing is that, because—I tried to coin this term, I hope no one else comes up with it, or names a book after it before I have a chance to, but, "virtual bread and cyber-circuses"—where I think there are qualitative changes occurring in capitalism, but that don't necessarily mean it's a new stage beyond imperialism. I'm very swayed by Fredric Jameson on this, that in a way it's stage "two-and-a-half," and it may never become stage three. But it's something where some of the new factors of production, and where electronic media, all the other stuff that is going on, "cybernetically," and in terms of the way that capitalism went into the "consciousness business," in a way that Marx never could have imagined. No one could have imagined what was to come—these developments have had profound effects on people, so that we have a normalization of meanness and cruelty and stupidity. Surely the idea that the most powerful nation-state in the history of the planet could have a president, who is on all accounts an idiot, this plays an ideological role, right?—the role of ideological training. And obviously there are people behind him making decisions and running things. But, I mean that in itself plays a big role in shaping things, and it's more than obvious that it's a hard thing to crack through. I guess the question is how do we understand that and how do we think about cracking through it?

AVAKIAN: I think with Bush, just on that, it's a sort of self-conscious philistinism and it's a deliberate promotion of philistinism. I think that is part of the ideological program serving a political program.

Another element, though, of this whole bread and circuses thing—it's not just the cruelty and so on, but another one of the spectacles that goes on, which is part of or related to the cruelty, is actually to enact a certain kind of cruel drama, or melodrama. People have sent me videos of a few episodes of things like *The Jerry Springer Show*, and a couple of other things like that. One thing that struck me in watching these things is that they have this sort of melodrama that's acted out where people come on who flout traditional morality and the customary and accepted ways of doing things—"I'm a prostitute and I'm proud of it," that kind of thing—and then the audience members are induced and encouraged to get up and chastise these people. It's almost like a verbal lynching: they get up and chastise these people, and point their finger at them, but all with the nostrums and bromides of the bourgeois system and its traditional values. In other words, "You have to take responsibility." And they don't mean it in the sense you're raising responsibility (or Derrida). They're talking about the bourgeois sense of "personal responsibility" in a very bourgeois and reactionary sense, and then they'll preach to them about basic family values. It's actually interesting how the audience will respond with these traditional, conservative bromides and injunctions, screaming at these people. It's a melodrama that's played out, and I think that goes along with the thing I was saying about the tabloids. There are some definite values being promoted through all that. In addition to the ones that we were talking about before and which you were mentioning—the cruelty, and all—there's also this reinforcing of the tried and true traditional values and the reactionary moral strictures and all that kind of stuff, even in this sort of rather grotesque and odd kind of way. So that's another dimension.

I see all that, but I don't see the picture as being, well, quite so bleak or as uniform or uncontradictory. First of all, if you look at the recent history, say, of the movement against capitalist globalization, that was something that even the bourgeoisie was admitting was, since the end of the Cold War, the first major and significant challenge to them on a mass scale, not just politically but also ideologically. In the sense of challenging their triumphalism: "No, your capitalism is not good, it's not right, it's not moral, it's not just; it's exploitative, it's causing tremendous suffering." And they were actually on the defensive—and I think surprised to find themselves on the defensive—in the face of this mass phenomenon.

And then, while among the oppressed there are a lot of bad things that reflect the influence of the system and the workings of the system, there is also a sort of culture of distrust and resistance on a certain level. Not that much of an active political resistance, spontaneously, at this point, but I would say broadly, for example, among the masses of Black people, there's a culture of distrust and feeling that the system on some level works against them and always has worked against them in whatever it comes out with. That's not to say that they're not influenced by the patriotic wave after September 11—you can't close your eyes and ignore reality on that anymore than on anything else. But there is definitely a countervailing trend of being suspicious and distrustful of what you're being told and of the high-minded morals that are being sounded by Bush and all that. So I think there are other trends—ones that are in opposition.

6
Legitimating Norms

AVAKIAN: On the subject of legitimating norms, I think that, with every twist and turn of what their system is doing, they always have to have their legitimating norms for it.

MARTIN: You do think that? Because that's what I am wondering about.

AVAKIAN: Even now, for example. It's very simple-minded what they're putting forward, but they have to be able to claim that they are going out not just to fight evil in a general sense, but that there are some moral principles that they're upholding in the world. I don't know if you have seen this letter that was published, mainly in Europe, by William Bennett and these other people upholding what they're doing. They actually had to go into some fairly sophisticated arguments and make some high-minded moral-sounding elaborations. They couldn't just say, "We're evil"—I mean [*both chuckle*] "We're good." They couldn't just say we're good, and the people we're opposing are evil, like Bush does in his speeches. In order to reach, particularly, a European audience and an audience of European intellectuals in particular, they had to try to go into some more sophisticated arguments—which do provide the basis for their undoing. The fact that they have to make them means that they're trying to establish a standard, which then can be examined and, if you will, deconstructed and opposed.

MARTIN: Uh-huh.

AVAKIAN: But, even for the populace, they have had to go out and argue that they are trying to achieve certain things in the world. We can recognize readily that their arguments come down to "might makes right" in a certain kind of sense. But they are still having to camouflage them and to present them in a way that isn't simply that. And whenever you have to do that, whenever you have to argue about what that means . . . and then the world also creates complications. In other words, Bush wants to say it's this very simple world: "You're either with us or with the terrorists." But then everybody, including all these bourgeois commentators, are saying that when they get into the Palestine situation, they can't just superimpose that simple-minded model over the Palestinian situation, to say nothing of situations even more complex than that.

So reality throws up problems for them. You know, I actually think that, while we have a lot of problems with this—there is a lot of reality to what you are saying, we have a lot of problems with this post–September 11 situation in terms of the points you're raising, though we're actually not doing that badly at this point given that this is "different" in the sense that, whoever is behind it, this was an actual attack on American soil where a lot of ordinary Americans, civilians, were killed—but given that, from my sense of things, while there is what you're talking about, people walking around feeling "Yes, we're very good because this evil has manifested itself," there are also a lot of people going around questioning and even people protesting, in a way that I think is actually, to the bourgeoisie, pretty disconcerting. I think they felt like, "Well now we got it—we got something that happened to Americans on American soil, it's World War II, it's Pearl Harbor, we can just go, go, go." And they have been going, going, going. But they haven't been going, going, going without a lot of opposition. Some of it is openly manifested, and a lot of it is on the level of people questioning.

MARTIN: Uh-huh.

AVAKIAN: And a lot of the way in which they've dealt with that is by just rolling on with the public opinion, as well as rolling on militarily—rolling on with a public opinion offensive in which they've told the people, who number in the millions, who have questions about this—or are troubled by it, at a minimum—that they're the only ones and everybody else agrees with it. And that is actually setting up a big contradiction for them, because part of their legitimating norm is also telling people that "the whole world is with us"—they'll use phrases like "the world" or the "civilized world," but actually the world is not the way they're presenting it . . .

MARTIN: Uh-huh.

AVAKIAN: . . . and that's what that example of Palestine shows. That also is true in Europe—not just in the Middle East but in Europe there are a lot of people who do not see the issue the way Bush et al. are presenting it. That gets manifested and that reality asserts itself. So, even here they have to have a legitimating norm: "We represent the civilized world against uncivilized terror." Well, let's face it, the main legitimating norm is a mafia one: "Hey, we got the nukes, you know whadda mean!"

MARTIN: Uh-huh, uh-huh.

AVAKIAN: "You don't like our argument, well *how about this* argument"—the nukes and all that.

MARTIN: Right, right.

AVAKIAN: But they cannot just do that, and I think they are still trying to formulate a legitimating norm, but it is actually wildly in conflict with the reality that they're dealing with and with the reality that they're trying to create. So, all these things give us something to work with, and all the things that were motivating the antiglobalization movement before September 11 are not gone. And they have everything to do with this military offensive, this open-ended declaration and carrying out of war that the imperialists are involved in. So that the things that were drawing people into questioning and opposition and protesting around globalization are also going to be asserting themselves and coming to the fore again. Because they haven't been changed, they have only been accentuated by what the imperialists are doing.

MARTIN: I want to go with that . . .

AVAKIAN: Go ahead.

MARTIN: . . . in terms of something I thought was really interesting and I'm still trying to understand it. You wrote in the "Challenges" document about this sense that the imperialists were presented with a certain opportunity after the collapse of the Eastern Bloc. But, that a certain significant faction of the capitalists in this country didn't feel that Clinton really had capitalized on that situation and so now in a certain sense they are trying to come from behind, but very quickly, and grab what they can out of it that they didn't think they were able to grab, in the eight years of his administration. I think that's really interesting in terms of what you just said about the antiglobalization movement pre-9/11. And, how, 9/11, and given what you said too, whoever exactly was behind it, because, of course, who knows, but it's not, you don't have to be at all conspiracy-minded to say, gee this has worked out so well for these guys, you kind of wonder if they didn't have some hand in it. And, I think it's quite appropriate to say, and not even in any kind of speculative way, that for groups like the Taliban and Al-Qaeda there seems to be a strategy where imperialism tries to set up groups where, if they were to at some point flip over and go into opposition, it would be in the most reactionary way . . .

AVAKIAN: Yeah.

MARTIN: . . . so that you've got some good enemies. You try to set them up as friends, but such that if they become where they're not friends anymore they're great enemies, too. And that works out really well for this Orwellian "war without end" sort of strategy. But, like you're saying, then out of this, they're intensifying certain of their own contradictions and they're opening up certain things. All right, but then to bring it back to this normativity and legitimation question, on one level they've got their ideologists out there formulating justifications, and you can say on a certain level if they're putting that into the discursive realm, some people are going to step forward with counterarguments and so we're still going to have questions about legitimation.

AVAKIAN: If I can just insert one thing, just on that one point, as another example, I've been told that wherever Chomsky is asked to speak, he'll get an audience of anywhere from hundreds to thousands of people . . .

MARTIN: Yeah.

AVAKIAN: . . . which reflects—you have pointed out certain shortcomings of his in terms of analysis, theory, and program, which are one thing, but he does do, as you . . .

MARTIN: He's doing a great job.

AVAKIAN: . . . he does a great job of exposure.

MARTIN: I'm really happy with what he's done since . . .

AVAKIAN: Yeah, and I think what it reflects is that he's put tremendous energy into this, and this is a sort of lifelong, I won't say crusade, but campaign of his. But, just quickly, because I didn't want to interrupt your train of thought, I think that reflects something, that he gets a significant audience every time and everywhere he speaks. And that's true of other people, too, like Howard Zinn, and so on. Anyway, I'm sorry . . .

MARTIN: No, no. And on that same thing, and obviously a very, very, very much lesser example, but I had been scheduled to give a talk that had been scheduled for months, if not a year, at a state university, out in rural Kansas, on music, but then when everything happened—I was asked, it was sort of interesting—they asked me just as I was about to ask them, "Well, can I address these events?—we've got to get into this stuff."

So, everyone was amenable to that, I mean I would have done it anyway, but it's cool that everyone was amenable to it, and during the discussion, it came up that, I think a day or two or three after 9/11, I think it was Peter Jennings, who is often presented as sort of the smarter, more intellectual anchorperson, said, well, people had previously questioned the legitimacy of this president, "but nobody is saying that now." And I just said in my talk, I said, well hell, I'll say it, I'll question it. [*Avakian chuckles*] I mean, there's no longer any question about how those votes were counted and all that kind of stuff? I'll say it. And I went down into that situation. So I'm going to a school in rural Kansas and to be honest I was worried; I didn't know what kind of situation I would find there. And, I have to admit when the actual events happened, I just felt for a week, just pure dread. So when I said that, plenty of people in the audience, I think there were about a hundred people there, were, "Yeah, sure, it's still up for question, why wouldn't it be?" So, I mean clearly, it was a nice example of where this idea of everybody just thinks one thing and everybody is unified and all this.

AVAKIAN: Look at Michael Moore's book, *Stupid White Men*— for some time now it has been on the *New York Times* "best-seller" list, and for a number of weeks it was number one. That's also reflective of . . .

MARTIN: What is that book about?.

AVAKIAN: It's about Bush and basically what you're talking about. [*Martin chuckles*] It's about Bush and his illegitimacy and the critique, from Michael Moore's point of view, of the whole Bush program. But I think he's actually added a postscript or something after 9/11. So it's from that oppositional point of view but, as indicated by the title, it's very direct and unapologetic. Well you probably know the story of the book, right? There was a whole attempt to suppress it.

MARTIN: I guess I don't know.

AVAKIAN: Well, we can talk about it, I don't want to take you totally off your train of thought. But, anyway, it's reflective of something also, that was my point.

MARTIN: Right. So I agree with all of that, but there's a flip side. For example, what does it mean that in the weeks after 9/11, if you were to take a blank map of the world that just showed and outlined the land masses on the globe and said to a lot of people, "All right, tell me where Afghanistan is, [*Avakian chuckles*] what languages do they speak there, who are those people, what's their culture?" "Well, I don't know but wherever the hell it is, just start dropping stuff on it." In a way the whole "virtual bread, cyber-circuses" idea is an extension really of the "society of the spectacle" sort of idea. And, I don't go all the way down that road, I don't want to go all the way down the road of thinking: and now we're just stuck in the spectacle and we can't get out. But there's something to it, and it has had its real effect, and it has transformed questions of normativity and legitimacy such that there are a lot of people, I think, in this sort of giddy, "We're good, I'm good, we're just so bloody good we can't believe it" kind of thing. "Why are we good?" Because "we're us!" Why are "they" bad? "Because they're them, they're the evil ones." And that's why we're the good ones. Yeah, it's easily taken apart, discursively, but I don't know that that particularly matters once you have that sense of things. And it's frustrating because it seems as though this situation in a sense poses an insoluble problem, because, well, what do you say about that when the very thing is that there's a kind of short-circuiting of discursivity about right and wrong and what kind of society should we have and that sort of thing?

AVAKIAN: Well, not to make too much out of just our own experience, but it is one significant indicator of things. When we did up our party statement right after September 11 [this refers to a statement put out by the RCP on September 14], in the six weeks or so after that we distributed something like 400,000 copies of that, not counting reproduction on the internet or whatever. Of course, not everyone agreed with it, but I think even a lot of our own people and other people who work with us taking it out were surprised that the overwhelming response to it was to seriously engage what was said there, and a lot of people were saying things like, "Well, I didn't know this" or "I'm going to find out if this is true, because if this is true it changes the whole way I look at things." And, I don't want to overstate that, both because it's only one experience—although it's not an insignificant one, that's not an insignificant number of people to reach even on that level—but also because it's contradictory. People say that, but then the grind of going on and living in this society and the effects of what you are raising weigh on people and wear them down in various ways.

MARTIN: It's a little like saying when they say, "Oh, 85 percent support it," you ought to come back by saying, "oh, so you're saying 45 million people are against it?"

AVAKIAN: I know right away—and we can calculate right away—that that's a lie. Because, for example, there's probably—I don't know, let's just say 25 percent—of the population in this country is that section of people who are proletarians and others who are really impoverished and oppressed in this society, very different sections of people, but as an aggregate let's say they represent 25 percent of the population. Well, I can tell you, from reading reports on the work of our party as well as more general knowledge, that there is nothing like 85 percent of those people that supports what the government is doing. I'm not saying that there's not a sizable number that supports it, but nothing like 85 percent. And that section of the people is not insignificant, that's a quarter of the population. And then there's a fairly broad strata of more educated people—not just intellectuals in the sense of people in academia or people whose work is in the realm of intellectual work but people more broadly of the "educated classes"—there are a lot of students and others, and there is nothing like 85 percent among those people that supports this. So, while there is a broad swath of support, and it would be silly to ignore it, it's definitely not the case that it's anything like what they say. Even what I just said, which I think is undeniably true, indicates that 85 percent is a way overstated figure. I agree with you that even 15 percent wouldn't be insignificant. But we can know, just from those few examples and extrapolating from that, that it's nothing like 85 percent.

MARTIN: Uh-huh.

AVAKIAN: So [*chuckles*] maybe they just sat around and said: "Oh, what should we say, 93 percent? No, that's too high. Let's say 80 percent—no, that's too low. Okay, 85 percent." I think it's actually almost that crude. Plus, to the degree that it's not, they are taking a poll among certain strata of society. And then think of it this way: If you just have a sort of general level of opposition, and you get a phone call from someone who says "I'm from *X*, *Y*, or *Z* poll," when the stakes have been framed that "you're either with us or with the terrorists" and people are being rounded up and held in secret and so on—and they got the Patriot Act, and Ashcroft is on the TV every other day denouncing somebody—and they say to you, "Well, do you support what the President is doing in Afghanistan [*chuckles*] or in the war against terrorism?" Even if you didn't support it, you'd probably think long and hard before you'd say no. How do you know, maybe it's the FBI calling, or maybe they're going to be keeping a list of the people who say no.

MARTIN: Totally, totally.

AVAKIAN: So that kind of thing is also going to influence and skew their polls.

MARTIN: Totally.

AVAKIAN: Again, I don't want to overstate that, but I don't think that's a small factor, either.

MARTIN: You know the famous incident when Freud was able to get out of Vienna and the Nazis allowed him to leave, but they made him sign a statement that he was not really opposed to what they were doing. They had typed up a statement, but he wrote his own comment at the end. He said, "I cannot support the Gestapo and their methods highly enough." [*both laugh*]

AVAKIAN: Yeah, a lot of people say what they have to say to keep themselves from being . . .

MARTIN: No, but I mean he had a double entendre there, right.

AVAKIAN: Right, exactly, right. I cannot support . . .

MARTIN: They were stupid enough to think that he was accepting that when, of course, he was messing with them.

AVAKIAN: Right. And, I think a lot of people either refuse to answer, so that they don't get counted in the poll; or they fudge and equivocate and say something that gets put into the "undecided" or even into the "supporting" category because of the way they carefully construct their answer. And anybody who doesn't think people are thinking about that now is not really taking account of what kind of atmosphere they're not only trying to create but are creating—where Ashcroft went and told senators that if you raise questions about what I'm doing then you're aiding the terrorists. Well, everybody might not be aware of that exchange and that hearing but the general atmosphere seeps out into the society at large, where they see people like—

what's his name, that guy who is actually a jerk overall, but that guy, Bill Maher, says one thing that has a little ounce of . . .

MARTIN: Fairly innocuous, but a little bit of . . .

AVAKIAN: . . . little ounce of truth to it, and he gets jumped on and almost lost his show from what I understand. So that has a chilling effect. [This refers to when, Bill Maher, the host of the TV talk show *Politically Incorrect*, made a comment to the effect that the people who crashed the planes into the buildings in the U.S. weren't cowards—the U.S. is much more cowardly because it bombs people from a safe distance.] Or, this thing they're doing where they're charging this lawyer, Lynn Stewart . . .

MARTIN: Right.

AVAKIAN: . . . with abetting terrorists. That's obviously intended to create a chilling atmosphere among other lawyers and more generally among people who pay attention to that kind of thing. So, with that kind of atmosphere, of course it's going to influence what people are gonna say and how freely they are going to express themselves.

MARTIN: Well, let me just ask you, because again to go back to that analysis you gave with Clinton and the, quote/unquote, you might call it the missed imperialist opportunity or something, and then what they're doing now. I guess I thought, and we've talked about it a lot, that in the United States, in Europe, Western Europe, I mean there are particularities here but I guess I've just thought it would be a real mistake for the powers that be to launch significantly into fascistic sorts of ventures. That speech that Ashcroft made to the hearing, that was really ugly stuff and straight up ugly stuff and no two ways about it. Sometimes we throw around the term "fascism" a little bit loosely but this was pretty fascist-looking stuff. And I guess I thought that that would be kind of a mistake. We think of fascist measures as actually something that to enact broadly, as opposed to just the fascist-like conditions under which certain segments of the population always live, but to enact that as a broad program, I mean, there might be a perspective on that that would say, "Gee, wouldn't that be kind of a strategic mistake on their part because it just would open up so many cans of worms?"

So why would they do that unless there's a kind of desperation there? It's like that faction of the bourgeoisie and its apparatus is usually kept somewhat under wraps, even to the point that after awhile they don't even actually want Pat Buchanan in the Republican Party. He has to do his thing in another forum. They'll still have him out there doing it, but they don't broadly want to advertise that "Hey, we're going to go over to a very directly authoritarian kind of thing here." So why are they doing it? You can say that it's partly in response to 9/11 but a lot of it also looks like "Man, these guys were so ready to do this anyway." I mean, even on the very day, on the very morning of 9/11 when they started saying, "Yeah, this must be Bin Laden," I was sitting there that very morning thinking, "Well, they're so damned sure about this right now then why didn't they know already?" Gee, they're right on top of it now.

AVAKIAN: [*chuckles*] Yeah.

MARTIN: So, I mean, just why do you think, in terms of political economy and the whole world structure, I mean, why do it this way?

AVAKIAN: Well, that's a . . .

MARTIN: Because on a certain level I was really thinking that they weren't even going to put G.W. in as president. I mean, up until pretty near the so-called election, in the sense that I thought Clinton represented certain newer factors and forms of production. So why would they want to open all this up, do you think? Like I said, I thought, why wouldn't they be happy with the course they had with Clinton and therefore put in Gore? I thought it was interesting at the Republican Convention when Colin Powell made this speech that was practically one he could have made at a Democratic Convention.

AVAKIAN: Right, well, first of all before we go on to that, I just wanted to say that I don't want to give the impression that I think there's nothing of importance to what you're raising about the difficulty of penetrating this whole bread and circuses—or what did you call it. . . cyber . . . what was your phrase?

MARTIN: Virtual bread and cyber-circuses.

AVAKIAN: I think there is something really . . .

MARTIN: Trademark! [*laughter*]

AVAKIAN: Okay. It sounds like . . .

MARTIN: You could use it. I just don't want some other . . .

AVAKIAN: That's all right, it sounds like it could be a good book title but you obviously have an idea for what . . .

MARTIN: Maybe not for one of your books . . .

AVAKIAN: No, it sounds like you have an idea with it, so go with it. But anyway, I certainly don't want to say there's nothing to it. In a certain way, this came up even under Reagan, and I do think there is a point to it—there is a particular role for culture or counterculture in relation to that. Some people also are trying to evolve some sense that you have to strike a pose of either using irony back against it or standing outside of it. I think there is a role for that kind of stuff. Even back in the Reagan years, I wrote this little piece that ended up in the book *Reflections, Sketches and Provocations* about the challenges for communist stand-up comedians . . .

MARTIN: Right, right, I know that piece.

AVAKIAN: . . . which I was also using as emblematic of the whole broader question: how *do* you expose these people? Like someone said even earlier, irony stopped when Henry Kissinger got the Nobel Peace Prize.

MARTIN: Right.

AVAKIAN: This has been with us, but it was accentuated with Reagan and it has been accentuated again, so I think we do have work to do—and many other people who are opposed to what's going on are also going to contribute—in terms of finding forms, as well as content, that can break through this. I think a lot of creativity has to go into that and is going into it. People are trying, I know, in various ways to come up with this, both as part of the political movement but also in the cultural dimension in its own right, and there's a lot more that has to be and should be done in that sphere. So I just don't want to leave the impression that I don't think there's a real contradiction there that you're pointing to. I was just trying to point to some of the contradictory things for the other side. Sometimes we see all the difficulties on our side and forget the problems of the other side. Sometimes we don't see all the positive things, even though sometimes we're accused of being Pollyanna-ish or whatever—we're just blowing all out of proportion the positive elements—but I think from the bourgeoisie's point of view, they do have some problems. Even, for example, the point you make about people not knowing where Afghanistan is on a map: one of the things that has been very concretely manifested here is that a lot more people know where Afghanistan is now than did before, millions more, and not all of them only with a "Let's go bomb it" sensibility.

MARTIN: Right, right.

AVAKIAN: In other words, they've had to, as Lenin said, drag the masses into political life. In the aftermath of September 11 and then with the whole juggernaut the imperialists have unleashed, people are debating a lot of big world issues, people of all different strata of society, as far as I can tell. Not continuously, and not always on the highest level or in the most informed way or with the most progressive outlook, but there is a lot more discussion and debate. People are being dragged into world affairs, and from our point of view, strategically, that's always good.

MARTIN: Uh-huh.

AVAKIAN: Even if the initial expression of it is mainly bad, it's potentially positive. So, anyway, I just wanted to say that about . . .

MARTIN: But it does segue very nicely into this whole question of whatever we want to call this wind that's blowing, this sort of fascistic wind. I like Bob Dylan's "Idiot Wind," you know that song from *Blood on the Tracks?*

AVAKIAN: [*chuckles*] I don't know that one.

MARTIN: "There's an idiot wind blowing from the Grand Cooley Dam to the Capitol."

AVAKIAN: Oh, I do know that one, yeah.

MARTIN: That's a great line.

AVAKIAN: Yeah.

7

Strategies of Imperialism and the Culture Wars

MARTIN: That also raises questions for people. I don't understand why the reactionaries want to do that [enact a controversial fascistic program]. So, then I'm wondering, what position do they think they're in where they think that's a good strategy?

AVAKIAN: Well, this is something we were also agonizing over, going back to the whole Clinton impeachment thing.

MARTIN: Right.

AVAKIAN: Why go after Clinton like that, even on the first day of Clinton's presidency, essentially, with the whole Jesse Helms thing: "He'd better not come down here . . ."

MARTIN: North Carolina, yeah.

AVAKIAN: Why do that? That's something we've been wrestling with and trying to figure out. It seems to me, part of the answer is . . . there is an immediate dimension, that you can't carry out this kind of an open-ended war internationally and not tighten the screws up and try to hammer things into place domestically, as well. But I think there is more to it than that. I think it does go back to—you mentioned Buchanan. It's true they've sort of put him on the "outs," but they also put him out there, like that. I think that's right . . .

MARTIN: Right . . .

AVAKIAN: . . . and he's got this latest book which I've just started to read. It seems to me the title is consciously modeled after the Spengler book, *The Decline of the West*. Anyway, Buchanan's got this book *The Death of the West* . . .

MARTIN: Right, right.

AVAKIAN: . . . and it's partly about the declining birthrates—of Europeans—in the West, but it's also about the culture wars. I've also been noticing a big theme of Bush's speeches, particularly the ones that are written for him, so it's more a conscious thing—it's not his off-the-cuff mumbling and stumbling around—they have been emphasizing this theme of people sacrificing for the greater good and people being motivated by something bigger than themselves. This thing that we were speaking to in the supplement on the Clinton impeachment, "The Truth About Right-Wing Conspiracy". . .

MARTIN: Right, right.

AVAKIAN: They're feeling that there are these centrifugal forces that come about, together with these economic changes—things that were promoted by Clinton, both in his program but also in a certain way by his demeanor and behavior: this self-indulgent individualism. Obviously, from a communist point of view, wanting a whole different kind of society, we have real problems with this and can recognize that it's a product of the system and something that has to be overcome and transformed. But, from a certain standpoint, the bourgeoisie as a whole and this section of it in particular has real problems with this, because how do you get the population to go along...and this whole thing about we can't have casualties in war. That was a Clinton thing that was taken to a high pitch in the . . .

MARTIN: Kosovo.

AVAKIAN: . . . Yugoslavia war, where basically they did have as close to zero casualties as you can have. But there was a whole line that was beginning to be put out—that we can't have any casualties, we can't commit ground troops, we can't do anything that would cause any serious loses, because the American people won't support it, they won't stand for it, they'll rebel against it, or lose faith in it or whatever.

MARTIN: I guess I was identifying that more though with the Gulf War in the sense of this incredible statistic that the half-million military people who were sent over there were actually safer than if they had stayed in the United States; that the death rate was actually lower. They would have naturally had other accidents here and more of them would have died.

AVAKIAN: Well, that was true in the Gulf War; they had minimal casualties. I mean, they did have some pilots that got shot down and they did have that one barracks that was blown up at the end.

MARTIN: So you think with the Kosovo thing it was actually then taken to the next level which is like literally zero casualties.

AVAKIAN: Or almost, I don't remember if they literally had any, but it was as close as in anything that was actually a war.

MARTIN: Yeah.

AVAKIAN: It was a small-scale war, but it was a war. It was probably as close to that as you can get, but there was a whole ethos being developed around that and it was almost raised to a doctrinal level. Well, with the program that Bush et al. are pushing forward—whoever is actually formulating and leading and developing this—they recognize, and it's already been proven true, that they can't have that as an operational principle. I think it is a little bit like the point we were talking earlier, about how "all that's holy is profaned"—these things from the *Manifesto*. As that supplement in our paper on the Clinton impeachment pointed out, there has been an element of that, sort of like wiping away the sentimentality and getting down into naked self-interest and cold cash—which, again, we see as a real problem from our point of view, but from the point of view of trying to get the population to be willing to make sacrifices and to sacrifice its sons and daughters for something bigger, it's a problem for *them*, that they have that kind of an ethos and that sort of whole "gold rush" mentality. I mean, you had people like, what's his name—Bork—saying, "The only thing that might save us is a good depression."

MARTIN: Uh-huh.

AVAKIAN: And, if there's anything better than a good depression, it's a good war. [*Martin chuckles*] Which is not to say that they don't have real objectives with this war and they're just having it for ideological reasons. It's not literally like the *1984* thing where you can't even tell if there is really a war—I mean, there's an element of that, you can't really tell [*chuckles*] if there's a war going on sometimes . . .

MARTIN: Uh-huh.

AVAKIAN: . . . but they do have real international objectives and real warfare they're waging and going to wage too. But I think . . .

MARTIN: Just to get into that, sort of from the military angle, I mean this goes back to some stuff you were saying in the aftermath of the Gulf War, can we, how did you put that? Can we still really win? or

AVAKIAN: Could we really win?

MARTIN: Could we really win? Yeah. Isn't this wrapped up with the so-called Vietnam syndrome and this whole way of recasting the very meaning of war where, on some level, it's an utter insult to even use the word "war" as regards the quote/unquote enemies, in the sense that the actions that were carried out that led up to the Gulf War, and then the Gulf War itself, were more like just high-tech massacres than what, anything you would traditionally call a war, where forces are engaging. Something where there's little or no casualties on one side and immense casualties on the other isn't ordinarily what you'd call a war any more than somebody just going into a public school with a machine gun and shooting. I mean, that's not a war either. And so if part of what you're saying is that now there's maybe an attempt to say, "But we can't sustain that," ultimately, that the kinds of struggles in the bad sense that the U.S. is going to face to maintain its position in the world are such that there's going to have to be more sacrifice than that, I mean, is that sort of where you're going?

AVAKIAN: Yeah, that's part of it. I do think they also . . .

MARTIN: So people do have to get a little used to the idea that they may have to . . .

AVAKIAN: Yeah, I think there are two things to it. Even leaving aside the international war dimension, I think they feel even internally that the center may not be able to hold with just this rampant individualism, and you need some higher values and sort of like the military culture . . .

MARTIN: Uh-huh.

AVAKIAN: . . . which is a highly hierarchal, authoritarian sort of culture of subordination of the individual to the collective. This is what they're actually promoting.

MARTIN: Yeah, but to be extremely crude about this, I wonder what effect this has on ordinary people, because I think there are ordinary people who will say, "Oh that was just so bad what Bill Clinton was doing," I mean the whole sort of sexual aspect of it—but in terms of these reactionary politicians, not a single one of them would have any compunction about casting a vote to impeach Clinton for getting a blowjob even while they were getting one themselves, you know what I mean? [*laughs*]

AVAKIAN: That's one of the things Engels pointed out . . . the hypocrisy . . .

MARTIN: But, I mean, I think most people know that on some level too.

AVAKIAN: Yeah, they do, and there's no shortage of hypocrisy in the ranks of the ruling class.

MARTIN: But it's even beyond hypocrisy because I think a lot of people actually know that too.

AVAKIAN: Yeah, they do, I think that's true but it doesn't change the fact that there is a section of the ruling class that really feels that without some . . . [*chuckles*] some sort of "transcendental ethic," which they want to root in tradition and biblical values and sort of the William Bennett program, they're not going to be able to hold the society together. They're not going to be able to maintain the core of the society in the way that they need to. That there are going to be too many centrifugal influences. And if you add to that the dimension where they feel like, yes, they're going to unloose a lot of stuff in the world—in other words, they're trying to proceed surgically, they're trying to proceed systematically, they're trying to proceed in an echeloned way, as we put it, but they also know, and they're already experiencing, that you can't control everything that's going to arise as a result of undertaking this sort of open-ended war that they're embarking on. And they know that a lot of stuff could get out of hand.

For example, take Saddam Hussein. If they actually go after Saddam Hussein, and as opposed to the last Gulf War where he may have felt, with some justification, that he had a good likelihood of being able to survive that war, and that if he could survive it there would be a certain way in which he could actually enhance his status even while his power was diminished on a certain other level—that's one thing, but in this war they're making clear that removal of him, and whatever that means . . .

MARTIN: Right.

AVAKIAN: . . . that nothing less than that is acceptable. And people like Gore are also saying, we have to go after Saddam Hussein and failure is not an option. Think about the implications of that. Well, if you're Saddam Hussein, you're going to approach this time around differently than you did last time. And partly what he's trying to do—and I think some of the accusations are true, not in the way they are framed, but I think he is trying to stir up the Palestinian thing . . .

MARTIN: Uh-huh.

AVAKIAN: . . . and contribute to the volatility of that, because he knows it poses an obstacle. For whatever other reasons he might have from his own viewpoint, he knows it poses an obstacle to the U.S. going after him, without the whole Middle East just erupting and boiling over. But if they do turn and go after him—or maybe we should say, *when* they do—who knows what he'll do in response? He launched scuds against Israel last time. Who knows what weapons he has? But he may try to do something more dramatic and extreme against Israel on his way out, on his way down, if he figures he's going out anyway. And, look, here the U.S. has already come out with a new nuclear weapons doctrine of aiming these nuclear weapons at lesser powers and small states that defy them—"rogue states," as they call them—so it's quite possible that Israel and/or the U.S. could end up—I'm not saying they will, I'm saying it's within the realm of possibility that the U.S. and/or Israel could use nuclear weapons in this whole thing as it goes down the road.

MARTIN: I think that's the "failure is not an option" sort of point.

AVAKIAN: Right, yeah, and I think they themselves know that's in the realm of possibility. Plus, they know that, whoever was behind September 11, if the U.S. keeps going with this, they're going to call forth more stuff, and maybe it will only be outside the U.S. but maybe it won't. So I think they're calculating all that. If you're calculating all that, then the ethos of "nothing is higher than me" . . .

MARTIN: Uh-huh.

AVAKIAN: . . . and "I'm the only thing that counts". . . they have this dualist thing, telling people "go out and shop, it's your patriotic duty to shop" because partly they want people depoliticized, even while they have to drag them into the political arena on another level, but if it gets down the road and gets heavier, they know that if you have all this mentality that we can't have any casualties—we can't undertake any military operations unless we have absolutely minimal casualties, and so on and so forth—that kind of thing won't work if you actually unloose and unleash a whole eruption in a major part of the world, like the Middle East, and you get nuclear weapons possibly—or, if not, other forms of mass destruction that are committed by the imperialists and their allies. Then you've got to have something that's holding the population together. You've got to have this

notion—which Bush keeps popularizing, or trying to popular-
ize, but anyway he keeps propagating this ethic, as he puts it
forward, of sacrificing for the greater good and thinking of
things higher than yourself.

So, if you look at all this—and, yes, they'd like it to go with
one victory after another without it getting really, really messy,
but they also have to plan that it may not. And looking at everything that they have in store, plus just the dynamics within U.S.
society itself, I think they are preparing for these eventualities.
In other words, Buchanan's got his own shtick and his own axe
to grind and his own view of this, but I think he is also speaking for some larger concerns of the ruling class. There is a section of people—and of course they identify it all with
self-indulgence, but there is a section of the people that's not
récupéré from the sixties. And then, in addition, there are people who've been unleashed by the whole heightened commodification, if you will, and consumerism and everything of the
recent decade. And all that creates a mix that's a real problem
for them.

MARTIN: Uh-huh, uh-huh.

AVAKIAN: And then, when you add the international dimension, it heightens the problem, so they're not just rushing to . . .

MARTIN: I just wonder how to get inside this strategy and
how they could think it's good. I mean, the moment that the
United States uses a nuclear bomb against a small, nonnuclear
power, the galvanizing and polarizing effect of that could be the
most extreme that's ever been seen. I could easily see pretty
much the whole rest of the world going into polarization against
that. Now maybe that's extreme, but even the fact, even when
they changed the doctrine, in other parts of the world and in the
United States itself, there were people who were immediately
polarized by that. It just seems like a really dangerous strategy
for them, I mean, it seems like saxophones and a sexually loose
president is [*laughs*] sort of preferable to our present form of
bourgeois society, *from the bourgeois standpoint.*

AVAKIAN: Well, obviously there's a section of the ruling class
that agrees with that.

MARTIN: And for that matter, the guy who's the figurehead
of this very agenda, cokehead, alcoholic, frat-party boy, lost
years . . .

AVAKIAN: But he's been born again.

MARTIN: Yeah, yeah.

AVAKIAN: And that's part of the picture too. He was all of those things, but now he's been redeemed, he's been born again, see that's . . .

MARTIN: Right.

AVAKIAN: . . . that's part of the program too. I think there's a section of the ruling class that agrees with you, but they have no initiative now. They did during the Clinton years, but I think there's a feeling that, more strategically...I don't think it's narrowly related to economic interests. Obviously, those underlie all this, in the ultimate sense, but I think that the strategic considerations they have are nothing like one-to-one with economic considerations. This section that has the initiative now, and is represented by "Dubya"—whatever the actual configuration that's actually making decisions, he's a part of that but he's obviously not the leading light of it in terms of formulating it.

MARTIN: He's the dim bulb, not a lot of light there. [*laughs*]

AVAKIAN: Yeah, right. But I think they feel—they were critical of Clinton all along for not paying enough attention to developments in the world—just going after Milosevic, that's kind of piecemeal and paltry.

MARTIN: Uh-huh.

AVAKIAN: And there are other constellations of power that are forming. I mean, Weinberger and others wrote that book which was full of a lot of nonsense and hyperbole in terms of the threats that were out there, even the way they pose them.

MARTIN: Didn't he write that with the elder Bush? Is that the one you mean? Weinberger's book?

AVAKIAN: Maybe there were some people who were around, officials around Bush, the elder Bush, who took part in writing this book, but anyway some of the scenarios were silly, on the one hand, but on the other hand they were trying to look down the road and they were saying, "if we don't step in and seize the initiative on this, then there could be new constellations of power that could emerge that could challenge us down the road." And they're not going to sit around and wait for that to happen. And then there are other factors. Whoever was actually behind September 11, what would happen for the U.S. imperialists if they didn't respond to it? Not only in terms of how they look in the world and the way it would give encouragement to other people to challenge them in various ways, but

also looking at it in terms of the centrifugal forces for a lot of
these regimes that they work through and that they prop up, all
the way from Pakistan to Indonesia and a lot of places in
between.

A certain dynamic could set in, where these regimes could
become unstable, these countries could become unstable and
these parts of the world could become too volatile for them to
actually effect their interests in them. So, especially if they did-
n't respond to this, if they didn't seize the initiative in it—step
in and say, "Okay, we're going to hammer some things into
shape here" . . . I think it's both freedom for them that they're
trying to seize, but there's also necessity involved. You can't
allow this to happen, both in the sense that you can't even allow
the appearance that somebody could do this to the great, powerful United States and "get away with it," and you also can't
allow the further instability that would occur in a lot of these
key places for them by their not responding and by the message
that would be sent and the forces that would be further called
forth. So it's not an easy thing for them on another level. And
by responding they are also calling forth forces of opposition.
But I think the line that they're acting on—besides the longer-
term strategic considerations I was just trying to speak to—is
their logic of force. Bush said at the beginning of this, let's do
future generations a favor. He couched it in terms of fighting terrorism but basically he was saying, "okay, this may take us a
generation or two—we've got to hammer this stuff into shape,
even with all the volatility we're going to unloose, even if it goes
through several rounds where it gets more wild and erupts even
on a greater level—before we can bring it all under control. If
we don't go hammer it all into shape, it's just going to get more
out of control, and more volcanic forces are going to be
unloosed, and then it's going to be that much harder for us to
get the initiative and run with it down the road.

A lot of things about this are accompanied by and rational-
ized through lying propaganda, but I think there's some truth
that they're telling there—that they do feel both that they have
the freedom to seize the initiative, and they can really run with
it—and that they also need to. As you were alluding to, one of
the things which was interesting to me was that RAWA
[Revolutionary Association of Women of Afghanistan] made this
point that in Afghanistan, with the whole Brzezinski thing of the

"Afghan trap" and then when the Soviets invaded, the U.S. actually sought out and rounded up the most reactionary, obscurantist forces they could possibly find. They didn't just go find people who'd resist the Soviet Union. They actually made a point of seeking out and drawing forward the most reactionary, obscurantist ones. But it does [*laughs*] create problems for them too. There is a certain Frankenstein monster thing: even though they may be overstating it themselves, these forces do feel like—there are at least some of them who say, "Well, we defeated the Soviets, why can't we defeat the U.S.?" Plus, even beyond defeating the U.S., they have their own strategic objectives: they want to bring down some of these regimes—like the Egyptian regime and the Saudi regime—and these regimes are sitting on a volcano. Even the Kuwaiti regime. Now in Kuwait, in a reactionary direction—in terms of a fundamentalist response—there is developing in this present context a whole growing opposition to the Kuwaiti regime and to the U.S.

So, I think all those things are factoring in. I don't pretend to understand all of it myself—or fully understand why they feel this is a necessity—but I can see factors that weigh in that direction, and it is a big gamble they're taking. That's why they're talking in these semiapocalyptic terms and they're talking in terms like this is a great—well they're not using the word crusade anymore, but basically . . .

MARTIN: Uh-huh.

AVAKIAN: . . . they started out with that word "crusade," and they tactically dropped it for reasons we know, but they are putting it in these very grandiose terms. And not just to make themselves sound glorious and highly moral, but also because they are conceiving of it in terms of big stakes.

MARTIN: And protracted . . .

AVAKIAN: Yeah, I don't think they're lying when they're saying this is going to last—I don't think it's just Orwellian that they want people caught up in this for a generation. I think they actually conceive of . . .

MARTIN: . . . the new normality and all that.

AVAKIAN: Yeah, I think they actually think that there's a good possibility that all that is going to be required. And also the section of the ruling class that's got the reins right now, more than any other, does want to recast the society internally along these lines, too, for some of the reasons that I was saying. They want to defeat the whole—the Vietnam syndrome was also a metaphor or an emblem for everything that came out of the sixties. It isn't just the international dimension of "we're afraid to go fight abroad because we might suffer a lot of casualties." It's also everything associated with the sixties. They want to purge that—defeat it and purge it out of the society on a much greater level. And they haven't had that much success doing it. I think you actually spoke to this in something you wrote.

MARTIN: Well, in part what's fascinating about it is the *waves* . . . so that you had Carter, part of what's funny about that is people forget, he was the first born-again President.

AVAKIAN: Right.

MARTIN: He was the first one declaring that Reagan had no real religious history to speak of. Do you know the famous story where the Reagans [Ronald and Nancy] went to church with the Bushes—to the Episcopalian church? I guess they had communion that week and Barbara Bush accidentally dropped her wafer in the grape juice and Reagan just thought, "Oh, that's how you do it" [*Avakian chuckles*]—so he dropped his in too. [*laughter*] So that shows you how religious he was. What I always loved about him was that he (of course I mean "loved" in the sense that I hated him) was that he had this whole thing with rural values, church and family. Most of his own family wouldn't even talk to him, he never went to church, and even though it's true he grew up in a small Illinois town, he basically was the product of Hollywood.

AVAKIAN: Right.

MARTIN: So, pure facade . . . so, it was sort of like, Reagan/Thatcher, that was a good representation of the antisixties, of the just-go-at-it-frontally approach.

AVAKIAN: Right.

MARTIN: Then you have Clinton who's in a certain sense recuperating it, so he takes up a lot of the rhetoric of the sixties, mainly then to say, "I feel your pain," but nothing structural.

AVAKIAN: Right.

MARTIN: But now clearly this isn't just part two of the earlier Reagan/Bush "Okay, now we're going to go at it frontally again." There's some of that, because in fact even in having the rehabilitated cokehead as born-again conservative, some of it is, not to be narrowly economic about it, that capital is having to ask itself, "What do we do with ourselves now?" I mean, I've tried to frame it in that last chapter of the Sartre book. The ruling class is not really going to throw itself into a tailspin just because somebody has oral sex or something, so what was really going on? And, I think you're getting at it more deeply than I did, I was looking at it that there were certain new economic factors and then there's a reassertion of a more traditional economic base, not to be reductivistic about it, but almost a kind of Microsoft versus GM, more traditionally industrial kinds of stuff. But I also do think that is still a larger question with capital and new forms of capital where it goes into the whole globalism question and, I mean, I agree with the basic analysis that there aren't really transnational or multinational corporations in the sense that they've somehow set themselves up above nation-states, but there are new forms of capital that do raise problems for the nation-state in terms of how they will be rooted and how capital can flow around. Also one of the great ironies: George Soros is critical of this flow, even though he's one of the leading actors in that sort of thing.

AVAKIAN: Right.

MARTIN: That actually is a real problem that capital has to confront now; in fact, I heard somebody at the Sartre meeting [the March 2002 meeting of the North American Sartre Society]— who is a bit conspiracy-minded, and so I had to take it with a grain of salt—but he was saying that he thinks part of what's going on in Afghanistan and the way it connects with Colombia and Plan Colombia is heroin and cocaine, and that you have to crack down on the forces that are preventing the flows of heroin and cocaine and that part of the new situation is that money laundering is now done electronically and that this presents new problems from the days when guys would go into banks in L.A. or Miami, literally with grocery sacks filled with greenbacks and trade it in. And the way capital can flow, there are elements of it where the bourgeoisie can pick up a rock and drop it on their own feet and they've got to get a handle on that, and I just wonder if that's playing a role in . . .

AVAKIAN: I don't mean to say there are no economic factors. Obviously, oil does have its strategic importance, and that's a significant factor. I just mean it would be wrong to reduce it to saying this is about oil . . .

MARTIN: Right.

AVAKIAN: in the more limited sense. And I also think there are other factors we need to continue to investigate to understand more fully how some of these contradictions of the imperialist system at this point—with some of this heightened globalization, how they are playing out and what contradictions this is presenting for the imperialists and what struggles within their own ranks is it giving rise to. It's a field that we need to do more investigation into and try to understand more about.

But I think that, in an overall and larger sense, what's happening is being driven, as they say, by larger, geostrategic considerations which ultimately find their foundation in economics but have a life and importance of their own, and they're not narrowly and immediately, in a one-to-one kind of way or linear sense connected with specific developments, either of particular parts of the economy or particular interests of the ruling class, like Bush or Cheney, or oilmen generally. Well, that's good as a metaphor up to a certain point—this is an oil war, etcetera—but it doesn't get to the essence, and it's too narrow in describing the really driving and underlying forces here, I think. So, we need to do more work to understand more about this, but I think they are operating at this point largely out of geo-strategic considerations. That's my sense of it—this is what's motivating them. Plus, although I don't think they're doing all this just to purge the sixties out of the U.S. culture, I do think that is one objective that they've had: recasting things in terms of the "culture wars" as well.

MARTIN: Yeah, I was just getting ready to say I wanted to come back around to that, but, gee, it's hard to see why they'd want to open up that can of worms. If they want people to read Shakespeare they've got to have some schools for them to read Shakespeare in in the first place, right? [*laughter*] Don't they have some questions that they have to answer about why they don't have a school system that's worth a flip? If you think people ought to be reading Shakespeare, or Plato or the great classics of Western civilization or whatever. Or that people need to know how to read to begin with, when instead the deal is, well there are a lot of Johnnies who don't need to know how to read if all they need to do is to be able to recognize the icon of the Big Mac on the cash register at McDonalds.

AVAKIAN: Yeah.

MARTIN: It sort of connects up with the other issue, or another aspect of it, not the way it's maybe going to sound, but it goes a little bit to the spectacle and the legitimation question.

I mean, it's clearly a brilliant thing on the part of the system when it can get people to blame the breakdown of the family on feminists and homosexuals. I mean, that's *brilliant*. That's brilliant, given that there are millions of people out there who come from families that are broken down in one way or another; I'd be one of them. There's no feminism or homosexuality that played any overt role in any of this. I didn't see any gay people out on the edge there somehow fomenting any of this. I mean, that's a brilliant scam, and it's part and parcel of this sort of culture war thing of where, "Yeah, damn it, we gotta get people to read Shakespeare"—I'm just using Shakespeare as the symbol of the great works of Western civilization that we have to recenter on, when probably a lot of people would be happy to go read some Shakespeare if they had some background, some situation in which they could do that instead of living in some burned out inner city. I think most people in the inner cities would say, "Hell, yeah, set me up with some Shakespeare, man, let's talk about Shakespeare."

AVAKIAN: If they can be introduced to it . . .

MARTIN: So that all these things are just battering rams that they're just banging people over the head with. When the so-called culture wars got going in the early nineties and the whole anti-PC thing, I just remember this one *Newsweek* article, I think I wrote about it in the *Impasse* book, where this was a big cover story. What was it? You know the "PC Controversy" or something to that effect, there was an article that played a key role in all this. But the person who wrote it said things like, "There are these academics who want people to be reading homosexual writers instead of Plato and Virginia Woolf and Wittgenstein . . ." Of course, all the writers they named were homosexual. [*laughter*] I thought, if these are the protectors of Western civilization, it's not going to last too . . . so again, it's really about something else.

AVAKIAN: Well, I think there are some actual economic and social things that are involved in this dimension of it. In other words, in a certain way it goes back to our earlier discussion about the agrarian life and farming and so on—that there have been changes in the U.S. since World War II which have come more fully into effect now, which have undermined a lot of the traditional values. And, when you're in a largely urban setting, even the question of having large families, for example, doesn't make the same kind of sense that it did in a rural setting. And even having families, or even traditional marriages, for certain sections of the middle class doesn't present itself as the same sort of necessity, including for a lot of women who are able to work. These are centrifugal forces that they don't really have an answer for.

They don't have anything to replace these traditional values and relations with, so they can celebrate the acquisitiveness, the heightened individualism, all that sort of stuff; but, on the other hand, it does cause certain problems for them. They can tell people it's their patriotic duty to go shopping, but on another level that doesn't really work and it works against their strategic considerations. So I think a lot of these changes actually have undermined the traditional foundations on which the system has rested—not its economic foundations, but some of the social foundations on which it's rested—and some of the key ideological elements of the system have been challenged by this.

For example, feminism, in a certain sense, even the more bourgeois variety, while it isn't a fundamental challenge to the system, does pose real problems for them on another level, both because of the basic fact that this is a society that can't produce equality and emancipation for women, but also because it does actually undermine some of the traditional foundation stones of the social relations. So, besides just the international dimension—or maybe interpenetrating with it, is a better way to say it—these concerns are real. Even while what you are saying is true that there's a self-conscious fabrication in terms of "feminists and homosexuals are undermining the whole society and are to blame for all the evils of society," there's another level on which feminism and homosexuality represent phenomena that are a problem for them. They don't have a synthesis.

MARTIN: Right.

AVAKIAN: They don't have a synthesis out of all the changes that have gone on. They try to promote a lot of "small town values" but this is not a small-town, rural-based society. The whole society is straining against the constraints, even socially and culturally, if you will, of what have been its historical roots. But it can't break out of them within the confines of this system. And I think that kind of tension is creating real problems for them.

MARTIN: Yeah. But there are even problems where, on some level it's even remarkable how foolish some factions of the bourgeoisie are about how they think they are going to deal with them, unless again it's just a battering ram in the sense that, as with more bourgeois forms of feminism, it's the case that this society can't create a situation of egalitarianism and respect in the sense that we would want to valorize those terms, but it can't even create that in the sense that *they* would want to valorize those terms. You know what I mean? It can't even create equal wages for equal work, it can't even create decent jobs, it can't even create a situation where you can work at say the board room of a corporation and see anything that's very different than what you would have seen however many years ago. So, yeah, you have a few Black faces in high places, you have a few women in positions where they weren't there before, you have a few very high profile folks . . .

AVAKIAN: Right.

MARTIN: . . . but most people know. I remember even when everything went down in 1992 in the Rodney King aftermath, even Michael Jordan, they went to Michael Jordan and said, I think I even read this in the paper [the *Revolutionary Worker*] actually, they thought they could get some sort of reactionary comment out of him—because after all aren't you doing really well in America?—and he said, "Well, that doesn't mean anything in terms of the way most Black people live," I mean even he said that. So, they can't even do their own thing much less anything even remotely like our thing. And they also can't, I absolutely agree with you when you say, they don't have anything to replace the traditional structures and what counts for values with them or what they're calling values. But, I mean it's also like you say, these centrifugal forces are such that this humpty dumpty ain't gonna get put together again. There's no going back to the traditional family now, there's no putting all these things back under wraps. It's sort of like, gee, could they really go forward with the *Kinder, Küche, Kirche*, get the woman back to the stove, have her chained to the bed, chain just long enough to reach the kitchen kind of thing? I just don't think that's in the offing, and so what is this really about?

8
Legitimation and Fascism

AVAKIAN: Yeah, going back to your earlier question [about why they would move in a more fascistic direction], I think this is a big contradiction for them in terms of legitimating norms and the undermining of those norms. In other words, if they actually would try to do something like that, that would cause a tremendous eruption. Plus, moving in the direction of a more fascistic operation of the bourgeois dictatorship—of this big machinery, this political apparatus, however you want to put it— this does run counter to a lot of the things that they advertise as what makes this country so special and gives it its right to go impose its will on the rest of the world.

MARTIN: Right, right.

AVAKIAN: So, I do think that's a real contradiction for them. As to whether they could really do the Nazi *Kinder, Küche, Kirche* program, I would say that they would try to do that only in the most extreme of circumstances. I mean, there are people who have that program—get the women back into the home— there are these Christian fundamentalists who actually give financial advice to couples on how to scale back their living standard in order that the woman can return to her rightful place in the scheme of things, as the breeder of children, homemaker, and helpmate to the man; but as a program for society as a whole, it would cause a tremendous convulsion, to try to do that. I think they're reaching for a synthesis that doesn't literally require women to do that but reinforces a lot of the traditional values at the same time, and that's what I meant in saying that, even though in some ways bourgeois feminism and similar trends actually embody and incorporate a lot of the bourgeois values themselves, there's another sense in which they do pose real contradictions, given some of these things that we're talking about in terms of changes in the system and trying to keep the center together and maintaining the cohesion of this kind of society. I think there are real tensions there, and they're reaching for a synthesis that reinforces the traditional values and recasts them to a certain degree in terms of the present conditions, without literally returning to the conditions of fifty years ago. Which, as some people have pointed out, were not normally the conditions for generations either—there was something particular about that period, that immediate post-WWII period. But, in that early post-WWII period, there were the particularities where women were working a lot less than they had in World War II, but also less than they had worked in some earlier periods in American history. Anyway, I think they are trying to reinforce certain traditional relations and values but do it on the basis of not totally reversing all these changes that are, in a significant way, if not irreversible, very difficult to reverse— along the lines of what you were saying.

MARTIN: Uh-huh.

AVAKIAN: But that's very volatile, to try to do that, and I think they felt like Clinton, not only in his own personal demeanor but in his political program, if you will, represented giving free play to that. And he represented to these other sections of the ruling class the wrong attitude, if you will, toward it. You were talking earlier about this interview where he was mentioning this saxophonist . . .

MARTIN: Peter Brotzmann.

AVAKIAN: I mean that's the kind of thing, like you said, "I feel your pain," [*Martin laughs*] or "I'm one of you."

MARTIN: He's hip.

AVAKIAN: Yeah: "I'm one of you culturally and socially." But I think there's a section of the ruling class that believes that's exactly what you *don't* need, to deal with this volatile mix of shifting ground underneath and shifting mores with it. There is a significant section of the population that thinks that "live and let live" should be the ethos and the mores, and basically, "Okay, politicians are hypocrites and a lot of people, like Clinton, engage in these sexual adventures that are exploitative or whatever, but to bring down a president for that would be worse than the fact that the president does that." They may not think it's a very uplifting model to have a president do that, but it would be worse to bring down a president for that. It's sort of

like live and let live, and it goes along with diversity, multicul-
turalism, all these sorts of things which are a real significant
trend, and strand of the society, if you will. There's an acute tension between that and "We've gotta bring forward and fortify the
traditional values." Both of them are contending sharply in this
society but also, in a concentrated way, within the ruling class.
And, again, they don't have a solution for this, so whatever way
they go with it, it's fraught with a lot of tension and a lot of
potentially volatile elements for them.

Take the whole abortion issue. They had to make adjust-
ments because of both underlying material and social changes
and because of a massive women's movement. And then to a
certain degree they've used that to call forth this whole reactionary movement in opposition to it—which is misnamed "right
to life," because if these people who are religiously motivated
actually read their Bibles, they'd see that there are many, many
celebrations of the killing of babies—bashing in the heads of
babies—all the way from Psalm 137 to other passages.

There's that reggae song "By the Rivers of Babylon," and I
always liked that song, but I recently reread the whole Bible,
and that song is taken from psalm 137, which ends with the
bashing in of the heads of the babies of Babylon—celebrating
that—joyfully proclaiming that this is going to be the fate of
Babylon. So, if those peoples really read their Bibles—it's sort of
farcical for them to be pretending that they're concerned about
the lives of babies. What these Bible passages are referring to
are babies who have been born—these are not embryos or
fetuses, these are living children whose heads are going to be
bashed in by the righteous God and his people.

So, anyway, abortion is something they've used to call forth
a reactionary movement but it's a real contradiction for them.
They cannot just stuff this whole thing of everything that has
arisen, as expressed by feminism, for example—all those social
and cultural changes—they can't stuff that back into the bottle,
so to speak; but they also can't really fulfill all the aspirations of
it, even as they're being expressed now. As you were pointing
out, not only can they not really provide, obviously, a communist solution to this and real emancipation for women, they can't
even fulfill the aspirations that are being spontaneously
expressed now. That's a particularly volatile contradiction for
them.

And there are a lot of things also in terms of the question of homosexuality. The constraints on people, as to why they have to be in traditional marriages, are not as great as they were in the past—the material constraints, the social constraints—so this is a big problem for them too. All these things are, actually, on one level, what you say—they are battering rams they're using to try to get across a lot of reactionary shit—but there is real social volatility there. And they don't have any easy solution for that.

MARTIN: Well, I mean, one of their solutions with people like Ashcroft, or Bush himself for that matter, G.W., it is clearly to have people who, at least in bourgeois terms are, I was getting ready to say constitutionally elected, somehow . . . [*Avakian laughs*] They got in under the constitution, pledged to defend the constitution, uphold the constitution, they don't give a damn about the U.S. Constitution, and they're breaking through elements of their own setup that they've pledged to defend.

So, for example, around the whole question of marriage, why is it, and Clinton himself is a great example here where, apparently what was it, he got up at five, six in the morning to sign this so-called Defense of Marriage Act so that it wouldn't be done in the light of day and, of course the act itself was put together and signed by people including Clinton himself but including people way on the right wing who would have a very hard time defending their own marriages. But, not a one of them, I realize this is sort of within the bourgeois logic, but not a one of them had the wherewithal to just even say, well wait a minute, I mean if two gay people want to enter into a union and call it a marriage why isn't that covered by freedom of association in our own constitution that we're supposed to be upholding?

I realize that's just asking a question that's in an arena that's not really our arena, but it's significant that they now, with the things that are going forward under the Patriot Act and stuff like that, are seeing that they have to reforge it may not ultimately come to actually rewriting the Constitution. But there are parts of it that they have to push into the background or make it fashionable to sort of say, "Well," that may be in the Constitution but, whatever, we've got this other thing we're doing here.

AVAKIAN: Yeah.

MARTIN: Now, you spoke to that some in the "Challenges" document as I recall.

AVAKIAN: Yeah. I haven't read his book but from what people have told me about it—Rehnquist's book on the history of the Supreme Court—he more or less justifies, not only states the fact but justifies, that in times of acute crisis, like war, when the national interest is really at stake, the Supreme Court has more or less allowed the government, in particular the executive branch, to do whatever it wanted to do, one of the salient examples being the internment of the Japanese in World War II, where the Supreme Court said it was perfectly constitutional, basically. That ruling was similar, in logic, to the ruling that the Supreme Court recently passed on the "one strike and you're out" in the housing projects: they said, essentially, "drugs are a problem in the housing projects, so we need to be able to have this law." [*laughs*] Which is not constitutionally founded reasoning at all. It's just a purely utilitarian argument that we need to be able to have this level of repression over this section of the people—so that's the Constitution. [*laughs*] And that's the same thing they are basically going to say, with maybe some fine tuning, about most of these things which Bush is pushing and Ashcroft is pushing, and which we have far from seen the full unfolding of, in terms of overall repression in the society.

That does, on one hand, pose a real danger to the people as a whole, and particularly to those who are seeking to oppose what the government is doing—and, more than that, ultimately make a revolution—in other words, to our side. But it also poses some real contradictions for the other side in terms of their legitimating norms, and this is not a minor thing to them, that "We're a country ruled by laws and not by men." That letter that Bennett and others wrote, for largely European intellectual consumption, makes a big deal out of this. The basis on which they can invoke the doctrine of limited sovereignty of other countries, and so on, is that they mistreat their own people, and "We don't do that." Which is a farce of course, when your police are shooting hundreds of people every year, almost all of them unarmed—just on that level, let alone the executions of people and everything else, but just on that level you have no right to talk about somebody else mistreating their own people. But, they insist, "We have a Constitution that protects the rights of the people here." This is one of the big things that not only holds this society together—legitimating norms for this society—but also provides the "moral authority," such as it is, for their international marauding and aggression.

MARTIN: But at the same time that they're saying, "We have this piece of paper," they are also saying, "Now we're going to ignore it, mostly," for a while here, at least for a while.

AVAKIAN: Yeah, that's what I'm saying. When we're talking about problems of legitimating norms, and the undermining of that, I think these are not insignificant factors, exactly what you just said.

MARTIN: Right.

AVAKIAN: You know this point of being a constitutional society where the rights of the people are protected, not just at the whim of the rulers but by deeply embedded principles and structures—to undermine that, as they're beginning to do in a significant way, is a real problem for them, even while obviously they feel a necessity to do it.

MARTIN: It's a real problem. I had friends where we were joking about this, still joke about it, I was at a big philosophy conference with a colleague whom I'm pretty close to, and we just got into kind of a whole groove of joking about, "I'm going to go get a Coke—*or the terrorists win*!" [*both laugh*] Everything we said we would add "or the terrorists win" to it.

AVAKIAN: Right.

MARTIN: And it fits in nicely with, "We've been attacked, we're at war, let's go to the mall."

AVAKIAN: Yeah.

MARTIN: When you can get those kinds of levels working together that's not quite not the situation of Weimar, Germany, with the rise of the fascist movements, and the Nazi party having what was it, your Goebbels, the famous "1933 cancels 1789" statement, the "going directly at it" kind of pronouncement but where it really had a lot of meaning in that context. Most people here wouldn't even know—what's 1933? What's 1789? What's 1776 for that matter?

AVAKIAN: Someone was making an important point recently, which figures in here, that when Americans think of freedom a lot of them don't think of the loftier principles of dissent and protection of the rights of dissent and that kind of thing. They more think in terms of the Magna Carta: the authority of the government has to stop at your own castle.

MARTIN: "Negative freedom," that's the term.

AVAKIAN: Right, if the government's not kicking down your door or literally supervising everything you say, and repressing things that you say that it doesn't approve of, if it's not literally intruding into your daily life, if you can still go to the mall and drive an SUV, for a lot of the middle strata, then that's freedom. This ties in with some points you were raising earlier—I do think this is a real contradiction. But, I still think in the maelstrom of everything that's likely to be unleashed by this juggernaut, some of that, or a lot of that, is going to be broken down, because people—it's true that they are atomized, but there are also these larger winds that blow, these larger social and even international forces that people get swept up in. And September 11 was sort of a concentrated example of that. It was one very sharp episode where people were shocked into thinking about the world and being drawn into big discussions. I know one of our people in New York said that, on a certain level—obviously not on the same profound level or to the same positive extent, but that parts of New York reminded people of what they read about with the Cultural Revolution in China: the immediate aftermath of September 11, with people writing "big character posters," people writing everywhere, about all kinds of things— their thoughts about September 11, their thoughts about life in general, whether they did or did not want retribution for this, big mass debates, and for a while it was allowed to go on because the ruling class figured this could all be steered towards its ends at a certain point, or "rendered harmless." That kind of thing does wrench people out of, "I'm in my castle, I'm master of my castle, and as long as the government doesn't kick down my castle door or intrude by some other means" . . . even though of course they are . . .

MARTIN: Or cut off my cable TV.

AVAKIAN: Right—or my connection to the internet or whatever—then I'm fine, regardless of what's happening to everybody else. There is that sort of mentality and a certain material basis for it, but there are also things that sweep against that— that's what I'm trying to say.

MARTIN: Yeah, that's where you have to look at that question of, in order for the system to get people behind it, it has to activate people politically in ways that then can be dangerous for that system.

9
Postmodern Capitalism

MARTIN: I like a lot of what Fredric Jameson says about some of the cultural shifts in society in recent decades and I think one thing that characterizes what I sometimes call postmodern capitalism (I'm really getting it from him), is in a certain sense where you don't have an operative sense of citizenship, and it's not just that, "oh, this is a consumer society now," but there is something to that in the sense of the level of depoliticization of at least large parts of the population. I mean for example such that you could have TV commercials saying, "I will go to the shopping mall to fight terrorism."

AVAKIAN: Yeah.

MARTIN: I mean, not even "Plant a victory garden" for heaven's sake, but "I will go to the mall and buy something for my garden," something that however many years ago would have just been laughable and bizarre to most people is now the norm. And it does speak; when people get repoliticized, still that has its effect, too. And, maybe this is the next phase, that also feeds into discussions about what people's interests are, what their sense of norms could be, maybe that's my sense of where to . . .

AVAKIAN: Where to go next?

MARTIN: Yeah, or even how we could break it off.

AVAKIAN: One little point I was thinking of—something you were saying before was causing me to think about something, but now I can't remember what it was [*laughs*], there was something about the shopping and the atomization, well, anyway, maybe I'll think of it later . . .

MARTIN: Citizens, consumers?

AVAKIAN: Oh, that was it, it's a very small point, the taxpayer becoming the paradigm, or whatever you want to say, instead of the citizen, is another phenomenon.

MARTIN: Right.

AVAKIAN: People are trained to think of themselves as tax-payers, which of course is a kind of reactionary social construct in terms of how people identify themselves. It's narrow—it is, if not literally then metaphorically, the petty property owner—this is this whole thing that's been promoted, the taxpayers, and the whole persona of the taxpayer. Anyway, that was just a small point, I think it's another part of this point, the taxpayer instead of the citizen, it's something that is maybe worth exploring. I can't really go any farther with it right now, but, I agree.

MARTIN: It connects with the consumer point in that it represents in its own domain an aspect of commodity fetishism. The products and processes of labor are taken as being apart from any sense of what that process is, and so then one has some notion of, "I *earned* this and now the government wants to take part of that away from me and I don't know if I want my money to go to that, I would rather for it go for this other thing, or for me to be able to keep it, because I *earned* it," without any larger sense of, what does that word mean exactly, in terms of what's the fabric of social relations that . . .

AVAKIAN: Right.

MARTIN: . . . has one person living in a mansion and another in a cardboard box?

AVAKIAN: Yeah, I think it also obscures and inverts the actual way in which value is created, and not just in this society but in the world: Here you have this whole system that's exploiting people all over the world—on the basis of which you have money in circulation, and even the wage levels of people in this country and their earning levels are determined in relation to that. The whole parasitism of imperialism and the fact that you can make x amount of money doing x job in this country is founded in all that, or even the fact that you're able to work in a certain sphere of labor is related to, that underlying exploitation and that whole division of labor internationally, not just within one country. And then the money that comes to you as a result of all that, you look at it as if somehow you individually earned all that and now it's a question of how much you're willing to have taken back from you. It obscures and inverts—not that there isn't some legitimate complaint about the way the government taxes people, but more fundamentally it inverts and obscures the way in which all this circulating pool of wealth is created in the first place, and by whom and by what means, and so then it individualizes people. But it's embedded in parasitism in a certain sense.

MARTIN: Utterly. And it grounds this whole sense of entitlement.

AVAKIAN: Right. Which is founded on this underlying, ongoing thing. Well, maybe we should stop on this now and then come back and get into this later. Interest/ethic is what maybe we're verging on right now . . .

MARTIN: Yeah, I think I even have a way . . .

AVAKIAN: Go ahead.

10
The Ethical, Interests, and Calculation

MARTIN: Well, these political theorists and social theorists, I can't remember when this term first came up, but sometime in the eighties, there started to be this discussion of what some people were calling the "two-thirds society" and they were mainly applying that to Europe and to some extent to the United States. I remember Habermas talking about it, but probably other people were too, and their argument was that it seemed that you could have in some capitalist countries what they were calling a two-thirds society, where, as long as about two-thirds were able to get along well enough, and as long as they had the mechanisms in place to keep the other third down, and a lesser part of the society in such abject conditions that they couldn't rise up no matter what, you could base a social compact on that for some period of time. I mean the way it was raised with people such as Habermas, it helped thematize something, but it didn't give it hardly any of its imperialist context. It didn't talk about what the material situation of the two-thirds was really based on internationally, nor did it talk about how in Third World countries the percentage or the portions are much more skewed.

But once you bring all that in, it raises this great difficulty. There was a bridge to that from what we were talking about earlier, so that, it's always two things. But to try to get people in a country such as this used to the idea that there might actually be a conflict, a war, an action, where there will be casualties, where there will be real costs that the population more generally will have to bear, this will obviously thematize the question of where people's interests lie, but then you do get into this question of percentages in the sense of, it's one thing to get people used to the fact that there will be real costs and some casualties, some deaths, but *how many?* How many people will really be affected by that? If they are still able to carry out relatively high-tech warfare where the social costs and casualties are still somewhat minimized, then I don't quite know how much that'll get thematized.

But the other level is one on which, so that when it gets thematized at least you can say to people, "But where do your real interests lie?" that sort of thing, but the other level, where I think the real difficulty comes up is, *given that*, if there's something like the two-thirds, but based on the utterly skewed portions in the Third World, in the much, much, much larger part of the world where more and more people are, and then, even if the question becomes thematized, OK so this social system is asking you to do *X*, it's asking you to give up *X*, "but where do your real interests lie?" Why wouldn't that just invite a kind of calculating view of "Well, gee, I don't know, let me think about that, where do my interests lie, where am I going to put my money down, what am I going to bet on here, should I bet on the imperialist's force or should I bet on some new thing that I have never seen before and that's very iffy about whether we can really pull it off?"

And, then, that leads to the other question, which is that there's probably some levels on which you could say certainly in a kind of narrow economistic perspective, but a perspective where we're talking about social transformations that are going to take a long time, people could say, "Well gee, yeah I guess my interests do lie with the present system, or, I'm more willing to bet on it."

But, then that raises the further question and that's where I think the ethical question gets thematized, or where there's that gap, where there is a certain level on which I want to say, "Hey, screw your interests. You think your interests lie with supporting this system? You may even be right in some sense, but the hell with your interests."

Then you have to get into philosophically nuanced conceptions of interest. I don't think that's what Marx was getting into. I think he was getting into that people would see that they would really have a material stake in one society or another and that they could find they could no longer have a material stake in this society. And I think imperialism and the lopsidedness just skews things to the point where that's just not going to get thematized for people that way and even if it does, I don't see how we could really get into the question of, "Well, what would be the *just* thing to do, what is the *just* view of this thing?," through that category.

AVAKIAN: Well, to use a double negative, there's not nothing to what you're raising [*both laugh*], on a lot of different levels. In other words, even your two-thirds point has an aspect of truth to it—taking that as a rough, not an exact, quantification, which isn't the point anyway. And, if you view things only in static terms, if that's the only way you could see things, then there would be a lot more truth to that. But I think things are actually much more dynamic and have to be seen as being much more dynamic. So just on the first point—I want to get to the ethics thing as we go along, we'll get into that more, but let me put it this way: I think, first of all, the great majority of people, even in the imperialist societies, would be a lot better off in a socialist society, and even more so in a communist world. And I don't just mean that in the sense that ultimately "even the bourgeoisie would be better off." I mean the "trade-off" would actually be to the advantage of broad middle strata in terms of the social relations and everything else that goes along with it, the culture and everything—this would actually be something that would be better for them. It's not just a matter of my saying it would be better for them but, could they experience it, they would feel that it was better.

But, on the other hand, that fact will never lead to a revolution, just abstractly posed like that. I think the point is—one of the points that we were trying to make in the *Draft Programme*—is that, to put it in extreme form, if you didn't have a force in society, including the U.S., that is strategically and powerfully situated and that has a kind of driving need—or at least a fundamental interest, a fundamental need to have a different kind of world, where that need could be expressed in a driving powerful way under certain conditions—if you didn't have those things, I don't think we could ever get anywhere. But we do have that, that's the first thing: our analysis—not just our analysis, but the investigation we did and the analysis based on that investigation, of the configuration of classes and strata in the U.S.—tells us it's highly stratified, there are caste divisions within it, but there is a significant proletariat in the U.S., although, again, it's very variegated and not one uniform proletariat. There are different strata and even castes within it, in a sense. But we do have that proletariat, and under the right conditions—both internationally and how that takes shape within the U.S.—I think that force can and will come forward ultimately as the driving force of a revolution (or at least a good part of it, especially its more politically aware and conscious section).

But then there's the question: what about the other strata? They are not a monolith, either. That other two-thirds of society, if you want to put it that way (not quibbling over the exact numbers), I think it breaks down into many different segments, some of which have different interests, particularly in more immediate terms, some of which have more, or less, "adhesion" to the system at various times, but broad sections of which have to be won over, even if they're not going to be the driving force and even if their adherence to the revolution is going to be much more conditional and limited and partial, or even just takes the form of not opposing—"friendly neutrality." I think that's the way it has to be looked at—dynamically and in terms of what are the conditions, both in terms of world contradictions and how they actually express themselves and, within that larger context, what's happening within the U.S. We can see ways in which that could all come together to produce a revolutionary situation, and then there's the question of the conscious element, as we say, working within all that—not just at that time but all the way up till then, as well as in a magnified way at that time—to turn that into a conscious revolutionary struggle.

But, let's take your point about some people saying, well, by cold calculation, I guess it is in my interests to go with the imperialists, if I just make a balance sheet on a piece of paper . . .

MARTIN: Right, right.

AVAKIAN: Well, okay, on the one hand, I sort of sympathize and agree with your point about "fuck your interests." And I don't think we'd ever win them to the revolution just by arguing with them about their balance sheet. That's too abstract, and if they're not compelled by things larger than that into motion against the system: or into motion which can be, without trickery, more consciously directed against the system, that's what I mean, I don't mean by chicanery or manipulation, but by actually winning them to a more revolutionary position—if there isn't something compelling that, just sitting down and arguing with them about the balance sheet and how to calculate it would never lead anywhere. If there weren't larger events in the

world and society, and if there weren't the force of the proletarian movement, and of other strata and forces in society who
are aligning with it, if this weren't exerting itself, then I don't
think that we could win these people over. I do think part of
winning them over is to present to them the larger picture
beyond their more narrowly calculated interests. And that does
include an ethical element.

In other words, I don't think it's correct to say that ethics, or
the ethical, the moral, plays no role in this. I don't think it's
wrong when we say what the U.S. is doing around the world,
or what they did in Vietnam, is immoral. We used that phrase,
"This war in Vietnam is immoral." We didn't just say it was ille-
gal, or something like that, or just politically bad, whatever—we
said it was immoral, and we said that for good reason in my
opinion. I think we'd say the same thing about what they're
doing now. And we didn't argue in narrow utilitarian terms.
That's more what the revisionists did and various allied tendencies—they put forward the equivalent of Jobs Not War or whatever it was at that time—and it might have been literally the
same, kind of like Stop This War, and Put the Money into . . .

MARTIN: Right, right.

AVAKIAN: . . . some of these vulgar economist arguments.
Which, in fact, isn't what was going to happen if you stopped
the war anyway, as we've seen. There's been no peace dividend—where's the peace dividend from the end of the Cold
War? Remember that, the peace dividend?

MARTIN: Of course, yeah.

AVAKIAN: [*laughs*] You know where it is? It's going into whatever the latest weapons systems are, as well as other interests of
the ruling class. But anyway, we didn't argue like that. I'm talking about the people who—even before I was a communist, I
didn't argue like that, and after I became a communist, I didn't
argue like that. We argued on the basis of, if you want to put it
that way, what was right and wrong, what was represented by
the one side and the other in that war . . .

MARTIN: Uh-huh.

AVAKIAN: . . . and which side represented something that
should be supported and which side represented something that
should be opposed. Now, our arguments, our moral arguments,
were based on socially established things. In other words, it
wasn't an abstraction what was moral or immoral, what was

right and wrong, what was liberation and what was imperialist domination. There are objective things, on the one hand, but there are also socially established and class viewpoints on that. What we call imperialist domination, they call bringing freedom to the world . . .

MARTIN: Right, right . . .

AVAKIAN: . . . and it isn't bringing freedom, but that's their view of it. And what we call liberation, they call communist tyranny, etcetera, etcetera. So it has a social content and a social context, and it's historically evolved. But, then, it isn't totally contingent. My view of the ethical, just to put it out there, is that it has a material grounding, it has a social context and a social content, it's historically related, but it isn't totally contingent. In other words, to put it in a certain way, it has a life of its own at the same time . . .

MARTIN: Uh-huh, uh-huh.

AVAKIAN: . . . just like the superstructure in general does. A superstructure may arise, or does arise, on the basis of certain modes of production or economic relations, but then it has a life of its own. Culture is not reducible, art and culture are not reducible, to what goes on in a factory . . .

MARTIN: Uh-huh.

AVAKIAN: . . . or "one to one" an expression of even the sum total of economic relations.

MARTIN: Uh-huh.

AVAKIAN: It arises on that basis, but then it assumes a relative autonomy and life of its own. And I look at the ethical in the same way. In other words, there are ethics that are—the way I see it, they're not transcendental in the sense that they can be applied regardless of condition, time, and place and in any society at any time. But they have a transcendental quality for the epoch that you're in, and they're not totally contingent—today I make a calculation so my ethics are . . . In other words, there are some overarching principles that are bigger than what's happening on Tuesday [*Martin laughs*], and therefore my ethics are not just directly related to what's happening, and they have a relative autonomy in that you're motivated by, and you seek to motivate other people by, a set of principles that has to do with a whole epoch you're trying to traverse, if you want to put it that way.

MARTIN: Uh-huh, uh-huh.

AVAKIAN: And then sometimes you have to compromise. Like Lenin said in *Left Wing Communism*, there are compromises and compromises. It's one thing if you're held up along the road and you give up your wallet. It's another thing if you join in with the bandits.

MARTIN: Right.

AVAKIAN: Sometimes you have to make tactical compromises but you cannot compromise your fundamental principles; and actually figuring that out in the real world can be very complicated.

MARTIN: Yeah, I like all that, that you're saying, but what's motivating the fundamental principle? To go back to something that was said a long time ago . . .

AVAKIAN: A long time ago here?

MARTIN: Yes, a long time ago here. [*Avakian laughs*] It seems forever now, and I'm not actually sure if we said this "live," so to speak, but the business about, where I had raised in what I sent you, the whole question of "to create a good society, people have to intend to create a good society."

AVAKIAN: Uh-huh.

MARTIN: That's what they have to be aiming to do. That would speak to something more like fundamental principles, trying to persuade people of those, trying to motivate people by those, and maybe people come to something like that through those forces of society that push them around, including their interests, including their needs. Maybe the word "needs" actually does help us sort some things out about how people find out what they really ought to be about. I try to frame it a little bit in terms of the Romans and the Christians. The Romans had a mode of production that arguably, I mean, I know Marx and Engels always valorized the early Christians in a sense, but in another sense, from their own scheme of things, why not see the Romans as the rising mode of production and the ones who have the system of production? I don't know that the early Christians had any system of production that was representative of who they were. And I think that actually is a good model for imperialism, for this whole question of imperialism.

Part of it is that imperialism divides the working class. I think Lenin's analysis of that is profound, and he opened up some questions that are, I think, still deeper than we've *ever* even gotten to. I think it's interesting that some things calling themselves

Marxism have only been able to keep going by either only paying lip service to that or by severing themselves from that altogether, because it presents a difficult reality to accept. It presents the difficult reality that in the United States, I don't know. I don't know if it's so different from western Europe in this, but it's got its particularities at this moment as the kind of superpower it is, where, obviously, I wish this thing would fall tomorrow, and I don't know when it will fall. But it seems like there's a kind of solidity around the question of interests that doesn't really quite speak to what we need to speak to. And I realize that's different in terms of different strata of people.

AVAKIAN: Let's go back to your example about the Romans, because you said something in there that I thought was interesting, which is, "Once something better becomes possible, then damn it, we're for the something better"—which I agree with.

MARTIN: Uh-huh.

AVAKIAN: And, to me, that's part of the answer to your own question. In other words, it doesn't matter at this stage in history whether imperialism's rate of growth in the imperialist countries, especially given how parasitic they are, is higher than what it was in China in 1972 or 1958 or whatever; but, because something better is possible, then that's what we should support—that something better. So I think that's at least part of the answer to where the ethics come from. They actually do arise out of the actual contradictions of society, of the world, which I would say are fundamentally rooted in the ongoing contradictions between the forces and relations of production and between the base and the superstructure, although not understanding that narrowly or mechanically. In other words, that brings forward certain contradictions that get posed, and the new comes forward out of that—something that's better, that you can say is better for the people of the world. In other words, communism.

MARTIN: Uh-huh.

AVAKIAN: The basis for it has emerged out of the contradictions of the real world. It is better so you don't have to keep arguing about interests in a narrow sense. Once you can say that there's something that's better—and not just in our heads but actually has a basis in the world that's better—then you support it no matter whether imperialism has another round of expansive growth and however distorted and disarticulated that is in most of the world and how parasitic it is overall. From my point of view, the trickier part is what you're raising about the Christians and the Romans, because the Christians didn't represent a more advanced form or better form of society. And when Christianity rose to the ruling position in the Roman Empire, then Christianity became . . . I was reading this book, *The Harvest of Hellenism*, by F. E. Peters. It's an interesting book, and he made the statement that once Christianity became enshrined as the official religion of the Roman Empire, then they turned against the other religions all the persecutions that had been carried out on the Christians, only on a much bigger scale.

MARTIN: Right, right.

AVAKIAN: I think that's not totally accidental. The Christians did not represent a way at that time to . . . in the beginning they were sort of a primitive distributive communism. In other words, not in the mode of production, but in their distribution, they had sort of an early communal form, in which there are some things to learn from. Even the slogan "From each according to their ability, to each according to their needs" is taken from Acts in the Bible, I believe. So Marx and Engels did learn, they were drawing some lessons from that and they did sympathize with that, but I guess my view of it is this way: It's kind of hard because we read back into history, looking at it the way we do now—and other classes and other forces in society in its earlier stages wouldn't look at it the way we do—but reading back into history, and looking at things now that are contemporary, I would say when people are resisting their oppression, you support that, you don't support the oppressors, and you try to make all of that serve the bringing into being of a better world.

MARTIN: Uh-huh.

AVAKIAN: You don't calculate which one has a higher technology, because the question now is that—to go back to your point—something better has become possible.

MARTIN: Uh-huh, uh-huh.

AVAKIAN: And you don't go "case by case."

MARTIN: But some of it has to do with how you define the "something better." I mean, for example, what if it really meant, if we were to have a revolution in the United States, what if it really meant that the material, the narrowly material level of the so-called standard of living, what if that actually had to go down for a significant number of people? But it would be better in the sense that we would have a society not based on exploitation. So, I mean, you have to sort of look at the relationship of those two "betters." Yeah, I mean, just think about Lenin and the Bolshevik Revolution, and I think you even wrote about this very sharply in *Conquer the World* as I recall, where Kautsky and crew were basically saying to Lenin, "Well, we'll think about having a revolution here, but can you guarantee us that our wages won't go down."

AVAKIAN: Right.

MARTIN: And I think the right answer to that is, "Screw your wages" and even if they do go down, "better" has to have some other definition and the definition is something like "good" or "a better society because it's not based on exploitation," which has something to do more with the kind of moral imperative than "better" in terms of our material standard of living. I mean obviously there is that strata in the United States who, like you say, is positioned such that they are in desperate straits and that is a very, very living question for them. And like you said, we side with the oppressed against the oppressor, that's right, but the lopsidedness makes it a very difficult question.

AVAKIAN: Yeah, it does. I think Lenin's answer was that we have to tell the workers the truth, that a revolution might bring their wages down in the short run. If it were true that our revolution would mean, as they charge, that the people's basic material needs couldn't be met . . .

MARTIN: Right.

AVAKIAN: . . . they couldn't eat, their health would deteriorate, that they would be living in squalid conditions—not just for a year or two or during a civil war, but beyond that, even once we "got our house in order"—then I think that would say there was something wrong with our vision of society. But I agree with you that that's not all of it . . .

MARTIN: Uh-huh.

AVAKIAN: But the fact is we can transform these structures, not just restructure from the top down, but we can lead a revolution and people can make a revolution to transform these structures and institutions, social relations, and even ideas in a way that meets people's material needs and at the same time, in an overall sense, on an ever-expanding level, frees them up to do lots of other things. And this also gets back to my point earlier about how for the great majority they'd be better off.

MARTIN: Uh-huh.

AVAKIAN: I've had people tell me, going way back years, middle-class people, "I'd gladly pay more taxes to see a more just society." That's obviously a reformist approach, but people say, "I don't mind giving up some of my income if people could have a more decent life," which I think is a good sentiment to unite with.

MARTIN: Uh-huh.

AVAKIAN: It's utopian under the present system, but I think it's a good sentiment to unite with. But if you look at the oppression of women, if you look even at some of the things that drive people in bad directions spontaneously, like crime and those kinds of things—which are real problems, not just for the middle class, they're real problems for the masses—the bourgeoisie does something reactionary with that to strengthen its dictatorship over people and its repressive apparatus, but these are real problems. We have answers for those problems, and they're not to institute a police state.

MARTIN: Uh-huh.

AVAKIAN: To the degree that there have been tendencies like that, we have to learn from that, but our answer doesn't consist in a police state. It consists in the masses increasingly and ever more consciously transforming these conditions to where those things can actually be eliminated. I remember the first time I went to China and we got to Peking (or Beijing, as they say now) late in the evening. We were driving in and the first thing that struck me—there was this old woman walking down the street all by herself at about ten o'clock at night, and the first thing that struck me was: that would be entirely impossible or extremely dangerous where I come from. [*laughs*]

MARTIN: Uh-huh.

AVAKIAN: And, to me, that's also part of the life of people. It's not just what your wage scale is at any given time. There is a lopsidedness in the world, and people need basic things, and they don't just need the barest things. They need to have some play. They need to be able to have entertainment. They need to be able to have not just entertainment, but art in a broader sense. They need more than just bread, in other words.

MARTIN: Uh-huh.

AVAKIAN: Our vision encompasses those things. But some things they don't need, they have in imperialist countries. You don't need—the absurd thing of everybody owning an individual car, or two or three, these gas-guzzling machines. You don't need a lot of that stuff, and people would give it up in exchange for this whole other society that we're talking about, even if they don't know it right now. A lot of them are not going to know it until it actually becomes a practical question for them. Which doesn't mean we don't talk to them about it now.

MARTIN: Uh-huh, uh-huh.

AVAKIAN: But the reality of that is not going to hit them until the actual choices are presented in a much more acute way.

MARTIN: Uh-huh.

AVAKIAN: So, we do have to say, "Well, the wages may go down for some, but we will have a much better society." If, as I said, things went to such a situation that people's basic needs couldn't be met, or if the whole life of people were consumed in simply meeting their basic needs, and they could do nothing else . . .

MARTIN: Uh-huh.

AVAKIAN: . . . and if that situation were perpetuated over a period of time, then I think our society would be a failure.

MARTIN: Uh-huh.

AVAKIAN: But it doesn't equate to whether the wages go up or down, especially in an imperialist country. I associate the "good" with all that.

MARTIN: Right, right. Well, I do too. Look, I think there's a standard interpretation of "the good," talking in terms of ethical imperatives or the role of the ethical, and where a lot of that goes back into Kant, where there's a kind of assumption that that immediately leaps to the real transcendental, the "way, way transcendental," or philosophical idealism, and I guess I don't think that's the right interpretation of what Kant was doing, or at least I don't think one has to give that interpretation to it. I mean, I don't really think you need any more for Kant's understanding of this than to say that the ethical has to do with doing the right thing because it's right, and not for some other sort of utilitarian or calculated sort of reason. And I don't know why that's not a good materialist principle because there's nothing in there about saying that this falls down from heaven or that you don't have to then ask yourselves, well, what is the concrete situation, what is the world in which we find ourselves, what are the social relations?

If you read what are called the "postcritical" essays of Kant, such as "Idea for a Universal History," to me he's opening up the very kinds of questions that Hegel is going to pursue, and then Marx is going to pursue, about the unfolding of history. I just don't see it as being unmaterialist or just sort of saying that it is "materialist," but then there is this transcendental aspect that is ahistorical, or any of that. I think it's more like, well, what would structure any conversation? The philosophical upshot may be transcendental in this sense: what would structure any conversation that two or more people could have, about what they ought to do? The answer it gives is one that, at least on some level, I find unexceptionable. It's very hard for me to see how this answer could be challenged. What we ought to do is the right thing as we understand it in our historical situation and we ought to do that because it is right. And I guess I think you see that sort of imperative, or that sort of thing coming through, in Lenin, I think you've expressed it dramatically. I can't remember whether it was in *Conquer the World* or it might have even been in a tape I heard of a talk you gave about *Conquer the World* and so we're going back like twenty-some years when I heard this, but Lenin saying when Kautsky and all the western European so-called Marxists were saying that "Russia's not really ripe for revolution and this and that condition isn't met and what Marx said in *Capital* isn't met." I think the way you put it was that Lenin was basically saying, "Just because it says in some book somewhere, even if it's a book by Marx, that's not going to stop us from playing our role in history; history will hold us accountable." If we say, oh, we could have had a revolution, we could have tried to do what we could have done in the situation, but instead there was a book that said we're really not ready to do that. It seems to me, though, it's that kind of thinking, and then the example I always like to bring up and I sent it to you, is just what Mao said, that Marxism consists of thousands of truths but they all come down to one thing, and the one thing he said wasn't some bit of political economy. Instead, it's what sounds like a kind of ethical imperative—"It is right to rebel."

AVAKIAN: But you know, what's interesting about that is that he felt the need to add the phrase: "against reactionaries" . . .

MARTIN: Right . . .

AVAKIAN: . . . because he felt that it had to be given some social content.

MARTIN: Yes, yes.

AVAKIAN: In other words, like when the slave system in the U.S. rebelled against the Union . . .

MARTIN: Uh-huh.

AVAKIAN: . . . that was not—obviously it wasn't Marxism, but it wasn't right, it wasn't righteous, it wasn't just. So, my point about this is . . .

MARTIN: Well, but, wait a minute. Okay, so suppose we just gave a slight spin to that. It is right for the oppressed to rebel against their oppressors.

AVAKIAN: Yeah.

MARTIN: Don't we accept that?

AVAKIAN: I do.

11

Romans and Christians: History, Oppression, and Meaning

MARTIN: And don't we accept that regardless . . . I mean, what if the oppressors really do represent in world-historical terms the rising mode of production?

AVAKIAN: See, that goes back to the Christians and the Romans.

MARTIN: Right, right.

AVAKIAN: I think you support the Christians even if they don't represent a rising mode of production.

MARTIN: Right.

AVAKIAN: I think you support the oppressed in any situation. That's going to be part of "the working out of history"—but not history with a capital "H" that's an independent force with its own consciousness, or its own sort of almost religiously endowed will or something.

MARTIN: Like a god that's calling . . .

AVAKIAN: Right, I don't . . . I only believe in history with a small "h" not a big "H." But that is part of history, in the sense that people are gonna rebel, it's gonna propel changes in society. Some of them are gonna be dead ends. Some of them are going to be absorbed into the present system, but it's all part of the process that's going to lead to the transformation of society, even if it doesn't lead to it directly.

MARTIN: Right.

AVAKIAN: But, for example, if you take a slave in the South in 1856, or somebody Black in the South in 1940, for them to get rid of the slave system, or for them to leave basically semi-feudal conditions in the South and come to the North, means in one sense, in a real sense, that they'll just be exchanging one set of oppressive relationships for another; but it also makes a real difference to them. Abolishing the slave system made a real dif-

126

ference. It was of real import to the society and in particular to the masses of slaves, even though they would then be living under, first more semifeudal, then more capitalist forms of exploitation and oppression.

MARTIN: Uh-huh.

AVAKIAN: So, you support the North in the Civil War, you support the slaves against the slaveowners.

MARTIN: Uh-huh.

AVAKIAN: Even if the immediate result is not going to be the abolition of capitalism, even in that case, if the short-term result was the strengthening of capitalism, the result of the Civil War.

MARTIN: Uh-huh.

AVAKIAN: . . . but the end result of all that is that it all contributes in one way or another to the process which leads to the continual transformation of society and eventually the abolition of all these forms of exploitation and oppression. That's the way I look at it, in other words . . .

MARTIN: I think any, for what it's worth, I think almost any social theorist or philosopher concerned with the question of history would say that you just gave as much of a description of big "H" history as anybody would ever want, in the sense that it's heavily teleological and it's that teleological element that gives you the big "H."

AVAKIAN: How so?

MARTIN: Well, I mean, not necessarily entirely in a bad sense either. Don't get me wrong.

AVAKIAN: No, I'm not offended. I'm just trying to understand what you're saying.

MARTIN: To me, one of the, and maybe I'm just a little sensitive to this because I'm from the South and the whole context of that question is changed somewhat and part of that's just in the sense that just in terms of the more recent decades in the United States, I mean I certainly saw racism in the south, growing up there. But I see forms of racism in Chicago that I *never* saw in the South. You know, I see forms of racism in places like Boston and Philadelphia that I *never* saw in the South.

AVAKIAN: That's true, but the South is where that whole thing was anchored and where it's . . .

MARTIN: Well, no, it wasn't. Yeah, it was anchored on one level. It was anchored in New York City on another level in the sense that New York City actually opposed having the Union attack, start a war against the South because that's where all the money was flowing through. It was anchored in Liverpool in another sense because that's where all the ships were coming and going, Marx describes all of this—the whole circuit of it. And there's also another level in which that kind of purely, I don't mean to get into this old sort of argument about stagism or whatever, there are some aspects of that I never entirely understood, but I mean it's something about capitalism that it can take certain systems that are horrible and replace them with something even worse. I don't necessarily mean in *that* example, but I mean especially when we talk about certain feudal and semifeudal, and we use that kind of whole, I think, teleology.

Well, maybe this is a point where something like the ethical makes its appearance because, I guess this is where I do probably disagree with Marx some, that yeah there are some levels in which capitalism gives us some tools and develops them such that we could solve the problem of production in a way that couldn't be solved before, so in some sense it's a higher stage of society than what came before it. But I guess I want to think on another track that it's the most evil, fucked-up form of society that can possibly exist. That even under feudal systems or systems where there's a heavy religious element, for instance there's, I don't know, you might not like this point at all, but [*Avakian chuckles*] people had some sense of why they were living, maybe, I don't know, as God's children or something, whereas capitalism gives you nothing. You live for no reason. You die for no reason. There is no reason, other than to just . . . , when Marx says "accumulate, accumulate, accumulate" is Moses and the prophets to the bourgeoisie, that's maybe even a better formula than he realized. That's why people live and that's, and even just for the sake of others accumulating. In the *Manifesto* when Marx and Engels are actually waxing pretty favorably toward the bourgeoisie as the most revolutionary class in history, I guess I think, well, on some level, but on another level, I guess I want to find a way. I want to find a way because I believe that capitalism is not just this system that has had its day that we could supersede now, we could take these tools, and some of them we want to get rid of altogether, but some of them we could use in a different way and assimilate to different social relations and all that. There's another level in which it's just *evil*. It's the worst disaster that has ever befallen humankind.

AVAKIAN: Well, I think . . .

MARTIN: I mean, feudal society, whatever you want to say about it, never gave rise to the possibility of just destroying the whole planet altogether, just blowing the whole thing to smithereens. I'm not saying that you or Marx or anybody else would excuse that.

AVAKIAN: Well, it's true, I mean . . .

MARTIN: So that's not just the form of society that ought to be historically superseded. It's an *evil* form of society that ought to be superseded by a *good* form of society. And we can talk about, well, yes, but doesn't capital create some tools for that, set the stage for it, don't you have to put that in terms of a historical dynamic? Yes, right, I agree, I agree, what else can I say, we're historical through and through. It's not that.

AVAKIAN: Well, I don't want to . . .

MARTIN: I want to go from the bad society to the good society, I guess that's what I'm saying.

AVAKIAN: I feel odd being in the position of being an apologist for capitalism [*both laugh*], but I think you're seeing one side of the contradiction but not fully the other side, although you did just speak to it, but not fully. In other words, it's true that capitalism, because of the nature of it—it continually keeps transforming things in a way that earlier systems didn't—it has brought us to the threshold where the whole world could be destroyed, or all of humanity could be destroyed. It's also, however, brought us to the threshold where by negating it (to put it that way), by overthrowing it and transforming the conditions which brought it into being and which go along with it, there are unprecedented possibilities for humanity—that's the threshold we're on. We could go one way or the other.

MARTIN: Uh-huh.

AVAKIAN: It's not a question of giving capitalism credit any more than it is, in another sense, blaming capitalism. This is the threshold we've been brought to. But I will say—I don't want to say any good words for capitalism, but I do want to say some bad words for feudalism. [*laughs*] First of all, people under capitalism are motivated—they do have some beliefs about what they're doing. They're trying to make life better for their families or trying to realize their dreams. They're trying to find, express themselves. They do have a purpose. People do feel they have a purpose, however degraded it may be—even in their own

minds, as well as objectively—or how illusory it may be, if not
degraded.

MARTIN: Uh-huh.

AVAKIAN: People even are motivated . . . some people actually do become doctors because they want to help people . . .

MARTIN: Uh-huh.

AVAKIAN: . . . which didn't happen under feudalism. You did-
n't become a doctor. You were either born a doctor or you
weren't a doctor, insofar as there were doctors, or whatever. So
I think it's a little one-sided to say that there was motivation or
that people knew their place in the universe under previous systems, but that doesn't apply here. It applies differently under
capitalism. I was thinking of this thing I read—I can't remember
the guy's name, this professor, who wrote a book on lynching.
I've quoted this before, where he made this statement—to me
it's absolutely astounding in its understatement—that "It's doubtful that a single Black male growing up in the rural South in the
period between 1900 and 1940 was not traumatized by the fear
of being lynched." Now to me that's a profound indictment of a
whole system, in just that one statement.

MARTIN: Uh-huh.

AVAKIAN: And I know, as the other side of the picture, to try
to put it in historical perspective, when I first moved to Chicago
I went looking for places to play basketball, and people told me
about this one playground that turned out to be in a Black
neighborhood on the west side. So I went there and was playing basketball, and then we were sitting down, talking—I guess
our team lost a game or something [*chuckles*] and we were sitting down and talking. There was this one guy, who was probably in his late twenties or early thirties, and we started having
a conversation, which turned into a friendly argument—the
terms of which weren't entirely clear, at first, because he thought
I was saying that nothing had changed over the last period—and
this was particularly centered around Kennedy . . .

MARTIN: Uh-huh.

AVAKIAN: And he kept saying, "Well, this has changed, and
that's changed" and finally he said to me, "Well, maybe you have
to be Black to see it." He didn't say it in an aggressive or an
antagonistic way, but in just a matter-of-fact way, "Maybe you
have to be Black to see all the changes that have come about."
And I said, "I'm not arguing that there haven't been significant

changes, but I'm arguing that there were bigger things in society and in particular there was a tremendous struggle and people sacrificed and even died, and what Kennedy did was not initiate these changes, but respond to the struggle and make certain concessions."

And kind of a funny postscript to this story was that after I said that, there were about five seconds of silence, and then he didn't respond directly to what I said—instead he said to me, "do you play baseball?" [*Martin laughs*] And I answered, "No, not really." Then he waited a second and he said, "Because we're looking for another pitcher for our semipro baseball team." [*Martin laughs*] And I said, "Well, thanks a lot, but I don't actually play baseball." But that was really a way of saying to me, "Okay, now I see where you're coming from: you're not arguing that these are unimportant changes, but you're saying that they came from someplace else, from the people themselves."

MARTIN: Uh-huh.

AVAKIAN: That's the way I interpreted it, because there was no context for asking me about being on his semi-pro baseball team, other than the fact that I was playing basketball with him: and he obviously knew enough to know that this doesn't mean you can play baseball.

MARTIN: Uh-huh.

AVAKIAN: Well, what I'm trying to say with that story is, yes, there are institutions of white supremacy as well as horrible racist attitudes all over the country, and yes there is an international dimension to the cotton production and everything else, but those conditions in the plantation South—not just the economics of sharecropping and everything, but the whole superstructure over it and the terror that . . . Now you got the policeman's gun . . .

MARTIN: Uh-huh.

AVAKIAN: . . . instead of the lynch mob. So it's changed form and you could say in a way it's just as bad. But that terror in the South . . . Or I remember Carl Dix [national spokesperson for the RCP] telling the story—sort of like the Emmett Till story, except it didn't end up the same way, fortunately—it was when he went down to visit some friends in the "deeper" South, and they were walking down the sidewalk and these white kids come by and his friend got out of the way to let the white people pass. So Carl turns to his friend and says, "What are you doing? We can take on these guys—we don't have to bow down to them, we can handle them." And his friend said, "Yeah, but are you going to deal with the Ku Klux Klan and everything else that's going to come behind them?"

MARTIN: Uh-huh.

AVAKIAN: You know, to me, this . . .

MARTIN: My parents told me stories like that.

AVAKIAN: Yeah, this is the reality of what it means to live with the form of white supremacy that corresponded to the feudal base, if you want to put it that way, and all the superstructure that grew up on it. It's not like capitalism has put something nonoppressive in place of that, I've made this point, agitation-ally—I've urged that this point be emphasized agitationally—that you could rewrite that statement I cited before and say: In the U.S. as a whole, it is doubtful that there's a single Black youth- -particularly males, but Black youth—growing up today who is not traumatized by the fear of being brutalized if not murdered by the police.

MARTIN: Uh-huh.

AVAKIAN: So that's capitalism for you, in its particular form in the U.S., with the whole history of white supremacy and national oppression and everything else.

MARTIN: Uh-huh.

AVAKIAN: But, it's not like that stands out as being more horrible than what you had in the South. You had it in the North, too, but when I say it was anchored there, in the South, that's where most Black people were. They were chained to the land, first literally, and then almost literally by the share-cropping system and the fact that they couldn't break away from it.

MARTIN: Uh-huh.

AVAKIAN: They couldn't break away from it economically, and it was very difficult to break away from it even superstruc-turally, even to get free, they were terrorized to get back on those plantations. That's really a big part of what the Ku Klux Klan was in the first place . . .

MARTIN: Uh-huh.

AVAKIAN: . . . to prevent them from getting independent own-ership of land and to force them back into where they would have to do sharecropping. And that was reinforced for decades, for generations, by terror. So, just to take that one manifestation—it's not a minor manifestation, but just that one manifestation—I can't say capitalism is more horrible than that.

MARTIN: Uh-huh.

AVAKIAN: Capitalism is horrible, but I can't say it's more horrible than that.

MARTIN: Uh-huh, uh-huh.

AVAKIAN: That's one point. But I still want to understand this other point, because if I'm actually falling into being teleological and conceiving of history with a capital "H" in it, then [*chuckles*] I actually don't want to—I don't believe in that, so I don't want to do that. But I'd like to understand better why you're saying that my argument amounts to that. In other words, to give one other example, Engels supported the peasant rebellions in Germany, even though what was on the agenda was the bourgeois mode of production and not anything that the peasants actually represented at that point.

MARTIN: Right.

AVAKIAN: He didn't support Luther and the bourgeoisie when they brutally suppressed those peasant rebellions. He looked at that peasant upsurge and saw some communistic elements in it, but he said it was also shot through and through with a lot of naive and religious obscurantist ideas.

MARTIN: Uh-huh.

AVAKIAN: But he recognized early communistic or partial communistic elements within it, he realized that they were striving for something like that, even though they weren't capable of bringing it into being from an historical standpoint. He supported that, and not the bourgeoisie, even though the bourgeoisie was bringing the new mode of production into being.

MARTIN: Uh-huh, uh-huh.

AVAKIAN: In other words, what he was sort of saying was that the limitations of the time meant that the bourgeoisie was more likely to come out of that stage and bring its mode of production into society than anything the peasants represented, but that doesn't mean we should support the bourgeoisie in suppressing the peasants. And that's what I was trying to say. Maybe I didn't say it well.

MARTIN: No, you said it very well. I'm for that too. The teleology, just to be simple about it, comes in when we talk about successions of modes of production. There are succeeding stages of society and the whole little chart that is set out at the end of *The German Ideology* where Marx and Engels even just write the words "primitive tribal societies, slavery, feudalism, capitalism, socialism, communism," I mean that's teleological, which is, I'm not saying it's necessarily a reason to give it up either, but that does have an element of . . .

AVAKIAN: But I'm not arguing that that was foreordained . . .

MARTIN: Yeah . . .

AVAKIAN: I think there were material factors that shaped things to a significant degree. I'm not arguing that there's some Hegelian idea of the unfolding of history that has to—first of all, history didn't develop the same way in every part of the world, and the more we learn about the world, the more we know that.

MARTIN: Right.

AVAKIAN: It didn't go through . . . always marching neatly through these stages. Once we got to the era of imperialism, then things were much more globalized and that had its effect on all the different parts of the world and whatever was developing in different places in the world; hardly any of it escaped and was not skewed by imperialism, and influenced and reshaped in some way by imperialism; but before that, it isn't everybody marching through these successive stages. I don't see this as some Hegelian unfolding—I just think that, in Germany in the fifteenth century, it was much more likely that you'd get the bourgeois mode of production than that you'd get anything else. I don't say that this was foreordained . . .

MARTIN: Uh-huh . . .

AVAKIAN: . . . by some whole process that was unfolding since the beginning of time or whatever.

MARTIN: Uh-huh.

AVAKIAN: You look at Germany at that time, that was much more likely. The fact that that's what emerged doesn't prove that that's the only thing that could have emerged, but I think there were reasons why it emerged. To say there were reasons why, and certain things that favored it at that particular time and given that history, doesn't to me mean the same thing as saying it had to happen that way—and, especially, it had to happen that way because there was some whole unfolding pattern.

MARTIN: Uh-huh.

AVAKIAN: Capitalism didn't develop in China, or its development was arrested, because of the imperialist system; but Japan cut itself off from the world for a few centuries essentially, yet it ended up imperialist and China didn't. You know what I'm try-ing to say? It isn't all sort of one neat pattern . . .

MARTIN: Yeah, absolutely . . .

AVAKIAN: . . . marching straight . . . Maybe what I'm saying amounts to that, but it's not what I'm intending to say, it's not what I believe.

12

History and Contingency

AVAKIAN: To divert for a second, I'm interested to hear what people like you think is important to read. I just have to try to figure out, in the context of everything else, how I can get to what and in what time frame . . .

MARTIN: Sure, yeah.

AVAKIAN: I'm glad other people, including you, are reading and wrestling with a lot of these things, I've often wished that I could clone myself [*laughs*], not for egotistical reasons but just to be able to do a lot of different things that one person just can't do.

MARTIN: I say that all the time too, that I wish I could just go through some sort of time warp and come back in at the same moment and also not age while I'm over there. [*Avakian laughs*]

AVAKIAN: Anyway, you were responding to what I was saying about history with a capital "H" or not a capital "h."

MARTIN: I think what Sartre argues in the *Critique of Dialectical Reason* about historical contingencies is fascinating and in some ways he doesn't develop it in quite the ways that I would. Clearly there came a moment when "pockets of people," here and there in the world, developed social surpluses so the question arose, "What do we do with the surplus?" and I think there's a little bit in Marx and Engels that seems to imply that everywhere they divided into class society. And then there are other writings, such as Engels's *Origin of the Family, State and Private Property* that are different from that. Because the way Sartre delineates it, well, maybe some societies divided into classes and maybe others—"Hey, more for everybody, we're doing fine here." Eventually colonialism and imperialism are, in the ugliest sense, the "crowning achievement" of class society. This virus finally gets imposed on everybody, whether they're dividing their society that way or not.

AVAKIAN: Uh-huh.

MARTIN: In some sense, you could even say that capitalism truly comes to fruition as a mode of production with imperialism and I was thinking in terms of something you were saying before, about the way imperialism takes that around, that debate, I forget when this went down exactly, but this whole thing where there was this anthropologist, I forget his name, but he was attacking Margaret Mead's interpretation of Samoa because Mead presents a sort of slightly utopian picture of Samoa in terms of how the natives lived there before. This anthropologist doesn't really quite give enough of the details and maybe Margaret Mead's picture was off in some respects, I'm sure it was conditioned by her outlook and all that, but he basically said, "Well, I went to Samoa and it wasn't like that at all," and his point was almost the opposite of what Engels was trying to say with the *Origin* book, that she just had a rosy ideal of the way those people lived but I went there and there was all this and that. Of course, what he didn't, what he managed to leave out, although others did point it out, Clifford Geertz and others, was that, "Gee, there were twenty years of much increased imperialist incursion into Samoa in the meantime."

This kind of gets at some of these historical contingencies, but I think then there is the other element, because Sartre wants to really push the contingency. And I think it's important because really what he's pushing is that there is a sense in which we could make the leap to freedom and that we *ought* to, because the basic ontological condition of being a human being is such that we could form projects; we are the sorts of creatures that can think about the future and try to go there. But what's left out of [this position] is that, and Sartre recognized this later . . . he said these things during the Second World War when he was actually interned in a camp. He made this famous statement that was somewhat offensive, as he recognized later, "We were never so free as when we were in these camps." He was probably spitting in the face of bourgeois society after the war as well, which was good, but he also recognized later that he clearly had left out some pretty crucial aspects concerning material conditions . . .

AVAKIAN: Uh-huh.

MARTIN: . . . and it goes a little bit to that materialism/ethics question, the ethical sort of consideration that, and I think part of what I hear you urging toward me, is that there are certain dynamics—economically, historically—that may have been contingent how they got going, where they got going, the exact forms they took, the ideological, the way the superstructure fit around it and all of that. But there's also—I think this is the teleology—that once these dynamics get going, they do unfold in certain ways. I think the key text there is the *18th Brumaire*. That's the one in which Marx is talking about the way Louis Napoleon III, is that who that is?

AVAKIAN: Uh-huh.

MARTIN: . . . is trying to sort of use something, he's calling it, trying to make it look like peasant ideology . . .

AVAKIAN: Louis Bonaparte, yeah.

MARTIN: Right, but, of course, what's really going on is that he's advancing the bourgeois mode of production, even while trying to give it this outward form of appealing to the peasants. And, of course, that text was then taken up as one that can teach us something about the way Hitler and the Nazis tried to, they had peasant pageantry around advancing the capitalist system and they would even denounce capitalism . . .

AVAKIAN: Right.

MARTIN: . . . even while . . . And part of Marx's point there, as I understand it, is, What else could happen? Even if Louis Bonaparte himself thought, "Oh, I'm now taking the side of the peasants." So, what else could happen but that the bourgeois mode of production would develop further because once that mode of production has implanted itself, unless there's just something that falls out of the sky and completely shatters society, you don't go back to the feudal mode of production. Why? Because the things that have been accomplished by the feudal mode of production are subsumed into the bourgeois mode and then raised to another level, or *taken* to another level, if you want to get that "raising" metaphor out of there. And so, in some sense, there's no felt need on the part of anybody to go back because everything's been carried over into this other level. I think there's teleology in that kind of scheme of understanding things. I'm not saying it's wrong necessarily, but once you see that, I think that's saying there are laws of history, there are ways that history develops, broadly speaking. It's going a certain direction and I think that's as much of the big "H" as . . . it's in the nature of things.

AVAKIAN: Well, I think you could have had and did have forces that arose that were striving for a return to feudalism, even some ways into capitalism, and under certain conditions they might be able to win out. My point is that, once the basis had developed and capitalism emerged, and once capitalism did "implant itself" in a certain fundamental way, there were definite material factors going in the direction of favoring it. I think that's true.

MARTIN: Uh-huh.

AVAKIAN: To me it's not the same thing as declaring that this is absolutely irreversible. We had this argument with people back in the seventies, when we were doing investigation into the nature of the Soviet Union, back before it became "Gorbachevized" and it became rather clear what it was—which then shed light on what it was before Gorbachev—but people would argue, before that, that you can't have a reversal of history, you can't have a restoration of capitalism. I remember this one guy who wrote that once the baby is born, you can't stick it back in the womb. It was absurd.

MARTIN: I remember the metaphor and I kept hearing it; in fact, it was at the big debate at Columbia University, because I was at that. [This refers to the 1983 debate on the nature of the Soviet Union.] I remember one group kept saying, over and over, and I think they were quoting Trotsky or something, "The film reel of history cannot be made to run backwards."

AVAKIAN: Well, see that . . .

MARTIN: Why the hell not? You can make a film reel run backwards. [*chuckles*]

AVAKIAN: Well, that kind of reasoning is completely ridiculous. There are particular reasons why socialism is more easily reversed than capitalism, once capitalism is deeply entrenched. Capitalism had reversals "on its way to the top," but I think there are particular reasons about the nature of socialism—that it has so much capitalism still within it, so to speak . . .

MARTIN: Right.

AVAKIAN: . . . and still in the world there is so much capitalism—which makes socialism much more vulnerable to being reversed.

13
History and Redemption

MARTIN: I don't know if we can really go too far with this [theme of redemption] right now, and the subject will get taken up a little bit, I think, in the discussion of the secular and "redemption" and mourning—those sorts of themes. A whole other dimension of this question is, if we have a revolution in the United States, we're still going to be, one would hope, most of the people who are part of the United States now. Suppose we had a revolution today, most of the people who are part of the United States now will be part of the United States, or whatever it is, tomorrow, and the debt we owe to the people of the world is enormous. On some level it's even unpayable. The things that capitalism and those of us who grew up in imperialist societies and especially the more privileged strata, owe to the world in some sense is even unpayable, but which, according to an old Jewish precept, doesn't mean that we shouldn't start paying it. Just like these arguments concerning reparations for slavery, on some level you can make that argument on perfectly bourgeois grounds in a lawsuit for lost wages or whatever. On another level, it's conceptually impossible that there could ever be reparations for slavery. What does that mean? But it's also, I think, a just demand and it's a demand that exposes the nature of the system.

AVAKIAN: Right.

MARTIN: And so, even though I think it's, there are problems with it, I also think it's a just demand and that the larger sort of question is that as people restructure society, we have to address those historical wrongs and those historical imbalances, and on a global scale, it's even much greater . . .

AVAKIAN: Well, here . . .

MARTIN: . . . and to me that, to be crude about it, has to be thrown on the balance sheet of our discussion of interests, what motivates us, what could make us create a better society and . . .

AVAKIAN: Well, here's an example, just briefly, that I think speaks to what you're getting at. Let's take the situation of Native Americans. Now you had this whole juggernaut coming at them—the expanding slave system as well as the expanding capitalist system, competing with each other but also both rolling over the Native peoples, sometimes all but literally exterminating them—genocide and everything else. Two points. Was it foreordained that this juggernaut was bound to win out? No, there were efforts by people like Tecumseh and others to rally all the different tribes; had he succeeded, it might have changed the whole course of everything. There were difficulties in doing that. There were reasons why things turned out as they did. Again, it goes back to what I was trying to express earlier about the dialectical relation between contingency and necessity. There were reasons why Tecumseh had difficulty rallying the tribes, but it wouldn't have been impossible; and if he had, again, they might have been victorious. It might have changed everything, and then the course of development in North America would have been very different. Whether it would have eventually led to a "Native capitalism," I don't know. That would have to be examined concretely. We may never know, because things didn't go that way. So, the question is: was it inevitable? No.

Two, should we have supported that juggernaut because it brought about capitalism, even though for a while that included this mix together with slavery? No. In other words, I don't think that you can—or should—say, well, this is a higher mode of production, therefore, it will all come out in the end. It's all good . . .

MARTIN: That's why I use this word "theodicy"—in other words, retrospectively, it'll all be justified.

AVAKIAN: Right, well . . .

MARTIN: And that's what we don't want.

AVAKIAN: Yeah. That's not what I think of and what I understand when I talk about—what I understand to be—dialectical materialism.

MARTIN: Uh-huh.

AVAKIAN: I don't think there was that kind of inevitability, nor do I think there was that sort of justification. All that didn't have to go on "so we can get to communism" in what I think *would* then be a teleological sense, or history with a big "H." So, to me, that's an example of where I don't think it was either inevitable that things happened that way, or "historically justified." On the other hand, there were reasons why it happened the way it did. There were factors favoring one side as opposed to the other. That's not the same . . . well, to put it simply, there's neither inevitability nor justification.

MARTIN: Uh-huh.

AVAKIAN: I think if we examine . . .

MARTIN: What do you make of that word "justification"? I mean, I agree with all of what you just said, I'm *for* it, but . . .

AVAKIAN: What do I make of the word "justification"?

MARTIN: Well, in other words, that's a bit of the language of ethics, that even if the European invaders were bringing a more advanced quote/unquote mode of production, it couldn't possibly be justified that they would come and wipe out the native population of the Americas.

AVAKIAN: No, it wasn't justified. I think, we . . .

MARTIN: Because it was *wrong*. I mean, is that the reason why it's not justified, because it was wrong? And then where do we get our sense of that wrongness?

AVAKIAN: Well, I do think we get this sense of right and wrong from our historically evolved and socially developed sense of what corresponds to where we want humanity to go.

MARTIN: Right.

AVAKIAN: That does get us back to the Kant question. I think that's where we get it from—from historically and socially evolved criteria—and when we, standing here, read back into history, that's the way we look at it, and rightly so. There were people at the time who opposed it also, from a different standpoint, for whatever reasons—religious reasons, whatever reasons—but our basis for opposing it would be different than that: we're looking at it from the point of view that the society we want to bring into being and believe can and should be brought into being is one that depends on people, above everything, in other words, above technology and above mechanical forces, whatever you want to say. This is not the same as humanism in the sense that it's not ahistorical . . .

MARTIN: Uh-huh.

AVAKIAN: . . . but it does have that element of recognizing the role of people, and you don't bring about that kind of world by wiping out people. That's not to say you don't have to have wars to bring it about, people are going to have to die, but that's different than genocide. On the other hand, obviously, I'm thinking of Mao's . . .

MARTIN: But how often do you hear Marx talking that way? See, that goes back to when we were trying to frame that in terms of "Is this something we can really get out of the Marxist framework? or do we need to work on it a little bit, at least?" I don't know whether it's a supplement that's really something else that we are adding to it. I would hope that it could come out of Marx, but Marx did not tend to talk that way and, I think of that famous passage about the people who shed crocodile tears over imperialism/colonialism in India and maybe his views evolved on this, but there was a certain point where he was basically saying, "They're just naive about how history really works."

AVAKIAN: Well, let me raise two points here. I think it is within the scope of Marxism. You made the point, in something you wrote in preparing for this conversation, that communism is bigger than Marx or Lenin or Mao. And I agree. It's bigger than any individual or any group of individuals at a given time.

MARTIN: Uh-huh.

AVAKIAN: And it's a developing, evolving thing. That's my understanding of communism. And what we're talking about is encompassed by what I understand to be communist philosophy and methodology.

MARTIN: Uh-huh.

AVAKIAN: That's one point. The other thing is, again, to be fair to Marx, Marx made some analyses that were just incorrect (I think you were pointing this out) based on incorrect information about what was happening in some of these societies, before and after British colonialism got there . . .

MARTIN: Uh-huh.

AVAKIAN: . . . and the nature of these societies. They were more complex and contradictory than he recognized. That's the nature of things, that people make mistakes, both because they don't have all the information and/or because they make methodological mistakes, which is not to say we should embrace their mistakes, but on another level that's part of what happens.

MARTIN: Uh-huh.

AVAKIAN: Secondly, it's like the Irish question. Marx, as he learned more, he did change his mind about some of these things.

MARTIN: Uh-huh.

AVAKIAN: What he said about the Irish question, I believe also applied in India—that he thought for many years that the Irish question would get settled by the proletarian revolution in England, then he came to recognize that there would never be a proletarian revolution in England without taking up the Irish question, that is, the question of the emancipation of the Irish from England. The other thing is, even Mao, who was, if anything—he was certainly not soft on imperialist depredation in the Third World, if anything maybe he sometimes had somewhat nationalist inclinations in relation to some of that, although not essentially, but he was certainly not soft on it. In his essay "The Chinese Revolution and the Chinese Communist Party" he talked about all the things that imperialism did to China, but he also said it did, on the other hand, bring into being, or hasten and accelerate, the development of the proletariat, which made possible a different kind of revolution in China. And I don't think he was being determinist . . .

MARTIN: Uh-huh.

AVAKIAN: I don't think he was saying that's the only way they could have had a proletarian revolution there, or that's the only way China could have gotten out of feudalism—if imperialism came in . . .

MARTIN: Uh-huh.

AVAKIAN: . . . but I think he's saying, "This did happen." To me there's a fine line there, but I think it's a real line, between saying, "Okay, this is the only way that something could have happened, therefore it's good". . .

MARTIN: Uh-huh.

AVAKIAN: . . . and saying, "This did happen and it divides into two: on the one hand it did all this—it brought all this depredation and suffering—and, on the other hand, it did bring certain conditions into being, and now we can do something with what it has brought into being."

MARTIN: Uh-huh.

AVAKIAN: And, I don't know, maybe I'm drawing a line that isn't a real line, but to me there's a fine line but a real and important line between those two statements.

MARTIN: Uh-huh. Yeah, I think, on Marx the one thing I would come back to though, sort of the two things but it's on the one thing . . . I could imagine one of my postcolonial theorist friends saying, "I guess that's a great step in the right direction where Marx got it right on Ireland, but gee, after all, it's too bad he only came around to that with northern Europe and not the south of the world, so to speak." I don't know that he really fully developed a whole lot in terms of understanding that and yes, look, I understand that this divide was opening up in new ways and opened up even much more after he died, and you can only ask so much. I never want to throw out the baby with the bathwater here, but the other thing is that, yes, there are the facts and maybe he had some of his facts wrong, maybe there were ways the methodology should be extended, but I don't know if we want to dig up his passage, we probably don't really have to, but I know I quote it in my *Impasse* book, there's also actually the *tone* of voice. What I mean—it was kind of a sneering tone toward these people who are showing concern for what England is doing in India. I mean, it really has this sort of, and you can say, "Well that's the tone, why do we make that a point?", but there really is a sort of, "They're just sentimentalists"-tone to it.

It's funny how this returned in 1992 around the 500th anniversary of the Columbus invasion. In fact it's our old friend Christopher Hitchens, if you recall, who was, I think, being reactionary then as well, so it's interesting that he's really come out much more fully here around 9/11, where he was saying—how did he put it?—he was referring to, who was the guy who wrote *From Yale to Jail*, he was an early antiwar activist, anti-Vietnam War activist, I'm trying to remember who that is again. It's a name we'll all know if we could think of it. [The name we were looking for was David Dellinger.] He wrote this book called *From Yale to Jail* that was part history and part biography. Anyway, Hitchens said, "My dear old friend so and so, he's waxing sentimental about this Columbus invasion, but doesn't he know that's just how history moves forward" and really sort of repeating this whole . . . He's actually even trotting out this whole "Doesn't he know that if you want to make an omelet you have to break some eggs" sort of thing and I guess you can credit him with sort of laying it right there on the line but . . .

AVAKIAN: He's got a bad case of white man's burden, Hitchens. [*laughs*]

MARTIN: [*laughs*] That's an interesting way into the question. [*both laugh*] I don't know, I don't know, I sort of wonder if he ought to have a bigger case of white man's burden . . . well, not a white man's, oh the white man's burden of . . .

AVAKIAN: "Civilizing". . .

MARTIN: Yes, the "civilizing mission."

AVAKIAN: European . . .

MARTIN: I guess I was thinking some more white man's guilt might help him . . . but I mean the return of that same tone that I saw in that passage of . . . he's quoting Goethe in that passage, Marx is, and there's just this sneering tone and I think it is exemplary of a certain view toward, and it's well known, there was this whole period where there was a spate of books on Marx and ethics, like Steven Lukes's book, and whatever the strengths and limitations of those . . . I mean, they almost all began by pointing out how Marx tended to sneer or laugh whenever anybody would talk about ethics. We could save some of this for later, and I know it divides into two, and I did say I think it divides into two in terms of laughing at bourgeois moralizing. But I think he also thought, "Hey, get real, that's just not really part of how things fall out," and if we've changed our view on that, I know I have, and what I hear from you is, the ethical is a real thing, if I can put it that way. I guess we could have a whole other debate on what its metaphysical or onto-logical status is, but it's real, it's meaningful, it's something that we have to answer the call of, that we have to have *responsi-bility* to. We have to have responsibility, then that's a different language than you find in Marx and maybe there's a way to build a bridge from Marx to that language and I'd like to think so, I'm happy to think so, but it's just not the way Marx tended to talk.

AVAKIAN: I think you can make an analogy to Darwin, for example. That was a world-historic breakthrough that Darwin made: it's still exciting to ponder it, especially in the face of these reactionary—I want to say medieval, but whatever—attacks on it. But there were things that Darwin didn't under-stand about evolution and there were things that are yet to be "worked out" about it—more to be learned about the reality of how it works, how it has worked, how it is working. But we, the people who uphold this and want to continue to learn about it, are working within the tradition and the framework, in a broad sense, established by Darwin, even if we don't agree with him on everything. We may end up disagreeing with certain important particulars that Darwin raised—and Darwin had his shortcomings, certainly socially and politically, which were not minor, but he established a certain new framework, which enriched our understanding of a very important part of reality. I look at Marx the same way. Marx saw the revolution coming out of Europe—he saw it coming in more immediate terms than it's been, unfortunately. And I think that, to the degree that there is truth to what you're saying—and, frankly, I'd like to not only think about it but actually read more to try to understand better to what degree I think there's truth in what you're raising and to what degree that Marx . . . I remember reading things where he did condemn the British East India Company and British colonialism in pretty sharp terms with regard to India, so it wasn't like he just celebrated it, but I think there may be an aspect to what you're saying in Marx—and I'm just thinking out loud here—that to the degree there was, he was sort of expecting this revolution to come sooner: You're expecting it to come quickly in Europe, and your view is that this will take care of things, in the sense that these are the advanced countries, where the proletarian revolution will first succeed, and once these become socialist, then the rest of the world will be transformed and "the problems of history will be cleared up."

MARTIN: Uh-huh.

AVAKIAN: Well, I don't want to sound too . . . pragmatic, but I think there is something to the truth that, once you begin to get a longer view of things, two things stand out to you. One, proletarian revolution is not coming, at this stage at least, mainly from Europe—or, to paraphrase that saying from the sixties, "Revolution is coming from a Black thing," revolution is *not* "coming from a European thing." That doesn't mean there's not going to be a revolution [*laughs*] in Europe, or the U.S., but it's not coming from a European thing.

MARTIN: Uh-huh.

AVAKIAN: And second of all, we've gotten a longer view of history and we understand more the complexity and variegated nature of history over the past, but we also see that this epoch we're in is a much longer epoch than Marx anticipated. And not only does that tell us things about the nature of this epoch, in a certain sense it gives us, I think, a different perspective on past epochs and even on the beginning of capitalism. I still think capitalism divides into two, but maybe to the degree that, provisionally, let me say, there is an aspect of this in Marx . . . I would like to look into it more, but my sense, provisionally, is that there is this aspect in Marx, not single-mindedly, or not unilaterally—there is the other side to it, he did condemn a lot of these colonial depredations—but to the degree that there is, I think it has something to do with what I was just trying to sketch out in my head here, just thinking out loud—maybe it has something to do with where he was in the process and how he saw it and how he saw these problems were going to get "cleaned up" from history, and from that perspective sort of saying, well look (I'm exaggerating here) why cry over spilt milk? Here's where we are; we're going to clear all this up now, so let's not read back through history and focus on or be preoccupied with these things that happened, because they were part of getting us to where we are now.

MARTIN: Right.

AVAKIAN: And I think where we are now, 150 years later or whatever, we understand more about what the reality in these countries was and what actually happened, but also more about the fact that it isn't just going to be like we'll have a revolution and we'll just—let me put it this way, we'll just go forward—but instead maybe we'll have a revolution and we'll go to the side as well as going forward, and maybe we'll even go back a little bit to take in some of these historical problems. It's not that we can go back and undo everything that's been done . . .

MARTIN: Uh-huh.

AVAKIAN: . . . but this gets to your debt point. You have to, in going forward, take into account and, in a certain sense, compensate for what was done in the past, as part of your going forward—not in order to go back—it's one thing to criticize that crude metaphor about the reel of history, but you can't actually, literally rewind the tape and I wouldn't be in favor, frankly, of trying to. It would be impossible, and I wouldn't be in favor of it. We can't recreate the world of 500 years ago.

MARTIN: Uh-huh.

AVAKIAN: If you read about the history of the Roman Empire, for example, you see how one people, or an amalgamation of peoples, in the Steppes of Asia gets pushed west by another one, and they in turn push another one—and there's sort of this concatenation, almost like a domino effect . . .

MARTIN: Uh-huh.

AVAKIAN: . . . that then impinges on the Roman Empire and impinges on Europe. You can't go back.

MARTIN: Right. Before the Aztecs there were Toltecs.

AVAKIAN: Yeah, you can't go back. But what we *can* do is say, "Okay, things were done here, they have consequences"— and, yes, viewed in that sense there is right and wrong and there are obligations that do stem from that.

MARTIN: Uh-huh.

AVAKIAN: We've tried to envision that in our *Draft Programme*, and I'm sure that's something that can and should be strengthened, but I think the basic position we're taking there is a correct and important one, that we have to take into account this history and we have to do something about the consequences of this history.

MARTIN: Uh-huh.

AVAKIAN: So, I don't know, to me . . .

MARTIN: To me, that's . . .

AVAKIAN: I think Marx probably was looking at this from a little different vantage point, and coming out of Hegel, too . . .

MARTIN: Uh-huh . . .

AVAKIAN: . . . if you want to talk about things methodologically, he's coming out of Hegel. He's negating Hegel but, you know how it is, he's carrying . . .

MARTIN: Well, I think one element of Hegel that's very clear in his perspective about Europe, and that's been addressed somewhat in the discussion of Darwin and the whole idea of punctuated equilibrium, is: Where does change ultimately come from? Does it really come from the center or from just kind of growing and growing until it breaks out of the center, or does it actually come mainly from the margins? And, I think that is a good example of where, I don't want to say we're with Marx and against Marx, we're coming out of Marx but we're seeing that that transformation and the understanding also has to be made and it's imperialism that especially forces us to make that development.

AVAKIAN: I mean, in accordance with the same principles we're talking about, we could have had a revolution, a socialist revolution in Europe or in some of these European countries. That would have changed the course of history, too, and some of these problems would have been dealt with in a different way. It wouldn't have changed the essential principles, but things would have been dealt with in a different way—the whole history would have been unfolding differently.

14
Kant and Hegel

AVAKIAN: But it [a revolution in Europe] didn't happen, so now we're where we are. And I think that, methodologically—besides that sort of situatedness, if you will, of Marx—methodologically, he was coming out of Hegel and he made a leap beyond Hegel, but when you make a leap, usually the phenomenon is that you carry a bit of what you're leaping beyond with you.

MARTIN: See, I think that's good. I like Hegel. [*laughs*]

AVAKIAN: But there are bad points . . .

MARTIN: But that doesn't bother me. I think that . . .

AVAKIAN: But there's good Hegel and bad Hegel.

MARTIN: I think it bothers you in ways that it doesn't bother me.

AVAKIAN: But I think the part that would bother you, or if you . . .

MARTIN: Or should bother me?

AVAKIAN: Well, consistently with what you're arguing for, it should bother you. By the logic of your own reasoning it should bother you in the sense that . . .

MARTIN: Yeah, but when we say that Marx in significant ways negated Hegel, the very principle of his negating Hegel in significant ways, that comes out of Hegel as well.

AVAKIAN: Right, but . . .

MARTIN: That sense of the unfolding comes out of Hegel . . .

AVAKIAN: Right, but there's also a way . . . of carrying a little Hegel with him [that] is a little bit of a "closed system" and a little bit the lower to higher kind of thing that was carried along by Marx and Engels. And the part of Marx that's good and essential, and the core of what we uphold, basically comes from Hegel and making a leap beyond Hegel and integrating

and synthesizing that with materialism. The part you are raising—and which I agree, at least in part, is a problem—also
comes from not enough rupture with Hegel. And a little bit
"Here's history unfolding one thing after another" and a little bit
like everything has to fit neatly into the system and everything's
sort of—this is a vulgarization, obviously—but "everything's
accounted for" and . . .

MARTIN: Right.

AVAKIAN: . . . everything is part of this unfolding historical
process. And Hegel's idealism only made it more absolute.

MARTIN: Right.

AVAKIAN: Because if you're a materialist, you'd recognize
more of the complexity and contradictoriness of it, ironically.

MARTIN: Right.

AVAKIAN: I think this goes back to the point that you can't be
thoroughly dialectical if you're not a materialist, and you can't
be thoroughly materialist if you're not dialectical.

MARTIN: You know, though, we're actually learning some
things in just recent years about Hegel that weren't known until
quite recently, based on notes that his students took—only in
recent years did the lecture notes get discovered. And in the
actual lectures, he said things that he leaves out of the book
[*Philosophy of Right*] because of the censors and the Prussian
repressive apparatus, and he talks about the right to revolution
and he refers to the proletariat directly and then that didn't make
it into the book . . .

AVAKIAN: Yeah, that would be very interesting. But maybe
what we should do here is go back from Hegel to Kant.

MARTIN: So, why don't we come at what we're calling the
Kant question, and maybe even this question of where we stand
in terms of history, philosophy, the Western philosophical
canon, that sort of thing, because I find resources there that I
wish that we could draw on and I don't always understand why
we don't.

AVAKIAN: Could you elaborate on that?

MARTIN: [*laughs*] Well, in particular . . . I think there are elements of Kant that very much enable conceptually what Marx is
doing later on. We've already talked about where Marx stands
with Hegel, and I was trying to argue that even where he stands
somewhat in negation of Hegel, it's a kind of Hegelian dialectical negation. There is a sense in which Marx can be seen, if

someone was just writing a kind of formal academic history of philosophy as, of course, many people have done, there's a way in which you can situate Marx as a culmination of the German idealist philosophical trend, but then turning it on its head and bringing Kant, Fichte, Schelling, and Hegel into materialism. There are all sorts of interesting things about that, in terms of others who also came from that same trajectory but went in very different directions, such as Nietzsche and Kierkegaard, but I mean, if you were just mapping in a kind of narrower philosophical way, that tells somewhat against doing that kind of mapping, but it also may be of significance in terms of just understanding where this came from. I think there are operative concepts that we might disparage in some ways if we are talking about them in purely Kantian language, but it actually turns out that they're fully present in Marx and that his whole intellectual project wouldn't have come together apart from those concepts and they simply appear in other forms.

AVAKIAN: Could you give an example or two?

MARTIN: Yeah. I think autonomy is one that we appeal to whenever we talk about human freedom and I think there are ways in which . . . there's a tendency, from a Marxist perspective, to give to Kant the most bourgeois-individualist notion of autonomy. But those more individualist notions of autonomy really come from quite different places than Kant. I think Kant gives us actually a very *thick* sense of autonomy as not, "I'm going to get my autonomy" meaning if you get in my way I want you to get out of my way or I'll sue you or I'll run you down or something like that. It's much more, "My autonomy is bound up with others;" it could not exist without others; it begins in a fundamental regard for others; it begins in the intersubjective and the interpersonal; it's only in relation to others that I'm in the world to begin with. I think it's a very thick notion and that when Marx talks about freedom, and ultimately the achievement of a society in which the free association of producers individually is the precondition for their freedom collectively, it seems to me that that Kantian language of autonomy is brought forward into his, or at least that conceptual framework is brought forward into what Marx is doing.

15

Social Animals and Their Visions: From Moses and Plato to Heidegger

AVAKIAN: You know, two things occur to me. One, I was just looking over Marx's "Introduction to a Contribution to a Critique of Political Economy" and he made what I thought was a very important statement, it struck me again as I was reading it, which is that man is a social animal, not only in the literal sense that he lives in society—that is Marx's saying "he," but people, let's say, are social animals and they live in society, but also *they're only capable of individualizing themselves in a social context*. Which, I think, is actually a very profound point and goes against a lot of the bourgeois-conservative notions of the individual and individualism, and the . . .

MARTIN: So-called self-made man . . .

AVAKIAN: Yeah . . .

MARTIN: Robinson Crusoe and all that kind of . . .

AVAKIAN: And even the idea that the individual, each individual taken by himself/herself, is "the subject of human relations," or whatever. In other words, people don't live outside of society; and, if they do, then even individuality doesn't have much meaning, if you're living all by yourself. Individuality only has meaning in a social context, to put it another way. So, . . .

MARTIN: See, I think you could take that even further. There is no living by oneself because if one truly lived by oneself, there would be no meaning, period, through which to understand, through which a person could say to him- or herself, "I am by myself."

AVAKIAN: Right, yeah, that is part of . . .

MARTIN: That isn't even understandable apart from a social matrix.

AVAKIAN: Right, that was what I was trying to say. So I think that when we talk about autonomy or individual flourishing, it has to be put in that kind of context, that there's always going to be a social context and a social foundation for individuality, for individual flourishing, for the relations among individuals, etcetera. So, I think that's one important point. The other point is that throughout history, whether Plato or the Bible or other scriptures, or Kant, or anyone else, anyone who has talked about justice or fighting against oppression—any of these kinds of terms—those things have always been infused with a definite social content and always have had a certain historical context. For example, I was reading something you wrote—which I thought was very well put—I believe it was in a chapter of a book that you're writing, I think it's *Ethical Marxism* and you posited a dream that someone would have of an exploitative society . . .

MARTIN: Uh-huh.

AVAKIAN: . . . and you said—I thought it was a very effective way to get at the point—what kind of dream is that? What kind of society? What would we think of someone who had a dream like that?

MARTIN: Well, or a dream, actually this was in my book on progressive rock music *Listening to the Future* and the idea was to imagine having a dream where just a handful of people among an immense population are sitting at the feast table, so to speak, or that one dreams of being among the very few at the feast table, and basically saying, "I dream of a world where society is divided by classes and I'm in the small minority who's in the well-fed class, and I have a dream that society will be divided by genders and I'll be the top dog in every way and everybody else will be down there, and . . . " On one level, that's a very sick dream, obviously, and on another level, it's not a "dream." What would it even mean to say, "I have a dream and my dream is I'm one of the few at the top and everyone else is beneath me"?

AVAKIAN: Well, I think that is a very good way to make a point, but it also occurred to me that if you take a lot of these figures—whether Plato, Moses and the prophets, or whatever— actually, the content of what they put forward as a model or guideline for society is very close in many ways to that "dream"—or even Kant, for that matter—the content of what they put forward, or what they supported, is very close to that perverse dream that you're talking about. [*Martin chuckles*]. In other words, women are subordinated, and, yes, you fight to free your people, but then you plunder and murder other people and carry off the women as prizes of war, or you at least support a class-stratified society. And my point is not these people were hypocrites. That's not really the point or the important criterion. I don't have any way of evaluating that. I don't really know, but I doubt if in Plato's case, or certainly in Kant's, they were hypocrites. I think it's more like they were products of history and of a certain class in history, or the society in which they were living and working, and they reflected that in their concepts of justice . . .

MARTIN: Uh-huh . . .

AVAKIAN: . . . and in their concepts of the ethical and the good, and so on. As I said, if you go to Moses and the prophets, for example, there was this instance where Moses excoriates his people when they come back from a war because they didn't kill every last male of the other tribe. [*Martin chuckles*]. They just carried off loot. So he tells them, go back and kill every male and then carry off the females as slaves and objects of sexual plunder. And that's not just one isolated thing—Joshua is the same, it's over and over and over again in the Bible. You go through the prophets, and there's talk of justice and there's talk of ridding their people of oppression by another people or empire or whatever, but then—even in their internal relations, but especially in their relations with others—there are all these things, the plunder and the exploitation, the subordination and oppression and plundering of women, and all that sort of thing, including slavery.

With Kant it's not that kind of thing, but there is the monarchy and there are the class relations of the society of which he was a part. That's not to say—I'm not saying that therefore we should throw out the concept of justice, or the ethical, or that anything they said about it is irrelevant or should be considered to be just mere talking with no substance or no importance.

For example, I read something where you referred to people saying, "Well, Heidegger supported the Nazis, so we don't have to pay any attention to his philosophy," and you commented, "That really makes me mad"; and I said to myself, I really agree with that. But I was reading this book *Heidegger's Children* by Richard Wolin, who has his obvious limitations, but he was actually trying to show how there was a link between Heidegger's philosophy and his Nazi sympathies. I think that is valid. In other words, to be able to explore the question, "Is there something in Heidegger's philosophy that lends itself to, or would make him inclined toward, supporting the Nazis?"—I think that is a legitimate and important question. It doesn't mean that you just take Heidegger's philosophy and throw it on the garbage dump because of his Nazi sympathies—and still less Kant, who supported the monarchy in essence (but not the Nazis, obviously). So, even more in the case of Kant, I'm not saying we should discard everything he says because, after all, he supported sort of a monarchial-bourgeois form of society with all its class relations of oppression and exploitation. What I am trying to say is that anyone's view of justice, the right, the good, and whatever, is historically and socially determined, or is conditioned by and reflects the society they're in and what class viewpoint or what social viewpoint they take.

MARTIN: Uh-huh.

AVAKIAN: And that's true for us as well. For example, when we were talking earlier about how we support the oppressed against the oppressors, even how we identify the oppressed and the oppressors is historically and socially conditioned. For example, in the Civil War, the South, the southern slaveowners, presented this as they were being oppressed, invaded, and occupied by the North; but the essence of the matter was that they were fighting to uphold the slave system, and even though the bourgeoisie was the leading force in fighting them, in terms of the Union government, you support—as Marx did—you support that Union government because, from our standpoint, the essence of the matter was that the oppressed there were the slaves, and the issue immediately on the agenda, the important question being fought out, was whether to abolish slavery or not, regardless of the degree to which various forces may have been fully conscious of that or fully desired that to be the issue. For example, Lincoln didn't necessarily fully desire that to be the issue, but he was in a certain sense overwhelmed by events and ended up having no choice but to recognize that *that* really was the issue that was being fought out.

So, all I'm saying is that all these concepts—I don't think it's not important to talk about the good, the ethical, or whatever, that Marxism shouldn't encompass that, it should—what I'm trying to say is that this still has, it can't be divorced from, a material foundation. In other words, it can't be divorced from the social relations and from the historical context.

MARTIN: Yeah, and I absolutely agree with all of that. But I suppose I want to make some emendations to it that might change the understanding of that a little bit. I actually function professionally in a milieu where this Heidegger thing gets kicked around quite a lot, and I have to admit in some ways you can say I'm a bit two-faced about it, in the sense that, among the Heideggerians, I'm probably one of those who more often says, "Well, what about the Nazi thing?" And among the non-Heideggerians I'm more, "But we need to learn from this guy on some points and not let us get stuck in thinking that that's the totality of it." But I haven't read Wolin's book, partly because I have such serious disagreements with him, I don't really want to go there. One thing that I think would be an interesting "test," and I propose this occasionally as sort of a joke, but I wish somebody would actually do it—someone should write a novel that would be one of these historical fictions, on what Heidegger might have been doing if the Nazis had won the war. There are all kinds of historical contingencies. Richard Rorty once wrote a famous article that tried to push the contingency to the point of a scenario where Heidegger could have conceivably run off to Chicago with Hannah Arendt and had a very different life, and that was possible too. Instead, he stayed with his wife Elfrieda who was deeply fascist in all of her sympathies. I think Heidegger, someone who's much more deeply into this than I am, once described it this way, that Elfrieda was truly committed to rabid anti-Semitism, whereas for Heidegger it was more on the level of, "How can the German people shine forth," and the Jews were just this incidental element in the way—which is of course extraordinarily horrible in and of itself.

I gave a paper a couple of years ago, that made some people angry, pointing out the fact that Heidegger's famous "Letter on Humanism," which was responding to Sartre's popular lecture "Existentialism is a Humanism," was written to a French philosopher, Jean Beaufret, who himself was a rabid anti-Semite who later got involved in Holocaust revisionism. So, part of what was interesting about Heidegger's letter—you had a letter being written from, and the reason it had to be written as a "letter" was because Heidegger was under a publishing ban at that time for his political activities, and after the war this publishing ban was imposed upon him for some period, I think five years or something. And he's writing this letter as one person involved in violent anti-Semitism to another, who at least is sympathetic with that, *about* the philosopher Jean-Paul Sartre, who had written this book that had come out about the time that he gave his lecture, *Anti-Semite and Jew*, that more or less blew the lid on French and European anti-Semitism at a time when a lot of people after the Holocaust were not wanting to talk about it. And especially in France, you had this whole mythology that after the war everyone had really been part of the resistance and no one had really been a collaborator and so Sartre was blowing the lid off that. There are many interesting aspects to this whole episode. *Be that as it may*, I don't think that's the end of grappling with the thought of Heidegger.

But I partly make this entrée into this point because, yes, on the one hand I agree with you that whoever has spoken of freedom, liberation . . . of course, the term "messiah" really means "liberator." It was applied to Moses as well as to King David in the Bible. As you say, and I agree with you, this language always has social content that essentially comes down to, I hate that word "essentially" here, but if we have visions of a future society, they will be shaped by our social structure today and our place in it and the role we're trying to play in it. That's certainly true for, back to Moses and before, and you especially point out and I agree with you, on the situation of women, the limitations were rather extreme, to say the least.

With Kant, I think, yes, those limitations apply, as they always apply, and yet I think he's also coming at a time when things are in transition to new forms of society. And so, then, just to go back to where you started, in terms of the sociality of all of this, as opposed to a kind of individualist framework, just as Aristotle had this whole formulation of the good life, the good person, the good society and the idea that there's no separation of these things. You can't be a good person in a horrible society; in fact, the only way you could be a good person is to work toward a better society. For Kant, the categorical imperative that he proposes and explains in the *Groundwork for the Metaphysics of Morals* has three formulations and he sees these as integral. The first one is the famous, act only according to that principle that at same time can be a universal law. That's the core of what I wanted to get at anyway, that in certain traditions

(I'm looking at the Jewish and Christian traditions), there is this ideal of ethical, political universalism, however inadequately applied, but it's significant that it arises as a concept at least. It's a contribution, I think, to what ultimately we're after. The second formulation seems to move from what should "I" do to the interpersonal level: treat others and treat oneself as ends, and never as a means only. And then the third one is, act so as to try to bring about a universal kingdom of ends. This has its limitations but it's significant and I think it's right in that same text of Marx's "The Contribution to the Critique of Hegel's Philosophy of Right," that you were mentioning, that Marx proposes what can be called a "fourth formulation," the categorical imperative to basically tear down the walls, to take apart all of those structures in which humanity is debased and he puts it in that categorical form. And I'm sure that there's an element at least of irony in that, but I think there's also an element of carrying forward this tradition of ethical, political universalism.

But then my larger point is that, look, here's the problem one gets into. In a way, you were more generous to Heidegger than I expected. Maybe we can come back to that, and my point isn't really about Heidegger per se, but that there's a tendency in Marx and in Marxism to think that once we get to Marx, you have either a culmination of philosophy or you have a kind of turning of philosophy or an "end" to philosophy where it then turns out that the only philosophy you need is what's coming from Marx and you don't need any of it before Marx, and you don't really need any of it after Marx, and especially not any that's not coming pretty directly out of Marx. And, okay, you might not be saying that, but that's definitely a trend.

I also like the way Althusser put it in that essay "Lenin and Philosophy," which otherwise I have some serious problems with, but he said that Marx has this famous eleventh thesis on Feuerbach, "The philosophers have only interpreted the world, the point, however, is to change it," and that from time to time Marx would express his desire to, I think the way Althusser put it was, to write up in a few sheets of paper the basics of dialectic per se, but what Althusser says is that instead Marx more or less initiated a long philosophical silence, and I think it's true that since that time there's been within Marxism a kind of basic skepticism toward philosophy and a wariness of it. It's not even that I think that that's wrong. It's not that I don't think that has its place in some sense. I think it is good to be wary of how people can just move words around and seem to construct castles in the sky and whatnot. I don't think there's anything wrong with being a bit wary of that. Maybe this is sort of a naive, bright-eyed way of looking at it, but I always loved Lenin's statement that "communism comes out of every pore" and that one can find it even in the most unlikely places and that one should try to marshal those resources to what we're trying to do.

I find that expressing itself in more explicit form and with the desire to do so in somebody like Jacques Derrida, a book like *Specters of Marx*, but even, in a certain sense, "out the back door" with somebody like Heidegger. I suppose there's the question of what we have to do with Heidegger the person and the question of what we have to do with his works, his writings. Those aren't unconnected questions but we don't want to cut off our noses to spite our faces here. If there's some good thinking that lends itself to showing why humanity should have a communist future, then I want that. I try to have sort of a "team concept" about them [*Avakian chuckles*] and I guess I want that on my team. I think different people on the team are doing different things but I want that in my team.

AVAKIAN: Well, we've talked a couple of times about how Lenin went back and read Hegel—not to adopt Hegel wholesale, but to see what he could learn in the context—and how important that was in relation to his carving a revolutionary path out of the events after February 1917. So in that sense I agree with what you're saying, especially in terms of this stage in history. There are lots of people with lots of different viewpoints wrestling with questions, and not only in the natural sciences, but more generally; we should not say that we can't learn anything from someone who has a viewpoint other than the communist viewpoint. I think that would be wrong and we would miss out on something. Lenin's reading Hegel is a sharp example of that.

That takes me back to Engels's statement in *Ludwig Feuerbach and the End of Classical German Philosophy*, where he sort of says: well, that's the end of philosophy. And I'd like to divide that in two. On the one hand, I think the essence of what he's getting at is that from now on, once we have the dialectical materialist viewpoint and method, it's a matter of seeking out the connections between things in the real world and not in the fantasies in people's brains. In that sense, I not only agree with it, I think it's important. On the other hand, if by "the end of philosophy" there's an aspect which could be interpreted as, there's no more need to think about philosophy, then I would not agree with that.

MARTIN: Uh-huh.

AVAKIAN: That's why I said I agree with you about Heidegger: it's wrong to just dismiss out of hand—a priori, so to speak—his philosophy, just because politically he was a sympathizer of and worked in the Nazi regime. That was the point I was trying to make. I don't agree with just discarding everything, even in the case of someone who's clearly a political reactionary like that.

But, I noticed—I guess this links up also with something you were writing—how you really don't like this Lenin statement about the omnipotence of Marxism.

MARTIN: Uh-huh.

AVAKIAN: Well, let me try to get at it in a little different way. Mao (I think it's in *On Practice*) says that dialectical materialism is universal because it is impossible for anybody to escape from its domain in practice. Now I happen to think that's a true statement and an important one, but anyone who'd say, [*chuckles*] "That's the end of the discussion" rather than in a certain sense the beginning of more discussion and more work misses the point, in my view.

MARTIN: Uh-huh.

AVAKIAN: I think Marx did make a breakthrough, and communism has made a breakthrough, in understanding the world—a breakthrough with dialectical materialism. But that doesn't mean we understand everything about dialectical materialism at any given time—or that we ever will—and, as a deeper reflection, it doesn't mean that we understand everything about reality and the universe, or ever will.

MARTIN: Uh-huh.

AVAKIAN: So, there's always more to be learned and things that we'll continually find out, as in every other sphere. It gets back to your point that communism is bigger than Marx or Lenin or Mao or any individual, or even bigger than the collectivity of communists at any given time.

MARTIN: Uh-huh.

AVAKIAN: I think that's an important point. And the fact that dialectical materialism is universal, in the sense I'm trying to speak to it here, doesn't mean that there's nothing else to learn from anybody who doesn't uphold dialectical materialism because that, to me, would be nonmaterialist and undialectical.

MARTIN: Uh-huh.

AVAKIAN: So there's the question—you have to ask concretely—"What is there to learn?" If you want to evaluate Heidegger, you have to read Heidegger, you have to put it in a certain context and wrestle with the question of what is he saying and what do you think is correct or incorrect in it—the same as with anything else. Or, for that matter, Kant. At some point we should probably turn directly to the categorical imperatives and talk about them. In the same essay on Ludwig Feuerbach and the end of classical German philosophy, Engels said, basically, that Hegel took care of that by pointing out that the categorical imperatives are nowhere applicable, therefore they really have no meaning.

MARTIN: Empty formalism.

AVAKIAN: Yeah. We should talk about that. What would they mean—and not just what have they meant in history and what did Kant actually uphold politically, but what would they mean if you tried to apply them in different circumstances? I think that is something we should come back to. But more generally on your point, one of the reasons Mao talked about one hundred flowers and one hundred schools of thought blooming and contending—even though they had some problems with that when counterrevolutionaries used it as an opportunity to do a lot of bad things—it was still a principle that Mao continued to uphold, and I think the reason is that, even if everybody said they upheld dialectical materialism, there would be lots of different ways that people would be coming at that . . .

MARTIN: Right.

AVAKIAN: . . . and lots of different angles and different things they meant. There's also Mao's statement that Marxism embraces but doesn't replace all these specific fields of practice and knowledge . . .

MARTIN: Right.

AVAKIAN: . . . and that's also a very important point. Just being a dialectical materialist doesn't tell you about Einstein's theory on gravity, or quantum mechanics, or whatever. You still have to go into those spheres and understand them, and there's still a lot that's always going to be there to be learned. I believe the more you're able to apply dialectical materialism, the more thoroughly you'll be able to understand things. Let's say I try to apply dialectical materialism, but I know a hell of a lot less about physics [*laughs*] than a lot of physicists who don't believe in and maybe are very strongly opposed to dialectical materialism.

MARTIN: Right.

AVAKIAN: It's important not to confuse those two things. That's the point of "embraces but does not replace," as I understand it. It also means to me that, in any field, including the field of philosophy, people who don't apply, and are very much opposed to, dialectical materialism may hit upon important aspects of reality—and they may hit upon it in a way of actually understanding something about it—that those of us who are communists don't understand at a given time. Or they may hit upon something and explain it all wrong but in so doing they raise questions for us that are important for us to grapple with. I think the old CP used to expel people for reading Trotsky at one point.

MARTIN: Uh-huh.

AVAKIAN: That's just ridiculous, worse than ridiculous. [*laughs*] How are you going to understand Trotsky if you don't read him?

MARTIN: Right.

AVAKIAN: And it's not that you should read only to refute— that's not my point either. You should read to understand. You should be looking for the truth. And, in my view, the more thoroughly you apply dialectical materialism, the better we'll collectively get at the truth, ultimately; but along the way there are a lot of things that come into it—including people who come at it from a different viewpoint. So you have to take each of these things concretely. Heidegger? Well, what's he getting at? What can we understand? What do we think of it? Or the same with Kant, or anyone.

MARTIN: Uh-huh.

AVAKIAN: So, on that general philosophical point, that's how I look at it.

16
Art and Vision

MARTIN: What if we were to shift the terrain from the history of, say, Western philosophy to art and culture? We know that there are many artists and cultural leaders who make contributions to changing society in a good way. They not only don't have a dialectical materialist outlook, but they haven't even particularly thought about those questions. Take one example, the discussion around Paul Simon's album *Graceland* which I liked, I think it's a fine album and musically very good stuff. I don't like to reduce a work of art to its quote/unquote outlook but I think its whole thrust I like. It's something I would want to affirm and yet we recognize that Paul Simon isn't . . . he's sort of a "good liberal"— I suppose is probably how you'd characterize him politically—with all the bad resonance I always put on, as they say, "the good liberal." But on the level of practice, it makes this positive contribution to what we're about. As a cultural work, as an art work, that's where materialism really matters, in its practice, and this probably goes against the grain of something we talked a little bit about earlier, of how can you create a good society without intending to, but I think in this case, of course, Paul Simon wants to make that positive contribution and in some sense as an artist he's able to make a more positive contribution than perhaps he even has the conception of. But the practice of it is ultimately where it really matters and I think that's true, as strange as it might be to say, of conceptual works such as philosophical works if they contribute in a certain sense a kind of energy to the project of transforming society; in some sense that's enough materialism for me. We could then say, "But yeah, what if these folks really grappled with, really wanting to be materialist, or whatever?" I supposed that's a little bit like, "What if these physicists grappled with really wanting to be materialist? What if mathematicians grappled with it?" That might be a good idea. It probably is a good idea, but it doesn't cancel the materialism of that energy that's already been contributed from those works and it's an energy that I would think we'd want to try to marshal to our cause, so to speak.

AVAKIAN: On one level, I would agree. You do have to sift through the content, though. I mean, two things. One, you have to sift through the content and see whether something really is positive or not in its content and in its effect. I'm thinking about what Mao said, in his "Talks at the Yenan Forum on Literature and Art," that the intent of the artist is important but more important is the objective effect.

MARTIN: Uh-huh.

AVAKIAN: And there he was talking about artists who were more or less following the lead of the Communist Party, but I think you should apply that more generally. You can see sometimes where the two, intent and effect, are not the same. For example, Bruce Springsteen wrote this song "Born in the USA." He had one intent, but it was taken over by other forces and it had a different effect. It became like a jingoistic anthem in the way it was mainly treated.

MARTIN: Right.

AVAKIAN: He tried to combat that after the fact, so to speak—after he began to realize this—but that was pretty clearly not his intent in writing that song. And Mao didn't say the intent was not important—it is important. That's why Springsteen tried to do what he could to correct the misuse that was being made of that song. So it can be complicated in that way. I like that Paul Simon album too. I'm not sure I understand fully the Graceland metaphor. I have a different view of Elvis than some other people of my generation—a more negative one. I was reading the book *Empire* (by Michael Hardt and Antonio Negri), and in one of the chapter headings they quote Jerry Rubin on how the youth movement, the counterculture and all, developed out of Elvis's gyrating pelvis, or something like that. [*Martin chuckles*] I don't agree with that at all. I think that's missing something much deeper that was actually, as they said at the time, coming from a black thing.

MARTIN: Uh-huh.

AVAKIAN: And Elvis represented something different. That's a whole other discussion, but without getting into that whole discussion now, I too like that album, the *Graceland* album. I think Paul Simon had, from his own perspective, a good intent with it, and it had a good effect overall in various ways, including introducing certain kinds of music to a broader audience. That, too, is complicated. For example, Ladysmith Black Mambazo, I think they're really religious and stuff, so it's complex.

MARTIN: Uh-huh.

AVAKIAN: Things are contradictory. It's not all simple. Or, "Because they're religious, therefore their music's no good"— that is not correct either.

All of this is much too complex to be treated simply as if the only people who can do something good are people who are trying to apply dialectical materialism. So, again, we have to evaluate concretely: what's the intent and, most of all, what's the effect—what's the content and what's the effect. On the other hand, I do think that with artists—with scientists, with others— without having a heavy hand, we should engage them and struggle over why we think dialectical materialism is the way to understand reality most fully and why it should be applied in the correct way, in the Maoist sense of "embraces but does not replace" and not in a crude sense or along the lines of some of the errors Stalin fell into. Dialectical materialism should be applied to every sphere. But there are going to be a lot of people we're not going to convince of that.

MARTIN: Uh-huh.

AVAKIAN: And you can't put everybody who doesn't agree with that in some kind of category that they can't make any positive contribution. That would be terrible.

MARTIN: Uh-huh.

AVAKIAN: They can make positive contributions. One thing I thought was an important point in that Skybreak article on working with ideas—it was actually made parenthetically, but it is an important point—is that even incorrect ideas can contribute to humanity's understanding of reality, but mainly after they've been shown to be incorrect, and until then they mainly have a negative effect. That's an important point, but even that's complicated.

MARTIN: Uh-huh.

AVAKIAN: So, whether people like Heidegger—or other philosophers of Western or Eastern (or other) traditions, whatever you want to say—whether they contribute even by just shaking things up, so to speak—yes, I think there may be an aspect to that. Even when what they're arguing for is wrong, even when what they're arguing for has a really bad content from the point of view of where we're trying to go with society, there still can be a role for that, but you have to distinguish— you have to identify what is the role. In other words, what is there that's positive in it? Is the content positive, even if not fully communist? Is it mainly positive? Or is the content negative but some questions they're raising and the way they're "forcing us to think" is positive? You have to distinguish those different things. To go back to the example of the CP not having people read Trotsky, I would definitely be against discouraging people, let alone—if you had state power, for example—preventing them from reading these things. I would, however, be for giving people some leadership, in the sense of trying to help them sit-uate this and understand it, without spoon-feeding them or shackling them in terms of their own initiative in grappling with things and coming to their own conclusions—and maybe seeing some things that weren't previously seen. You were giving the example earlier about Hegel and the notes from the lectures, and things he couldn't say because of the censors. We're always learning more, even about things we "know a lot about."

MARTIN: Uh-huh.

AVAKIAN: So, to me, that's all part of the picture.

17

Calculation, Classes, and Categorical Imperatives

MARTIN: What is the conclusion, what does it point to when we're not yet in a position, for example, where we can grow food a whole other way even if we thought that it would be much better to do so and maybe it would? But right now we're not in a position where we can make those decisions and yet people are; as I said, people have to. But it perhaps poses this in the most acute form, where I would argue that (I'll call it the point of underdetermination) the way that people are mapping themselves onto and understanding themselves in the context of the swirl of world events gets worked out mainly or purely in the form of: "Where do my true interests lie?" or "Where do my real interests lie?" or even, "Where do my basic interests lie?" That there's this moment of underdetermination, and that the only way, well, I'm trying to understand this myself, but what has to happen in that moment is something other than the calculation of one's interest. Of course, people don't just sit down and draw up the balance sheet and check off on either side and see where it comes out in the end. It's a living thing; it's a grappling thing; but where people are grappling not just with their minds but how they're going to live their lives this or that day, this or that week or year or whatever. And there's that moment of undecidability where what has to decide it is something like, "What would be the right thing to do? What's the right way to go here?"

And something like Vietnam, who knows where the current wave of what are called wars or actions by the United States on Third World countries will go eventually and whether it will go into an arena where there are more casualties, there is more "feedback" so to speak, the actions come back onto the home front in more direct ways. Obviously it's coming back now after

9/11 in the form of strengthening of the repressive apparatus, but, I mean, as they always say, "when the bodybags start coming home." Who knows where that will go.* I tend to think, not that the existing system has anything like perfect freedom in this case, but I tend to think they're going to be very careful about ever—they may be forced to go into this no matter what they want, but I think they're very aware of the Vietnam syndrome. I think when George Bush "the first" announced, I think this was on the day when Saddam Hussein surrendered in the Gulf War, Bush made a big point of saying something like, "And by God we have kicked the Vietnam syndrome." He said it very loudly. I don't think that's true at all. I think it's very clear that the whole war-fighting strategy is still very much shaped in an awareness of that. Who knows where it's going to go, but even in the case of something like Vietnam, where even though the numbers on the other side were all out of proportion to what casualties were suffered on the U.S. side, even there, there's that point where we have to support the people of Vietnam. And the thinking on that isn't and shouldn't be—and when I say "shouldn't" that already has ethical connotations of the *ought*, purely on the basis of a calculation of what interests are served.

As you pointed out, I think quite rightly, part of what's interesting in imperialism—interesting and extraordinarily ugly, as ugly as anything that's ever been in the history of humankind—is that in the lopsidedness of the world, basically what you do have is systems that have advanced means of production decimating systems that are in a semifeudal condition, that are primarily agriculturally based, etcetera. And so then our thinking on that, I just don't see where interests will motivate it fully to where it needs to go. And that's the moment where a question like "What is the right thing to do?" has to come in. I don't mean that, but I also don't think Kant ever meant it, as some sort of, as Hegel said of it, "empty formalism." I think Kant was fully aware that we ask ourselves this question in the context of whatever situation we happen to find ourselves. But that is the *matter* of the ethical, to say "What would be the right thing to do?" and to do it because it is the right thing to do.

---

* [These conversations took place before the U.S. invaded and occupied Iraq in March 2003.—Ed.]

AVAKIAN: You were earlier sort of saying, well, you have to go from the more immediate and narrow interests to the larger interests. And I suppose there would be a point where that loses meaning, but I do think that, at least up to a certain point, that is not only real but important. There are narrower and there are larger interests. A lot of what we're trying to do in making a revolution is motivating people to go against their most momentary and narrow interests. That's a lot of what Lenin was polemicizing against on the question of revolutionary defeatism, and even in some ways in "What Is to Be Done" around economism, and so on. And in terms of the point you raised about how we have to tell the workers the truth, that a revolution might result in lower wages, but it would still be worth it, I would say that it would still be in their larger interests to be rid of a society like this and to bring into being a better society. And I think that is actually in the objective interests of most people, even in a society like the U.S., let alone most people in the world where it's much more clearly and decisively in their interests.

As I was saying, Bush keeps harping on this thing: they're trying to get people to sacrifice for the greater good, to be willing to have their children or young adults in their families die in the service of imperialism. And making a revolution requires all kinds of sacrifices—not just the most extreme of giving your life but all kinds of other sacrifices that run counter to your interests or even your needs in the narrowest sense. You could never make a revolution or motivate people to make a revolution on the basis of anything other than the most sweeping kind of vision of a whole different way that society not only should be but could be—and understanding that you have to strive to bring it into being. So, is there a role for the good? Yes. There is a role for doing something because it is the right thing to do. There is a role for principles, to put it another way. That's another way of saying the ethical or the good. There's a role for principles—you do things out of principle, as opposed to the pragmatic motivation that you're going to get some immediate gain out of it, and whatever gives you the most immediate gain you do. You do things out of commitment to larger principles.

My point, though, is that those larger principles are ultimately grounded in what your view of society is—your class viewpoint, in class society—without viewing that in narrow economist terms. I've even used, as a sort of ironic phrase, "the godlike position of the proletariat" to describe not the spontaneous view of individual proletarians but what, from the vantage point of the proletariat and what's required for its emancipation in the fullest sense, you can see in terms of the sweep of history and in terms of where society is going and needs to go. Not inevitably going, but where, in what direction, there are very strong tendencies—and those tendencies have not inevitably developed, but they have developed. There's a certain tendency that points in a certain direction. There is also—as you've pointed out, and I've pointed this out as well—there's also the possibility humanity could become extinct through the same contradictions that make possible a whole different and better world of communism. So there's nothing inevitable, but there are certain tendencies, there are certain things to build on in terms of going for communism. And what we think is right and good and principled depends on how we view that, how we view what kind of society it is that is both possible but also desirable, if you want to put it that way.

And then, as I was trying to say earlier, this does take on a certain life of its own. In other words, it does have a certain autonomy: you have certain principles, and you act out of those principles, rather than out of immediate calculation. When I wrote that book *Preaching from a Pulpit of Bones*, I was trying to give some examples of these principles. Like you have women from the ruling class: yes, we oppose them, but we don't call them "bourgeois bitches." We don't say it's all right to sexually assault them since they're women of the ruling class, because those things would reinforce the oppression of all women, and the oppression of people in society in general. So those things are against our principles and we don't narrowly say, "Well, maybe in this case it's all right to do it because it's a minor instance." We say no, those things are against our principles.

There is a relationship—that's another way to say it—there is a relationship between means and ends (here I'm not speaking about the Kantian imperative regarding people being ends in themselves and not means). This accusation that communists believe that the ends justify the means—I believe it's the other way around: you have certain ends, or objectives, and your means have to flow from that and be consistent with it. Which, as I was trying to say earlier, doesn't mean you never make compromises, but you can't compromise the fundamental or essential principles. Sometimes you have to take a step back, but you don't take a step into the swamp.

In my book *Harvest of Dragons* there's a statement near the end about how we have to get down and fight the enemy in the trenches, literally as well as figuratively—literally when it comes to that, and figuratively all the way along—and we have to defeat them without becoming like them. And that's another way of saying we can't just adopt any old means, and certainly not *their* means. We have to adopt means that flow from and are consistent with and build toward our ends, our objectives—what kind of society we're trying to bring into being. We can't bring it all into being now, and we can't "live it all now"—we can't live without commodities, for example, as much as we want to eliminate them eventually. Even in socialism you can't live without them. But we don't want to worship them. We don't want to make a conscious fetish of them, to go along with their objective "fetishization." There are things you have to live with because you can't yet eliminate them; but that doesn't mean that principles don't matter. And it doesn't mean that you don't try to live as much of the future as you can at a given time, both in your personal dealings and in the larger way that you deal with society and what you're trying to do to affect society.

So I do think there is a role for principle, there is a role for morals, for the ethical, but it's "situated" in that sense, it has a certain content, and different people with different views of society, and how it ought to be and could be, have different views of the same phenomena and of what they regard as the good, the moral, etcetera. For example, let's take exploitation. You wrote something saying, "Well, we could take it as sort of fundamental that one person exploiting another is the definition of evil."

MARTIN: Right.

AVAKIAN: Well, yes—except that we and the bourgeoisie don't agree on what constitutes exploitation.

MARTIN: Exactly.

AVAKIAN: You read Ayn Rand and she says, "Well the communists they take business enterprise and creative initiative and call it exploitation."

MARTIN: Right, we call it "giving people jobs."

AVAKIAN: Right. "And yes, we're paying people low wages in Indonesia but if we didn't go there and do that, they'd be even worse off."

MARTIN: Right.

AVAKIAN: And they're only willing to partially call exploitation what we might call super-exploitation, where a kid somewhere in Haiti or Pakistan or wherever is working twelve hours a day, sleeping under the machine, seven days a week, and having their health ruined and their life stolen from them. They might say, "Well, yeah, that's exploitation"—unless they're doing it themselves. Some bourgeois theorists and apologists might say, "Yes, that's exploitation"; but we would say, as you were pointing out, the whole thing of being in a situation where other people's livelihood depends on, is conditioned by, the fact that you've monopolized the means to a livelihood and the only way they can have a livelihood is by creating more wealth for you—that's exploitation. That we got from Marx, but it's exploitation. This goes back to your statement I was referring to earlier about the Romans, when you said, once something better becomes possible then, damn it, we should support the better thing. Well, something better has become possible, and we don't have to wait for capitalism to play itself out to the nth degree. Because, for one thing, it never will.

MARTIN: Right.

AVAKIAN: So the basis has already been brought into being for something better. We view everything from that standpoint, that something better is possible. So it doesn't matter if you call it exploitation or rabba-dabba-dooba, there's a certain thing going on with people, the way in which people are being treated in this society, in production and the overall social relations, the culture and everything—something better than that is possible. And so we want that something better. And it's not just that we want it subjectively, we recognize that it's in the interests of the great majority of people. And so, from that vantage point, these other things are intolerable. And, again, it does get tricky. As we were talking about before, what about earlier times when the peasants rose up in Germany but they really couldn't bring into being a different mode of production or even a different society, or at least it was unlikely that they could. And maybe the bourgeoisie had a much better basis—not better but more favorable basis—for being able to bring its mode of production and its society into being. So why support the peasants, not only against the feudal oppressors but against the bourgeoisie, when the bourgeoisie went to suppress the peasants?

Because, again, what I was trying to say about that earlier is that the revolution that we're about is a revolution made by people and not by technology. Even though technology that is created by people plays some role in creating some of the material conditions—and even in providing, or requiring, some of the social relations—that establish some of the foundation for where we're trying to go, it's not made by those things. It's made by people, and just the wiping out of whole peoples doesn't contribute to the kind of world that we want to have, even back five hundred years ago. That's the way I look at it anyway. To me, that's some of the complexity of this question of the good and the right, principle, the moral, the ethical.

MARTIN: So, there's a lot there to talk about. I want to respond to a lot of it. But just as a provocation, I want to say that to me everything you just said was very Kantian in its general character. And even to just make a formula out of it: once something else becomes possible, for example, once it becomes possible to have a society where everybody can eat, starvation is intolerable. It would be one thing if there truly was some condition where only some would be able to eat. But once there is not that condition, to have some sitting at the table and others lying in the gutter starving is intolerable. That to me would be a very Kantian sort of thing to say.

AVAKIAN: Well, I guess we probably can't really get . . .

MARTIN: And it wouldn't be something that Marx would say. If you think about it, not to beat up on Marx, but when class society emerges from so-called primitive communal societies, that is in some sense for Marx an *advance*, even though it's also a fall. It's both the fall of humankind and an advance. It's partly an advance because it leads to the day when there will be a "humankind" in a global sense, which can only be seen retrospectively. But it is, for Marx, in some sense an advance to go from primitive tribal society to class society. And somehow out of this the good thing is going to come, ultimately. That's part of the teleology. But maybe just as a provocation, what would you say to my saying that a great deal of what you just said has a very Kantian sort of character to it?

AVAKIAN: I am going to resist saying, "I Kant understand that." [*laughter*] I'm not going to resist, but I'm not going to go any farther with it. Before, we were talking informally, while we weren't taping, about Marx—and saying that you have to recognize some positive things in Marx in terms of his statement about how capital comes into the world dripping with blood from every pore, and how the pedestal for child slavery in England was literal slavery in America, and many other statements of that kind. Or that famous statement about how the entombment in mines of the indigenous population in Latin America, and the hunting of black skins for slavery constituted the rosy dawn of capitalism. There were a lot of things like that from Marx, in terms of talking about primitive accumulation, in terms of colonial depredations and things that he did come to see more clearly, which he sharply condemned. So I think it is two-sided, just to be dialectical about Marx, too. But getting more directly to the thing about Kant, I guess we can't really evaluate that without talking more directly about what is the heart of, or at least one of the main things in, the Kantian ethic: treating other people never as a means but only as an end unto themselves.

MARTIN: I think the way he put it was never *only* as a means; as an end and never as a means only. So, if you're purely instrumentalizing people . . .

AVAKIAN: Okay. I want to comment on that, but first let's go back to your other point about Marx and class society being an advance. One of the things about some of these early tribal or communal societies is that they often had, generally speaking, a lack of exploitative and oppressive relations, as we recognize them in a more fully developed form in other kinds of society, like feudalism or capitalism or slavery. But they also contained some seeds—for example, the sexual division of labor, while it might not have been oppressive right there, had the potential to become that with changing conditions. But, even beyond that, I don't think we could say in every case—and I'm not in a position to know about this in great detail, but there are a number of situations that I do know about that have been studied where a people would have been nonoppressive, nonexploitative within their own ranks, but then in dealing with another people they could be very antagonistic and violent. There are different people, including Jared Diamond in his *Guns, Germs, and Steel*, who have discussed and analyzed that phenomenon.

MARTIN: It partly comes down to who is recognized as people.

AVAKIAN: Right. For example, when you look at the names that different indigenous peoples have given to themselves, even in different parts of the world, often the name means "the people." They kind of see themselves as "the people," and anything else they encounter is often not part of "the people." And they often have hostile relations and even warfare with these other peoples, which doesn't in any way excuse what European colonialism did on a whole other level and scale of genocide. That's a different matter. But I'm just making the point that they often were not able to relate to other peoples without antagonism. And I think that goes back to my point much earlier, by analogy with your statement that you can't do good if you're not trying to do good. I said I think you can do some good, but you can't do good in an overall sense if you're not trying to. And the analogy I was drawing is that you can't really develop a society and a world that doesn't have exploitation and oppression and antagonistic relations and violent eruptions among people unless you have, yes, the material conditions but also the corresponding ideological orientation that enables you to integrate the relations among people on a world scale in a way that doesn't say, "Here's the people, and everybody else is the non-people."

And I do think there's a question of science here, not understood in a mechanistic sense, or in the instrumentalist sense, but I think in the sense of really understanding reality or engaging and increasingly developing your understanding of reality in a comprehensive and systematic way. That's necessary to be able to handle all the contradictions that arise among people in a way that's not antagonistic. So I think it's wrong, in other words, to completely romanticize these early societies, even while we recognize that, as compared to the class societies that we contrast with them, they were relatively—and I stress relatively— free internally of exploitation and oppression.

I also think that here your point about reading back through history, or seeing it in retrospect, is also important. In other words, if you sit here at any given time and say, well, whatever's been done, it's all good—it's all going to lead to communism in the end, anyway—I think that would be (a) teleological and (b) wrong and (c) harmful. It would lead you to not oppose a lot of things you should oppose and to sort of mash all of reality down in a very crudely reductionist way.

MARTIN: The other term I apply to it is theodicy. In other words, nothing that looked evil really was evil, because in the end it all comes out good; it all works out.

AVAKIAN: Right, we'll all get redeemed or whatever.

MARTIN: Exactly.

AVAKIAN: In the end, yeah. Well, for all the reasons that you're pointing to and that I would also agree with, I think that's wrong and harmful. But to turn more directly to the Kant thing, I think that principle of means and ends as applied to people is not applicable in a class-divided society. First of all, we can see that it's not applicable on the part of the bourgeoisie or the other ruling and exploiting classes. They don't and can't apply that principle. By definition, what they're doing is treating other people as means.

MARTIN: As things.

AVAKIAN: Yes, they need to in order to exploit them in the way they do. That's built into the exploitative and oppressive relations. But even from the point of view of the proletariat, while there are still classes and still a need . . . even in socialist society there is still a need for the state, a need for the dictatorship of the proletariat—you have to prevent "the full flourishing" of some parts of society, individuals who make up the bourgeois class and counterrevolutionary forces, or else the rest of society is going to be prevented from flourishing and being emancipated, and you're not going to be able to transform society to where eventually it's not necessary for one part of society to be held down and restricted by another part. There are, we know, a lot of contradictions involved in that, and that can turn into its opposite. But still, for the proletariat, you can't avoid suppressing some of the "flourishing" of the bourgeoisie, if you're going to get to communism.

Okay then, when you get to communism, here to me is where it gets trickier. And I think it goes back to the statement from Marx we were talking about earlier—about how human beings are social animals and they can only individualize themselves in a social context. In other words, to me the flourishing of individuals, and their interrelations on a nonexploitative basis—that's also socially conditioned. It depends on what's going on with the relations among people in the society as a whole. And the realm of freedom for individuals is going to be dependent on what the society as a whole is doing and how people are interrelating. And how they're still interrelating with nature, for that matter. Because, as we talked about, people are still going to need to eat and have other necessities, and you're still going to need to put away stuff "for a rainy day," as well as to expand the sphere of people's freedom by being able to develop production so that less effort, less time in the day on everybody's part, has to go into just reproducing the things necessary for life. All that is still going to be operating, even in the various stages of communist society, a communist world. And the relation of individuals, as I see it, is not unimportant at all, but it's situated in that kind of a context. So, then, I'll end up my comments right now with a question back to you: how then does the Kantian maxim or principle fit into that?

MARTIN: Great. I like the way the word "flourishing" has entered into the conversation. I think the root of the use of this word in political philosophy really goes back to Plato but especially Aristotle in this Greek word *eudaimonia*. There are different translations of it. Sometimes it's translated as "happiness," actually. Kant would object to this translation, because he was very skeptical about mixing questions of pleasure and pain with matters of right and wrong. This is often seen as a kind of Puritan side to Kant or a very strict side. Sometimes Kant is seen that way, as having this very strict demeanor, whereas apparently he was a very jovial man, at least on some levels.

Kant did have a very strange side—I don't know if you know this, but Kant apparently never had a sexual encounter with another person and would even wrap himself tightly in sheets at night for fear of becoming aroused in the night. A friend of mine wrote a book where he partly used that aspect of Kant to interpret some other parts of his philosophy. It's a bit worrisome to me. [*laughs*]. And I should say, too, that Kant himself was somewhat aware, not as aware as we would need to be, of the contradiction involved in that whole means/ends question, especially around the question of revolution. Because in a revolution one class violently overthrows another, and with that violence those who are overthrown are instrumentalized in the sense that some of them are even killed. It's hard to put that into the mix of their supposed flourishing, if they're killed. So Kant found himself with this contradiction that, before the fact he couldn't justify the French revolution. But after the fact he thought it was a great thing and was very positive toward it. But that's a contradiction, and I don't think he necessarily has the full resources for resolving it.

But to go back to the flourishing point. Here's where I think it really makes a difference. I guess what I'd want to say is it comes down to the question of ideas that matter. And that one could talk about ideas that matter without being philosophically idealist. And what I mean by that is that, well, something Adorno said is helpful here. There was this interesting conversation that was recorded in some form, but we have it anyway, between Theodor Adorno and Ernst Bloch—these two Frankfurt School/Marxist theoreticians. And it's interesting that the conversation was given the title "Something's Missing." Adorno is talking about utopianism, and he's basically saying, we're really down the road in society toward complete philistinism when to call something utopian can just automatically be taken to be a criticism or . . . not just a "criticism," as Marx said, a "critical criticism" or a bit of critical thinking. Not a criticism in the sense of, "Oh, your idea is utopian," in that it's not really rooted in where we could really work toward. Or it's not really looking at the real divisions in society and what we need to do. But more the sneering attitude toward anyone who has any dream of something different and better than what we have now.

And that's where I think that you can see the importance of something like ideals, whether they be of flourishing, of not instrumentalizing, of working toward a world where people are not reified into mere things, where they are not under a commodity logic that then circulates them just like every other thing that is circulating. That it *matters* that we have those ideals. It matters that we think that that's what we need to do. And in that materialist sense, we *need* that idea. That's the materialism of it. We need that idea; it matters that we can talk in this language, that we want to create a world where . . . Because one way I like to spell out the word "communism" is that it's where we can attempt to create a global community of mutual flourishing. And I think mutuality is in the ideal of flourishing, as I've understood it historically, but it helps to reinforce that that's what flourishing is, it is a mutual thing. It is a "we" thing. It is a collective thing. It matters that we can use that language and that if instead all we had to fall back on was the calculative language, we materially couldn't get there.

AVAKIAN: What do you mean by "calculative language"?

MARTIN: Well, interest, I suppose. If that was all we had.

18
Postinevitablist Marxism

MARTIN: To speak of Marx more positively, if we no longer say that what he shows us is that communism is inevitable, as has been thought, or that "iron laws" will take us there, in some sense whether we want to go or not . . . And, of course, you could still even say that there's some sense in which either that's true or humanity will destroy itself. And I continue to believe that, myself, just on the simple level of either, we'll sort this stuff out or, it'll sort us out in the worst kind of way. And it does that every day and I do believe that the underlying forces are at least very capable of sorting humanity out in the worst kind of way. So I have a fairly dire view of that. What that all means for the concrete workings of what we'd call crisis or crisis theory or whatever, that's a question that has mostly empirical dimensions. But if we give up inevitability in the stronger sense that Marx was using it, then what we can talk about is his work as showing us possibility. And it goes to that point about, when something else that's better becomes possible, we're for that thing. And what Marx shows us is that the conditions have arisen where we can . . . and even in 1850 the conditions had arisen.

I like science fiction analogies. I always like to think of how they can help us, and I always find it interesting that in *Star Trek*, especially the second series, the Next Generation series, there's this strong idea that in this twenty-fourth century—I think it's a twenty-fourth-century society—basic social divisions have been healed. There's no poverty. There's no disease. There's gender equality. There's no racial subordination or any of that. There aren't really classes so to speak. Of course, most of this is coming from a spaceship that's organized according to military rank [*laughter*] and obviously it is that sort of utopian vision, but it's marked by the present in which the vision is formed. And then you always think, okay that's great, if truly that were a society that had overcome these divisions, great. And thank you for some images that are positive and helpful or at least the very idea that they're valorizing the idea that that would be a good thing to have, apart from how they're representing it necessarily.

But then you think that's great, but how did things get from where we are now, where these divisions are as deep as they can be and in some places getting deeper all the time, to then? And generally the implication is that technology did it. Technology enabled it. Marx thought, I think quite rightly, to the extent that technology enabled it, it was already enabling it in 1850, at least in some parts of the world. And certainly everywhere now. And that's maybe Lenin's point, to give a more positive spin to it. I think we've mostly been critical about the whole "We'll have the revolution then we'll get the technology, then we'll get the productive forces" line. But for instance, that's the positive thing; these things exist—that's no longer *the* problem.

The problem is the social relations, and we've got everything to do the technological aspect within that. So it's not that. So it's instead something that's underdetermined by that. I think it's more determined in Marx because I think that in Marx technology does play a stronger role in terms of what are the more efficient means of production, more productive forms of production that allow us to create the basis for shared abundance. And once we have that basis, in fact, it will be such a strong basis that nobody will need to fight over anything anymore and we can all eat, we can all have a place to live, we can all have our basic needs met and beyond. And in some sense, you could call that the calculative basis for the possibility of communism.

There's also what you might call the ethical basis. Namely that if society collectively is producing that which would enable society, and through highly socialized forms of production, that which would enable us to have a community of shared flourishing, then that's what we *ought* to have. The ethical imperative is that that's what we ought to have. In this postinevitablist Marxism, that "ought" assumes, and I think it always should have assumed, a heightened role. But especially in our postinevitablist Marxism I think it absolutely has to assume a heightened role.

AVAKIAN: I think there is a unity between interests and ideals, to put it that way. The two can and should go hand in hand. Taking interests in the broadest sense, in the case of proletarian principles and outlook, they should and do correspond to interests, and vice versa. In other words, looking at it in the broadest sense, I think there is a role for ideals. Just because we reject idealism in the philosophical sense—and don't think that ideas are what creates matter or that ideas predate matter, or whatever—doesn't mean that there is no role for ideals, in another sense: people having principles and a vision and a sense of what's possible and what should be striven for, and motivation corresponding to and flowing from that. And self-sacrifice and lots of other things that go into realizing such a vision. So that's the way I look at that: I see that they are mutually reinforcing.

On the question about post-inevitability, the problem for us, on one level, is that there's the lopsidedness in the world exactly in a certain sense, or in large measure, because the world didn't turn out the way Marx and Engels anticipated. And the lopsidedness has been even accentuated and taken some particularly grotesque forms—or accentuated grotesque forms—so that we have this funny situation where, in the world as a whole, taken as it is right now, there are plenty of productive forces to meet all the needs of the people and to provide a material foundation for advancing rapidly to communism, insofar as the element of material foundation is concerned. And if we could simply wake up one morning and communize—or socialize, as a beginning step—all the major means of production in the world, then we'd undoubtedly be a lot further ahead, and we could go rather rapidly. There would still need to be transformations in the social relations and ideology—the "four alls" of Marx—not just the production relations, but the social relations and the ideas, the superstructure as a whole, the political institutions, the structures of the society. [The "four alls" refers to Marx's statement, in *The Class Struggles in France, 1848 to 1850*, that the communist revolution consists in the abolition of all class distinctions (or "of class distinctions generally"), the abolition of all the production relations on which those class distinctions rest, the abolition of all the social relations that correspond to those production relations, and the revolutionizing of all ideas that result from these social relations.] But we'd be way far ahead.

The problem is, given the nature of imperialism and the lopsidedness and uneven development, we don't get to do it that way. So one big complication is that, first of all, revolution tends to happen country by country, or in a few countries at a time, and then you emerge into a world where most of the productive forces, as well as political power and military power, are still under the control of the bourgeoisie and allied reactionary forces. But there's also the fact that, as opposed to how Marx saw it, revolution is coming from the other direction: without making an absolute out of this, the main revolutionary impulse and thrust in the world is coming from the countries where the productive forces are the least developed (or the technology, anyway, is least developed). And that's another expression of the lopsidedness.

And then, even in countries like the U.S., if you conceive of what would actually have to go into making a revolution, to begin making possible all these things we're talking about, there would be tremendous destruction of productive forces—including, unfortunately, the people. I could very easily see—not that I like it, but I can very easily see—the imperialists using nuclear weapons and other things which are then going to mean that there is going to be a big problem, in a certain sense, of production and even, in one sense, of efficiency, without making a fetish out of efficiency. Efficiency based on socialist principles will still remain a question, and a somewhat acute question, for quite a while, for all the new socialist states that come into being—even in the imperialist countries—especially if you add the point you were making earlier (with which I agree and we also spoke to in our *Draft Programme*) that there is not just the internationalist dimension in general, but there is a question, first of all, of breaking all these exploitative international relations. Not just trade but outright export of capital and international exploitation in all these grotesque forms. And there's the importance, even with all the destruction, of recognizing, as soon as you get back on your feet, a special obligation to use what will still be advanced scientific knowledge and technology to aid the world revolution, and not just narrowly turn inward. Even in the midst of tremendous destruction and sabotage by the old ruling class, you can't turn inward and only pay attention—nor, in a fundamental sense, even pay primary attention—to just building socialism in that one country.

So, all that makes it extremely complicated. But it doesn't in any way obviate or eliminate the questions of principle that we're talking about. That's not my point. I'm just trying to say it's going to be very complicated to know how to apply these principles and to be able to apply them. We're still going to have class differentiation within these socialist societies. And some classes are going to have more interest than others in seeing this revolution through. And there is the point that you have referred to, which I raised in "Conquer the World?" where workers have nothing to lose but their chains and then they make a revolution and they have a state, and they have some material gains that they make, and that has a conservatizing influence. There are other contradictions that come to the fore as well: the contradictions involved in the emancipation of women, for example, will assume even sharper expression in some ways. Not in a negative sense, but more in the sense of the potential for that to be realized, but that potential coming up against whatever the limitations are at any given time, and how to continue breaking through on that. There are a lot of these kinds of complicated contradictions. Yes, some of them are questions of material production, and a lot of them are political-ideological questions. So how to apply our principles to all that? I agree, there are ideals; there is a role for ideals and for the ethical and moral in that whole context.

How do you move through all that? And how do you change the "we" while you're moving through it? In other words, there is the "we" who are the communists sitting here discussing this. And there is "we" the communists who lead the revolution. And there is the "we"—let's be honest—the communists who, in the early stages of socialism, have a greatly disproportionate influence on everything that happens in the society. And that right there, that is fraught with contradiction that can take the society backwards. How do you change the "we" so that the "we" is ever more collectively the masses of people, and the contradictions among the people—the social distinctions among the people—are being overcome as you continue to go forward? And it's true that, in trying to do all that, if you're not guided by something beyond immediate interests, you'll never get there.

So in that sense, and I think it's a very fundamental sense, the role of vision, the role of what's possible—and therefore, and together with that, what's desirable and what's required in terms of principles to be upheld and applied to get from here to there—to me all that has a tremendously important role. But I think it has to be situated within all these objective contradictions that we're dealing with. Not to say, "Well, we can't have principles, we have too much necessity," but how do you apply the principles to transform necessity? Mao made this criticism of a Soviet economic textbook where it just contained the statement that "freedom is the recognition of necessity"; he emphasized that it's the recognition *and transformation* of necessity—we have some work to do. Which I believe is in the same spirit of what you're wrestling with and emphasizing.

19
Principles and the Real World: Vision and Viability

MARTIN: I like this phrase that Raymond Lotta gives us in his afterword to the Shanghai Textbook: "a visionary and viable socialism." Those two elements have to interrelate. If it's just "visionary," well then you can say that you're *just* a philosopher in kind of the worst sense. You're dreaming up stuff in your armchair and not even saying that's bad necessarily, but if that's all it is, so what? And that would be empty formalism, because, of course, even in your armchair you're going to be thinking out things. And especially if you're in the position to have an armchair in the first place and be sitting around dreaming up stuff, you're going to be dreaming up stuff that is just going to reflect your social background and position.

Let me find these two other ways of coming into it. I think we're really coming to something here that's not the end of this theme among us by any means, but I think we're reaching something here that . . . there are sort of two tracks for coming into it. You mentioned that things could reach a point—clearly they could—unfortunately we're living in a time when there's a certain preparation before it, where the capitalists could use nukes on whomever. And from an ethical standpoint the point is, they could use nukes, they could use whatever, they will use whatever. There's no limit and there is certainly no ethical limit on what they would ever do. All there is, in a certain sense, is a calculated and strategic limit on what they might do, depending on how they think they can play their advantage. Maybe they'll dress it up. Of course, they'll dress it up in something that is supposed to look like a justification. We talked about that in terms of legitimating norms and whatnot.

But as for many of us of your generation and my sub-generation, or half a generation apart from you, let's say you came out of the sixties and I came out of the aftermath of the sixties but at least very aware of the sixties and things like '68 and some awareness of the Cultural Revolution and, of course, Vietnam shaped how I started to think about a lot of things. And for me, one crucial moment was the fact that this system would formulate such substances as napalm and Agent Orange and drop them on people. And napalm in particular, the heinousness of it, is just beyond description in the sense that it's meant to kill a lot of people and to torture them in the process, and it's also meant to torture people and leave them alive as grotesque reminders to what happens if you oppose this system. And thank whatever goodness there is in the world that this mostly doesn't work. It mostly doesn't cause people to say, "Oh they're using something horrible against us, let's give up." At least in that case it just made the struggle more determined and in some sense that's the best that can be hoped for and that is the real world of what our principles have to deal with, ultimately. And the real world is one where we have to think about our principles in an ethical way and in a strategic way and a visionary way and a viable way. *They* don't. They only have to think about "principles" in terms of what's in it for them and their class—the bourgeois classes in the world—they only have to think about what they are doing in a way that's viable for them. And to hell with anything ethical. And even beyond, then to bat ethical language around, to play with it, which is even sicker. So that is also the context in which this takes place.

To say it takes place in that context is also to say it takes place in the context where Marx tended to not speak that way, in part for the good reason that a lot of what made this sort of language circulate was just bourgeois moralizing either of a sort of milder sort or bourgeois moralizing of a very insidious sort, the type that we see today with people such as William Bennett, who has a Ph.D. in philosophy and even at one point said something about the justification for executing, I think drug dealers, he said something like, "I know I'm right because I was a philosophy professor." [*laughter*] Which, to put a little bit more positive spin on philosophy professors, I can assure you that everyone I know got a huge laugh out of that. No matter what their politics, the idea that "believe me because I'm a philosophy professor or I have a Ph.D."—I mean come on. So that's sort of the positive side of where Marx did not want to really get into this kind of language. I recognize that, I think he's right on that.

But, of course, there's always that question of in a certain sense the ownership of terms, and who gets to define the terms and who gets to mess with the terms. After all, we live in a world where capitalism can be called "socialism," so, what a mess, what a mess. And yet, in some sense if we don't go forward with principles, we're not going to go forward. And that's what I'm saying in a certain sense is the materiality. That's just one way to answer the question of materialism, that if you can't go forward without it then that tells you that it's a real thing, it's a material thing.

As to the question whether this is saying, "Okay, Marx, we need to add Kant to you. We need to make sure you get back in conversation with Kant, whether you need to recognize that there's something that was initiated there, and in Aristotle for that matter too—where Marx actually is, at least early on, fairly clear about the fact that he's taking up something from Aristotle. Is that the most pressing question? Well methodologically it's an important question. It goes to issues of monism and the integration of our ideas systematically, even if it might not be practically the most pressing issue, that we can't go forward till we get this fixed.

To bring the ethical in, to say that now this assumes a heightened role, as I'm urging, is that something that we can argue out of the kinds of principles that we knew we held already? Which then has the sub-question, what are the ontological commitments of our language, as they say in analytic philosophy, what are we committed to once we recognize the fact that we also have to have this as part of our thinking? I don't want to say that's for the philosophers to sort out by any means–that's for the masses to sort out. It's for the masses to sort out what we need to know to go forward into the future. To use one of Derrida's famous terms, is it a kind of "dangerous supplement," the thing you add in that looks as though it's supplementing but it actually transforms the structure? I guess I think on some level that is what it is. And yet I'm happy to just think of it as historical materialism. We won't go forward without it and so it's part of our historical materialism. It's part of our communism. To sort of make a formula out of it, in our postinevitablist world, certain things remain inevitable. Capitalism inevitably will continue to do horrible things. I don't think we have any worries about that. But in our "post-" thinking that there's just some trajectory that's going to unfold in a kind of— not that Marx thought it was highly predictable—but in some way that has much more of a pattern to it than we're really able to see at the moment. I think that's where you might say that in addition to being economically and politically communists, we have to be ethically communists as well. These other sorts of more abstract philosophical questions, I don't know how to resolve them myself. In some sense they'll get resolved historically.

AVAKIAN: I agree that we should be ethically communists as well. I've tried to speak to that as best as I understand it. One thing that was occurring to me—I believe it was in a letter from Engels to Bloch about 1890, where he's talking about the materialist understanding of history and he was saying, Marx and I had to spend so much of our life's efforts in establishing the materialist understanding of history and then analyzing how it actually applied in particular to capitalism, that we were not able to pay as much attention as we would have liked to the superstructure (he may not have put it exactly that way—"the superstructure"—but that was the essence of it).

He talks about the question of wills, people's wills. Not "will" in the Nazi sense, but people's motivation and how that relates back to the material base. He said we weren't able to pay as much attention to this as to the material side, because there was so much work to be done. So that may have been a factor, along with what you were saying about moralizing in the bourgeois sense, as opposed to the materialist concept and understanding of history. They were fighting for the latter. And, as Lenin said about "What Is to Be Done," sometimes you "bend the stick" when you're in the course of a polemic or when you're recognizing, as Engels was saying, the need to focus on a particular area of work because it really has to be fought for and has to be worked through to be established on a certain level.

But, in terms of the ethical dimension, I was thinking of how, in China, they popularized throughout the society Serve the People as the motivating principle. Once again, different classes interpret that differently. I remember reading somewhere about these party cadre in China a few years after the coup when, under Deng Xiaoping, they were starting to promote To Get Rich Is Glorious—one of his many perverse slogans—in place of Serve the People. There was a report of this conversation among party cadre, where one of them says: "Well, we used to say 'Serve The People' all the time, but aren't *I* a people?" [*laughter*] So that was the new ethos: let's take up this To Get Rich Is Glorious; let's take up the bourgeois outlook with abandon, so in the name of the people we can just gorge ourselves on the people.

MARTIN: By the same token, this is an issue with any of these things that are stated as formulas. I think in some ways that's the Kantian retort to Hegel's empty formalism charge, is that as slogan, as formula, even as thesis, even as social form, any of it can be not only an empty formalism, but . . . Serve the People— you could see that as a banner at a training institute for McDonalds as well. [*laughter*] Serve the People! You can put other class content into any of these things. And I think one of Mao's great achievements was to show, and obviously not to show as writing it up as theory, but shown in the course of the Chinese revolution itself, and especially after it came to power, that institutionalizing it, formulizing it, making a formula out of it, at the most that's just the beginning of it. That's just the beginning of the dynamic struggle that has to take place within those forms. Then none of the forms is permanent; they have to continually be re-forged. And there may be relatively longer periods of time where you could have stable forms, but nobody should think that they're here forever because the formulas are what are doing the work for us, either. And in some sense that's also sort of the ethical point. In other words, like you've kept saying, it's got to be people. It's not that you set up a structure and then the people will do it right, it's that the people have to do it.

AVAKIAN: And that slogan Serve The People also has a different meaning in socialist society than it would in communist society. I don't even know if that would be an appropriate slogan in communist society. Let's say it would; then it would have a different meaning than in socialist society. Precisely in response to this degenerate—politically and ideologically degenerating—cadre, Serve the People doesn't mean serve the bourgeoisie. There has to be differentiation not only in the sense that different classes look at that slogan differently, but also that in different contexts it means different things. The bourgeoisie is not part of the people that gets served. The workers, the peasants, the intellectuals, and other strata that are broadly the 90-plus percent which, even in class-divided society, are included among the people, even with the class differentiations among them—that "people" is what you're supposed to be serving, the broad masses of people. When you get to communism, if you would still apply that slogan—or something equivalent, corresponding to those circumstances—you wouldn't have those class distinctions. You wouldn't say, there are some people who should not be served, whose interests should not be served—some people whose interests should be worked against. In socialist society, you have to work against the interests of the bourgeoisie in order to implement the slogan of Serve the People. So that's as to the social and class content of it under different conditions—or lack of a class content in classless society.

But there is also Mao's recognition that people have to be ideologically—and, in a real sense, ethically—given the foundation of it, have to be ideologically and ethically motivated. That was his criticism of "goulash communism" with Khrushchev. Sure, you have to meet the needs of the people but . . . I've visited some of those places in China where they dug the Red Flag Canal out of this mountainside. It took tremendous heroism and sacrifice. I forget if people actually died—I think some did—but anyway they had to risk their lives all over the place to do it. And, because they were diverting a river, some of the people who were more favorably situated, with regard to that river, actually lost out in terms of narrow self-interest. In order for the water to be spread over the larger area, to benefit the larger collectivity of people and ultimately the society as a whole, and through that the world revolution, some people who had a more favorable situation, as far as irrigation, had to sacrifice some of that. So there had to be an ideological struggle—which has a dimension, obviously, of principles and ethics—about what do you put first? Self-interest or the good of society as a whole? Which in turn is rooted in materialism, because if it weren't true that by putting the interests and the needs of society as a whole first, people overall would be better served, then ultimately it would fall apart. And the motivation of individuals to go for their own personal gain or personal safety or personal protection would overwhelm the ideological line or ideological commitment to pursue the common good. This is something you were speaking to here, in terms of how ethics doesn't in and of itself have the necessary purchase (I think that was the phrase you were using).

MARTIN: It doesn't have the necessary purchase to itself be ethical. That's the rub, so to speak. Ethics by itself can't be ethical.

AVAKIAN: Part of the reason why it can't is because ethics by itself also can't be effected.

MARTIN: That's what I mean.

AVAKIAN: Well, yeah, maybe we're saying the same thing— if you can't actually bring it into being, if you can't transform it into a material force in reality, then it can only remain an idea, and then some other idea is going to actually be operative in reality, if you want to put it that way. But, given that there's a material basis, then there's the class struggle—or even in classless society there's a struggle among people—about which world view, which principles, which ethics are they going to uphold and apply. In socialist society that's a big question of struggle. What ideological outlook—Serve the People or To Get Rich Is Glorious—is going to motivate people. And that's connected to where are you trying to go with society and how does the nature of the society you're trying to bring into being relate to the needs and interests of individuals and, as you are formulating it, to their ability to increasingly mutually flourish.

I have no problem with the idea of a society of mutual flourishing, it's just that what I'm trying to emphasize is that it has to be grounded in material reality. Not in the sense of being slaves to the present material reality, but you have to be constantly transforming material reality in order to create more and more of the basis for that and to give it more and more expression. That's what I mean by the materialism of it. It gets to Mao's point that ideas and matter can be transformed into each other. Certain material conditions give rise to certain ideas, and those ideas can become a powerful force—and that includes ideas of the right and the good, and so on. Obviously, our ideas are different than Aristotle's. Aristotle thought that the concept of happiness didn't apply to slaves, for example—it didn't apply to slaves any more than to animals is what he said, if I remember correctly. Well, we don't see it that way. But, at least in my understanding, that doesn't mean that the question of the right and the good has no meaning at all, period.

MARTIN: Right. Another way to put it, in more philosophical-sounding language, is to say that *ought* implies *can*. That we're talking about what is and what ought to be. That we don't make some disconnect with what is, we aren't just utopian. We have to deal with what is. That's what ethics is about. That's what the ethical is about. I myself am hesitant about the term *ethics* for reasons that are similar to Marx's skepticism. As a discourse it circulates in certain areas and is mostly used in a not even necessarily insidious way but in a trivializing way, really. In a certain sense I mean trivializing, when you compare it to the idea that the most ethical things we can do are to fight imperialism, to be for internationalism, to fight for communism. To work in whatever ways we can to bring about a communist world. Those are the ethical tasks. And they are also the tasks that we would never get to if we didn't do political economy, if we didn't do scientific investigation, if we didn't try to understand what is going on out there. If we didn't try to understand that many many people experience exploitation and alienation and reification and commodification. That also systematically there are common sources to all of that. Most people in this world feel that something isn't right. There's no question about that. Even people who are conservative politically know that something isn't right. But to then dig deep into what materially is causing that, we'll never get there if we don't do that, and if we don't engage in the struggles where people are coming up against that and that's where we mainly learn how this thing is working, and to put all of that together. I think in some sense we're both saying, apart from whatever sort of differences we might have about the ontology of it or something, that we're for putting all that together.

AVAKIAN: Let me ask you a question in that connection. There was this excerpt from something I wrote, "Great Objectives and Grand Strategy," that was published in our party's newspaper, where I spoke to Lenin's point about dreaming, and I was told that you thought that the way this was presented was too narrow or too limited. So I was interested, in light of the conversation we're having here . . .

MARTIN: Well, I did . . .

AVAKIAN: What you meant by that?

MARTIN: The part of it that I had a problem with was (I think I'll probably not get the exact words quite right) that dreaming is fine, dreaming is great, but it has to be done in a sense "in accord with reality." And I think it's more that I think one has to be very careful with formulations like that. There's some sense in which reality's taking care of itself just fine, and in a certain sense what we want to unite with is the "to hell with this reality" trend. And I think you just have to be careful with that word, *reality*, because it just becomes so constraining. And that actually some of the dreams that go the furthest from that reality are great stuff. I guess I think of Adorno's understanding of the art work. And obviously that would be another two week's conversation if we really wanted to get into that, but his argument about avant-garde art, apart from every aspect of that, part of the core of his argument, is that through its formal properties experimental art jars the sensibilities away from that which can be immediately reappropriated to the commodity system. And it does even have sort of a bit of a—sorry, I shouldn't even get into this, it loads it too much—but it almost seems to have a kind of, almost Zen moment aspect to it. But I think he thinks of it as dialectically . . . it has that aspect of pushing one toward a leap into imagining a world where the world is not subject to commodity relations. And that without that kind of vision, and Adorno had tremendous shortcomings in terms of—All right, great, but what do you do with that, how do you get somewhere out of this moment? There's no question that there are shortcomings. But in some sense you could say, well that's not a dream in accord with reality. In fact that is a dream absolutely against the reality. You might even unite with that, I don't know. But it comes down to, let's be careful when we talk . . .   It sounds a little, what's the word, paternalistic, even—"It's great for you guys to dream, but just make sure you do it in accordance with reality." [*laughs*]

AVAKIAN: I actually didn't mean that as a limiting statement. My intent was the opposite. What I was trying to say, and the reason I raised it here, is that it has to do with a lot of the themes we're talking about. I was trying to say, as I think I put it there: it's good to envision the way the world could be and then to strive to bring that into being. But the point of the reality criterion was what we've been stressing here—there has to be some sort of material foundation. You have to be in accord with reality—you can be anticipating where reality can go, but there has to be a basis for taking it there. That's what I was trying to say. Certainly, it wasn't meant to be a limiting statement particularly with regard to art—whether it's science fiction or avant-garde art or surreal art or other things—that they should all be limited to holding a mirror to reality. That was not at all what I intended to say. Some art is more directly related to reality, and some of it is very "oddly" related to reality. Some of it's very unrelated to immediate reality. And I think there's a role for all of that. There's a question of the content and what it points to, but there's a role for all of that. I understand the point you're making about "be careful with how you present reality," but my point was actually the opposite: to try to find the unity in having a vision but a vision that's grounded in reality, ultimately. The same Lenin I was taking this from—about dreaming—said the essence of revisionism is that "what's desirable is what's possible, and what's possible is whatever is being done at the moment."

MARTIN: Right, right.

AVAKIAN: So that's along the lines of what you're raising. In the same spirit, I certainly wouldn't want what I was trying to get at there to be interpreted to mean that people's dreaming should be limited to reflecting what already is—and that what already is, is all that is possible. I was trying to emphasize the opposite—that, as opposed to being mired too much in what is, it's good and important to be looking at what could be. But then there's the question of what actually can be, and how you actually get there. Can we realize the anarchist vision of immediately no state? No. Can we eventually get to no state? Yes.

MARTIN: So let me just provoke you on that. What about images of a future society where there are no states, no classes. That, of course, will be marked by the present in which an artist attempts to create these images. But be that as it may, and when we get there it may not be like that image. It seems to me, though, there's a very positive role . . .

AVAKIAN: Like Marge Piercy or Ursula LeGuin—like that?

MARTIN: To me, those are just great examples.

AVAKIAN: Yeah, well, I agree.

MARTIN: So inspiring to me. When I read *Woman on the Edge of Time* I was like, man, that's the future I want to go to. I have certain questions about it, but on the whole, that's where I want to live.

AVAKIAN: That's provocative to me, in the sense that those things provoke you to think, but not in the sense that I disagree with it. In other words, some aspects of the picture they paint you might agree or disagree with—and certainly there are aspects that won't actually be the way it will turn out—but it is important that people, in science fiction and other means of art, other forms, be trying to envision the future, even beyond what we have imagined so far. I think we know some of the fundamental things that are going to go into the struggle to achieve communism, and some of the fundamental things that have to be transformed, but a lot of the particulars we don't know right now, and a lot of them are going to change. So it's a unity of opposites right there too. But even for people to "play around" with things where there is not really a basis to know whether they're going to work out that way or not—this can also be positive, at a minimum in the same sense that we talked about earlier in terms of philosophy: coming at things from different angles and provoking us to think and to question and to broaden our horizons and turn the world upside down, or our image of it upside down, and shake it around a bit and see what falls out, so to speak. I think all that's very important. So I certainly wouldn't want my statement about dreaming, which had the opposite intent, to have the effect of suggesting that those things aren't important and positive.

20

Defining "Secular" and Introducing "Postsecular"

MARTIN: I think there's a way to go from the ethical question to some other questions that I'm very interested in that have to do with religion, the rise of secularism in the West, the question of what I like to call the "postsecular"—of course others have used that term as well. Part of it has to do with what I think of as the underdetermination of the ethical or of the ethical moment. That moment where I don't think you can just fall back on or rely on scientific analysis. Not to cancel it. And there is a series of questions that have a similar status. And in some sense historically you might say they've been the "religious" questions. Obviously that's a very loaded term. And just to narrow them down a little bit, and we've certainly touched on them in one way or another: the question of meaning, and the question of the meaning of life, of purpose for life. The question of evil. Is that a word that does us any good, or is that kind of language something we'd do well to avoid? The question not only of the meaning of life but the meaning of death. The fact that we are the sorts of creatures who don't live forever. And in the grand scheme of things we don't really live very long. And I guess lastly and maybe not something we can develop very fully, but it relates to the meaning of life, is the question of home, so to speak. Being at home in the world. Is there some sense in which we can be at home in this world? And it seems to me that historically these are questions at the intersection of politics and religion.

I think we have to be careful with the term *religion*. What I mean by that is there's a tendency, for people who talk about religion in the modern period, at least in the West, and I mean in the last three, four, five hundred years, to talk about it in a secular way. In presecular times, there wasn't some discrete thing called religion. There was a form of life that had dimensions that appealed to something fundamental in the world; I know I'm giving a highly abstract, philosophical slant to it. But something in the nature of reality that situated us and made it such that we belonged here and that there was something "larger" about us. I guess I think there's a sense in which, on the one hand, sure, why not have scientific critique of religion and look at the things that religion in some senses attempted to give an answer to. We know that it's a better explanation for how the human biological organism came about to look at biological evolution than at some story about Adam's rib or whatnot. But these other questions, that are these larger ones: Why do we live? Why do we die? How do we live? What's the meaning of our mortality? Do we belong here? etcetera. These are questions that stay around and the answers to them are not, it seems to me, so easily given by science.

In effect, it seems to me that once Western society starts to move into a more, I would say *positivistic* frame, the kinds of answers that are given, including by at least many strains of Marxism, really sound a good deal like positivism. In other words, they sort of say, well, really the terms of those questions don't make sense and so that's how we'll answer them. They're pseudo-questions, so we can get rid of them that way. And yet I find that they just continually assert themselves in people's lives. And so apart from this or that particular religion, this or that theology, it seems to me there are some questions that have that structure, that don't go away. And that we ought to be able to discuss these questions, and look for the answers to them.

AVAKIAN: Once again, there are a lot of big questions wrapped up in that. At some point I was intending to ask you about this statement from your book *Humanism and its Aftermath*, on this subject of the meaning of life—or your quote from Wittgenstein about it's not *how* the world is that's a mystery but *that* it is. You say that you raise this with your Marxist friends, and they tell you to go find something better to do. [*laughter*] So I won't fall in that trap: I won't answer it like that. But I did want to come back to that.

I find myself once again wanting to say a word for science and materialism. Not to *exclude* the question of meaning, but in order to *address* the question of meaning. In other words, I think this is similar to what we were saying about non-inevitability and on the other hand how that doesn't mean there's not a material basis. The way I look at it, the contradictions that have been classically identified by Marxism as fundamental (like the contradictions between productive forces and production relations and between the economic base and the superstructure—understanding that, and everything that gives rise to, in all its richness and not just as some formulae that are abstract and dry), I think those are still the dynamic, driving forces in society at whatever stage. That doesn't mean it's going through some sort of pre-choreographed dance. Or, to put it another way, the straining of the new to come forth out of the old and the contradictions that involves—I think Marx used the phrase about straining against the integument, particularly as applied to capitalism, the socialization of production straining against the integument of private appropriation. That has meaning. There are actually things straining to come forth out of that. And I think we're correct in what we've said here—that this could lead to the utter destruction of humanity at this point, but it could also lead to something new and beautiful, from the point of view of how we're looking at society. So I think that's a material force there—that's a material basis underlying and driving certain things. Which doesn't mean it's inevitably going to go one direction or another. And it certainly doesn't eliminate the need for people to consciously understand that and act on it, and all the initiative that goes along with that and, as we talked about earlier, all the principles and ideals that arise from that and that also have to be fought for and have to motivate people.

But I want to raise this in connection with the question of meaning. I think that, if we try to invent meaning, we won't succeed. That's essentially what religion has sought to do. Now, to put it like that is vulgarizing—I don't mean that somebody sat down and said crudely, "Let's invent a meaning"—but I think it has been an attempt of people to come up with some meaning, some way in which they place themselves in the universe and give meaning to their existence individually, and often as a people, in the larger scheme of things, as they're able to understand them at the time. But then that has run into all kinds of contradictions. People run up against questions—questions that Nietzsche was also dealing with in a certain way—like how can there be a god or gods in a world in which such cruel things continually happen. And, as for the answers religion provides, they do offer, as Marx points out too, consolation in a cold world, however you say that—the soul . . .

MARTIN: Heart of a heartless world.

AVAKIAN: Right. They do. But, on the other hand, they also provoke a great deal of anxiety themselves, because they don't really answer . . . and reality keeps throwing up these horrendous things that happen to people, and people are put into this hopeless position of trying to reconcile the reality with—to put it in boiled down terms—with the gods that they've invented. And again, I don't mean that they sat down and invented them one-to-one themselves. But I think—this is a Marxist answer, but I believe there is something in it that overlaps perhaps with existentialism in a sense—that the meaning that we have to our lives as individuals, as human beings, is the one we give to it.

And the reason I raise materialism again is because those things also arise out of the conditions we find ourselves in. We give a different meaning to life now than people did 5000 years ago in many important ways. We find meaning in the striving for the resolution of these profound contradictions and the advance to a whole different kind of society: the transformation of society, and even of people, even of our whole way of looking at the world. All that to me is full of meaning. It's a meaning that has no larger origin or motive force outside of human beings and their society, but on the other hand it doesn't have to, in my opinion. In other words, there's plenty of meaning in striving to be part of making a different kind of society where people could relate to each other without all these barriers and obstacles and divisions and alienation that are embedded in the present form of society and previous class societies.

So getting back around to . . . I've always meant to ask you this and I'm glad I've got the chance, because I underlined this and made some markings by it to call attention to it and to remind myself to raise this in one form or another if I got a chance—this question of how we're here: I believe there is an important role for mystery—I have referred to this phrase "the need to be amazed" and I think that is a need that human beings do have. There's the continual mystery posed by the many things that we can contemplate but can't understand, and then on the other hand to me there's also a great thrill, if you will, in seeing something explained that was previously unexplained or even previously thought to be inexplicable. That's a continuing process. And both parts are amazing to me, and awe-inspiring—not "awesome dude," but they do genuinely inspire awe, at least in me and I think in others too. But I meant to pose a question to you about this. To me this question of not *how* the world is but *that* it is—to me it's a very interesting scientific and philosophical question. I have read books by various physicists, theoretical physicists, and others, grappling with the question: what is there about matter that enabled life to be able to emerge, without having to have the intervention of some external force—a god in other words, in one form or another. And they're actually trying to examine matter in its development, not just on the earth but in the larger cosmological sense, in order to understand that. I don't think we're right immediately on the threshold of having an answer to that, but wrestling with that is to me very worthwhile and, again, awe-inspiring. But if you mean it in some other sense—like why are we here, in some metaphysical sense—then I think I would have to say that *that* question, in that sense, doesn't make sense to me. But what are we going to do now that we are here?—that is a question full of meaning. And how did we get here?—in a scientific, not in a metaphysical sense.

For example, not to go on and on but just to try to scope out what I'm thinking of here, I know one of the things I've talked to people about—it's one of the hardest things for people in general, including myself, to get your mind around—in a certain sense it's almost impossible: If you think about matter being infinite and existing infinitely and (to use a poor metaphor, I guess) if you try to go to the edge of that and peer over the edge, you can't do it. Your mind just won't go there and can't get around that. Because, if you pose the question as religion does sometimes—what was there before matter?—then you've really got the same question in another form. The answer again is matter. There isn't anything there "before" it. But, on the other hand, if you actually try to think of matter being infinite and infinitely existing, it makes your head hurt—at least mine. So I think that's a kind of big cosmological question which is extremely interesting to explore, in a scientific sense. And I know this word "science" is a word that can be greatly misused and vulgarized, but by "scientific sense" I mean just exploring reality in all its complexity as it actually is—I don't mean the vulgarized view of science, I mean exploring reality in all its complexity and changingness, but reality and not something else. But I've always wondered what exactly you were getting at with that question: not the *what* but the *how*—how did you put it exactly—that we're here?

MARTIN: Not the "how it is" but the "that it is."

AVAKIAN: Right, the *that* it is. Not how the world is, is a mystery; but *that* it is. So I've always been meaning to ask, what did you mean by that. So maybe those are some questions that will help us move this.

MARTIN: I'm going to affirm, from my own perspective, a lot of what you said. And just say, too, I don't believe in some non-material, guiding consciousness for all reality or anything like that either. And somewhat for scientific reasons in the sense that we were discussing, just casually I was mentioning Diderot's famous retort to Napoleon, where Napoleon read a work of Denis Diderot's and said, "Well, why don't you talk about God?" and Diderot responded with the famous line, "Sir I have no need of that hypothesis." [It was not Diderot, but rather the mathematician Pierre Simon LaPlace (1749–1827) who said this.—BM] And I'm certainly not for inserting the hypothesis just for the heck of it or if you run into something that's a gap or we don't know what to say about it or whatnot. That's foolish on many levels. I would also find it objectionable in a more philosophical sense in that if you get yourself into a model, and this is one of the things where occasionally I'll speak with a religious believer and they'll say, "Well, you can't not believe it just because you don't like it." And I'll say, "Well I really don't like it, and I'll just keep not believing it and that will be one of my reasons."

You find yourself in something that's come up before—theodicy. Some forms of traditional Western monotheistic theology supposedly give you an answer to why we are here, except that the answer is, you're just here so when it's over you go somewhere else. And that's no good because to me that's an answer that says that nothing we do here *matters*. And I was thinking about this the other day; I don't know why this came to mind. I was riding the El [the elevated train in Chicago] and as usual just letting my mind wander. I was thinking of the story of the loaves and the fishes from the New Testament, about Jesus feeding the multitudes. And I was thinking of the way that in some sense you could divide Christian theology at least into two just around the interpretation of that story, in the sense that the mainstream of Christian theology focuses on the idea that "it was a miracle!" and therefore some divine intervention in human affairs and magical beyond explanation or whatever. And one response to that would be to say something like, if that was true then what that is saying is that human beings can't find ways to feed themselves, they can't work out these problems themselves. Which is another way of saying, you know you guys are just like toy soldiers in a sandbox and some large force is playing with you for whatever crazy scheme. I've seen bumper stickers in the wake of 9/11 that say things like God Is Still in Control. And you want to say, "Well, he's not doing a very good job!" I mean if you're going to say that, take responsibility for it. So what you're saying in other words is this is God's plan, to have this mess happen, I mean, come on!

AVAKIAN: That's theodicy, right?

MARTIN: Right, that it will all work out in the end. Of course, that becomes extraordinarily offensive, it seems to me, in the case of horrible historical disasters like the Holocaust. An explanation for why the Nazi officer takes the baby out of its mother's arms and gasses it or puts it in the oven is that, well, somehow, somewhere down the road something is going to happen that makes that all work out okay. And part of my response to that is that one can only wish that there would be something. I don't think that anybody can help but just wish on some level that there was something. But on another level, there's nothing and there will never be anything that could possibly make that such that that was not the horrible thing that it was. So there's nothing there that I want to get mixed up in.

So, just to get back to the loaves and fishes thing, it's interesting that what you might call the mainstream, which would include both fundamentalism and most sorts of "vanilla," blasé religious believers who are mainly looking for what they think of as fire insurance, or they're mainly looking for middle-class religion in First-World countries—"Well, I have everything else I need materially I may as well have that, too, I may as well keep that fire insurance policy in my back pocket, too." The focus from that perspective is on, that's a miracle. What's interesting is that the focus isn't on, they fed the people. Interesting that it's on the magic; the magic is the point of that story. Whereas another point of the story might be that all of these people came together and they found some way to eat, despite the odds. I realize that, in a certain sense, is what in more recent times would be called a kind of secular reading of the story. But it's the question of where's the emphasis. I tend to think in these stories the emphasis originally was more on the feeding than the magic of it because to me there's always a non sequitur at work in this idea that first you pull a rabbit out of the hat and show people you know how to do magic. Then you give some ethical precept or something and somehow the fact that you can pull a rabbit out of the hat "proves" the ethical claim. That seems ridiculous to me. So instead, I have to think it's about something else.

The term I've fastened on recently is *ongoingness*. I'm trying to capture that element of faith that it takes to believe that the human project is worth pursuing and that it hopefully will have a future.

Back in the eighties when I was getting involved with certain things politically, I found myself having an argument with my grandmother. This was the time when we were talking about, basically, revolution or nuclear war. It's interesting, all the scientific investigation we can do around why that dynamic did not work out the way we thought it would at the time, and I accepted it too, and I think it was right to accept it. Because after all, the stakes of that . . . whatever allowed humanity to pass through that period without obliteration, I don't know what it was exactly. My point here isn't to go off into "God saved us" or something of that nature. But sometimes I think what saved us was the call of the future. I don't mean that Gorbachev heard it or something, or Yeltsin or something like that. Something allowed us to live and fight for another day, and that's a good thing. Occasionally I think sometimes we feel a nostalgia for a time when the dynamics that were driving the world were polarized in such a way that there was a little more clarity, but, of course, I think the analysis was right, that if that kept going much longer, who knows, it's quite possible we wouldn't be here to have this conversation in the first place. But my point is, I got into this argument with my grandmother, and I was trying to put it in terms that she would relate to, and I said, "I don't want the world to end. I want us to go on. I want us to go on and create a better world." But there's a point where she asked me, "But why? Who says humanity has to have a future?" On some level, not to run my grandmother down, but that is kind of a sick question. Why does an answer have to be given to that? But on another level, in the larger frame of things, just to go back to that statement of Mao's that goes something like, "If a big meteor hit the earth and destroyed everything that would be a major event for the solar system but a relatively minor event for the galaxy." [*laughter*] So from the galactic perspective, so to speak, you can imagine, just as one day maybe we'll be able to look out into the cosmos and see that other conscious civilizations have come and gone. That's a fantastic sort of thought.

I want it to go on. I want us to go on and create a better world: a world where we share the world and we flourish together and where we create beauty and we have ethical relations among ourselves and we have sweetness. As I said before, I'm a bit sentimental. And what allows me to say that I want that rather than just, "Hey if it ends it ends"? I realized there's an underlying material question that those who have their backs against the wall will tend to fight. And that's the material basis on which ultimately we'll go forward. When people find themselves unable to hold body and soul together they have to do something about it; they're going to do something about it. Then the question is with what vision. How are they organized? Can they effectively go forward and really start to address some things? But when I think about what I would hope to see—you mentioned existentialism—I think one of Sartre's contributions is this idea that humans are the sorts of creatures who have projects, which means they project themselves into the future. They try to imagine themselves in the future.

We have to plan. We have to know where, try to know where we're going to sleep tonight, what's for dinner, etcetera. And hopefully . . . *if* there will be dinner, etcetera. And hopefully by and by something much larger than that. Then Marx's great contribution, didn't Engels say that this at the . . . I could see somebody taking this up in a narrow way. I don't think Engels meant it that way at all, at the speech at the graveside of Marx, where Engels says Marx's great contribution to philosophy was the understanding that people have to eat. If you have to eat you have to know where the food is going to come from. You have to make some plans. Then hopefully we go on to the stage where we don't live by bread alone, and that seems to be something that goes very deep. It's interesting that in some of the documents that have come out around the new Draft Programme, on art and changing this line on art as just being "entertainment." That speaks to part of that question, too.

Ongoingness is something that requires all the scientific analysis that we can bring to it, all the political economy. But there's also that element of faith. The structure of that faith looks to me like what we've known of religious faith before. That doesn't mean that it is a leap absolutely in the dark or any of that, but that one commits to the idea that we ought to have a future. We have to work for it. It would be a good thing. Let's keep going. That having that form of that commitment is actually what then spurs us on to do the scientific analysis that we need to do. Now obviously that's a very different way of configuring the question than saying, because usually if the "religion question" comes up, it's more like freedom of religion under socialism, or, What has been the effect of this or that religious group in the world? or, What things do people need to break through to try to understand what's really going on in the world? Whereas to me what's left over after all of that has been critiqued is this faith in and commitment to ongoingness.

AVAKIAN: Well, first, just one little thing in relation to those Skybreak articles on art. The party had actually rejected and criticized that line—Art Is Entertainment—quite a while ago. Skybreak actually wrote those things a while ago, having studied summations of that. But she was trying to further develop her thinking: okay, if art's not that, then what is it? I think that was the purpose—to get that discussion going more. Art is not just entertainment—then what is it? That is actually a line we had rejected a while ago. But there is still a big discussion that's ongoing about what is the social role of art, and Skybreak's articles were a contribution to that.

MARTIN: I didn't know that. I actually became active around a time when the entertainment line was the line.

AVAKIAN: Like in the early eighties?

MARTIN: Yes, and in significant ways I've found myself rubbing up against it. I had a lot of difficulty with that. So it's great that it's changed.

AVAKIAN: There are a lot of spheres where we would like to be able to pay more attention on many different levels than we are able to all the time. We have paid a lot of attention to art but we'd like to be able to pay even more. And those articles were a contribution that she offered in a sense to help propel some more wrangling in the theoretical realm, even while we've been trying to make advances in working with people in practice and the party overall has been trying to come to a better understanding. That was a line that had some sway in the early eighties—Art Is Entertainment—but not too long after that we summed up that that wasn't correct. But there is still a lot of work to be done. Besides working practically with people—to try to create art and to do criticism of art, in a good way, and things like that—we're also trying to develop our theoretical understanding of its social role overall and how, in a broad as opposed to a narrow sense, that relates to the revolutionary project, if you want to put it that way.

But that was just an aside. I wanted to say that I definitely agree: to use the language you were using, I want us to go on, too. But my feeling is, I want us to go on enough that I think the only way we have a real chance—the only real way to do that—is actually to be scientific in the way I've been trying to talk about that. Not in a narrow, mechanistic sense. For example, one of the problems I have with what I think you referred to as the "falliblistic" religious beliefs—or the more inclusive ones, the less dogmatic ones, the less literalist and fundamentalist ones—is that they're still caught up in a contradiction. A lot of people who hold these views take very positive stands on a number of different issues. They stand with the oppressed in a lot of ways, and that's all very good. I'm not saying this in any way to diminish that. It's important, and it's important to unite with that even while continuing to struggle with people about some of the areas of disagreement that are important. But the problem I have is that there's this contradiction where people want to say, "Okay let's not insist that Christianity is the only way, and let's take the life of Jesus, or the beliefs of Jesus, for example—just to take one form of that kind of religion—let's take the idea of standing with the poor and the downtrodden, the marginalized, and living a just life, let's bring that to the forefront." But there are two problems with that, that I can see. One, they still want to have, in the final analysis, a different kind of insurance policy, to refer to your phrase. Not that they're going to go on living forever necessarily, but they want to have an insurance policy that somehow this has backing that's bigger than just people. Somehow you have to have some supernatural force behind this, because people are not enough. And that's leaving aside that I have some disagreements about some of the content, too, if you examine what Jesus put forward—and I'm going to speak to one aspect of that in a second. But even leaving that aside for the moment, there's a problem of wanting to have a supernatural backing there. In other words, they're not willing to just say, "Okay, let's look at the programmatic essence of what Jesus is about as we understand it, and put that up against other programmatic ideas—other ideas about how life ought to be and ought to be lived—and see which ones really meet the needs." They want to have something supernatural behind it which gives it sort of a favored status but also, and even more importantly, gives it a force behind it so that just in case human beings aren't capable of doing this, there'll be something else that will make it happen.

The other thing is, I was reading this book by James Carroll—he's an author who has written novels and other things, and he's a former priest—he wrote this book *Constantine's Sword*, which is very interesting. It has a lot of good exposure about the history of the Church, particularly the Catholic Church, especially in terms of the persecution of the Jews throughout the history of the church, right down to the modern age, and ways in which that's still continuing. And then at the end, when he sort of puts forward his programmatic views, he wants to stand on the basis of Vatican II. He's trying to speak to being open—that we shouldn't have this exclusionary idea that only through Jesus can people live a good life, or is there a valid expression of spirituality or whatever. And he's part of this school that says that some of the Gospels, for example, were rewritten or restructured so the onus was put on the Jews rather than the Roman authorities for the killing of Christ—that whole Christ-killer thing through history. So he's saying a lot of the scripture is not really in keeping with the spirit of Jesus and it's more what the early church came up with through its own . . .

MARTIN: In coordination with the powers that be.

AVAKIAN: And more out of its own needs to survive as a community, under conditions where they were being persecuted, in the first century of the church, before there was an accommodation, or "merging," with the established powers. But the problem is (I made a note in the margin when I was reading this) if you go, for example, to a Gospel like John, right in there—not out of somebody else's mouth, not attributed to someone else, but attributed to Jesus himself—is the proclamation, "I am the way: the only way to everlasting life and to the Father and everything is through me." So it's not just that the Christian religion afterward, when it became institutionalized as part of the Roman Empire—or even before that, when it began to develop itself as a movement—"imported this from the outside" or "stuck this on"—artificially grafted this on to what it was that Jesus said (according to the Gospels). This was right in the words of Jesus himself. So you have got a contradiction there. You can't at one and the same time say, let's be inclusionary and not say Jesus is the only way to be spiritual, while the very Jesus that you still want to put at the center is saying, "I'm the only way." So to me these are just expressions of the problems that you get embroiled in with relying on something other than science in the way I've been trying to talk about it, and relying on people.

And just one other thing to mention here, for right now. I don't know if you have seen this book called *This Dark World?*

MARTIN: No.

AVAKIAN: It attracted my interest because it's called "A Memoir of Salvation Found and Lost." It's written by this woman named Carolyn S. Briggs, who grew up in an isolated rural area in Iowa and who—without telling the whole story, she got pregnant at seventeen, got married and was attracted to and got into one of the Christian fundamentalist movements. There are a lot of interesting things she talks about. She describes the group she was part of as sort of the "pseudo-hippie" part of the Christian fundamentalists. They saw themselves—this point you were raising about community—they saw themselves living, as much as they possibly could, the life of the early Christians. She describes how they shared with each other and how they had, not exactly communism, but communalism. Among the women in particular, one person would get sick, and all the women would come over and take care of her. But, at the same time, all this was bound up with very backward traditional relations—the women were subordinate to the men, the women's role was to have lots and lots of babies, and, of course, they couldn't have abortions. And it's odd, some of the things she describes. They sit around and drink herbal tea and talk with each other, but they're talking about "the rapture" and what it's going to be like when all of a sudden people are raptured up to heaven and others are left with the great battle with the devil. And she was so far into it that she talks about getting rid of statuettes and figurines in her house because she was afraid that the devil would lodge in them and get into her children. Really, genuinely psychotic stuff.

She's now broken with this and she teaches creative writing and lives somewhere in Iowa, but the thing that really struck me, out of all this, was at one point when she's beginning to break with this, she says (I don't remember exactly how she puts it, I'm paraphrasing but this is essentially it) she confronted the question of living in a world without absolutes, and she found it at one and the same time exhilarating and terrifying. It was like this need to believe in absolutes was the cement of all this, in a very obscurantist kind of way. The inability to deal with the complexity and even, in a certain sense—in a very central way—to be unable to deal with uncertainty. I think that is one of the hardest things we face, that you do have to give up a belief in absolutes. In this case she was believing in nonexistent absolutes like god, but they are all ultimately nonexistent—not just god but absolutes in that sense—the world is not really like that. Existence is not really like that. It is a difficult thing, I think, especially when you're living in this kind of society, where you not only have complexity but you have a tremendous alienation, oppression, and people being fragmented and people being pitted against each other, and the whole dog-eat-dog mentality, and all the rest of that. It's very hard to deal with the feeling of coldness that comes from feeling, like Bob Dylan's Mr. Jones, "My god am I here all alone?" [*laughs*] So I think you can understand why people get drawn to that kind of fundamentalism. That's why I was very interested in this book. It raised many other questions in my mind, and by the time I finished reading it I felt like saying, there are a hundred other questions I'd like to raise to have her speak to from her experience.

Anyway, to move on, Mao was alleged to have written—it was one of the things that came out right at the time of the coup, the bourgeois press printed some stuff about this, that he was supposed to have written a letter to Jiang Qing, just before dying, expressing that he felt like he'd accomplished some things but there was so much more that he'd wanted to accomplish, that what he'd been able to accomplish in his lifetime was very limited. Then he made the statement, "People's lives are limited but revolution is infinite."

MARTIN: Right, it was really a poem that was his last message to Jiang Qing.

AVAKIAN: Right. I don't think he meant "revolution" only in the sense of the stage we're at now in society and history—overthrowing capitalism and going to communism. I think he meant the continual confronting and transforming of necessity, transforming reality, the process of going on with that: as long as people are here, people will be doing that, even though any particular individual's life is limited. That is one of the things about our species: it is sort of an irony that we have the capacity to have the kind of consciousness that we do, yet also included in that is that you have the capacity to know that you're going to die—you know about mortality. It reminds me a little bit of the "intelligent designer" thing, a refutation of that: another one of these ironies is that the fact that you can speak also has to do with the fact that you can choke eating. [*laughter*] It has to do with how human anatomy makes both things possible. So, some intelligent designer would have to be extremely cynical to design like that. But that's one of the things that evolved, when human beings evolved, they had that capacity to speak but also you could choke to death, just because of the anatomy. In a certain way that is analogous to the fact that we can project, we can see the future, we can grasp, in the reality and the contradictions of the present and the way things are straining against the current constraints, the possibilities of the future. But another thing we can do is recognize that we're limited as individuals. And that there's even the potential, as we've been talking about, for the human species to go out of existence.

I can agree with ongoingness, not in the sense that there's something more that gives this meaning, beyond people and what people do, but in the sense that we want to . . . it's like, even as religious and metaphysical as he was, Peter Tosh had this song where he says, "I'm a man of the past, living in the present, and walking in the future." Well, there's something about what we're doing that is drawing from the past—we're not people of the past, in the same way he means that, but we're drawing from the past—yet we have to live in the present while we're trying to walk in the future, in the sense of seeing where the future is, where things are straining to go, and where they can go. Not inevitably bound to go, but where they can go. And yet, we're not going to see a lot of that. Maybe we're not going to see things get better before our time as individuals is up. And there is a threat of humanity's time being up, because these same contradictions could lead to that. So to get back to the first point, I want to see us go on too, and I can embrace the idea of ongoingness in the sense that we have to strive, first of all, for a better future—which in many ways is bound up with striving to have a future, but strive for a better future and see ourselves as part of what Mao was talking about, an ongoing thing that's "infinite." Not literally—at some point human beings will go out of existence, maybe, who knows what that will mean—we don't know if it means that human beings will evolve into something else or . . . we don't know. You can speculate, and good science fiction can be written about it, but we can't say for certain what that's going to mean. But for a long time, hopefully, human beings are going to be around, and we do have something to say about that. We can make our contribution to not only their being around but making a leap to a better world, from a real material foundation.

So, as I say, I can embrace ongoingness in that sense. Not if it's invested with some . . . look, if there were actually supernatural forces, the whole world would be different. All of our science would be wrong, all of our efforts, what we're trying to do, would be misguided or beside-the-point at best. But I don't believe there are those things. I think a correctly understood scientific approach tells us these supernatural forces don't exist and that belief in them is also a human-created thing to try to deal with certain contradictions, both class relations but also other things that human beings interacting with nature are trying to understand and deal with. So, if we are like Mr. Jones—my god, we're here all alone—in the sense that there's no god, that doesn't mean to me that we're forlorn. It just means we have to make the future on the basis of the contradictions we're dealing with now and where things have come to—not in some unfolding teleological drama, or something, but in the sense that things have developed to where they are, certain contradictions characterize our age, and certain freedom can be wrenched out of this necessity. On the other hand, disaster could result from it too, and we're here—it's up to us to fight for one path as opposed to another, I guess is the way I would say it.

Let me ask you a question. If that's not good enough, why not? I'm not trying to be provocative, I'm actually seriously asking: what's missing in that? Just to be clear, that wasn't a way to try to put you on the spot, I'm just putting it out to think about.

MARTIN: No, it's good to be put on the spot with this kind of question. It's also the case that I'm framing it in a way that's hard to deal with for me too, in that on the one hand I'm really kind of talking about a fairly abstract philosophical question about the structure of a certain kind of belief, and where one orients one's life, even while we're talking about a several thousand or more years' long history of religions and belief systems and institutions and movements and whatnot. And, globally, there are a myriad of belief systems that are really, radically different from one another, at least I think so. I'm not one of the school who, which again is a bit of a sort of a New-Age thing, thinks that, really, they all come to the same thing. I think Buddhism, for instance, which obviously has hundreds of millions of adherents, is different from Judaism, is different from Christianity, and so on. So it's not syncretism that I'm looking for.

So to me the larger question is, what is the structure? Well, here's a simple way to put it: what is the structure of a belief in a future that in fact we're not going to see? I guess I'm thinking of, and I hope we'll see part of it, God I hope we'll see part of it. But I think about what Mao said about five hundred years, and in a sense asking us to put in perspective what we have to do. And that the transition to a different world, the transition from feudalism to capitalism, which in some sense still isn't complete — and will never be complete, of course, because of the way that capitalism then incorporates feudal relations into it. Or at least we're not going to sit around and wait for it to be complete, let's put it that way. It took centuries, so why would we think that what has to be an even much more immense transition in terms of the work that it has to do to transcend class society, why would that take any less time? Certainly it will be even much harder to accomplish. And, mindful of the idea that when humanity hopefully one day reaches that point and then finds itself confronted with new tasks, the revolution that never ends—we'll be in a position to think about things in a way that we can't even, we probably can't even imagine, given the society that we're the products of.

So I think that's the larger question, when you finally come down to it, what is the structure of that belief? I think we could quibble about this or that scenario about Jesus and the Early Christian Movement. We could also quibble about whether it's worth quibbling about it or, in the grand scheme of things, what sort of difference it makes.

I always find it interesting when fundamentalists say that Jesus said, "By no other name are ye saved." I always say, well his name wasn't really "Jesus," for one thing—so I guess you're screwed. Jesus is what, a Hellenization or Latinization of the name. He was "Yeshua," and we don't really know how that was pronounced, so I guess those folks don't in fact, after all, have the secret password or the shibboleth or whatever to go where they want to go. And people knocking on your door . . . I got this repeatedly in college —"Do you know where you're going when you die?" And after a while I'd say, "Well, where are you going?"—and they'd of course say, "Heaven." Then I would say, "Well, you know that would be *hell* to me, if you're going to be there!" [*laughter*] Of course, it turned out that all my favorite people were going to be in the other place.

On the other hand, I guess I take inspiration from Jesus and the Early Christian Movement. I think it is very clear that not only was he executed by the Roman state, but that he was executed for political reasons, because he was a thorn in their side. We can talk about how much of a thorn and was he reformist or radical or revolutionary or what. And we can talk about how much that was then rewritten mainly for the early Christians to progressively distance themselves from the Jews, even though most of them were Jews up to a point. It's always been an embarrassment for Christianity.

There's at least a couple of major embarrassments for Christianity in its own history, and one was that with all of the anti-Semitism that then gets grounded in Christianity and carried forward, there's this embarrassing fact that Jesus himself was a Jew. They have to deal with that somehow.

The other embarrassment being that if Jesus was some sort of political radical, then the interpretation of it that says that, no, it's really about giving us some sort of ontology of salvation or, like I say, the password to the next realm, or that the thing that gets us in good with God is to make some incantation. I guess I just don't really ultimately think it's all about that because for sure I would never accept any version of that that says that human beings don't matter and I think that's where that really goes, ultimately. And I do think most forms of what calls itself Christianity, that's the path they go down. I always find sort of funny and weird the forms of it that say, "Well, you think it's all about human beings, but it's really all about God." I guess I feel that God will take care of himself—what does that mean, even, that "it's all about God"? I'm worried about humanity. I'd certainly agree with the idea that, for one thing it's just a version, just to sort of take your phrase, "liberation without gods," in some sense that can just be thought of as a version of the idea that the working class must emancipate itself; no one else can do it for them. I mean this in the sense that, even if there really were a god who could save us—and I have to admit, there have been days when I've wished there was. Last year, I was hearing on NPR these stories about people who during the Argentinean repression had been disappeared, and what had happened to them was that they were taken up in these military transport planes, out over the ocean, and dropped into the ocean, like 75 to 100 miles off the coast. And I was thinking of that old phrase, "ready to catch you should you fall." And thinking it was a hard moment, thinking not God save *me*, but if only there was a hand to reach down at that moment and catch them. And I guess, I started to think, what does it mean to want to be a materialist, trying to be a materialist, but in some cases just wishing, wishing for something for those people because otherwise there's nothing.

AVAKIAN: I remember saying, at the time of the Gulf War, in the piece you mentioned earlier, *Could We Really Win?*, that I wished there *were* Jah or Allah or something that would reach out and neutralize these weapons of mass destruction that the U.S. was using.

MARTIN: Right. And yet the flip side of that is that if we don't, if humanity doesn't liberate itself, if the proletariat doesn't liberate itself, then it's not liberation. And it is about humanity, . . . the ongoingness point is about humanity. What the distant future or the larger cosmos, the fate of the known universe or whatever, some sort of *Dune* scenario, a scenario of that scope—if you ever read *Dune*, that science fiction series [of six long novels] that takes place on a multi-thousand year level, it uses this term, "the history of the known universe." Well, if someday there will ever be a history of the known universe, and if we're there to write it, that means that we were a part of it and the same sort of trajectory. And we won't get to be a part of it if we don't, sometimes I think of it as, if we don't thread the needle—if we don't make the passage through all of these difficulties that history has set for us. And so to me it is about that.

I was starting to say I think Christianity traditionally has this embarrassment that, in some sense if the only point of it was just to teach us the proper metaphysics of existence, or what incantation one needs to say, and in that sense "believe," since, after all, it's just, "Do you believe in the correct ontology or not?"— then, why do you even need the other stuff? The point, too, is that the Roman Empire, and this I think has been established very well, they couldn't care less what . . . in fact they were actually quite intelligent in that they were not going to get involved in merely theological disputes within the peoples that were under their dominion. They couldn't care less about that and in fact they saw it as counterproductive. There's no way they were going to execute somebody because within some group that they belonged to one held to the ontology of this and another of that. If it's really about something else, I still take inspiration from that something else. I think that Marx and Engels did, too, in some sense. Then what is it that I believe about that? Well, it's not any of this ontological stuff, it's not any of the supernatural, I don't even know what "supernatural" means. Just to throw in my own, what would that mean anyway. I don't even know what it would mean. Other than in some sense a pessimistic human belief about what we could accomplish as human beings, I think that's really what it comes from, and that's really the role that it plays institutionally for most people. I agree that that's not something we want to affirm in any way.

And one thing interesting is that I think in more recent decades as the fundamentalist movement got more directly politicized, and you have these figures such as Jerry Falwell and Pat Robertson emerging, is that even though it presents itself with this sort of rosy demeanor, it's really extraordinarily cynical. It's actually part and parcel of the whole machinery of cynicism that basically says, mere humans have nothing to say about their own fate and don't ever think they do. There's nothing there that I want to affirm in any way.

I guess if there's any bit of anything even remotely related to that that I feel somewhat affirmative of, it is in a certain sense a reaction to the secular in the sense of a secular world being not only a world where we're alone, but a world where there's no, I mean in some sense I don't think we're alone in the world, not only because none of us is alone individually but even as a species and even as a planet, here we are in this wonderful cosmos. I think we almost started our conversations at this point, and I take inspiration from that. Here we are, it's great, let's do something with it, let's make something of it, let's make a home here. So that it's more what I call the *coldness* of secularism that I not only understand the reaction to, but I even to some extent take inspiration from—I don't want to say the reaction to it—but the *sense* of the reaction to it. That one does not want to live in a world that's utterly cold. But how do we warm it up? Well, we have to warm it up ourselves. I don't think any . . . because liberation isn't liberation unless we do it ourselves, unless we make this home ourselves.

But then finally to come 'round on that, come back to where I started this, the structure of the belief in that future—see this is why to me it is similar to the ethical question. There's a sense in which that commitment to the future is a part of making that future come about. And to me it's one of those things where the structure of it is, it's true because it *could be* true, and it will be true if we make it true. And that doesn't mean we can just make it true by conjuring or incanting or wishing. There's no other way then to make it true but trying to understand, as you like to say, the world as it is, by scientifically investigating. And I agree with you; there's both the mystery of it and there's the joy at seeing how this thing works. I mean I feel that joy, too. I love reading it at the level at which I can read it, from a very lay sort of level. I love reading material about physics, about biology, other sciences, explained at a level where I can understand it. And it doesn't diminish my appreciation for the world one bit, it deepens it. But my basic commitment to it, and I suppose maybe it even comes down to, maybe it goes a little to the point made earlier in Derrida's writings, that a class per se, the proletariat per se, is not some collective subject in the sense of having a collective subjectivity, some super mind or meta-mind or something. It's the aggregate and it becomes in some sense more what it is as people come to class consciousness about their situation in society and start to see the way forward. I think this expression Derrida uses, actually, about how there's a sense in which, and he's making an essentially Kantian argument here, there's a sense in which our consciousness is structured by, and in fact, what even gives rise to consciousness, is responsibility— in the sense of the ability to respond. But then one has to take what he calls "responsibility to responsibility," in other words, commitment structures us, the future structures us, the project structures us, but then there's the sense of making the leap to the commitment to that. And that's what I think is underdetermined by the science. And it doesn't bother me to say that there's something like what traditionally has been thought of as a commitment of faith that describes that structure.

AVAKIAN: I see the point about commitment. In other words, I think the recognition of the possibility of a different and better world—and the recognition that there are material forces pushing in that direction, even if they're ones that could lead in a totally different and destructive direction—gives rise to a need for commitment. It isn't going to happen just because these contradictions are asserting themselves. To me, that's a vulgarization of Marxism, which some Marxists have fallen into in one form or another and to one degree or another. But it's a vulgarization of Marxism to say this is all going to take care of itself. Lenin emphasized that: why do you need a conscious vanguard? He was dealing with a very profound contradiction. At the beginning of any movement it's mainly intellectuals and people from classes other than the proletariat, though not exclusively— Engels pointed out that Joseph Dietzgen worked out, independently, the same things that Marx and Engels worked out—but it's mainly intellectuals who have, for whatever reasons, the inclination as well as the opportunity to wrangle in the realm of ideas, who can grasp these things that we're talking about. And then, there's a big contradiction: what are they going to do with it? The contradiction is, they're the first to be able to grasp it, but they can't do anything with it by themselves. Both because they don't have enough force and because, as you were alluding to, if they could somehow do it by themselves, it wouldn't be *it* anymore. In other words, if a few intellectuals made a change, it wouldn't be the change we're talking about.

So that's a profound contradiction, and that's really a lot about the contradictions involved with having a vanguard and everything—you need one, but it's fraught with contradiction. How do you work your way through that? We've talked about this somewhat, and we need to keep talking about it, and wrestling with it in practice as well, because it's one of the big contradictions we have to work our way through in advancing. But there is a need for that conscious commitment, and that does make you—not in a metaphysical sense, but it does make you part of something larger. You stand up and you sing The Internationale—there's a real feeling that you're part of people, through generations and all over the world, who have sung and are singing and will sing that song, just to use one rallying point, so to speak.

But I guess this touches on the point you were raising about the cold secular society. I think bourgeois society, in the measure that it's *bourgeois secular* society—and it's far from wholly secular, I mean this bourgeois society is very nonsecular, it's very infused and suffused with religion, and religion is promoted all over the place, especially these days—but insofar as those secular relations, the kind of cold commodity relations that you're talking about, assert themselves, yes that is very cold and very alienating. It's part of a whole exploitative system, which both materially and in people's "spirits"—not understanding that in a metaphysical sense, but in how people feel about the world, let's put it that way—is tremendously destructive. As I said earlier, it's important to say some bad things about feudalism and slavery, too, in terms of what they do to people, but there's no question capitalism is very cold. And it's cold in its own particular way—that's true too. But, as you said, how do we warm it up?

I think we have models of community. First of all, capitalism is contradictory. It does atomize people in the way Sartre talked about it, as an example—there's an aspect of serializing people, making them just one more number in a faceless mass. But there are also ways in which it throws people together, both in production but also more broadly. We were talking earlier about how it drags people into political life. Because of the socialization and because people are social animals, they do constantly seek ways to create socialization even in the conditions of atomization. One of the big contradictory expressions of that is something like the internet, where it's very atomizing but also people try to socialize through it. Every movement that comes forward does create its culture and does create its community in a sense. And I think there is a need that that's responding to. The antiglobalization movement has done that on various levels: it's created some of its own culture, it's created some of its own community, people coming together, a community of resistance, and a community that's trying to assert an alternative. And I think, much more fully, that gets expressed a lot of ways through the all-around struggle against the system.

And where we've been able to take state power, there has been the ethos of Serve the People and the ways in which, even down to the architecture and everything else—where, in China, for example, they tried to make things so that you didn't have this mad crazy situation of capitalist society where you drive three hours to work so that you can live in X neighborhood, or even if you live in a slum, ghetto, or barrio or whatever, you have to go three hours across town to work, because that's the only way you can live—they tried to build so the work, and the home, and the neighborhood and the schools all developed together, while it all also opened out to the broader world and they raised people's sights to the broader world.

I'm sure that this was—and it was presented as—a subject of very intense struggle, but I remember you would go to a village in China and people talked about how the standard they were trying, with some success, to get people to strive for in the home, for example, was: the floor needs sweeping, and people would compete with each other in a friendly way to try to be the one to do it first. And the men would be sweeping the floor, not just the women. This was the kind of thing they were aiming for and the kind of standard they were encouraging people to strive for, rather than let's all find the way we can get out of doing the work and foist it off onto somebody else. You know, the typical sort of male trip where you wash the dishes and break them. I know of someone who, when he was a kid, used to have to wash dishes, and he would break them so that his mother would get frustrated and say: "Okay, never mind. *I'll* wash them." That's kind of a typical male device with a lot of household-type work and other things. But much more generally than that, there is a way that you try to objectify other people and you try to manipulate other people—that's all part of the deal in this kind of society. And in China, when it was socialist, they were trying to bring forward, and were making some progress in bringing forward, a different ethos, where people were actually competing in a friendly way to take up the tasks that needed to be done, and doing it in a collective sense.

There is a story I always like to tell about going to a real remote commune, where there was a woman who was too old to do a lot of things. But she was tending to a pig. She told us about what she did, and she concluded by saying, "So I'm raising a pig for the world revolution." Even though that was just one thing she was doing, but some of the money they raised through what she was doing—she knew that this was contributing to not only changing that society but to the world revolution. And that was being brought forward as what she was striving to do. And I'm not saying this was without contradiction or that there weren't a lot of influences of bourgeois ideology— there were plenty.

MARTIN: Or what the pig had to say about it? [*laughter*]

AVAKIAN: Well, we'll get to that a little later. That's later, we'll have to come back to that one. We did not talk to the pig and find out what the pig had to say about it.

MARTIN: There was also the dog-eat-dog metaphor, which I'm always a little skeptical of, since only in very, very extreme cases would a dog eat another dog. It lets us humans off the hook, because dogs could never do anything as remotely as . . .

AVAKIAN: It's true that the human species has more potential for doing harm to its own species than any other, that's true. We should come back to that—that's a whole big subject that I do want to talk about, but whatever the metaphor is, people being at each other's throats is very real. Whatever metaphor is more or less appropriate to express that, it's real, it's a real phenomenon.

But we have had the history where we've had state power, where we've been able to give people a sense of purpose and a sense of pulling together collectively in something. Not the George Bush: "Let's all sacrifice for the greater imperialist right to plunder and exploit and destroy," but our own—the morality that *is* part of the proletarian revolution to transform society and part of pointing to the future of people cooperating for the common good, in which, like we talked about earlier, their own individualizing and individuality can be more fully expressed as part of the broader common good. So I think this is a very cold world of capitalism, but the way we warm it up is by developing forms and means of struggle that will eventually lead to its overthrow and transformation and the bringing into being of a whole new society and world. Otherwise, any temporary warming will be overwhelmed by the coldness. And I don't believe that means there's no role for developing community and a culture of our own, which is both a culture of resistance and (if you want to put it that way) a culture of affirmation. I think we do need those things. But they won't be able to fully flower, and in fact they'll get turned into their opposites, unless we are able to go forward and get rid of this system and transform these structures, institutions, relations, and forces, and even world outlooks that reinforce all this—which embody and reinforce all this coldness.

MARTIN: I don't think we're talking at cross-purposes here at all. Not that we're agreeing right down the line, but we're not going in opposite directions either. And actually I think we've explored this pretty well. There are a few smaller points I wanted to just put on the table. One thing I love about these novels, like *Woman on the Edge of Time* and *The Dispossessed*, is that the characters the authors create give us a sense of what it would mean to live in a certain way—and theoretical works can't really accomplish this. And that's an important thing, that's a great thing. In some sense it plays this very practical role of making something plausible when in some of the theoretical kind of discussion plausibility can't really be addressed, in the sense of how you would live "in your body" in that society— how you would *be* there?

AVAKIAN: That was one of the points that was made in one of those Skybreak articles on art that was actually quoting Gould, Stephen Jay Gould, on that novel (I forget the guy's name or the name of the novel) about the Cro-Magnons and Neanderthals: a lot of these kinds of questions, even scientific wrangling, could be done in the form of a novel in some aspects better than it could be done in the form of more rigorous science. I thought that was an important point. I'm just reinforcing what you're saying. There is a very important role for that.

MARTIN: Another novel I'd mention in that connection, in connection with what you were saying about the friendly competition to see who could sweep up and whatnot is *Stars in My Pocket Like Grains of Sand* by Samuel R. Delaney. It's a very complex novel and there are a lot of things going on, but one of the interesting things about it is that there are these people who play the role, their work is to go through the garbage, and even the sewage, to basically recycle and to sort out all the garbage and try to get it back into the system in a sustainable way. And these are the most highly valued members of society who do this, rather than the most lowly valued members of society. In fact, they're considered to be the most privileged members of that society. That has its contradictions and whatnot, too, but it makes plausible the idea that even these kinds of activities perhaps someday we'll have in society—I think we would have to hope for a society where we value this work. We won't want, and in fact part of moving toward that society would be to overcome the sort of division of labor where it's just *relegated*, even if they were thought to be the most privileged, where it's relegated to one part of society. But the idea that that could be valuable work and seen as valuable, I think that's a good contribution from that novel.

I guess I still disagree on the whole point about this being a secular society but with all sorts of nonsecular stuff in it, it's filled with religions and whatnot. Because I guess I think most of these religions are pretty doggone secular themselves, in the sense that most of them do also just contribute to the idea that this world is pointless. And their form of contributing to it is the idea that this world is pointless, you have to wait until the next one.

AVAKIAN: What do you mean, then, by secular? Maybe that will be helpful, to me anyway.

MARTIN: I think that is all I mean, that there's no point to this human life.

There is a book that I find extremely interesting, extremely difficult, it's a very intimidating book in the amount of learning it displays—it's called *Theology and Social Theory* by this fellow John Milbank. He's part of this trend—the politics of it, in a way I don't even really understand the politics of it, I'm just not able to really sum that up at this point—for myself much less for anybody else. But he's part of this trend called "radical orthodoxy." There are others in this "school," so to speak. One of the arguments they make, or Milbank makes especially, and others have taken it up in other ways, extended it, is that you have to have the secular and capitalism arising at the same time in some sense to kind of—maybe it's in a certain sense to cross the narrow horizon of feudal right, if I can put it in sort of a provocative formulation—in other words to get us ready for a world where the profitable production of commodities is ultimately "Moses and the prophets" for bourgeois society. You have to get rid of any trace, no matter how imperfect, no matter how messed up, even, and often cruel in its application—any trace of the idea that human beings might be God's children or part of some plan of creation or part of some redemptive scheme— that all has to go out the window. And I think it's in the context of the rise of commodity production on a scale where it is inescapable, and the crossing over into the commodification of labor power itself, such that *people* then circulate as commodities. Then you get the assimilation of most religion to that secular framework as well, and so I think again, I would just sum it up as *overwhelming pointlessness.*

Maybe this takes two main forms or two forms that interact— one just being the pointlessness of having a social form for the production of nothing other than commodities, and commodities not meaning mainly this or that product or this or that item, but for the production of the logic of commodities that structures everything within it. Or maybe the other form is, "Yes, that's right, this is a pointless life and really the reality is elsewhere or whatever" and that's where you get all the supernatural stuff and all of that. But it all still comes down to this pointlessness, and that's why I say that there's a side to it with people like Falwell and Robertson and that whole crew where it's not just illusion but it's deeply, deeply cynical. I don't want to be conspiratorial about it, but if you wanted to come up with a cynical plot this would be a good one. This is a pretty good one. So that's why I think that in some sense the overcoming of that—that it helps to think—who am I to legislate that it *has* to be?—but the overcoming of it is in some sense "postsecular."

Look at it this way. What is socialism? And I mean socialism as opposed to communism. Is it the lower stage of communism, or is it in some sense the higher stage of bourgeois society? We think that it's the lower stage or the transitional stage to communism. But there's a whole school of thought that you can call "bourgeois socialism." It's the completion of the unfinished project of modernity. One major part of that project, and this actually speaks to something that I wanted to come at directly—in the "Challenges" document, at the end where you say there's kind of a start on secularism and then it's not until we get into socialism that we can really go all the way with that. I guess I feel that if I'm right, secularism is the production of pointless-ness. I'm sure you're not going to say that you want that either. But my point is that the world will never see anything better at this than capitalist society, or "more evil" at this than capitalist society.

A text of Marx's that has probably been the most central one to me in recent years and that I've concentrated a lot on is the *Critique of the Gotha Programme*. And even though there are tasks of socialism that include, and it's different in different parts of the world, but in some sense even the completion of bourgeois right, in order to transcend it, it's the "in order to transcend it" that we're ultimately about. By the same token, I think if we look at what we're about as trying to overcome bourgeois society and to begin to open up socialism as the transition, then it's not to complete the secular-bourgeois task that we're mainly about. It's to do something else. It's to have, and it can't be disconnected from wanting humanity to go on because it's terrible the way it's going now, and it has no, and we've said this many times, that ultimately, without being "inevitable-istic" about it, but, I still think it's right to say that ultimately, humanity won't have a future with capitalism. Obviously, lots of humans, individual humans, have no future, but even our whole species. So to get to be a part of this other unfolding, I call this "postsecular."

AVAKIAN: When I'm talking about secular, what I mean is people confronting, engaging, learning about, and changing nature, themselves, their interrelations, their interactions, their thinking, by themselves and by their own initiative, without the invention of illusory and imaginary means for attempting to do so. That's what I mean by secular. And I include in that people giving meaning and purpose to human existence themselves, out of the social conditions that they are enmeshed in and are transforming at any given time—the meaning will change in some ways as we go along. Even under communism, the sense of the specific meaning, aspects of the specific meaning, of human existence will change and will undoubtedly be viewed differently by people in the future. To use a somewhat awkward phrase, even a hundred years into communism it will be viewed differently than it will be to two thousand years into commu-nism, because they'll be in different places, to put it simply. By secular I just mean clearing away those things that obscure and obstruct human beings from doing that, including finding on their own, and without invention of some artificial means, the meaning and purpose to what human beings are doing and what their society is about at a given time.

I agree that bourgeois society is cold, but in slavery one person is literally the property of another person—and if that slavery is in the context of commodity production, as a lot of it has been, then you're the commodity of another person. Not your labor power, but you yourself. I read this book on the history of slave trading, which is actually an important book, because it is a polemic against the idea that slavery wasn't so bad. It was written quite a while ago actually, I think early in the twentieth century. [This book is *Slave Trading in the Old South* by Frederic Bancroft, first published in 1931.] This book was making the point that, when the slave owners would exhaust the soil, one of the ways they would make a profit was to raise slaves to sell further south and west, say from Virginia to Mississippi. They would raise slaves as a commodity to sell to plantations where they could still profitably employ them, where the soil hadn't been exhausted, etcetera. It was horrendous. The author was making the point—which I always like to think about when I hear all these literal as well as political descendants of the slave-owners talking about the "irresponsibility" of these women on welfare having "children out of wedlock"—here these slave-owners were not just encouraging but coercing these women slaves to have kids. They didn't care if they were married or not married. They wanted more commodities to sell, and then they would rip the children away from the mothers when they were eight, nine, ten years old and sell them all over the place. Part of this book was exploding the myth, the lie, that slaveowners didn't break up families and didn't sell small children. It was a very well-documented book.

The same thing under feudalism. You may have a place in the universe but your place, if you're the majority, if you're the peasants, is to be a beast of burden. And if you're a woman, a young woman, you can look forward to being raped and pillaged by the feudal lord on the night of your marriage to someone else—the Rite of the First Night, and all that kind of stuff. So that's a different kind of coldness. It's horrific too. We have to overcome all that—all the vestiges of anything oppressive that came before capitalism, and all the forms that are characteristic of capitalism too. Yes, to me there's plenty of meaning in that. It arises out of what we're confronted with. It arises out of what the society is straining toward, but it arises out of our need to make that a reality, too. To me that gives meaning. When religion has passed into art, [*laughing*] then it will be different. What I'm trying to say by that is that there is plenty of room, and there always will be, for the imaginary—but *as* the imaginary. When we are no longer asked to believe that the imaginary is literally true, is really reality—and not only that but is the essential and defining and determining reality—then I think humanity will be a lot farther ahead.

That doesn't mean that we won't need and won't have a purpose. I think we'll have a purpose that's "better," just to use that word. I won't hesitate to use that word. It will be better because it won't be obscured and obstructed by mysticism—in the sense of mysticism presenting itself as reality, as the defining and determining reality. Maybe we're not using secular in the same way. You're talking about postsecular; I mean postreligious, which doesn't mean post-*imagination*, or post-*wonderment*, or post-*awe*, and all those kinds of things. I think humanity never should and never could get along without or do away with those things. I'm looking for a postreligious society. I'm looking for when humanity gets to the point where it doesn't need religion, which doesn't mean humanity doesn't need or won't have a purpose. But it will be one that humanity itself will establish—and will change even, but will continually recreate on a new basis.

MARTIN: Yes, there are differences in how we're using "secular." There are probably differences in how we're using "religious," but I don't mean that to be a squirrely way to try to get around the point you're raising. I think I would want to go further in the formulation of something you said, in that we find meaning and purpose in the struggle. I actually think there's a sense in which we can *only* find meaning and purpose in the struggle. It's only in the struggle for, and again I realize it's a very vague term, but the *ongoingness* of humankind, and the things we need to do to try to secure this ongoingness, including, and we're not just *including*, but very centrally *solving* the problem of production in that very, very broad sense that Marx gave to us and that wasn't reductive at all, even though sometimes people want to say that it was. That we can secure our place here where humankind doesn't have to scrap over the basic necessities of life. And then humanity can in a certain sense orient itself more toward the imaginary, as opposed to just holding, trying desperately to hold body and soul together.

So, if anything gives meaning to our lives today, it's that we take part in that, even though, including people who do it in ways where maybe that's not even their conception of it, just to be sort of broad-minded and generous about it. As opposed to— I sort of joke with my students, especially when I teach, when we do a course on Marx, that bourgeois, sort of suburban middle-class kind of idea of, "at least I got to do X in my life", like "at least I got to go sky diving," or "at least I got to play in Carnegie Hall." "I'd like to be able to say that at least I did so and so." What's funny is, who were you planning to say that to, ultimately, St. Peter or somebody? [*laughing*] What's the meaning of that? You think about people who do extreme sports, and the idea is to confront an existential condition and it's the sort of thing where . . . sometimes we find ourselves confronting some extreme conditions. Some of us do things like ride bicycles or whatever where we might get run over by a car someday. But we're probably not going to go out and purposely do the things where, "Man, you could get killed, and that's what makes it so cool!" [*Avakian laughs*] Because we want to live our lives for something else. And we know that if we're lying there two seconds away from death having ridden our mountain bikes off the side of a cliff because we were trying to negotiate some very iffy passage there—we're not going to be able to lie there and say, "That gave meaning to my life, because at least I got to do X."

I want to go back to the whole question of mortality, in the sense that for me there has to be something like a redemptive scheme to what we're doing, in this sense: If ultimately what we can hope is that the point of human existence is that there has been a long, long struggle and one that in our time is exceedingly painful, to achieve a kind of conscious collectivity on this earth, then in some sense what we will have to take forward into the future with us is humanity itself. We would hope for a future when humanity is brought forward in some large sense into itself.

Humanity has a lot of wounds, and I think there's a sense in which ultimately it's right to speak of the body politic healing, and that if it doesn't have a sense of that, then it won't heal. The other reason is, it goes back to this very interesting exchange between two other Frankfurt School thinkers or people associated with that, one much more on the margins of it, Walter Benjamin and Max Horkheimer. There was a famous exchange between them, where Horkheimer was accusing Benjamin of being overly theological in his claims, in his thinking, and saying, "You have to accept that the dead are dead and will not rise again." And part of Benjamin's problem with that was that if we don't work toward a future that will also be a community of memory then what you get is a kind of triumphalism where the living live on the capital of the dead and reduplicate that relationship.

You spoke earlier of generations, and I think an aspect of that part of our mission of ongoingness, so to speak, is to bring the generations forward. And I guess I'm thinking, too, in terms of something you wrote in *Preaching From a Pulpit of Bones* where you were talking about something that Jim Wallis had said about being in a cemetery and thinking . . . How did that go?

AVAKIAN: That is my interpretation—that he's talking of "the noble long-suffering quality" of the people.

MARTIN: But that in some sense there's almost satisfaction in knowing that that's redeemed "on the other side," so to speak. Isn't that part of what you were . . . not redeemed, but at least in his Christian framework, that at least God will take care of them now.

AVAKIAN: Right. That they had suffered long, in this veil of tears, but then they would be rewarded.

MARTIN: I don't believe that in part because I don't think that's any answer really to their suffering . . . and I do think it's mere theodicy. Since I don't believe that, what I believe instead is that the community of the future has to be a community of memory in some sense for those who have, for all of humanity who has lived and suffered through what it will take to get to the future. Otherwise we'll find ourselves on that bright day, so to speak, in a kind of triumphalist state of, "Gee, the past was bad, but it's gone."

It's the sort of thing that I associate with secularism in the sense of the Clinton theme song, using that Fleetwood Mac song, "Don't stop thinking 'bout tomorrow, yesterday's gone, yesterday's gone" —you know, "It's all gone; now let's party." I think in some sense that's actually the return of capital itself because what it means is that the future will just use the past as fodder and that that will actually reduplicate itself in some form. That's why I think ongoingness has to be a kind of redemptive scheme.

AVAKIAN: I'm not quite understanding why the future would repeat the past—as you're speaking of it.

MARTIN: Because the living would live off of what has been accomplished by the dead, basically. Which I think is on some level unavoidable. That's how it works, so to speak, but on another level, if we don't give that its due, and take it up into ourselves . . . I'm just thinking again of these people where I wish some "hand" could have just reached down and caught them—that we actually have an obligation in some sense that they live through our human ongoingness in the future.

AVAKIAN: I guess I'm tempted to fall into the somewhat philistine response of saying, "We can't do anything for the dead—they're dead." That's literally true. But you're obviously trying to speak to something beyond that, so I don't want to respond that way. But I'm trying to understand. There's a way in which I was trying to speak to that in "Great Objectives and Grand Strategy," in terms of putting our arms around the past as well as around the diversity of humanity—that we don't just negate the past. We have to bring forward those aspects of it that we can learn from and build on, and also that we can recast and resynthesize, as we go forward. But it seems like you're speaking of something different than that, or something that maybe has to do with that but from a different angle. I'm missing something here.

MARTIN: I find it hard to understand myself. So maybe it's foolish of me to try to introduce it. But, maybe we could just approach it through the idea that there are wounds, where in some sense they're not healed, and that means that the past continues to be a reality among us, and if we don't attend to it as such, as opposed to just . . . it's a little bit on the model of personal relationships. Suppose one is in a personal relationship, or a familial relationship, that's very difficult. On one level, you could just move out, so to speak, move out of the apartment or the house, move away from your family. On another level where can you go? It's still in there. I don't mean to be heavily psychoanalytic. My mind doesn't go that way, anyway. But I think there is something to the idea that, "It's still in there," and if you don't attend to "it," it'll be in there and it'll be doing things and it'll structure the way . . . just like people who go, who leave one relationship like that and go right into another one. Because it's in there, and "it" has structured them. I think that actually is a real problem for our ongoingness and for our conception of the future, the way in which in some sense, that what ultimately is aimed for is a kind of redemption of this long struggle of humanity in that future.

AVAKIAN: I guess I can see an aspect, going back to what we talked about (it seems like a long time ago) earlier in our discussion, for example the history of genocide or near genocide, slavery, the reparations issue. The way we tried to address this in our *Draft Programme* is that there are things that weren't done by the proletariat—the proletariat itself has been brought forward out of the same process, again not some foreordained process, but the same process that brought forward all these other horrors, and in its self-conscious expression the proletariat represents the negation of the systems that have brought that forward—but that doesn't mean that in coming to power the proletariat can just say, "Hey, that's not us. We didn't do that, so that's not our responsibility." We still have to assume responsibility for deep wounds and scars from the past in various ways, including around national oppression and other things. We have to do something to compensate for the past, or there won't be the future we're talking about. In that sense I can see the point. I can't see it in a theological sense, but I can see it in that sense. That it's more complex than just, "Okay, let's go forward now—all that was done by somebody else. Hey, that wasn't us, you know." Even though, if you want to put it that way, the proletariat has more right to say that than some of these privileged white people who are still living off the historical results of slavery and wanting to claim that they have no responsibility for any of it. But we do—the class-conscious proletariat does—have responsibility for everything. The irony is, though—here's the acute irony— that the healing of humanity right now is proceeding through antagonistic expressions. First, it has to go through these antagonistic struggles.

MARTIN: Right.

AVAKIAN: And the proletariat has to defeat the bourgeoisie. It has to lead the people broadly, and ultimately all of humanity, to completely, as we say, cross over and beyond the horizon of bourgeois right and every form of exploitation and oppression before there can be a unified humanity—which won't be one undifferentiated mass, it will still have contradictions within itself, but it will not be characterized by antagonistic divisions. It will be "brought together again" in that kind of way, as humanity, even though with great diversity and with contradiction and with the new still emerging and struggling with the old, and right and wrong, and all that sort of stuff still being motive forces.

But that's the other thing, going back to your point about mountain biking—that example of "at least I could say I did this or that"—that goes back to Marx's point about being a social animal, that it's really only in a social context, and actually subordinating yourself to the larger social good, that you can find the fullest expression individually. And all these bourgeois ways of trying to . . . part of the reason I think a lot of these youth from the more privileged strata do things like get on a motorcycle and go as fast as they possibly can to see if they can escape death is because, ironically, their lives are privileged and they have no purpose—they're dissolute in a certain sense. This is not a personal condemnation of the individuals, but they're bound up in parasitism and they have no meaning that really sustains people. So they're looking for some sort of meaning, ironically. You'd think that it would only be people who have the least who would have the least fear of letting go of everything. But in another sense, this is an odd expression of "having too much," in the context of society and in relation to the general condition of the masses of people and of humanity. You're in this privileged position, but it's parasitic and it's unfulfilling. Even though people try to fulfill themselves, still it's unfulfilling. I think that's why a lot of these youth go and do these kinds of "daredevil" things. I mean, partly it's because they're youth—and we don't want to sound like old fogies, [*laughing*] you don't want to be an old fart—but it's not just that they're youth. The specific form this takes reflects their social position. There are other sections of youth, more of the basic masses, who go around getting caught up in killing each other and stuff. For them, it's not just the money. It's not just the competition for who's going to regulate this corner to sell drugs, or whatever. They're also, in an ironic sense, looking for some meaning. And under this system this often takes a very perverse form.

I think of this statement by Edward Luttwak, in his book *Turbo Capitalism*. If you want to talk about a stinging indictment of the system, here's a big apologist, one who celebrates the capitalist system, and yet he says, point-blank, that for millions of youth in the inner cities, leaving aside any alleged pathology, a life of crime is a rational choice, even taking into account the possibility of long prison terms or an early death. So what kind of system have you produced? What kind of system are we living under, where for millions of youth a life of crime is a rational choice? You want to talk about an indictment of a system. All this is owing to the same system and social relations and the influence of the same ideology, but it takes a different expression among the more privileged youth. I think what all of this really illustrates is that only by completely abolishing this system, and moving beyond it, can people's individuality even get fully expressed, and can their lives take on a meaning that actually can sustain them. And there is also that dimension of everything that has gone on, throughout the world, as part of what we have to take into account—that's what I meant by putting our arm around the past and around the diversity of humanity—there's a lot of complexity, a lot of diversity, there is the past and there are, in that sense, the wounds of the past, the consequences of the past, and it isn't just "Okay, everybody march forward now. Let's forget about the past." In that sense I can see it. We have to overcome the consequences of the past, even while we bring forward what is positive from the past and recast and resynthesize it as we're going forward.

So that's as far as I can go in understanding that point. Maybe you're getting at some whole other thing that I'm still missing, though . . . I did want to—maybe we've talked about this indirectly, since I did raise this quote from *Humanism and Its Aftermath*, the Wittgenstein thing about, "It's not how the world is that's a miracle, but *that* it is": have we spoken to that indirectly, or is that a whole other thing we really can't get into here?

MARTIN: I see that as an expression also of, what in philosophy is called the "question of being." I think Leibniz gave the formulation of it that's usually taken up, and Heidegger takes up that formulation of it—"Why is there something rather than nothing?" And the idea I think both on the part of Heidegger and Wittgenstein is that that's in a certain sense a kind of limit question, of science. That you can investigate the "something," but as to the why there *is* something rather than nothing, then to the extent you can talk about it, science isn't going to help you.

Part of what's interesting about that, and I'm almost afraid to try it out on some of my Heideggerian colleagues, is that quantum mechanics now seems to give something like an interesting answer to this. It goes back to something you were saying earlier about the infinity of the world, whatever edge you go to and try to look over, there's more of it, and even though I don't agree ultimately with the positivist response to that, there's sort of a point to saying—not to saying that it's just meaningless, "Don't ever, let's don't talk about that again, I don't want to hear that question coming around again," but more that there is also a point to saying that infinity in some sense is just not of our ken, except insomuch as we go further out into it. But in terms of thinking, if you're saying to me, "Gee, how can you wrap your head around infinity?"—well, I don't know, because I don't have an infinite head. [*laughing*] Sometimes we get puffed up and think we have infinite heads. Then infinity and the part of the world that's even much "closer in" than infinity tells us otherwise.

Quantum mechanics has started to lend more credence to what's called the "many worlds interpretation" in physics, and there are many interpretations of the "many worlds interpretation." This physicist, what's his name?—Lee Smolin—argues for a kind of "Darwinian" view—some universes make it, some don't, but in principle there's no limit to how many of these there can be, and to say that in principle in some sense is to say the world exists because it can exist. And that gets out there a little bit beyond what I can imagine conceptually, to be honest, I mean I think it's fascinating that there are people who can actually pursue the mathematics of it, so to speak, the physics of it. That's awesome. I think that a comeback to that from the perspective of the idea that it's not the how that it is that's a mystery, it's the *that* it is, would be that to say well, quantum mechanics gives something of an answer, by saying the "that it is" is "that it can be." I think Heidegger and Wittgenstein would say that's to beg the question because then we'll just ask, "How can *that* be? Why is it that way and not some other way?" On some level I take that sort of question as being heuristic, or a sort of stand-in for the idea that for however far scientifically we push the barriers back, there will be infinitely more, and that it's that infinity that in some sense also structures our purpose. Even just in the simple sense of, gee, I hope we're around to find out more and more. I hope we will find out someday if there's life on Mars. I hope we will find out someday if someone else is out there, all of those things. I hope we'll be around to do that. I hope we'll have a worthwhile society to present to them when we do find that out. I don't want guys showing up in flying saucers and saying, "Why did you tear down that forest? Why did you cut down that forest?" "Oh, because we own it." "Oh, you own it. Okay, there's a good reason. You own it." I hope someday that happens, that we'll have a decent society to show whoever else is out there, and that inspires me also. So, just as it's inspiring in Mao's last message to Jiang Qing, where he says, "Human life is limited but revolution knows no bounds," I find that cosmic sense of infinity tremendously inspiring.

I think this is enough from me on this question. My faith in the future, and sometimes my faith in the future against all odds and everything that this society sets up to make me, to make all of us sometimes find it hard to have that faith . . .

AVAKIAN: Just to put out my final point on this: We hope that humanity will be around to pursue infinity—if not infinitely, then at least for a long time. One thing we do agree on—and there's a lot more to be said and explored about this, so I'm not putting this forward as the end point—but the future of humanity and the meaning of existence for humanity has to be, can be, and will be forged by humanity itself. That's an important point, out of all this.

MARTIN: Amen. [*both laugh*]

AVAKIAN: Before we move on, there's this question: We've given different definitions of what we mean by secularism. I've tried to define what I think is a positive and important meaning to secularism. What do you think about that? You've spoken of a negative secularism. Is there a positive secularism along the lines I've spoken to, or is something else needed?

MARTIN: Yes. If secularism means or includes, just to be blunt about it, that humanity has to "do it for itself"—it's got to be humanity, if there's meaning, we're going to make the meaning.

I believe that, too. I absolutely agree with that. Just two very straightforward, simple things.

One thing I really love about Marge Piercy's novel, *Woman on the Edge of Time*, is that it sets up this question of the call of the future very nicely. Because, as you know, the scenario is a woman who's been institutionalized. She gets out but she has a history of that, and she's visited by somebody from a future society that I suppose just for shorthand we'd call in some sense "utopian." And the worry, though, is that there's an awareness that there's another timeline in which it doesn't work out that way. The question is, the call of *which* future? And the call of "the future that has a future," if I can be very redundant about it. What is the *physics* of that? Interestingly enough the novel raises the idea that there's a physics of that, so to speak. I mean there can be many timelines from this point. We want to try to get us on the right one. That's what I'm ultimately interested in, is the call of that future, and our answering that call.

So that when we talk about the idea that it's up to humanity, it is up to humanity, part of what it is up to humanity to do is to answer the call of that future.

The other thing is just that Kant, in the famous essay "What is Enlightenment?"—"An Answer to the Question, What is Enlightenment?"—describes this as . . . basically, enlightenment is maturity. It's when humankind in some sense doesn't need God to be speaking to it on a level of, "This is what you ought to do to sort out your affairs." But more, "You're on your own. Now there's stuff you've got to sort out for yourselves." And apart from, just leave God out of that, so to speak, for Kant that's the good side of secularism, too. That humanity is now in a position . . . In some sense, when he was talking about autonomy, he means, and this gets refracted through a Eurocentric framework that I don't want to accept either, but humanity is reaching a point where it's got to confront itself and sort itself out. And that is what I believe. That humanity has to sort itself out. If that's secularism, then I think that's the good secular.

21

Sexuality and Homosexuality

MARTIN: I want to get into the question of homosexuality, and some of the analyses that the party has had around the question and some of the more recent turns that have been made on this question. We've talked a lot about the question of ethics and its role. One thing that's interesting about that is the way that sometimes in the past it seemed as if something called "proletarian morality" turned out to focus a good deal on sexual morality, so to speak, and, of course, relationship questions in general, and very much oriented toward the woman question, which is very important. But I know for myself, and just from some of the experiences I've had and others I know have had, I've felt like I got to a place to where I just didn't feel a lot of trust on this sort of question, and in fact actually a good deal of distrust, and I know that this gets "personal," so to speak, but I think not just in a bourgeois individualistic way, because these are issues that are intimate issues, and they're bound up with our direct experience with materiality, in our embodiment. And I think it also gets into the question of conversations that will tend to be nonreciprocal and where authoritarianism and top-downism are real problems. And I want to open that up. I wanted to come at the question, or I'd love to hear what you've got to say on this question, in and of itself as regards homosexuality. But also I want to look at the methodology that seemed to be behind the previous line and the way that the new line on this question came about, and whether . . . because I wonder whether in some sense on the surface the line is changed, but I'm worried that a kind of reductivistic methodology is still at work behind the line even though I think it's very good that the line has changed.

In the past it seems to me that there's been this idea that an organization (such as the party) could have a doctrine or a line on homosexuality without really having any kind of developed analysis of sexuality or embodiment or desire generally except at the most general level of saying that these are historically-conditioned phenomena, they relate to classes, to class struggle, class interest, etcetera. [Even though the party stated that it opposed discrimination against homosexuals, for a long time and until recently the party regarded homosexuality per se as a negative phenomenon.] On the specific question of homosexuality it seems to me that the new material that's been put out is good, and of course I affirm the change in the line. But I think it doesn't do two things that I wanted to see in this material. And one, just to pose it sharply, is that it didn't really explain, to me anyway, it made a few comments on this, but in some ways they were to me very cursory and just didn't do enough of something I thought needed to be done, which is to explain why it took twenty-five years to get anywhere on this question, and even more, why it didn't offer an apology that I think is needed, for what I see as really messing up on this question for twenty-five years in such a way that a lot of people were alienated.

And again, not to be personal about it, but I myself had some estranged relationships, including ones that were very important to me, not only because of this, I mean, gee, if only I could lay all of my relationship problems on this sort of thing, and I clearly can't, and I struggle with the woman question myself and I mean materially in my life and how I try to live my life. But even so because of working with this policy, there has been this estrangement (or at least the estrangement has been related to that). In the kind of milieu where I tend to work, with intellectuals and artists, I've felt a need for a kind of constantly defensive posture on this. It seems to me that the damage the previous line did was really quite large and that it goes way beyond just the question of homosexuality per se, or for that matter beyond the question of particular people who are gay.

And then second, what I think is perhaps even a greater problem is that I think the line has changed but I'm not sure the outlook that was underlying the line changed. I worry that changing the line on the surface but without digging deeper can just be one way of keeping the basic, what I see as the basic reductivism that led to the line in the first place intact, and to me this is a good case where historically people have a right, even a responsibility, to fear philosophical reductivism, because it leads to authoritarianism within structures, organizations, states, what have you, whatever kinds of structures. Because it hits people in a very intimate way.

And I think certain strands of the history of the international communist movement bear this out, with very bad consequences, and I've seen in the past times whenever the term such as authoritarianism is raised there is a tendency to just say, "Engels said that a revolution is the most authoritarian thing there is," and I just don't buy that as a very good response on this kind of question. I suppose that a more simple gloss on this is that people are rightly suspicious of any attempt to mess with their sex lives, so to speak, for all kinds of good reasons. Of course, people should aim at relationships of mutual respect and, of course, nonrespectful behaviors toward other persons, and especially women in the context of the kind of patriarchal society we have, is not just a "private matter," and I don't mean to imply that it is. But beyond this it seems to me there's a basic *fraughtness* to intimate relations that can't be gotten around by some uniform set of rules, or [you can't] just think that you can really describe what goes on in real relationships, which is why even in bourgeois society, attempts to get the law involved in some aspects of this look really screwy.

I frankly feel, by the way, that there was something about the previous line on this that was shaped by the historical experience of the sixties, where a kind of indulgence turned into a seventies form of puritanism and workerism.* This doesn't mean there weren't aspects of the previous line that were largely correct or at least were concerned with the right things, as regards both patriarchy and some sort of hallowed public/private distinction. But it was also indicative of the sort of reductivism that attempts to capture hugely complex particulars under a too straightforward and simple set of categories. So that's a lot to respond to, I realize.

AVAKIAN: Well, there are lot of important points there, and I'll try to speak to them as best I can. Besides what's in our *Draft Programme* on the question of homosexuality, we did put out a position paper to amplify and elaborate on that position in the *Draft Programme*, and this position paper has also been put

---

* By "workerism" I mean a narrow and superficial sense of "working class culture."—BM

online. But here I can't go fully into that position in anything like the way the position paper does. It sets forward what our previous position was, how we've come to a different position, what the essence of the position is now, and it tries to sum up why we made the errors that we did, and at the same time indicate that we think that this is an ongoing process of learning more about it. So that's kind of the backdrop, because I can't—it's a forty-some-page position paper, and in the time that we have, I can't hope to try to even summarize all that. But I will try to speak to what I think are the important points that you raised, as best as I can.

On the first point, of having a doctrine without having any developed analysis of sexuality, or embodiment, or desire generally, and also why—there's also the question of why it took so long. Our position did go through several changes over a number of years. On your suggestion that this is a matter of sixties indulgence turned into seventies workerism/puritanism, that's something we should think about and look into further—there may be some aspects of truth to that, in terms of what our position was at the time the party was founded, which was in the mid-seventies, in 1975. First of all, I just want to say that our position has always been—and if you look through the pages of the *Revolutionary Worker* over the years you'll see this brought out very sharply—it's always been to oppose discrimination, pogroms, brutality, government repression, bedroom policing, etcetera. We've always been actively opposed to that and have done a lot of exposure against it. Within some corners of the movement, there's been a certain amount of, a fair amount of, distortion about that, and I think it is important to make that clear.

At the same time, we did have a position that went through changes. In 1975 we more or less put this phenomenon [homosexuality] in the category of being part of the decay of imperialism—although some time after that we summed up that this was way too crude, a vulgarization, an incorrect analysis of a very complex phenomenon, and we started doing more looking into it. And there was a two-line struggle in the party shortly after—only a couple of years after—it was founded, which came to a head over the question of what stand to take on what had happened in China, what was in fact a reactionary coup in 1976, after the death of Mao. And that concentrated a lot of issues, including a lot of this workerism that you're talking about. Not that the party as a whole was free of that, but it was particularly concentrated in the people who took a stand of supporting the revisionist coup in China. So when we had a struggle that led to a complete rupture with that, we also began, as part of the whole trajectory and momentum of that struggle, to reexamine some other things in light of that. And this question of our analysis of and stand on homosexuality in its various expressions was one of those things we began to take a look at. But it was still the case that, even after that internal struggle, the Programme we adopted at the beginning of the eighties still treated this phenomenon as a part of the decay of imperialism. Nevertheless, shortly after that, and as a result of continuing struggle against workerist and related tendencies, we began approaching the question of homosexuality differently than we had previously—seeing it not as a matter of the decay or decadence that comes with imperialism, the urban decadence of imperialist parasitism or whatever, but more looking at it in light of how it relates to the oppression and the emancipation of woman (or how it relates to sexual relations generally, but within that, how it relates especially to what is pivotal to sexual relations in this society, which is the woman question). So that was a key change we began to make, looking at it more in that light.

For example, in the article we wrote in *Revolution* magazine (I think by the time we actually published it, it was 1988) we did attempt to make some analysis of the "love question" more generally and to situate the question of homosexuality within that. But it was partial, and at the same time, even though we were trying to examine it with some new eyes, we were also carrying along some incorrect methodology—our outlook and methodology was marred by some incorrect assumptions and some incorrect approaches.

This came out, as one aspect, in relation to the question of the role of biology in this. We had a tendency, from what we knew, to not accept the idea that this was biologically determined. Now, we didn't do nearly the research at that time that we've done since, and there's much more to be done, even into that aspect of it—looking at the biological studies. Plus, there has been, independently of us, a lot more study of that whole phenomenon—the biology of sex, the biology of particular sexual expressions—there's been a real leap in how much of that has been done from, say, the late eighties up to the present time (more or less the last decade plus a few years). So we looked into it some back then, but not nearly as thoroughly as we've done since—and we still have much more work to do in that sphere, we recognize. But a serious methodological problem came out this way. We were approaching this by saying, "Well, it doesn't look to us like this is biologically determined" and—here's where the reductionism came in, or at least one manifestation of it—we said, "Well, therefore, it's a matter of conscious choice. That's the way it presents itself to people." We knew of a number of women who had made a conscious choice to be lesbians, rather than being heterosexual, and we kind of generalized off of that, to conclude: that's the way it presents itself not only to lesbians, lesbians in general, but to gay men, to homosexuals, in general—this is a choice they make. And, along with that, we made a further methodological error, which was to say, "Well, since this is a conscious choice, this is essentially an ideological question." And, following that logic, we concluded: for men who make a conscious choice not to enter into intimate relations with women, this means that they're consciously rejecting women, and therefore it's a kind of concentrated statement of misogyny. And, not surprisingly, just as there are among heterosexual men and in heterosexual relations, many concentrated expressions of misogyny, this can be found also among male homosexuals. But, again, we were making these unwarranted leaps and these reductionist conclusions, applying some reductionist, mechanical methodology, first of all to say it's a conscious choice, because it's probably not biological in most cases. And, second of all, it's a conscious rejection of women, on the part of male homosexuals, and therefore it's a concentrated expression of misogyny.

With regard to lesbians, we have always said that this is a different phenomenon, but we saw it as an incomplete and essentially reformist attempt to deal with the oppression of woman by simply avoiding men in any kind of intimate way and having intimate relations only with women—and therefore it doesn't really measure up to the oppression of women, it's not a solution to the oppression of women—although, as we've since recognized, and stated, most women who are in lesbian relationships don't make any such claims, that this is an answer to the oppression of women.

We have gone back to this, we have continued to wrestle with the question overall. But then we came to a point, toward the end of the 1990s, of saying we should come out with a new Programme—for various reasons, not primarily because of the homosexuality question but because of the overall development of the world and recognizing that, while there are many good things in our party programme from 1981, basically there are many things that have changed. Some things no longer apply; the world situation is different, plus we have learned a lot, so we really needed to come up with a new Programme, which we've now done in draft form, to take into account those changes, both what's happened objectively and what we've learned, what the communist movement has been through and what lessons can be drawn out of that, as well as what the world has gone through and what lessons can be drawn from that. So, when we did that, that became a concentrated occasion to reexamine a lot of questions. And there had been a lot of questioning and struggle within the ranks of the party on all levels, as well as criticism from outside the party, about the question of homosexuality—the party's position on this—so this was one of the main questions we focused on, at that point, looking at it in a much broader way than we'd been able to do before and looking again at all the various criticisms from outside as well as what was coming from within the ranks of the party itself.

At that point we did go back and try to do a much more broad and deep study of, among other things, the question of the biology of sex and the various studies that purported to show that different kinds of sexuality, including different kinds of homosexual attraction and so on, were biologically based. We also went back to study the history of sexuality, and homosexuality in particular, more broadly. It's not like we had ignored the history of the question, we'd looked at certain historical experiences before, but we tried to do a much broader and more sweeping study of the history of it and what other people were saying about it, what other scholarship and study had been done on it. As a result of this—as well as some other methodological grappling we were doing in general, and further summation of shortcomings in the history of our movement internationally (with Stalin, the whole Lysenko thing, for example) and trying to understand more fully what led to those very serious errors of instrumentalism and reductionism and so on—

all that kind of came together and we saw that, with regard to the question of homosexuality, we've been vulgarizing on many different levels.

What we have now come to understand more fully, to this point, is that while our study has still led us to believe that, speaking of this as a general phenomenon, it does not seem to be something that's primarily biologically determined, it is a complex question and there is more to learn about it, including about the biology of sexuality in general—sexual attraction and many different aspects of it. We are not convinced by what studies we've read (and we did do some fairly deep and systematic study of what's been done so far) that homosexuality is primarily biologically determined. We saw a lot of problems methodologically and otherwise with studies that attempted to show that this had a biological basis—either in genetics or in hormones, or something else, at various stages of development, even of the fetus, or of a person after they're born. So we are still inclined to think that this is more of a socially determined phenomenon.*

But, on the other hand, here again we saw the need to break with certain kinds of mechanical and reductionist thinking. For example, okay, it's a social phenomenon, or likely to be primarily determined by social factors—we think that's what the preponderance of the evidence points to, although we're still looking into the question more deeply—and the woman question is very influential in society in all kinds of different ways, including ways in which individuals themselves are not necessarily fully conscious of; but what we now recognize is that it would be wrong to say—to make the leap from that to saying—therefore, if men are attracted to other men sexually and not to women, that derives one to one from

---

* In the time since this conversation took place, in 2002, the RCP has continued to study this question and has come to the conclusion that it is not correct to say—that there is not a scientific basis to conclude—that homosexuality is more likely a socially-determined, rather than a biologically-based, phenomenon; in fact, as the RCP now recognizes, not enough is known to draw conclusions beyond the fact that both biological and social factors are involved in all human sexual attraction, that more needs to be learned about this whole subject, and that methodologically it is very important not to draw conclusions, or even to formulate "inclinations" of this kind, for which there is not a real, scientific basis.

the fact that the oppression of women is a pivotal and central and fundamental social relation in this society and pivotal to intimate relations generally in this society. We recognize that it's much more complex than that, and there are many different levels of it and many mediations of it. All men are influenced by patriarchy and the attendant ideology, but for some men who are very influenced by this, and even by outright crude forms of misogyny, it results in heterosexual attraction, while others are not attracted heterosexually but to the same sex (men). So there's obviously more than just the oppression of women when we talk about social factors. There are both individual experiences of people and there are also other social factors, besides the oppression of women, which go into all this. And while we still believe the oppression of women is pivotal, it's very complex and needs to be understood more fully than we understand it. There's a lot to be learned—more about the interaction of social and biological factors but also about the interaction of different kinds of social factors. Even if the oppression of women is ultimately pivotal, it's not reducible to that.

So this is what has now informed our position. That's a very thumbnail sketch. As I said, we put out a position paper that's forty-some pages long. I'm trying to condense that—it's difficult to do that—I'm doing the best I can, but the position paper is important to keep going back to.

Now, as to the question of why it took so long. I tried to speak to that a bit. It's true, it would have been better if we had recognized these errors and corrected them more quickly. Part of the reason we didn't is—this may sound tautological, but we didn't recognize our errors because we were using some flawed methodology. And we did make some changes previously: we moved away fairly quickly, at least in some significant measure, from some of those workerist influences, particularly after we had the rupture with the people who were fighting for a revisionist, economist line within the party, and who exerted some influence—not that they were entirely responsible for that. But while we made those changes, and moved to a position that I think was important and was different than the way a lot of people approach this—we put the question of the position and role of women in society, and their oppression in this patriarchal society, at the center of how you evaluate these things—we still had these reductionist and other methodological errors that I was talking about. So we didn't see some crucial things. We listened to criticism, but the criticism didn't penetrate. Partly, the criticism itself contained errors, but nonetheless we might have been able to assimilate what was correct in that criticism more readily and better if we ourselves weren't still proceeding from certain incorrect methodological approaches. You could say it would have been better if we had been able to shed those reductionist and mechanical, mechanical materialist, approaches earlier. And that's true. It's not that we don't listen to criticism. We do, but we didn't think the criticism was essentially correct because we were still proceeding from methods that didn't enable us to recognize what was correct, even in criticism that may not have been entirely correct itself, and to correctly assimilate that and arrive at a better synthesis.

As I said, certain things came together, including certain ways in which we were trying to critically sum up more of the history of the international communist movement—which, as you know, we've been trying to do over a whole period of time. But it kind of goes in stages, and with all the various responsibilities we were trying to assume—of actually being a vanguard party and trying to bring forward a revolutionary movement and ultimately the revolutionary overthrow of this system in this monster of an imperialist state—given all that, we were able to pay sometimes more, but also sometimes less, attention not only to this particular question, which is an important question, but also to other key things, including important history of the ICM [International Communist Movement] and major questions that are posed by the international movement, and challenges we face now, like all these major demographic and social-economic changes in a lot of countries in the world, the whole massive movement of a lot of the peasantry into the shantytowns, and so on. All these are big challenges not just for us, of course, but for the whole international movement, and particularly for the Revolutionary Internationalist Movement. But we were able to pay more, or less, attention to these different things at various times, as we tried to explain in our position paper. We did say, in that position paper, that it's probably true that it took us too long to come to this recognition of our errors and begin to make a serious rupture and leap away from and beyond them, and we have more work to do, as we recognize. But it was that whole combination of factors: some things in terms of the requirements on us, in trying to lead an all-around revolutionary movement, and some things having to do with our methodological shortcomings, which persisted for a while.

As for taking our responsibility around this seriously. We do take our responsibility as a vanguard and our responsibility to the masses and to the whole movement, including internationally, very seriously. I look at it this way: if anyone who has an influence on other people makes errors, then that's going to have a bad effect—it's going to cause problems in all kinds of ways. I think anyone who's trying to do right in the world, to put it in general terms—trying to analyze the world as it is and trying to change it in a way that leads to liberation for people— has a responsibility to understand the world as well as they can and to develop lines and policies and programs for changing it accordingly. That is what we did try to do. For one thing, you could say we took up a position that was extremely unpopular and stuck with it for a while, not because it was bringing us any short-term advantage, or that people liked us better for it. Not only did you have difficult experiences, but many people became alienated from our party over this question, although there may be other reasons why they did not agree with us, and there are various people who just don't like our party because of its revolutionary position overall, who jumped on this as a way to attack us.

MARTIN: You couldn't be accused of opportunism on this, that's absolutely for sure.

AVAKIAN: Yeah. But the main thing I'm trying to say is that it would have been better if we had been able to recognize our errors more readily. And had we recognized them, we would have changed our position earlier. We were doing what we thought we should be doing, and what I believe you should do—even if you're not a vanguard party, if you're a person who's trying to be responsible and to seek out the truth and to change the world in a positive way—you try to understand things the best you can and you act on that. You can't agree with things you don't agree with. If people raise criticism and you're not able, at the given time, to agree with that criticism, whether it's objectively correct or not, you obviously should not agree—it would be opportunist to say you agree with something just because it's causing lots of problems for you that you're sticking to a certain position. But it is your responsibility, if and when you do recognize that you're making an error, of whatever magnitude, to frankly acknowledge that error, to seek the means to correct that error, and to let people know that you recognize this error, what you understand about why you made that error and what you're setting out to do to correct it. So that you're accountable to the masses, but also so that other people can learn from the error you've made and the way that you're seeking to correct it. That's what I think we have set out to do and are doing.

I guess what I'm saying is that I don't think it's appropriate to talk in terms of an apology. This is not a personal thing. We weren't setting out to do it for personal reasons, or with individuals in mind. It wasn't something we did out of personal motivations. We have a responsibility to make a self-criticism, and that we have done. We also have a responsibility to continue to deepen our understanding of this, and if we come to more understanding of our errors, or why we made them, then we have a responsibility to make *that* public. Not because we want to beat ourselves up, or something, but that's your responsibility if you want to change the world and especially if you're assuming the responsibility of being a vanguard—which is what it is, it's a responsibility, it's not some sort of capital you're proclaiming. It's your willingness and determination to take responsibility for the whole revolutionary process. In other words, I think it's a matter of self-criticism, not of apology. It's not that we don't think it did damage, and it's not that we don't regret the damage that it did. But I think a self-criticism in the way we've done it, and not an apology, is more what's appropriate.

Let me give an analogy. There are parties and organizations, some with much greater influence than ours, who took a completely wrong stand on what happened in China and supported the revisionist coup. That's a phenomenon in many countries. In my opinion, as important as our errors on the homosexuality question are, what these people did around China caused infinitely greater damage, in terms of the struggle for liberating people. We've struggled with many of these different forces, but we haven't said, you should make an apology; we've said, you made an error, it's important that you correct the error and take the correct position, and then educate people as to what the correct position is and why you made that error. That's what I

believe the correct approach is. You have a responsibility to recognize your error—and, if and when you recognize it, to correct
it and let people know—both so that you're accountable to the
masses, as I said, but also so that people can learn.

That's the way we struggle with other people who have
made errors of a very serious nature. If you support the bourgeoisie and the imperialists when it comes to a head over who's
going to hold power in a country as significant as China, that's
a major thing. Again, that's not in any way to say that our errors
around the homosexuality question weren't serious, that they
didn't have serious consequences, that we don't recognize those
consequences, or that we're not upset about it and don't regret
it. We do. And we do take seriously our responsibility to correct
this in the most thorough way that we can, and to learn from it,
so that not only do others learn from the errors we've made, but
also that we don't make other errors, either around this question
or on a whole range of other questions, by making the same
methodological mistakes. I mean, we are going to make mistakes, but we should try to learn from and minimize our mistakes, and that's what we are trying to do.

Which, I guess, leads me to put a question back to you. I
understand your point—I want to talk more about this too, this
whole authoritarianism thing you raised. I think the Engels
quote is appropriate to use when talking about why you need a
dictatorship of the proletariat over the bourgeoisie. But I agree
with you, I would never use that statement about how a revolution is the most authoritarian thing there is in relation to—as
a way of answering—the danger of a party acting in an authoritarian way toward the masses. I agree with you that that's a
completely inappropriate use of that quote. I don't know exactly
what experience you're talking about, but that is not correct,
and I can see why hearing that would be infuriating. I just
wanted to say that on that point. We can come back to it,
because I do think the question you're raising about how this is
a particularly sensitive issue—I don't remember if you used
exactly that term, but I think that's what you're getting at,
because it does involve very intimate things, and one of the
things we did say in our position paper is (to quote it):

We, as Maoist revolutionaries, want to liberate all of human expression and social relations from the weight of thousands of years of

traditional (oppressive) morality and institutions. So when it comes to matters of sexuality, we do not approach things in the manner of a "bedroom police." We recognize the great variety and complexity of human sexual expression—including historically—and that the practice of human sexuality is not a static or unchanging thing.

This is part of the fuller and deeper understanding we've come to, not only on homosexuality in particular, but sexuality and intimate relations more generally. And we don't want to be, and we're not going to be, acting in the manner of bedroom police.

There is a legitimate fear. That goes back to the thing about authoritarianism. There is a bad history of this in some aspects of the international communist movement and there are errors that our party made that, if they were persisted in . . . as Lenin said, if you make an error that's one thing. If you make an error and then not only persist in it, but seek profound justifications for it, it can become truly monstrous. So there is that danger. That does intertwine with the fact that this is a very sensitive issue. I was going to ask you a question, but since I'm on this let me first try to speak a little more to this, and then I'll get to the question.

I think any society has to decide—at least any society that has laws, and mechanisms for enforcing those laws, has to decide—what it is that properly falls within the sphere of law. How will this be approached under the dictatorship of the proletariat? Let's take a very obvious case: rape should be a matter of law. It should be a matter of crime and punishment. You can't allow that to go on, and it's not merely a matter of persuasion. But that's a fairly obvious case. Then there are other things you decide should not be a matter of law, and the enforcement of law, but should be a matter of, let's say, mass campaigns, which (as I have tried to point out, for example, in "Great Objectives and Grand Strategy") involve an aspect of coercion. Even if it isn't a matter of the police, and the state, and the courts and everything enforcing the law, still mass campaigns are developed against certain practices, and that has an element of coercion. And rightly so. But then, as I've emphasized in some things I've written, you have to make judicious use of even that kind of coercion, and you have to sort out the appropriate time, place, and way for even developing mass movements around things, because it does involve an element of coercion—what people are doing is made the object of mass struggle and criticism. That involves an aspect of coercion. So even that has to be done judiciously. And this is not fixed and firm, but I would say there's a general third category of things which are neither a matter of law and the state, nor a matter of mass campaigns, but more a question maybe of mass education in which you raise the question broadly in society without a particular target. For example, women in oppressive relationships: some aspects of it you want to make mass campaigns out of, but others (and here I'm not thinking of things like physical abuse—that's another question—but of more "subtle" forms of oppressive personal relations) it's more a matter that, as society develops overall, as mass education is done around it, they decide they've had enough of this, and they want to stand up against it and refuse to put up with it any more, and then it's a question of supporting them in doing that. And even there you have to be judicious, but it's more a matter of that kind of a contradiction, if you want to put it that way.

So I see those as three broad categories: things that should be a matter of law and the repressive apparatus of the state; things that should be matters of mass campaigns, targeting certain particular practices if not particular people; and other things that should not be handled in either of those two ways but more general education should be done around it and then you support people when they stand up and say they don't want this or that particular thing anymore. It's always difficult to sort this out, and when you get to intimate relations, once again I agree, you have to be very careful about this. As we said in that quote I was reading from the position paper, we recognize that there's a lot of complexity to this question, and that's something we're learning more deeply through all the work we've been doing around this and listening to and trying to correctly absorb and assimilate the criticisms, or what we can recognize as the correct aspects of the criticism, deepening our understanding, because it is complex, and we do have to guard against not just authoritarianism in general but a crude handling of this, which can get way out of hand and can actually lead to real tyranny over people in ways that are very intimate—are right where they live, so to speak.

MARTIN: That's a good expression.

AVAKIAN: So I agree with the spirit of what you're saying there, and we're trying to continue to evolve a more nuanced understanding of this and understand the different levels of it. We're working up to the question I wanted to raise. One other thing I did want to say, just to give an idea of the complexity of this. Let's take the question of pornography. In the *Draft Programme* it says that pornography will also be outlawed. But then there's the question, what is pornography? You can't have a crude approach to that. It's not just pornography as an abstract category, but things that degrade women and contribute to the degradation of women. That burden has to be lifted to even begin to carry forward the struggle for the emancipation of women in an all-around way. What constitutes that is not something that can be decided by crude methods, to say the least.

Take the sphere of art: is everything in which some degradation of women is portrayed a bad thing? Not necessarily. It depends on whether it's exposing that, making that an object of criticism, or is it furthering it? Obviously, everything in which there is nudity is not pornography, is not oppressive to women. Even nudity of women may not necessarily be that. You have to be very careful, I agree with that. This is something we need to continue to understand more fully and deeply. You have to be very careful, and sometimes take your time. While you can't allow a lot of harm to be done, you also can't create a lot of harm by being crude. So we are trying to rupture more fully with any reductionist approaches, not only to the question of homosexuality but to intimate relations more generally.

My question is: what do you see as the remaining aspects of this reductionism, or ways in which the position has been changed, but only superficially, and it hasn't really changed in a more fundamental or essential sense?

MARTIN: First of all, I want to say that I did read the position paper. I thought it did address many of these questions in a good way. Someday it would be interesting to know more in detail (and I'm not saying it's a priority) the history of struggle out of which all of that came. Because you were describing not only the way that this emerged as a leap, but also some stages toward that, that occurred earlier that I have to admit, I not only was not aware of, but I don't know that they were particularly available publicly, or to me anyway. In some of the periods that you were describing, where some of these things were struggled over, I heard things that sounded, if anything, sort of the opposite of that. I'm guessing; of course I wasn't "internally" a part of this process, but I'm sure there were many who struggled with themselves over this line and how they could sit with it. Others went the other way, and maybe went a bit overboard. For example, a big part of the way the new line came about is to show that there's no essential connection between the oppression of women and whatever it is that has some people go toward homosexuality. Although that maybe does get a little bit at something I would see as having a kind of reductivistic side: when we ask why people are homosexual. I don't know—why are they heterosexual? I know some theorists in the past have called that a kind of "hetero-normativity." In some sense one question is just as good as the other; in fact there's no really getting into either one apart from the other.

But I know in the early eighties, someone said to me, "No wife-beater's going to get into this party, and no homosexual's going to get into this party." And then on closer prodding, they were willing to admit that, for one thing, it's not that likely that anyone who's homosexual is going to be a wife-beater, but they are not one and the same or anything like that. You had to wonder how did someone get in a position where that kind of seemed to trip off the tongue, one right into the other. This was a woman who said this to me, and I thought that was significant, of course. And I was maybe less inclined to be as angry about that, as if a man had said it, I suppose. But it just seemed to show something to me. And now I see the struggle to get beyond that sort of thing.

Another thing that was said to me sometimes was that, in a way, homosexuality, especially male homosexuality, was comparable to drug addiction. In fact, I had a long conversation with somebody where that was really set out as though that was a systematically understood point of view. And this person at the time was also saying, when we [the party] did have this earlier workerist orientation, we're breaking with that, and yet it seemed to be not only reductivistic but to be coming from a kind of puritanical mindset. Another aspect to this, another way to go into this, when you say you have to be judicious about dealing with these sorts of things, because we are talking about intimate relations . . . I think the term "sensitive" here is fine. I understand the problem, or I think I understand, I want to understand the problem that's being negotiated here in the sense that, how do we respect freedom in this area but without creating another hallowed private-public distinction and especially without putting ourselves in a position where we can't really raise the real brutalities of patriarchy and the ways patriarchal social relations shape people in ways that are very limited, mean, violent, etcetera. All of these things absolutely are important in themselves and we can't change society positively without confronting them.

But one of the problems with "you have to be judicious" is the question of who is the "you" who has to be judicious? This is why I raised the point about nonreciprocal kinds of conversations. If somebody wants, and I guess I'll be a little personal about it, if someone wants to get into where I live, I guess I want to know where *they* live. I want to have some sense of, I don't mean just in a one-to-one kind of "I've got to know your whole history before I'm going to discuss my history with you." But on the other hand, if people are put in positions where . . . I know I certainly was personally and I saw other people in this. It can acquire, and I'm not Catholic and I don't have any kind of Catholic background either, but it has a bit of a "confessing to the priest your shameful past"-sort of aspect. And I know for myself, it just made me feel that not only was there an authoritarian aspect of it, but also that I'm just not going to have those kinds of conversations in the future. We can talk about general principles, but I'm just no longer going to have any of those conversations because they are intrusive in ways that I just don't feel are helpful to anything. And so I guess it's more like, when are we getting on that sort of thing, or have we moved things forward on that sort of question? Or is it still a kind of outlook that betokens, I think, what would still look like a kind of authoritarian vibe about all of this? That doesn't entirely go into the reductionism question. To be honest, I think a lot of what you said before answered me on a lot of that. I'm happy if in a certain sense the approach is . . . and, *look*, I think there's a danger of reductivism that has to be risked on some questions, so I don't think what I sometimes call reductivism is that simple a question of, "Yeah, you just don't be reductivistic." We want to find out how things work, and if they're oppressive we want to find out how to unwork them, so to speak. And that means trying to zoom in on the way things work. And so, on some level, it's a good response to simply say, "And we're going to try to not be reductionistic about it, even while we have to try to get into the nuts and bolts of these questions." So I feel like a lot of what you were saying addressed a good deal of that for me.

AVAKIAN: I don't know the particular arguments that were made, that you were referring to, but I would say two things. Those kinds of arguments, those kinds of comparisons, were not what we were putting forward as an organization, as a party. That's on the one hand. Especially after the *Revolution* magazine article, which was published in 1988, it was more that we made an analogy to religion. I ran down what some of the basis of our position was analytically, and what the methodological errors were in that, in as condensed a way as I could, but the analogies we were making were more to something like religion: a phenomenon that should disappear, or that people would voluntarily give up, when we transformed oppressive relations, and waged ideological struggle, in socialist society, although we said homosexuality in various forms might reemerge in communist society. But at this point we don't see that that's either an objective—that homosexuality will disappear under socialism—or something likely to happen. Frankly, as we've said, while there has been some experience, positive and negative, around this, and around intimate sexual relations in general, in socialist society, that experience has unfortunately been way too limited. Unfortunately in the sense that we need a lot more experience in socialist society in general.

There's a lot we don't know. We say in the position paper: what are intimate relations going to look like in the future—who knows? One thing we do know is we're going to struggle to uproot oppressive relations among people and in particular those that shackle women and diminish and demean women and degrade them. And, through the course of doing that, we'll see a lot of different ways that people have of dealing with intimacy—as we remove the weight of that oppression and the thinking that goes along with it, a lot of different things will likely flourish. It's very likely some of them will be same sex and some of them will be heterosexual, and for some people it will be bisexual. There are many different phenomena and we're not trying to prefigure or predetermine what they will be. We do say that the point is—whether different individuals are engaged in one kind or another of sexual relations, same sex or heterosexual, the key thing is to transform these relations so that we uproot the oppression of women and we uproot oppressive relations in general and the thinking and ideology that goes along with and reinforces them. And then, as we do that, we'll see what flourishes. This is our program and orientation on that now. We did analyze, even in the 1988 *Revolution* article as well as in this position paper, the *social* reasons heterosexuality has been the predominant form of sexuality, or seems to have been, through most of the history of class society—having to do with the patriarchy and other factors. So there are reasons why that's predominated, but it's not a question of "one is more natural than that other," or something like that—in some sense other than social conditioning.

MARTIN: Well, it's unclear though whether you can use those terms over the broad sweep of history and cultures. I remember the first time I took a graduate course in ancient philosophy and a fellow student who hadn't really read much Plato before, it was funny to the rest of us when he asked the professor, "Professor, I really get the sense that Plato was gay." There's, of course, a real sense in which Plato or Socrates or whoever, well, they weren't gay, because "gay" is a culture-specific term of a modern society, probably of European society, it's more complicated than that, still. But in some sense you will make a reduction, I think if you see those as sweeping terms in the sense that on one level you could say that they just apply to dispositions of bodies and what kinds of bodies are next to each other and doing what sorts of things. But obviously sexuality is a vastly more complex issue than that. And very specific to cultures.

AVAKIAN: I agree, and that's one of the things we did point out in this position paper. Just to round out the picture, I wanted to refer to this one statement toward the beginning of the position paper, where it says: "People engage in sex in many different ways and for many different reasons. One of the main reasons is, of course, that sex (at least when it is freely engaged in) feels good." So I don't think we're coming from a puritanical approach to this—or to the degree that our position may have had aspects of that, we're certainly trying to break with that. I think our orientation goes along with the thing about not being bedroom police. Our approach is not to try to keep people from having fun! The other side of the picture, though, is that what people regard as fun does closely inter-penetrate with all these other social relations and can't be free of them. So we have to sort that out correctly.

For example, there's this group (I guess they're still around) the MIM, Maoist International Movement. They made the highly reductionist argument that all sexual relations between men and women are actually and objectively rape, because after all men and women aren't equal so therefore a woman can never . . .

MARTIN: The Andrea Dworkin position . . .

AVAKIAN: To me that's just the crudest kind of reductionism and confounding of different levels. There's the societal level of social relations in general, but it's like relations between white people and Black people: could you never have a friendship between somebody Black and somebody white, for example? Because there's inequality in this society, you could never have a genuine friendship based on mutual respect? That would be ridiculous. And the same for any relations—you can't translate from the general societal level of social relations to each partic-ular individual relation, either friendship or a love relationship, an intimate sexual relationship, whatever. Those are different levels. That's one of the things we've been coming to under-stand more fully. I think it's important that we continue to grap-ple with that. And I agree with you, some of these things you do need to get into, because the whole sanctity of the home, for example, a lot of horrors—molestation, sexual molestation, and just physical abuse against children—are committed in the home. It was only in the last decade, I believe, that in all states in the United States marital rape was actually declared to be rape and outlawed. I did some research into that when I wrote *Preaching From a Pulpit of Bones*, and at least up through the eighties, and maybe beyond that, there were some states where it was still not recognized as rape, was not a crime. So you can't have the sanctity of the home.

That's the other side of "we don't want to be a bedroom police." And that's true, we're not going to go kicking down doors to see who might be molesting their children or who might be abusing their wife. That's not the way you're going to resolve that contradiction. When individual cases emerge, or when there's a basis to believe something may be going on, then there are different ways to look into that, which don't amount to acting like bedroom police or anything like it. And which don't amount to and isn't motivated by saying, like Paul in the Bible, carnal urges and lust are bad: you should resist them if you can, but if you must do it, then have a marriage in which the man is supreme so you won't give vent to those urges in bad ways. We don't want to have anything to do with that kind of outlook, just as we don't want to have anything to do with perpetuating, and even in some ways furthering, relations between people that are oppressive, particularly of women, but also in a more overall sense. We do have more work to do on this, partly because we've got to continue to understand more fully—and rupture more fully with—certain errors; but also because, as I think you were pointing to, it's a very complex question. And it's not one to be easily handled. With regard to individuals, it's not a matter of going around and having people step into the confessional booth or whatever.

MARTIN: Let me just say one more thing about that and I'm done. Although I think what you said about self-criticism and apology was something I would agree with, and regretting what's been done here—and what can one do but to try to go on and have a better line? But there's an element in a certain sense, if I can put it this way . . . my gay friends would not forgive me if they knew we were having these conversations and I did not raise this issue. And that in a sense goes to a whole set of questions. But that's why we've had the conversation, and I think we've done some good things in talking about it. So my last little bit on this goes again to that nonreciprocity point, that people don't want the cameras in their bedroom. But in a certain sense, they don't want the camera in their head either, if you know what I mean. There are ways in which, so to speak, the camera gets in the head. Even if it's not in the bedroom; as if there's somebody watching, even if it's coming out of your own eyes, so to speak. And that was in a certain sense the atmosphere to some of the way this got talked about before. And I recognize this problem, that people have sex, one of the reasons people have sex—probably the best reason—is because it feels good. And I think it can feel good on a deep level. I like thinking about the fact that the Greek word "eros" doesn't just mean the sexual things, it really refers to a kind of embrace. To embrace other people I think is a fine thing, sexually and otherwise. You don't jump from that to the desire that's beyond politics, or where there's no politics of desire, to in other words, "If it feels good, do it." There's more to it than that. To somehow get in between those things, again it's very difficult. To have the kind of discussion around this that doesn't ultimately still just amount to people feeling repressed; I think that's an important thing, especially given the past, and actually not even mainly the history of this organization on the question, but the large history of the whole ICM that hasn't been on the whole very good on this.

AVAKIAN: Well, there is one thing I wanted to say along with the point that this was not how we put this forward—some of those arguments and comparisons you mentioned. There were problems with our arguments, but those were not what we were putting forward, as a party. On the other hand, what does happen when you have a line that is erroneous, and people are seeking to defend it, is that they are going to find themselves making arguments that don't stand up, because they're having difficulty trying to justify a position that's not correct. So, even though those lines and the argumentation that you were summarizing were not what we were putting out as a party, I don't doubt that in individual discussions those arguments may have been brought forward, as well as some others that were specious or just wrong in significant aspects, because people were in a position of trying to defend a position which objectively was not correct. When that happens, you find yourself grasping for arguments that don't really stand up. And some of them may be more than just wrong—they may actually be insulting and offensive or whatever.

MARTIN: And I want to criticize myself for that as well. And on this issue. I know there were times when I dug in, so to speak. And maybe more than was even needed, given the requirements of the line. I don't want to make this a unilateral, *j'accuse* kind of thing; I criticize myself on this as well.

AVAKIAN: Our party is, as I said, taking the responsibility to be a vanguard, so we have to take responsibility for our mistakes in a scientific and in an open way, and not resist criticism. If a criticism is made, even in a bad spirit, we still try to listen to it. If we don't agree with it, we have to keep thinking about it, but as long as we don't agree with it we can't embrace it, so to speak. So we just have to keep on learning, and we are trying to not only learn but to do better. And we're trying to apply the lessons not only to this question but more broadly. One fortunate thing, or important thing, not just fortunate, is that our party has never—I talked earlier about the CP expelling people for reading Trotsky—we've never tried to have, and don't want to have, an "opaque" party, where we discourage our members from reading what other people have to say about anything, including by way of criticism of our party. We do have a democratic centralist party, where everybody doesn't just go off and voice their own personal opinions outside the party. There are channels within the party for there to be criticism and struggle. But we also try to be very open to people—as well as having criticism and lively ideological struggle within the party, we try to listen and learn from people outside the party who in various ways raise their criticisms. And if we didn't listen as well as we should have in this case, it's not because we don't want to hear criticism, it's because we weren't able to recognize—for the reasons I tried to speak to, including the fact that we weren't able to consistently pay a lot of attention to this question on the level that would be required to really dig into it, to come to some different understanding—but for all those reasons, we just weren't able to recognize the correctness of the criticism as soon as we should have. It's true, we should have been able to recognize it sooner. But we didn't, and we should learn from that, too. On the other hand, or more generally—not on the other hand but more generally on this question—there are two points I want to speak to.

One is your point about reciprocity. Yes, there should be discussions among friends, comrades, whatever, about these questions in a way that is not accusatory or authoritarian on one side or the other. But, beyond that, we're a party that's seeking to lead the whole revolutionary process—and, as I said earlier, this means we will play, to be honest about it, a disproportionate role in terms of influence and even in terms of decision making in the early stages of socialism. Even while we're trying to move beyond that, it will still be a fact for a while. Therefore, we have a special responsibility to handle these contradictions well. And part of that, again, is learning to be judicious but also to learn when it is we should take more time and when and where we actually have to come to a conclusion. That's another important lesson that we're trying to learn with regard to a broad range of questions. How do you draw the distinction between those things over which you have to come to a firm conclusion—both because it's possible to do so but also because there's a need to do so—and those times and circumstances when you don't have to, and you shouldn't even try to, come to any kind of firm conclusions. Maybe you can form some tentative opinions and put those out for people to respond to, but mainly you should be learning more—you're at the phase where you should be learning more. That's another important lesson that we're trying to absorb more deeply as well. So, yes, I agree with the reciprocity point; but then, so to speak, that doesn't remove the special responsibility that our party has to apply the correct methods and correct approach to this and not a crude and heavy-handed one.

22
The Animal Question

MARTIN: There's a question that hasn't been raised much within Marxism of whatever kind. I suppose some would call it the animal rights question, and I would tend to just call it the animal question. On the face of it even, it sounds like something that—"Yeah, that's rather foreign to the kinds of concerns we have." I guess I want to make an argument for it being not foreign, or that it shouldn't be foreign. And part of that has to do, again, to go back to our old friend the ethical, with the status of the ethical. The animal question, so to speak, thematizes that, I think anyway, in a way that shows certain dimensions of the ethical question. Namely, in terms of a kind of fundamental concern for the other when the other, if I can put it in this loaded way, isn't even human, but this is instead a concern for systems that perpetrate what I think can easily be recognized as cruelty. And I mean toward animals. However, there are also dimensions of cruelty toward humans in the way that animals are used for food, from a nutritional standpoint, from a standpoint of what it gets people involved in to shape a food economy, the economy of food, primarily around the production of, I hate this term, but "food animals." Even just around the question, something that's been studied by sociologists, that people who tend to be cruel toward animals are the sorts of people who would tend to be cruel toward other people as well. That sort of thing.

I think I would want to push that to an even deeper level. And I'm trying to develop this argument under the theme, I'm taking my cue here from Sartre, who wrote a famous essay titled "Colonialism is a System," and I wanted to develop this under the theme of "carnivorism is a system." I'm not ready to make the leap to saying it's *the* system, or it's somehow the broadest category of the system, but I think it's integral to the kind of system that we have. I would even go so far as to say that, to repeat what a well-known philosopher and theorist of animal rights has said, Peter Singer, that the dinner table in the First World is the scene of tremendous cruelty. And not just family arguments, so to speak, but because of how the food economy comes together and the way that it comes together there at the dinner table. But carnivorism is also in a certain sense a "school" of cruelty and even a school for the idea that there's nothing one can do about cruelty in the world. So one thing we know is, and this is very common, there often comes a point with young people, and I do again mean this especially in the First World, where they suddenly realize that they're eating the leg of an animal. They realize that's a leg suddenly and not something that magically has something on it that they happen to be able to eat. Children often reject that, and their parents will often go to tremendous lengths to get them around that—whether it's by authoritarian parental pressure or something more like argument. Whereas I would want to say that I think a child's instincts on that are, I don't want to say a natural reaction, but their reaction in any case has truth to it—and that, actually convincing them otherwise is part of the general culture of saying either, "That's not really cruelty, because . . ." and then putting animals in some category where it's not only, "Let's not apply human categories to them, let's not 'anthropomorphize' them," but more like, "They don't feel it," or because of some supposed priorities in society, such that it's right to raise them in certain ways so that they can become food. And the children are sometimes told, "Well, yes, it is cruel, but you have to get used to the fact that this . . ." Sometimes people say, "Well this is a cruel world. It's an unfair world, and there's nothing really that you can do about it." It actually is a way in which our consumption of something that in a certain sense, to continue our discussion of intimate relations, what's more intimate than what you eat and digest and process through your body? It is in a sense a school for accepting that there just *is* cruelty in the world, and what can we do about it? It actually spreads out to all sorts of spheres of society. I don't expect that we'll answer this question here. Maybe we won't even go very far. But I think it's an important question to try to get onto the table. To get off the dinner table and get on to our philosophical table, so to speak.

AVAKIAN: There are a lot of different dimensions to what you're raising. It's hard to know where to start. I think, for one thing, we not only have to differentiate between human beings and other animals but there are many different gradations and qualitative differences among different animals as well—some of which don't even have a developed nervous system, some of which have highly developed nervous systems and some have some forms of consciousness (which we're still learning more about). And then there are human beings, who have a whole other level of consciousness—including that human beings, as far as we know, are the only species that actually takes up philosophical questions and debates these things. Human beings are not the only carnivores. Other animals do eat other animals. There is that phenomenon in nature, and mercilessly so. Not out of any cruelty but just out of their need to live themselves—that's the way they've evolved. But they don't have the same consciousness as human beings—the question doesn't pose itself for them, and it does pose itself for human beings. So, I'm not saying: other animals kill other animals, therefore what's the question? But I'm saying there are differences among different animals, and that has lots of ramifications.

Another facet of this is that we are at this stage of human society, we are at the end of a long chain that began with domestication of animals and everything that has flowed from that. Different people have analyzed this, including Jared Diamond but also people who are Marxists. We're in a world where at this point two things are important to keep in mind here. Well, three things. One, the way that food in general is grown and animals are developed as food under this system is, on many different levels, not the way we would seek to do things under socialism and ultimately communism. But there is a lot of complexity to this, and exactly what that would mean I don't know, to be honest. There is a lot of complexity and ground to be traversed between here and where we could actually take that up in a whole different way. And right now one of the problems we have in the world, a very acute problem, is that most people in the world don't have enough food and enough protein, and they don't have a lot of options about where they get their food and their protein. That's not to excuse anything that's done, but this is a real contradiction that we're confronted with, even now before we've made revolution, even now when we once again don't, yet, have a socialist country. So that's one thing.

Another thing is that there are many ways—leaving aside other animals, just speaking of human beings—that most of the things that are produced that are essential for people's lives are produced under conditions that are horrifically oppressive and exploitative for people, for human beings, including children. And yet we don't have the freedom, as a mass phenomenon anyway, to say we're not going to consume those items. Individuals can say that, but masses of people are not able to get enough of those items. Which, again, is not a way of saying, "Who cares, people have to eat, people have to have clothing, so who cares how it's done." But we do have to somehow take that into account. And we also have to take into account, just to be crude about it, that there is a difference between a chicken, or a fish, and a great ape. There are differences all the way in between. Going "lower down the scale," sponges are animals. Technically they are. But they're very different than not only a great ape but also a lamb. So the question can't be just animals in general.

The other thing is that these criteria, going back once again to what I was saying earlier, are criteria that human beings make. What is cruelty, for example, is a criterion that a human being makes, and as far as we know no other animal does that. So we have to keep that in mind as well.

MARTIN: On one level I agree with you, of course, but surely the animal makes that criteria when it resists being treated in a certain way. There's not any question about what's happening in that situation.

AVAKIAN: Yeah, but different animals react even to that in different ways. A great ape, for example, a chimpanzee, reacts with much more consciousness about that than even a dog does, for example. And, again, there are other gradations. So it's not just human beings and one undifferentiated mass of other animals. There are different levels of that. And there are some tough decisions that have to be made. I think we can agree in condemning gratuitous cruelty—in other words, inflicting cruelty just to inflict it. There are frat boys and stuff who get off on doing that kind of thing. Growing up, I knew people like that, who did horrific things to animals. And those are the kind of people who extend that to human beings too. It does desensitize them and . . . there is some connection there. Then there's cruelty that's inflicted—or pain that's inflicted—on other animals so people can have luxury items, that aren't really necessary and just are part of parasitism—which, again, from the point of view of the standards and all the things we've been talking about, we would think are bad. But then you get to some things that fall into a different, more complex category: food, clothes, medicine for people, for example, which, at this point anyway, we're not able to provide—they are not able to be produced and distributed among people—without involving animals as either being tested and suffering, for medical purposes, or being killed and consumed. If you could show me, or if I'm missing something here, in terms of how we could do this without any of that, that would be a different thing in my mind.

MARTIN: I think it's been well shown. Of course, there are a lot of people who write and research this question; I think it's been well shown. A great deal has been done to try to show that in the category of medicine, which I think could be maybe put up as the most difficult example, that animal testing isn't nearly as necessary to the point that it's made out to be. But then a lot of stuff that goes under that category that will be labeled as "for science" is something more like some new shampoo or something where it's hard for me to see how the justification could be made.

But in the food area, one can make actually the opposite argument. Given the amount of resources it actually takes to sustain a "food-animal" food economy, a lot more people could be fed if things weren't being diverted in that direction. It takes enormous amounts of water, it takes enormous amounts of grain to fatten up the cows and pigs to be eaten. If this sort of thing were stopped it would raise a whole other difficult question, namely, that these animals have been domesticated for that purpose, so then what happens? That's not an easy question either. But more production of food-animals, and again it's a term that I really dislike even though I'm the one using it, isn't the key to how will the world's people be fed in any case.

AVAKIAN: Well, let's say, for the sake of argument, that food, medicine, clothing, and other things that human beings now use animals to get, in one form or another, could—under a whole different set of social relations, a whole different kind of system—could be gotten better without using animals. Let's just say, for the sake of argument—I don't know whether it's true, to me it's a complex question that we're not going to be able to unravel right now—but let's just say that's true. There is still the problem of we're here and we're not there. We're not in a different system where we even have the freedom to take that up, practically. We can talk about how things could be done differently, but as long as we have the classes that we have in power—and the systems that they are both the expression of and also, on the other hand, that they are the ruling force and directing force of—well, I hate to sound pragmatic, but what's the practical effect, what's the conclusion, what does it point to, when we're not yet in a position where we can grow food a whole other way, even if we thought that it would be much better to do so, and maybe it would. But right now we're not in a position where we can make those decisions; and, as I said, there is too little food, too little medicine, too little clothing. And something else is true—that the forms and means through which these things are produced, that people have too little of, not only involve inflicting pain on and even killing animals but they involve horrific suffering and oppression for people, including even children in the tens of millions at least. Obviously we want to put an end to that, but in the meantime, how do we reconcile it? What's the right synthesis of that?

MARTIN: Right, and why raise this question? In a certain sense, why burden us with this question now? I'm saying that.

AVAKIAN: I'm not saying why raise it.

MARTIN: You're not saying it, I'm saying it.

AVAKIAN: I'm just trying to raise some things on the other side of it, to round out the picture.

MARTIN: Right. I think there are three reasons. One is that even though I don't think this is a dividing line question, I think there is the question of what we are aiming to do when we're able to make big leaps in transforming society and what our "disposition" is and what people see our disposition as. I think it says something about how seriously we take the ethical. It goes way back in our conversation that when there's a better possibility, we're for the better possibility. So that it becomes, at least on a sort of personal level, that if there is a better possibility—why don't we exemplify the better possibility? On a more systemic level, there are people out there who are working on various levels, and some militantly, some more ideologically, to raise this issue. I guess I think they're on the side of the angels, that they're doing something that ought to be done, and it does go to systemic questions. I agree with you that, in some sense, even if we were to take a position on this, what impact would that have? I think that myself. So I don't eat meat, but that's a tiny drop in a gigantic ocean, and it just becomes a kind of, looks like a kind of personal statement, I suppose. But what's the larger upshot of that? I guess I think it goes to that whole issue of how we understand cruelty, how we understand an exploitative system. I really do think it can be shown empirically that it's not for lack of producing more food animals or doing more animal experimentation that there is a need for more food, more clothing, more medicine among the world's people and especially in the Third World.

I also think it's a little bit different, the situation in the Third World. You mentioned a woman saying that she was raising this pig for the world revolution. I think that's quite different, I might still have questions about it, but I think there's a difference between people in villages raising animals and a massive, international system of industrialized so-called agriculture, basically food-animal production. Including things like where this fellow in this book, *Fast Food Nation*, has shown that it's also part of a system—meat-packing plants that are still the most dangerous industrialized jobs in the United States. It's part of the whole mythology. It's not to say that some people don't need more protein, but there's also a lot of mythology around this in terms of how much protein people actually need. And there's a tendency to sort of buy into the idea that protein's what it's all about, it's all protein. There's all kinds of stuff in food that we need in addition to protein and there's also ways in which we can get too much protein. And it's basically just a campaign of the meat industry to promote the idea that we just need protein, protein, protein. I remember growing up, what would we always hear about Third World countries or even the Soviet Union or China or wherever? "They only have meat once a week or twice a week." I haven't had meat for seventeen years, and I'm here having a good conversation. Of course, I had some nice tofu for dinner, and not everybody has the opportunity to have that either.

But I think it's mainly . . . you think about milk, this idea that "it does a body good." Everybody's got to get their milk. Well, for example, I don't know the current state of this research, but I know that at one point there was thought to perhaps be a connection between drinking milk or at least a lot of milk and sickle cell anemia in black people. So what does the dairy industry do? They go out and hire some black actors to be shown drinking milk and having their milk mustache and saying it does a body good. I heard a radio commercial where one of the Neville Brothers was singing a kind of soul song along the lines of, "God bless you mom for giving me my milk." Clearly it's playing into the feminine, I don't even know how to put it, mother's milk sort of thing. And it's easy for us to be swayed by this, that all these things are needed. Again, I would press the point that actually if things were organized differently the situation would not be seen as it is.

The last little point on that is in terms of medicine, too. I might take a rather extreme view on this and again I know it's different in the Third World. There's practically nothing coming from the medical establishment that I trust in any way. I tend to stay away from it to whatever extent possible, and its medicines. There is just not much there that I would put a lot of stock in. I've even written about this in my books, and I even wrote a little article that was in the RW some years ago, something I sent in and they accepted, about medicine in China, where one of the remarkable things about the whole barefoot doctor system was that it's not something we could look at condescendingly and say, "Yeah, that's doing pretty good for a Third World country." It was a better medical system than exists in a First World country like the United States. And better for the health of the people, and it didn't involve testing medicines on monkeys or chimpanzees or pigs or any of that. So I think there's a whole mythology that we could actually break with.

AVAKIAN: Well, I wouldn't make a principle that people must eat meat. Like, as a principle, you must eat meat.

MARTIN: There was this moment at the debate in New York City, what year was that, 1983? The Soviet Union debate over socialism or social-imperialism where the revisionist speaker on that, the pro-Soviet speaker on that, out of wanting to adopt a kind of workerist posture, said to Raymond Lotta up there on the stage in front of whatever it was a thousand people or more, "I don't know about you, but I'm sort of down with the workers and I want my meat and potatoes." There's something to that too. It goes back into the gradations point, because it seems to me that divides into two. On the one hand, sure on some level I even accept that cruelty might mean different things as concerns different animals, and sponges aren't really what I think I can be too concerned with right now. On the other hand, I don't actually think that shrimp would be a creature where I would be so worried about the cruelty to the individual creature except the way in which that's done is like clear-cutting the forest. They drag along the ocean floor and destroy whole environments and it's neither good for them nor for us ultimately. It's not sustainable. And it goes back into some of those earlier questions we were getting into about sustainable agriculture and sustainable food production. I don't know that meat is a very sustainable food production system by and by, even though it's the cruelty question that I think is most important and it's the cruelty question that in a certain sense says something about how seriously we take this category of the ethical.

AVAKIAN: I would like to say a number of things on different levels about this. One, I think there is a question of the analysis that some people are undertaking that needs to be done much more fully in my opinion, looking to the future: how do we want to approach the problem of meeting people's basic needs, through what means and using what kinds of resources, whether animal or plant or whatever. So that's one question, I think that's a valid question to be continuing to look into and struggle over, in terms of the future. And I certainly wouldn't take a position that, well, let's just dismiss anything that anybody raises about some of the points that you were making, about how there could be a whole better way to meet people's actual needs and their health requirements. I think that's valid, and it's important to continue analyzing and struggling over that and trying to learn more about it. That's one point.

On another level, while I can sympathize with what you're saying about the medical establishment, I don't really think we can do without them at this point. I don't think the masses of people can. There are some things that are important, surgery and other things, that do save people's lives and actually make their lives better. As screwed up as the medical establishment is, and as medicine generally is, and the insurance industry and all that stuff, there are valuable things that are uncovered by research that do actually benefit people, even though that's not the purpose—ultimately the purpose is, like everything else in

capitalist society, to make profit. Still, in a certain sense inci-
dentally because they can't entirely make profit without it, they
do things that are actually important for people and do actually
make their lives better in certain ways, even though (to use a
bad pun) to have a healthy distrust of the health industry, of the
medical establishment, certainly the insurance companies, is
very warranted and wise. But I don't think, on the other hand,
we can just say, oh we can do without it, people can do without it at this point.

The third thing is, similarly, I don't think we can make a principle, at this point in any case, of saying that for society as a
whole—I'm not talking about what individuals may decide they
want to do or think is right to do, but I don't think we can make
a principle, for society as a whole, that we can do without any
things that come to us by way of inflicting some pain on, or even
killing, some animals. I don't think that, at this stage of where we
are with human society, we could make a principle out of that,
and I think to make a broad principle out of it and to actually try
to apply that in practice is mistaken and will lead to some bad
results. And that's not to say that there aren't many instances in
which, even now, things could be done so that they don't inflict
the kind of cruelty that's inflicted, or even now we could say that
certain things should be done away with or dispensed with,
because they're not really necessary and they don't really benefit humanity, and on top of that they do involve inflicting pain
on beings that do have a central nervous system developed
enough to feel pain and even sometimes ones that have a certain level of consciousness (whatever level that is—we don't
really understand this very deeply at this point). I think there's
enough known to say that some animals, even below primates,
have consciousness on some level or other—there's more to
learn about that too. But I don't think we can make a principle
out of that—not injuring or even killing animals—at this point.

I think that those people who are making a principle—not
just for themselves, but are trying to actually make that an operative principle in society at this stage—it's a mistake in my opinion that's analogous at best to saying we can do without
commodities. It's an analogy; this is not to the point that animals
should be commodities. I'm just saying, analogously, that we
recognize that commodities have all kinds of problems, and they
contain the seed of capitalism. That's why Marx started out in

Capital analyzing the commodity. As Lenin pointed out (and Mao quoted him on this) Marx, in *Capital*, started with the cell of capitalist society, the commodity, and there's a reason for that, because everything does kind of unfold out of that, even though (as you've spoken to a couple of times) there's a leap when even human labor power becomes a commodity under capitalism—that's different than simpler forms of noncapitalist commodity production and exchange. I don't think we can do away with commodities now, but if somebody wants to raise that we should have the aim of doing away with commodities, I agree. But if they want to say we should do away with them *now* and they try to make that an operative principle, I think they'd be making a mistake.

Whether or not we should do away entirely with "animal products" in the future is something that I think is at least a valid question, and I'd certainly feel the need for not just me personally but for all of us collectively to look into that a lot more. To read what's being put forward by people who have been looking into it, to further the investigation, to raise the questions, or wrangle over them. But, again, even if I were to end up concluding that okay, that's right, we could see a way to do this better without using animals in these ways, I still think it would be wrong to make a principle out of that now, out of insisting on that now for society. If somebody is a vegan, or a vegetarian like yourself, I'm not talking about that. If to them it's a matter of principle—that's the way you or others want to live—it's not that I say you can make a contrary principle: you *must* use animal products, or you must eat meat to prove you're a mensch or whatever. [*laughter*] Or just not to be a "petit-bourgeois flake," or whatever. That's wrong. But, on the other hand, without repeating it all, I do think the other things I said are also true, or at least that's my understanding of it at this point. I admit readily that I have not been able to look into this question very deeply—and I don't think it's an illegitimate question to be raising. But at this point, to my level of understanding, that's what I'd say about it.

Unfortunately, I guess we have to stop this discussion of this question, for now at least, and move on to other things.

MARTIN: I think we've accomplished a great deal simply by making a start with this question.

23

Intellectuals and Revolution

AVAKIAN: I think an important question to explore—I'd really like to hear your thinking on this, I know you've done some thinking about it, I'd like to hear more—to put it a certain way, one aspect of it is the kind of conversation we're having here, and the question is: how can we contribute to that conversation going on, on a much broader level, among people who consider themselves radical intellectuals or people who are engaged in intellectual work on the one hand but are trying in some way to make that contribute to changing the world for the better? What are the obstacles? It's not just a question of this conversation, but these kinds of conversations—how do we develop that further, including what we're doing here in terms of the questions we're grappling with here, the kind of exchange we're having here, involving on the one hand the ideas that you are working with and that are represented and embodied in your work, which you're already trying to enter into the dialogue, so to speak, but also the things that I'm trying to represent from our party in terms of our thinking about some of this—how do we also make that part of the discussion and even make people aware that this is something they would consider valuable to engage and wrestle with? That they'd have something to say to us, and we'd have something to say to them, as well as more broadly getting more dialogue of this general kind going among intellectuals and people engaged in that sphere who have these kinds of concerns in a broad sense.

MARTIN: And it has to be spoken to on a lot of different levels, and part of the problem is integrating the levels so that one problem is just the present situation of intellectuals generally. And now I'm going to be slightly narrow and just sort of say, in the United States. Not that that's the only or perhaps even in any way the most important level to speak to it, but in some sense, how do we intellectuals come forward around these questions and get involved in them? And we can look at some of the history of that, and I've tried to grapple with that, for better or worse. And yet there's also another level in which in Russia, heading into the Bolshevik Revolution, there was this whole question of the intelligentsia, and which way they were leaning, and which ones of them would gravitate toward and even join and take up different roles in the process.

But intellectuals in the United States aren't situated the way the intelligentsia was in Russia leading up to 1917. Or in China, which is even much different from that. For example, it's not even clear exactly how to define what an "intellectual" is in this society. On the one hand, it's sort of like, anybody who reads books anymore is an intellectual, in our increasingly postliterate, in some ways anyway, society—anybody who thinks ideas are important. But then there's the other end, people who have a certain training, and who probably come or most likely come from a certain background. To go back to something you said earlier, there are people who want to get involved in this process, in a certain sense they have all these ideas but they can't do anything with their ideas until they, in one way or another, and whatever this means, have gotten involved with the masses. And prepared themselves to learn from the masses, and I do think that's a fundamental dividing line right there in the sense that who among those who come from that background have, and I struggle with this myself, and I struggle with all the pulls of society around this kind of question, who has struggled to get beyond the idea that somehow they've invented these ideas themselves and that they sort of condescendingly lend their wisdom as advisors to the whoever and whatever. And it's hard, because on the other hand, and this goes back to what I think are the tremendous strengths of that Ardea Skybreak article recently on intellectual work, there has to be not only an experimental outlook with intellectual work, but I'd even say a kind of funkiness to it. And sometimes it's hard to be a funky Marxist. [*laughs*] In some sense I think the Maoists have done the best job of being the funky Marxists, so to speak, but it's hard. There has to be not only a liveliness to it, but excitement. But in terms of then how do you go beyond a person just sort of saying, "I want to be a part of hopefully in the long run changing the world and I'm going to try to write with that spirit," to in a sense working more closely with those who are attempting to organize the process? That's where we've had a lot of struggle in the past and that's where ...

AVAKIAN: If I could just interject: if not working closely, in one sense, at least entering into a dialogue. There are different levels of working with, but there's also entering into a dialogue, even if you don't have much organic working relations on other levels.

MARTIN: Right. How do we promote that? On some level, it's how does that become the dialogue that is the dialogue to be had?

AVAKIAN: Or at least part of the dialogue to be had.

MARTIN: Right. Well, I don't mean the intellectual dialogue or the dialogue on what intellectuals might be doing to advance the process. I mean the dialogue coming more front and center, sounds very military, but the dialogue on what we need to do about society becoming more front and center such that intellectuals say yes, those are the questions. Those are the questions. So that on some level the question becomes one of how we break through to greater popularity of the party and its vision. I think that's a big part of this. As these become the questions, why wouldn't intellectuals gravitate toward those becoming the questions? So how do we make them the questions? And I'm just thinking out loud here. As you know, I've grappled with it for a long time.

AVAKIAN: Let me ask you something to get at part of it. There are a number—however much smaller it is than we wish it would be—for whom those are at least important questions. You obviously have contact with some of them, in one form or another or in one way or another. So that raises two questions in my mind: one, going in one direction, how in a general sense do we expand the number of those people, building on what there is, and two, how do we make what the party has to say a part of that dialogue, more than it is? Even beginning with that group for whom questions of changing the world are important, and then hopefully expanding as that group expands as well. I didn't formulate those questions too clearly.

MARTIN: No, you did, you formulated them very clearly. It's the difficulty of the questions that is the problem. I mean I know at a certain stage in my own grappling with this there were points where I was aiming toward closer relations, but then there were points where I really had to kind of back up. Let me put it this way, it was worth trying to do things that I thought were important to do as an intellectual, there was kind of a "proximity" question. I knew that I didn't feel enabled to do them, at least in a certain kind of proximity, and so maybe that's my problem, but then I also kept sort of saying, at one point there was a conversation that kept coming back, or I kept pressing it anyway. Someone from the party was telling me that intellectuals are doing this and that with the party, and we can have this dialogue, and I was saying, well, who are they? I didn't know who they were and I guess I felt like if they were there, I would more or less know who they were. Yes, I do know who some of them are, don't get me wrong. But let me put it this way, there wasn't much penetration that I saw into the milieu. And some of that has to do with overcoming certain historical issues about the international communist movement, about associations people have with certain things, rightly or wrongly, that sort of thing, as to whether they would get involved with this, so to speak. At whatever degree of proximity. So that there have been times when I have felt like, they're hammering away in the ways they are and I'm going to try to hammer in the way that I know how, and I know that what we want to hammer away at is imperialism and what we believe in is internationalism, a society of, a consciously-collective society. I think what they're doing is good, I hope what I'm trying to do is good, but how that work can be integrated—there have been points where I've thought, I just don't know how these two activities can be integrated.

AVAKIAN: Going back to what you said a little while ago, I think that, whatever problems or shortcomings there might have been on your part, the main problem—when I wrote to you that one time I tried to indicate this—the main problem has been our own limitations, on the part of the party, not in terms of our orientation so much . . . maybe there have been problems with that, too, but the point is this: just as the main way that, overall, artists are going to contribute to the revolution is in the sphere of art, the main way that people who work with ideas and work in the intellectual sphere are going to make contributions is in that way. I agree with you that it's very important that they not shut themselves off from the masses, that they both learn from the masses as well as bringing the understanding they have to them and having that back and forth. But a party that's taking the responsibility of being a vanguard has to relate to all those spheres. We're trying, and we have limitations—as I said, maybe partly in our orientation, but more just in what we're able to do.

We're trying to figure out how to build some bridges. I realize there are some ideological questions, some disagreements people have, frankly some prejudices they have, misconceptions they have—the influence of all this "communism is dead" stuff is not helping. Part of our uphill struggle is to make people realize that these are questions—the kind of things we're talking about—they aren't "settled" in the negative sense. We're trying to figure out how to begin, to really take the first steps to build more bridges, because if we jump in over our heads and try to commit ourselves to doing a whole level of things that we can't do, it will be worse than doing nothing. But we're trying to figure out how to build a little span, a beginning span in a bridge, to enter into some of these spheres more than we've been able to, without getting in over our heads, without trying to jump in and do everything all at once, which we wouldn't be able to handle—which, as I said, would lead to bad results and bad feelings probably.

MARTIN: Right, and I think you said something very important there, and here's one way to look at it. I think no person who is trying to be a radical intellectual, or for that matter an intellectual who is just, as you said, concerned to try to find the truth of things, could ask a group whose main responsibilities are not, say, to lead philosophy or quantum physics study groups, or to form a Derrida study group so they could then have a complex discussion with a Derrida scholar on Derrida's works, or something. But on the other hand I think there was a former attitude, and I hear you getting beyond that, and again, this may also be similar to the whole issue of some things that were said around the question of homosexuality that didn't at all represent the line of the party but that somehow came out of the *ethos* of the party, so to speak, of, "look we're not going to be reading Derrida, and we don't think you need to be reading that either, you're just wasting your time, and our time, and everyone's time, and it's not your time to waste anyway." And that's right, it's not my time, it's not anybody's time to waste, and there's no time to waste. But the idea that it is wasting time, I think that characterized a kind of ethos that runs somewhat deeply. And it goes back to what you said about the CP and expelling people for reading Trotsky. You've probably read Trotsky at a far deeper level than most people who are Trotskyists, so that already puts the question on a whole other level. And so I think that's the way to go. A kind of openness. I do like this formulation of Richard Rorty's, about being open-minded, just not so open-minded that your brain falls out. What's needed is openness of the sort where we can say, "You know, we might just learn something here." And in the dynamic interaction we're going to learn some things. Even when we're disagreeing, we're going to learn some stuff. That general orientation is what will help to unite with intellectuals.

AVAKIAN: But, in my view, on this problem of engaging these various intellectuals, one thing I'd like to say about that: going back to the example you gave about Derrida, we're not going to be able to understand Derrida the same way people who immerse themselves in that particularity and in that general field will understand this but, let's put it this way, we are striving to be in a position where we have people who can sit down with someone who is deeply into that and, assuming that person is willing to meet us halfway, shall we say, we can have a meaningful conversation with them about that. I haven't read hardly any Derrida, but you and I could have a meaningful conversation about that because you're willing to tell me what you think is important about what Derrida's doing and what are some of his main ideas and the implications of them, and I think I'm on the level of understanding and engaging that—without pretending that I'm deeply steeped in Derrida, which I'm not. There is that contradiction where some people are, by definition, deeply into a particular field and someone else isn't. You have to find a way to bridge that gap. You don't bridge it by one person pretending they know about something that they don't; but you also don't bridge it by the person who knows about it saying: unless you know on the level that I know, it's not worth talking to you. But there is a bridge of, okay, this is my field, I'm into this, I think it's important; if you think it's important, we can engage and I can meet you halfway to have a discussion about this—not the same way I'd discuss it with someone who's also deeply into this particular sphere (or this particular person's work) but with someone who's meeting me halfway. I think that's what our orientation is. I don't know, as I said, maybe there have been influences or wrong thinking in our party that reading Derrida is not worth anyone's time etcetera.

MARTIN: Or you just say, "Oh, he's just an idealist, we're done with him." But I think the larger way to frame that is that, of course, the contradiction is that our aim is a world where we increasingly overcome these kinds of divisions of labor. But in doing that, it's a little bit like the old point that you have to pick up the gun to ultimately get beyond it. There is a lot of great energy out there. There's a lot of, again not to wax sentimental, there's a lot of good people out there, and some of them are intellectuals. They want, in their way and as they understand things, and I don't mean that condescendingly, because I think there are many ways in which some understand some things in a way that's, to be slightly mechanical about it, on a lower level than the party, and there may be some that understand things on a higher level. But the point is, if we're about organizing this thing, we're about wanting to say, "Hey everybody, let's bring this energy to it, and let's be open to it. And let's encourage it." I think if that's our approach to it, and without being sort of smiley-faced about it either, or opportunistic, but on the other hand wanting to unleash all the energies, whether they're intellectuals, artists, or people in whatever field, or in no field or whatever. In a certain sense if that's the approach, I don't know what to say about it other than that, isn't that the approach?

AVAKIAN: Yeah, I think it is in a basic sense. I wrote some articles, which were published in the RW about five years ago, on anarchism. It was a critique of anarchism, but one of the points I made there was this: because we have these criticisms and fundamental disagreements with anarchism doesn't mean we think that anarchists have nothing that they can contribute and they should all be put in a negative category. And I went on to make the more general point that, because of the responsibilities the party has to take on—and this will even be true in socialist society—we have to focus on certain things, which means that there are other things we can't focus on, which other people do, and they're quite likely to know more about those things than we do, even if they have a different outlook on it than we do, and even if their understanding is limited in some ways by their outlook. So how do we correctly deal with that contradiction, how do we learn from that while at the same time struggling with people over how they should view the larger questions—and even the questions in their own sphere to the degree we are able to understand them at any given point? That was the principle I was trying to stress—the fact that we're taking the responsibility of being a vanguard for the revolution doesn't mean we know about everything better than everybody else—particularly in spheres that we're not able to concentrate on at any given time.

So how do we extend a hand, and how do we in turn take a hand that's extended to us? And, as you said, try to mobilize all positive factors (to put it in Mao's terms), and in an all-around way make it serve the cause that we're striving for? That's something we've been trying to grapple with. That was a particular set of articles, on anarchism, but we've been trying to grapple with the principles involved, both before that and in an even more concentrated way after that.

MARTIN: Two comments on that: and I think this actually characterizes our whole dialogue. The fact that we're asking questions is half the battle right there. I would even say in a sense it's more than half, the fact that we're looking at, and especially that way of asking that question, it's not just "How do we whip those people in line to get with the right thing?" Which wouldn't be a dialectical way of approaching any of this. And it wouldn't be liberatory, it wouldn't unleash people. So I think it's possibly even more than halfway there to just frame the questions this way. The second comment I have is hey, we've got an uphill battle. The party has an uphill battle. Intellectuals who believe in wanting to create a better society have an uphill battle. I struggle with this all the time. There are moments when this struggle is tremendously frustrating. But let me turn the question around a bit, perhaps this will help.

How do you see the role of intellectuals who are in the party as theorists, themselves functioning in certain intellectual arenas? Do you see them trying to get into positions where in a certain sense they can play leading roles as theorists among other theorists?

AVAKIAN: Well, I certainly see the role and importance for them entering into various spheres, both ones they may already be somewhat predisposed toward, or have a certain amount of knowledge and experience with, but also other spheres where there's a need to enter in and learn and become part of the dialogue, so to speak. Leading is—I think sometimes there's a misunderstanding about leading, and also our own understanding is developing, speaking of the party, about what it means to lead in various spheres, including this one. It certainly doesn't mean to come in and start barking orders, especially about things that—even if you know something, or know a lot, that would be bad methodology—but especially when you're just getting familiar with something or you're just really learning about it, entering into a sphere for the first time. I see leading more in terms of entering into a sphere and becoming part of the dialogue and having—as we do in other, even more directly political, work—a unity-struggle-unity orientation and approach. In other words, you enter in, you learn, you engage the subject matter, you engage other people who are also wrestling with it from various angles. You put forward what we call our independent line: our view of these things and how they fit into the overall project that we're all about, if you want to put it that way. And, at the same time, you try to work with people in diverse ways and have lots of friendly debate with people in ways that are both principled but also lively, and that can draw in more people.

It's through the whole process of that kind of thing that we would try to exercise leadership by trying to persuade people that our viewpoint has validity, while recognizing at the same time that there are going to be many people who can make many valuable contributions, even indirectly, to what we're trying to do, by the things they raise, as well as making contributions to the overall struggle in the larger sense. I don't mean the immediate political struggle, but the struggle to understand the world—and then you go back to the Feuerbach theses (Marx's *Theses on Feuerbach*) that the point is to change the world. But there is also the realm of ideas in its own right. Not in the idealist sense that it's divorced, ultimately, from reality and from practice. But that was one of the things that was being put out to provoke more thinking in that Skybreak article ("Working with Ideas"): there is this realm of ideas that does have its relative autonomy, even while it's grounded in material reality and ideas are ultimately either validated, or shown to be false, in the realm of material reality. There's a lot of back and forth with practice and reality, but there's also a relative autonomy in terms of the struggle in the realm of ideas and working with ideas. So

I see leadership as a whole process like that, an ongoing process.

Even in socialist society, I see it as essentially being the same, although then the party is in a position to lead in ways it's not able to now. Still, even at that point, the correct approach to leading involves the kinds of things I'm trying to emphasize here, as opposed to coming in and either "here's the truth"— without any investigation, without any healthy debate and dialogue and common work and struggle—or simply issuing orders, which would be even worse. I see leadership more as engaging in the whole process and having that unity-struggle-unity in a healthy way, which does actually mobilize all positive factors but also within which everybody puts forward what they understand to be true and then you have back and forth about what actually does ultimately conform to reality and what actually does serve the betterment of society. We're talking broadly here about people who are interested in the betterment of society, even though they may conceive of that differently as well. But that's how I see it, and we're trying to increase our ability to do that by taking small but significant steps—trying to build some further but still really beginning spans in the bridge to being able to do more of that.

MARTIN: Part of why I asked that question is to do with, to put it crudely you might call it the "fame" question. That's a very vain way to put it. I know for my own work, which I try to approach from the standpoint of understanding the world in order to change it or at least in order to try to change it—it's not that I don't think you can learn a lot from people who don't have that perspective, that's what I think is the approach the "engaged intellectual" would take. So I don't write what I do in order for it to just go in a drawer somewhere. I like to try to find ways to get it out there, so to speak. You can obviously get caught up in that in various ways and just become self-promoting, in a selfish way. You can also get caught up in it to the detriment of being able to do this work. But on the other hand, how do we "get it out there?"

I think there's some commonality in terms of, if I can put it this way, the ideas of the party and the aims of the party, and the aims of intellectuals who want their work to find some sort of influence. I think a lot of intellectuals, and I certainly am in this group, are in a real quandary as to how to do that, especially in a society where there's actually a certain stigma in a way to being an intellectual. Or at least the powers that be love to stigmatize that when they can. We talked in other areas about Noam Chomsky, who's somebody who needs to be grappled with. Now I mean this "narrowly," on this question of a model for that kind of work, and I've grappled with him and I've grappled with Sartre as a model, though the context for Sartre was very, very different—but wondering what inspiration I can take from the way Sartre went forward with that. And I remember on *Saturday Night Live*, right after the events of 9/11 there was an idiotic kind of commentary on the "Weekend Update" segment, where Colin Quinn was making fun of Chomsky. Without even saying what Chomsky in any way had said, but just saying, "Well, thanks a lot *Doctor* Chomsky" or "*Professor* Chomsky" or something to that effect. It was a very dismissive sort of thing. It sort of captured, though, this way of stigmatizing—"Yeah, you think you have some higher-level analysis or whatever, but you're just another of those pointy-headed intellectuals, so who cares what you say?" And how to break through that, and also, at the same time, to not *be* a pointy-headed intellectual. That's part of it too. People who are gravitating toward wanting to be engaged intellectuals have some sense of that, yes, indeed there actually are pointy-headed intellectuals, and instead we need to be something else.

But that's a hard thing, and by the same token, I guess part of what I'm thinking is, look, I consider Bob Avakian to be an important, not only political leader, but an important Marxist thinker, and an important thinker on cultural questions, on questions of political economy, on questions of the shape of society and where that's going and what might come of it. I consider Raymond Lotta to be an important thinker in that field. I consider Ardea Skybreak to be an important thinker in that field, and so on. And I'm wondering what the potentiality is, what the desire is for these important thoughts to kind of appear in certain contexts, such that they're grappled with by others who are thinking in those arenas? And then I also wonder, well, is that an important question? But I'm at least putting it out as a hypothesis, that the question is worth getting into. So that when one speaks of, suppose a person is thinking, yeah, there's this thing called Marxism and there's been this, by now, long tradition of Marxist thinkers analyzing society. And what would make, because as you know I cite your work in my own work, and I'd like your work to be more out there as something that others are taking up in that arena as well. That not being the main thing, but something where, in other words, other intellectuals would say, "Yeah, there's something I want to unite with there or at least grapple with."

AVAKIAN: Well, first of all, it is an important question. And second of all, we do definitely want to be part of that discourse. To be in those arenas—as I said, to make people who are in those arenas more aware that we have something to say to them and they have something to say to us—both ways. Partly, I see that connected with your other point, about the "pointy-headed intellectuals." It's partly learning both the concepts but also the language in which people discuss these things. There are specialized areas of work and of knowledge which develop their own vocabulary. That's certainly true for Marxism. We have all these terms that are sort of "technical" terms—"materialism," "dictatorship of the proletariat." They describe real things but to a lot of people who are not conversant with that, it just sounds like a bunch of rhetoric or dogma or whatever. And sometimes, unfortunately, it's presented that way. But they are real terms that have real meanings. Similarly, in other spheres—whether it's physics or philosophy or whatever—there is a language and there are certain concepts that people are conversant with who are in that particular discipline or field or sphere, or whatever you want to call it, and others are not.

I think there is a two-fold thing. For us to be able to do what you were just talking about, to have our voices heard more by people who are in some of these fields, we have to become more familiar with the terrain, so to speak—know what people are engaging, how they're engaging it, what language and concepts they're using. Even where we disagree with them, we have to at least know how people are approaching it, in order to be able to speak to them and have ourselves heard. And we're trying to learn more about how to do that as well as learn more about the content of things. On the other side, I think that, with people who are in a particular field, it's important for them to strive to also speak to a broader audience and not simply to talk to the people who are already conversant with what they're dealing with. And that's hard, because in order to speak to a broader audience, a lot of times there's a pull to vulgarize things. And we don't want to vulgarize things in order to be understood by people more broadly—you don't want to give people pablum. You don't want to vulgarize the thinking that you're doing or what's being wrestled with in the sphere that you're dealing with. So, this is a challenge, and this is a problem for many intellectuals. Leaving aside those . . . sometimes I think that some people are deliberately being obscurantist in order to turn this into capital and exclude other people from the discourse, but leaving that aside, let's talk about people, of whom there are many, who are not trying to do that—there is still a question of learning *how* to explain these things, or have discussion of these things, in a way that invites a broader audience and that brings them into the discussion. I think there is a challenge for many intellectuals on that side of it, to learn how to do that. Just as there's a challenge for us, for some of the individuals but for the party collectively, to learn how to enter into this sphere and to be able to address what people are raising—both in the content of what they are raising but also to understand the language and concepts with which they're addressing things—so we can speak to people there, too, in a way that connects, so there can be a back and forth. I think we have to learn that and, as I was saying, people who are in particular fields have some work to do also to be able to speak to both people who are, let's say, generally intellectuals but not knowledgeable in a particular sphere, but also people more broadly who aren't intellectuals. And it's a real challenge to be able to speak to the latter category without watering things down to the point where you've lost the meaning of it or you've lost the import of it. But I think it's something that can be worked on.

MARTIN: This whole discussion reemerged in the eighties around the idea of the public intellectual. There were some books, one by Russell Jacoby, especially, that kind of bemoaned the loss of the public intellectual in the United States. It harkened back to people such as John Dewey, a certain tradition of, really from Ralph Waldo Emerson to John Dewey, William James, etcetera. Apart from all of that, that's not really the point to evaluate them as intellectuals and their politics. But it seemed to me part of what Jacoby was posing was a difficult contradiction, but without appreciating all of the dimensions of it. It did seem that fewer intellectuals were interested in being public intellectuals, and he was bemoaning that, saying, in a sense, why aren't they getting out there more? But Jacoby did not really take account of the fact that the "out there" in which to "get," the shape of that had changed. Many of us would be happy to, say, go on the radio and talk about ideas or go on television and talk about ideas, but that doesn't mean that those who control the media are going to have us on the radio or television to talk about that. Even well-known intellectuals like Noam Chomsky, Edward Said, or Cornel West have a hard time getting into certain arenas to speak. Pierre Bourdieu addressed this in a short book not long ago—of course he died just recently, but in the last few years. The book was about the idea of the "television intellectual," and what it does to thought to "package" it for television. That has its own issues in terms of what you said about *pablum*—which is one of my favorite words, actually. What happens when you shape the discourse for certain arenas? —that's a very difficult thing to negotiate. I know some people, and I feel the pull of this myself, I sometimes think it would be better just to be in my office or wherever writing stuff down, working on ideas, than to go into those arenas. Because as I'm sure you know, whenever you talk, you know much better than I do, that when you talk with journalists god knows what's going to come out the other end or what they're going to do with it, or how they're going to set it up or how they're going to edit it and all that sort of stuff. In some sense that is something that has to be negotiated both by, broadly, intellectuals who want to get their ideas out there and want to engage with changing society, and by people such as yourself. I don't quite know where to go with that, but there are certain commonalities in the difficulties of doing that. And in some sense intellectuals just need some sympathy in terms of how difficult that is. I do know a lot of people who are trying to do that, to negotiate that space, but it's very difficult.

AVAKIAN: I think there are different vehicles and different occasions on which we can, even now, try to speak to a broader audience. We try to do this through the *Revolutionary Worker* in terms of taking up scientific issues and trying to make them understandable. The RW has a kind of unique audience in the sense that it's made up of many diverse audiences—all the way from people who have a lot of formal education and intellectual training and experience to people who have a very low level of literacy (a lot of times the articles are put on tape, because that's more accessible to them). So we have the challenge of trying to bridge all that and write in a way in the paper that meets the needs of all those diverse parts of that overall audience. That's one vehicle, and it's important. But I think there are other vehicles and occasions.

I was reading a report recently about how in Cleveland, I think it was, there was a big forum about evolution. And Stephen Jay Gould and some others spoke there—to an audience of more than a thousand people, I believe. The reason for that big turn-out is not only that the subject is interesting but also there's this whole struggle in Ohio about "Intelligent Design"—the "Intelligent Designer" version of creationism. In that kind of circumstance, where this became a big political and social issue, then there was an opportunity for a much broader audience, even though there are still some limitations, because it was mainly the "educated classes" who came out to that, although not entirely. So I think there are those occasions when something becomes a big issue in society where you not only can enter into the debate and struggle about the issue itself but there are questions of theory and intellectual understanding, ideas broadly speaking, that are connected with that, and there's more audience and receptivity for that. We should learn how to seize on those occasions when they arise.

MARTIN: What about something that is just as simple as interviewing more people? I realize then there will be different audiences for that, and maybe for some of those among the diverse audiences for the RW, it won't really be their bag, so to speak, and again I'm just hypothesizing. But it might be a way of holding that hand out in terms of wanting to talk with all of the intellectuals who believe we need fundamental change in society.

AVAKIAN: I think that's a good idea. We have done lots of interviews, in fact we have that feature, the RW Interview, and the whole point of it is to speak with people—not that we wouldn't do an interview with someone who agreed with us on 95 percent of the issues— but the main point is to speak to a range of people who are exactly in the place you're talking about: they're seeking some kind of fundamental change, as they conceive of it, but their conception may be different in significant ways from ours. We think they have important things to say and that it's important for the audience of the paper to hear what they have to say. So that's a good idea. But in that context it does present a challenge to the interviewee, along the lines of what I was saying—the challenge I was referring to earlier of actually, without watering down what you have to say and what you're engaged with, making it more intelligible to an audience that isn't immersed in or isn't already quite familiar with both the subject matter and the particular terminology and concepts that are part of the discourse in that field. But I think it's a good idea. The more we can do things like that, the more it will build on itself. You do a few of these kinds of things in various spheres, and then more people are interested in doing them. Also, one of the things that people feel is important is that we try to be very respectful of the people we interview. We try to provide a forum and format that enables them to say what they want to say, and in the way they want to say it. We don't edit or clip things so it ends up sounding more like what *we* would say. I think that's also important, that people have a sense that we respect the integrity of what they're saying. That's also why we have the brief statement, which accompanies each interview, that we don't necessarily agree with everything they say, and they don't necessarily agree with, and aren't responsible for, everything else that's in the paper. The point of that is not a "disclaimer"—the point is the integrity of the paper, on the one hand, but also the integrity of what people who are being interviewed are saying and want to say.

And we do have lots of sympathy for the difficulties of this. We would like to help to the degree that we're able, in terms of giving people support, and the interview is one way of giving them an audience they don't normally have, or at least to some degree they don't normally have. And then we'd also like to work together with people—even when we don't have those occasions when we can speak to broader audiences—to try to figure out how we can increase the number of people who do, in broad terms, share the orientation of wanting to contribute to changing the world in a way that gets rid of oppression and things like that. Find the ways to have more dialogue and engagement among those people, who may only vaguely know about each other—or even, in some cases, literally don't know about each other, or don't know that they have something to say to each other. They're sort of off in different corners and they're either ignorant of each other, or else influenced by certain misconceptions about what people are about and whether they

have anything to say. For example, our party: do we have anything to say to people, or do we just have a bunch of rhetoric
and dogma that doesn't really have anything to do with reality
and has been totally discredited. That's something that has to be
overcome.

On the other hand, going back to a point you were making
earlier about "why are you wasting your time thinking about
why existence is, or reading Derrida," our party needs to learn
more about this. You were referring earlier to something I wrote
around 1990, "The End of a Stage—The Beginning of a New
Stage." I said that in socialist society even some books by reactionaries should be published, because it will be part of the
overall process of challenging ourselves, challenging people
generally and learning. The point I'm trying to make here is that,
leaving aside reactionaries, there are many, many progressive
people (if you want to use that term) who need to be brought
more into dialogue with each other, and with revolutionaries
and with communists. I feel that sometimes we are not really
talking with each other. There are certain barriers, including
misconceptions and prejudices—not just toward us, but sometimes on our part toward others—that need to be broken down.
And, again, when we have the opportunity to speak to a
broader audience, it's important to seize on it and maximize it.
But even short of that, and in a more ongoing way, we need to
find the ways to build, step-by-step, so that even if, compared
to society at large, it is a small number of people at a given point
who could speak to each other, and have something to say to
each other, we remove some of the subjective barriers that are
in the way of our doing that.

MARTIN: I think that's a really important point. I really like,
and what's funny about this is I'm not really connected to this
person's writing at all, but I've always liked the little two-word
saying of the British novelist E. M. Forster, "only connect." I
think it's something that probably a lot of people don't realize,
and maybe even intellectuals themselves, that intellectual work
can be very isolated. I know I sometimes even feel isolated from
even my own colleagues in my own academic department. Not
for reasons that would actually be more interesting, but for sort
of stupid reasons — logistics, the way that this society just
makes you tired a lot of the time. This society makes most people, whatever their arena, it just gives us more and more and

more junk to deal with that wears us out. Just the general social fragmentation that plays a role in the lives of intellectuals just like anybody else who has to eat, sleep, get dressed in the morning, go to the grocery store, or whatever. And to forge these connections—in my own work connectivity is just a big, big part of it, just forging connections. And some of it, to use one of your favorite words, I know, is a bit *trippy*, in that I often make rather large leaps from one area to another and not always with all the spaces filled in in-between. I'm not saying that about your work but I will admit it for my own work. A lot of times the spaces in-between aren't very well filled in. In principle I'm in favor of filling them in, but then, *in principle* I'm also in favor of wanting to be able to see how one can, almost in a "science-fiction" way, go through a warp and go all the way from here to way back over there.

But connectivity . . . facilitating connectivity. Part of what's great about what I think I'm hearing you say, too, is that some of this is facilitating connectivity where these areas outside the party need to get connected to one another, even if it's not always right through the middle of the party, so to speak, but around that. In terms of, again, bringing those energies together. And even just letting those energies know that each other exists, so they don't feel that they're just voices in the wilderness or something like that. That's something that intellectuals need to break down in themselves, too, because sometimes there's a bit of a fetish for that—"I'm the solitary one, the only one who ever saw so-and-so." Of course, like you say, too, it can become capital in the sense that, just as I was joking earlier about my phrase "virtual-bread and cybercircuses, *trademark.*" I don't want anyone else to *own* that because *I* thought of it, and I've got to "get out there" with it. If it just becomes capital, that's something intellectuals need to struggle with, to get beyond. And I think the party can play a role in helping them to do that.

But the main thing actually is to speak to any intellectual who even begins to think about the relationship between knowing and doing. What's the relationship between the things, for whatever reason, whatever life path has been gone down that got a person to certain questions and certain investigations, and what's the connection between that and a better world? And even a situation where people are talking about these things such that it's not just some private enclave and tiny discussion group or something, but where more and more broadly people are taking up important questions, this would be a major step. There's a lot of energy to be mobilized there. Finding the ways to do that is, I don't think we'll change society if we can't mobilize that on some level. In some sense to me it goes along with Lenin's idea that without revolutionary theory there won't be a revolution. Without a broad culture of change and opposition and lively sensibility even just on the basic level of this society has essential problems—we need a new society, we need a new kind of society. Which I think is actually a broad sentiment. We need to find ways to sharpen this sentiment in those different arenas, and to give intellectuals the way to come forward around essential questions. I think we won't change society without doing that, so we have to find ways to do that.

AVAKIAN: I really agree with that. Also the sphere of art is another expression of that. A lot of times things happening in the sphere of art are harbingers of what happens in society more broadly, including in the political struggle. I think there are ways in which ferment . . . as opposed to this "pointy-headed intellectual" thing, it's never good when there is not intellectual ferment in society. Whatever the level of it is, we should be trying to increase it, and make it richer. That also goes back to what you were saying a little bit earlier about the question of leadership. First of all, since we want to be materialists and scientific, we have to face the fact the party is not at this point in a position where, even if we wanted to, we could be the center of the wheel and everybody else would be a spoke, we would be Rome and all roads lead to Rome—everything connects through us. But, more fundamentally, even if we were in such a position, when you talk about leadership, that's not our view. That's not what leadership means or how it should be exercised. We don't want a situation where it's just people trying to connect to us and through us; we want to create an atmosphere in which there's a lot of broad wrangling, debating, breaking down walls between people—among intellectuals and even more broadly among other sections of the people—bringing them into the discourse, too, to the maximum degree possible at every point. Have a lot of ferment and a lot of back and forth among many different people, in which the party will be taking part.

As I see it, our role as leadership—even in socialist society, and not just out of the necessity that we can't do it another way now—is to be in the midst of that and, yes, struggling for certain principles, struggling for certain methods and a certain outlook, but doing that as part of the whole ferment and striving to both learn from people and at the same time to lead them in the sense of being able to point to the synthesis out of all this and point to the way forward. To me, that's what it means to lead. It doesn't mean you're at the center of everything, not only in the sense of giving orders but even in the sense that everything goes through you, and you're the only one trying to systematize anything. But leading through that whole percolating process, working in that whole very exciting and rich mix to both learn more deeply and to point certain directions.

In socialist society, not to side-step the issue, you have certain principles of how things are done. Things have to be led one way or another. But even there, on the basis of certain broad principles, you want the kind of ferment and actually to learn more what those principles mean as applied to a particular sphere, as well as to learn more about additional principles or new principles that should be brought forward to replace the old. None of this is static. It is a matter of a lot of percolation, or ferment, or whatever metaphor you want to use—the party being in that mix and trying to lead through that whole process in the ways I've been talking about, as opposed to being at the center of everything. Which we couldn't do—but shouldn't do, even if we could.

I look at the U.S. and I wish there were more intellectual ferment. I'm always writing people, asking what's happening—how much intellectual ferment is there? Because I remember when I was coming forward in the late fifties, late in high school, some of the first things for me were in the cultural sphere: sitting around listening, putting the headphones on—I had to go up to the university library at Cal to listen to Allen Ginsberg reading "Howl" day after day after day. I also listened to Barbara Dane singing folk music. I listened to Leadbelly. Some friends of mine I used to play basketball with in the summers, we were reading Plato and Aristotle and Hume . . . and I don't remember who all else. Debating in between basketball games. Interestingly, we were a small group, some of whom were black and some of whom were white. We used to sit around talking and arguing between games, and other people would make fun of us. But there was a certain ferment, it was paralleling certain things happening in society, like the civil rights movement, things like that. But it wasn't directly one-to-one with them. It was part of the general upheaval, if you want to put it that way, that was beginning to break through, to break and strain at the oppressive relations of that time. It was a very important part, I know, of my own development, but it was also part of what was going on much more broadly in society—and we always need that.

MARTIN: Just to seize on something you said, I loved that phrase, "It's never good if there's not intellectual ferment." How could things be good if there is not intellectual ferment? Two analogies that might seem a little wack, but that express the way I feel sometimes in our present society, a society without intellectual, as opposed to what we call those "heady days," like those heady days of 1968 and their aftermath, when poetry was in the streets, when, as they said in Paris, "all power to the imagination"—and all these other great slogans. It's more like in present society sometimes I feel that the "ferment" is like looking across a big room and there's a single glass sitting on a table with an Alka Seltzer fizzing in it. And there's what "ferment" there is, over there. By the same token, to go back to the "bemoaning" point, regarding *The Last Intellectuals* by Russell Jacoby, I think it was in the mid-eighties that he put that out. Significantly, as I recall, I remember Carl Sagan, for instance, not being mentioned in that book. He was somebody, and Stephen J. Gould, they were people I thought of immediately in terms of Jacoby saying there aren't any public intellectuals out there, and I was thinking, well those guys are out there and they're actually having broad impact, they're doing a lot of good stuff. And so the conception was something like, "Why aren't people coming forward to be public intellectuals?" This goes to your point about the party being at the center and the spokes of a wheel coming into that center. The "bemoaning" point was set out as if, gee there's some big hill out there and if only intellectuals would go to that hill and climb to the top of it, they could just speak to the world. And the fact is, either there's not that hill, or if there is that hill it's invisible and we're sort of stumbling around looking for it, or, even better trying to build it in a certain sense. Trying to shovel a bunch of dirt in one area and build it up. And that's hard to do, especially under the more recent circumstances.

I think this was already seen in the fifties and in some ways the 1950s in the U.S. set the stage for this. And now we have the postmodern fifties, of hyper-homogenization in culture, and where this has had a huge affect on what intellectual arenas are, how one can enter into them, what can be done with them, what limitations they have. This goes to the powers of recuperation, the way these arenas have been shaped by the powers that be, by the media conglomerates and whatnot. I dealt with this in some of my writing on music recently, I recently wrote this book called *Avant rock* that deals with experimental trends in rock music since the later Beatles. And it was extremely difficult to write because there is so much music now. I was talking with a friend of mine who is a recording engineer and producer in New York. He was saying we don't even know what the number is, in terms of the number of albums that came out in 1969 compared to the number of albums that come out these days. But it's more than a proportion of a hundred times. It could be a thousand times. It could be even much more than that. And we're in the extraordinary circumstance of where on the one hand there's this quote-unquote mainstream culture that's under the thumb of, even though sometimes some interesting things happen in it, interesting things slip out from it, but truly under the thumb of about five or six gigantic media conglomerates. On the other hand, you have people who can make an album in their bedroom on their iMac computer or whatever, of the same recording quality as Abbey Road studios in London. Now it doesn't mean the music is going to be as good as *Abbey Road* or what's that Pink Floyd album that was recorded there, that's so famous, *Dark Side of the Moon*. It doesn't mean there's going to be the genius of George Martin, the producer of the Beatles doing it, but you could do it. It's become very democratized. So there's this sort of marginal culture but where there's tons of people who are getting involved in it, putting their stuff out and circulating it. It's changing the way, with people having the ability to download music. I think that's going to increasingly become a model for how culture in general is disseminated. How the specificities of that affect how intellectuals navigate these new arenas, I think need to be understood better. And understood in such a way that real resistance is possible. Part of the problem is, how real oppositional points of view can get expressed, but also how they can get expressed such that they don't just become immediately a part of the swirl of just, everything's out there, everything's "out there." I was talking with someone last night, we were in the car and the song "Louie, Louie" came on. We were joking about how when we were in junior high or whatever, bands would play this at dances. And of course the big thing about "Louie, Louie" was that you don't really quite know what they're saying, but it's maybe something vaguely obscene. We're supposed to titter at it, yeah, we really know what they're saying, it's really about you-know-what. And now it's like, turn on just the regular radio, and okay, another song about fucking, big deal. [*laughter*] I suppose that shows a certain development. It also shows a massive recuperative apparatus—sure you have countervailing currents, but in some sense it just becomes part of the game. You have people who put out that, and then you'll have the rebuttal by some fundamentalist who will then do their own bemoaning or whatever. That "game" itself needs to be transcended toward real opposition, toward, really, you might call it the "punching through" question. How to find ways to do that? In a way that's also a commonality between many intellectuals and what the party's trying to do: how to "punch through." It's not the same punch through, or it's not the same holes or whatever, but the general mode of operation is something that there's a commonality around.

AVAKIAN: I think there are two points. One is what you were just speaking to—which is how to get out to a broader audience and to broader arenas, including making use of some of these more newly developed forms that you were just speaking of. And yet doing it in a way that does actually break through, as you were saying, not just become . . . It's both the problem of quantity—there's so much that you can get lost, even in these forums where you can put anything out there, like on the Net. And, as you were also speaking to, there is the problem of not being coopted and turned into something tame and institutionalized so that it doesn't really have the impact that you want to have with it.

MARTIN: The "quantity question," it's a bit like, I know one bookstore I used to go into that was a great bookstore, one of the great intellectual bookstores, and it's too bad that it's gone under now, but, in a way it's part of the whole problem we're talking about that it did go under. But it was somewhat of a sloppy bookstore and things were often not in much order, there was a general state of disarray. And sometimes when I went in there, as somebody who writes books myself, I thought, why throw another book on this pile? That's sort of the quantity question. What are you going to toss into this pile? And the other thing, also, how to not get involved in something, and this is really, really difficult, because on some level you have to go out there and risk getting involved in this, and yet how to not get involved in something that's just a false debate. It looks like a debate, but the arena is shaped such that it's really like forming this integral whole where people can say yeah yeah that guy put out his views, this other person put out their view, and well, gee, "one man's opinion." That's again the "punch through" question.

AVAKIAN: Yeah, I think there are all those kinds of questions. Then there is the other dimension: without turning inward, at the same time those of us who, broadly speaking, are trying to make a better world, and can see the need for a different kind of society, however differently that may be conceived, we need to be speaking to each other more than we are. Everybody has problems, everybody's very busy, to put it in simple terms: Well, if I read *that* and engage with people about that, then I can't do it around *this*. And somehow we have to figure out how to overcome that and be able to talk to each other more, and in better ways than exist at this point. So we need to advance in both dimensions: how to speak to broader audiences, how to find ways to do that, ways that are meaningful and do (to use your phrase) punch through; and how, in a quantitative and a qualitative sense, to talk more to each other—have a better dialogue among ourselves even while we're not doing that in an ingrown way that works against also finding and maximizing the opportunities to speak to much broader numbers of people and to learn from them, to get feedback from them, to be able to engage them and hear what our ideas call to mind for them and how they respond to them, what they think about the issues we're raising. I think both are important: finding those various avenues to actually be effective in speaking to broader numbers of people, and be speaking more to each other, too, and breaking down some of the barriers that are in the way of doing that—figuring out how to get a mix going where it's not like, "Well, I'm too busy to do this, I can only do that," but actually there's a whole mix going where it's building on itself and you can be part of a dialogue without having to be speaking individually with every other person who's part of that dialogue. That's difficult, but I think it's very important too. That's going to take some "bridging," as I was trying to say earlier. Step by step, and through some trial and error—and through some working together on various things and then summing them up—we're going to have to figure out how to start building more of those bridges.

MARTIN: So the question arises as to how to unite a little better with some people. A specific example comes to mind. I won't really mention this person's name per se, because I don't really want to "implicate" them, so to speak. But suppose there are intellectuals out there who, broadly speaking, they, to be simplistic about it, like the idea of revolution, they think there's a lot to learn from the Soviet experience, they think there's a lot to learn from the Chinese experience. Some of them would even go so far as to say that Lenin and Mao are still setting the terms or at least significantly setting terms that we still need to grapple with and take forward. Some of them would perhaps even say, yeah I'm a bit of a Maoist or I dig that on some level. Then it's frustrating—Why aren't we uniting? And I think there's this sense that, it's just uniting in terms of this dynamic interaction going among our projects, and we're building an understanding, and we feel ourselves to be part of a common project. Why isn't that happening more? Obviously there's the old problem that the leadership that's attempting to guide this process is ultimately not a philosophical study group, it should have that as part of it, but it's ultimately not that and it's not a debating society, as Lenin wanted to say, although it should have that. But still, surely it seems as though there's just objectively out there the basis for getting together more or at least exchanging more. I think the problem in the past has been, and I know I've felt this sometimes quite acutely, is that it's not that I want or expect or think it would even be right for an organization such as this to devote lots of energy to reading and discussing my work and getting back to me on it, writing their own works about it or anything like that. But on the other hand, it wouldn't hurt if there was some sense that this work had been read and grappled with by some people who are in a position to do that, and then commented on in their own work in the sense of saying, there's an analysis by so-and-so that really fits into this point and that ought to be taken up; here's how we see that falling out. So that there's more of a real intellectual interaction because otherwise then what you get is the situation where the intellectual in question looks at it as though, well they're doing what they're doing and I'm doing what I'm doing and I guess I hope somewhere down the road that could come together if we're really for the same things. It's like that old poster from the sixties or early seventies—you're you and I'm me and we're on the road of life and if we happen to meet then that's beautiful. But there's no road map for knowing what mile markers we're at on the road or how that meeting might take place. So it looks as though it's just something that *might* happen, or might not or whatever, but we really don't know where we are.

AVAKIAN: From our side, part of the problem—there are different facets of the problem. One is our own limitations in terms of all the things that we're trying to do and how we array our own efforts and deploy ourselves, if you want to use a military analogy. Part of it is also the state and the enemy, which makes it difficult for us to do certain things, in terms of having dialogue with people, etcetera, that we would like to do—and they are likely to make it much more difficult, given everything that's going on in the world and everything they have on their agenda. And then part of it is probably limitations of our own in another sense—not appreciating enough the importance of certain things or at least not knowing how to go about them—either problems of orientation and/or lack of understanding of how to tackle the questions, or some combination of both. We're trying to deal with all those things because, particularly with regard to the orientation question, we are increasingly recognizing the importance of this whole process that I've been trying to describe—using the word "ferment," or whatever word you want to use—the importance of our being part of it, both to learn and also to contribute and to be able to lead better, in an overall sense, even to be able to lead the more directly political struggle. What we're trying to confront now, making some advances in our orientation around that, is how—maybe I can put it this way, how to begin connecting more. You connect more by beginning with the people you are closer to. It's kind of like concentric circles. People overlap, you have a certain broad area of unity with people and some area of disagreement, and then they in turn have the same with other people, and you in turn have the same with other people. How to get that all in the mix together, so it's not just separate isolated circles, with limited overlapping, but where there's more interaction.

That's one level of things. The other is how (to continue that imagery) to go to the next circles closest to us and not have it be that they're working on what they're working on, and we're working on what we're working on, but actually have more interconnection, interaction and dialogue. That's one of the important next steps we're trying to take, to figure out how to do that, how to do the kind of thing you were just referring to: actually have their work be "in us" and our work be "in them"— as you were saying, more systematically read what these other people are writing and generally what they're putting out, and then comment on it, and try to have them do the same with regard to us, break down some of the barriers and make some of the links that begin to get a more positive dynamic going. I think you do have to begin with, or mainly begin with, the "circles that you overlap with more" and try to both expand out more from that but also get this broader mix going. That is important, and we have to figure out—and we are trying to figure out—how to do that. Things that can be done with me directly are limited for various reasons, including the state, but taking the party more collectively, we can do more things, and I can have correspondence with people, too, which is one important thing. Everybody's busy, I'm busy, but I can still have correspondence with people, and I think that would be a very good thing if we can figure out how to do it. And there are other people who are in the party—or are close to the party and generally agree with its line and try to apply that in the work they're doing—who could also be part of, I don't know, sitting down in salons with people or having some correspondence themselves with people, or doing a combination of those things, maybe coming to each other's meetings occasionally to sit in and listen. For example, the Sartre association—just sitting in and listening, participating or contributing on whatever is the appropriate level. Or inviting people to come to a forum we have at one of the bookstores that are politically aligned with the party, finding ways to sort of cross-pollinate, something like that. Beginning modestly, since everybody is very committed and trying to do many things.

MARTIN: Also beginning modestly in part because people are deep into their stuff on whatever level and how else should you approach it except modestly.

AVAKIAN: And you have to get to know each other a little bit, too, so to speak—or to know each other better. So I'm thinking of things like that, which we need to explore in a more ongoing way. We're sort of tossing out ideas here but, in a more ongoing and somewhat more systematic way, we need to follow up and figure out what those first modest steps would be to get a more positive synergy going.

Bibliography

Adorno, Theodor W., and Ernst Bloch. "Something's Missing: A Discussion between Ernst Bloch and Theodor Adorno on the Contradictions of Utopian Longing." In *The Utopian Function of Art and Literature* by Ernst Bloch. Translated by Jack Zipes and Frank Mecklenburg. Cambridge, Mass.: MIT Press, 1988.

Althusser, Louis. "Lenin and Philosophy." In *Lenin and Philosophy and Other Essays*, translated by Ben Brewster. New York: Monthly Review Press, 2001.

Avakian, Bob. "Celebrate the 25th Anniversary of the RCP, USA. Message to the Youth: The Special Role of Youth in This Revolution—The Challenge For Your Generation." *Revolutionary Worker*, October 22, 2000.

———. "Conquer the World? The International Proletariat Must and Will." *Revolution*, December 1981.

———. *Could We Really Win? Prospects for Revolution.* Chicago: RCP Publications, 1991.

———. *For a Harvest of Dragons: On the "Crisis of Marxism" and the Power of Marxism, Now More Than Ever.* Chicago: RCP Publications, 1983.

———. "Getting Over the Hump." *Revolutionary Worker*, October 12, 1997 to January 18, 1998.

———. "Great Objectives and Grand Strategy." *Revolutionary Worker*, November 2001 to March 2002.

———. *Preaching From a Pulpit of Bones: We Need Morality But Not Traditional Morality.* Chicago: Banner Press, 1998.

———. *Reflections, Sketches & Provocations: Essays and Commentary, 1981–1987.* Chicago: RCP Publications, 1990.

———. "The End of a Stage—The Beginning of a New Stage." *Revolution*, Fall 1990.

———. "The New Situation and the Great Challenges." *Revolutionary Worker*, March 17, 2002.

———. "The Truth about Right-Wing Conspiracy . . . And Why Clinton and the Democrats Are No Answer." *Revolutionary Worker*, October 17, 2004.

Bancroft, Frederic. *Slave Trading in the Old South.* New York: Ungar Publishing Company, 1940.

Berry, Wendell. *Home Economics.* San Francisco: North Point Press, 1987.

Brien, Alan. *Lenin, the Novel.* New York: William Morrow and Company, 1987.

Briggs, Carolyn S. *This Dark World: A Memoir of Salvation Found and Lost.* London: Bloomsbury Publishing, 2003.

Buchanan, Patrick. *The Death of the West.* New York: Thomas Dunne Books, 2001.

Carroll, James. *Constantine's Sword: The Church and the Jews – A History.* New York: Mariner Books, 2002.

Courtois, Stéphane, Nicolas Werth, Jean-Louis Panné, Andrzej Paczkowski, Karel Bartosek, Jean-Louis Margolin; Mark Kramer, eds. *The Black Book of Communism: Crimes, Terror, Repression.* Translated by Jonathan Murphy. Cambridge, Mass.: Harvard University Press, 1999.

Dellinger, David. *From Yale to Jail: The Life Story of a Moral Dissenter.* New York: Rose Hill Books, 1996.

Derrida, Jacques. *Specters of Marx: The State of the Debt, the Work of Mourning, and the New International.* Translated by Peggy Kamuf. New York: Routledge, 2000.

Diamond, Jared. *Guns, Germs, and Steel: The Fates of Human Societies.* New York: W.W. Norton & Company, 1999.

Engels, Friedrich. *Ludwig Feuerbach and the End of Classical German Philosophy.* In Karl Marx, Friedrich Engels, *Selected Works in One Volume.* New York: International Publishers, 1969.

———. *The Origin of the Family, Private Property, and the State.* New York: International Publishers, 1975.

Hardt, Michael, and Antonio Negri. *Empire.* Cambridge, Mass.: Harvard University Press, 2001.

Hegel, G. W. F. *The Philosophy of Right.* Translated by T. M. Knox. Oxford, U.K.: Oxford University Press, 1967.

Heidegger, Martin. "Letter on Humanism." In *Basic Writings*, edited by David Farrell Krell. Revised and expanded edition. San Francisco: HarperCollins, 1993.

Jacoby, Russell. *The Last Intellectuals: American Culture in the Age of Academe.* New York: The Noonday Press, 1987.

James, William. *The Will to Believe.* New York: Dover, 1956.

Jameson, Fredric. *Postmodernism, or, The Cultural Logic of Late Capitalism.* Durham, N.C.: Duke University Press, 1991.

Kant, Immanuel. *Grounding for the Metaphysics of Morals.* Translated by James W. Ellington. Indianapolis: Hackett Publishing, 1981.

———. "An Answer to the Question: What Is Enlightenment?" In *Perpetual Peace and Other Essays,* edited and translated by Ted Humphrey. Indianapolis: Hackett Publishing, 1983.

———. "Idea for a Universal History with a Cosmopolitan Intent." In *Perpetual Peace and Other Essays*, edited and translated by Ted Humphrey. Indianapolis: Hackett Publishing, 1983.

Lenin, Vladimir I. "'Left-Wing' Communism—an Infantile Disorder." In V.I. Lenin, *Collected Works*, Vol. 31. Moscow: Progress Publishers, 1978; pp. 17–118.

———. *What Is to Be Done? Burning Questions of Our Movement.* In V.I. Lenin, *Collected Works*, Vol. 5. Moscow: Progress Publishers, 1978; pp. 347–529.

Lotta, Raymond, ed. *Maoist Economics and the Revolutionary Road to Communism: The Shanghai Textbook*. Chicago: Banner Press, 1994.

Lukes, Steven. *Marxism and Morality*. Oxford, U.K.: Oxford University Press, 1987.

Luttwak, Edward. *Turbo Capitalism: Winners and Losers in the Global Economy*. New York: Perennial, 2000.

Makdisi, Saree, Cesare Casarino, and Rebecca E. Karl, eds. *Marxism Beyond Marxism*. New York: Routledge, 1996.

Mao Tse-Tung. *A Critique of Soviet Economics*. Translated by Moss Roberts. New York: Monthly Review Press, 1977.

———. "On Contradiction." In *Selected Works of Mao Tse-Tung*, vol. I. Peking: Foreign Languages Press, 1967; pp. 311–47.

———. "On Practice." In *Selected Works of Mao Tse-Tung*, vol. I. Peking: Foreign Languages Press, 1967.

———. "The Chinese Revolution and the Chinese Communist Party." In *Selected Works of Mao Tse-Tung*, Vol. II. Peking: Foreign Languages Press, 1967; pp. 305–34.

———. "Talks at the Yenan Forum on Literature and Art." In *Selected Works of Mao Tse-Tung*, vol. III. Peking: Foreign Languages Press, 1967; pp. 69–98.

Martin, Bill. *Avant rock: Experimental music from the Beatles to Bjork*. Chicago: Open Court Publishing Company, 2002.

———. *Humanism and Its Aftermath: The Shared Fate of Deconstruction and Politics*. Atlantic Highlands, N.J.: Humanities Press, 1995.

———. *Listening to the future: The time of progressive rock, 1968–1978*. Chicago: Open Court Publishing, 1998.

———. *Politics in the impasse: Explorations in postsecular social theory*. Albany, N.Y.: State University of New York Press, 1996.

———. *The Radical Project: Sartrean Investigations*. Lanham, Maryland: Rowman & Littlefield, 2000.

Marx, Karl. *Capital*, vol. 1. New York: International Publishers, 1979.

———. *The Class Struggles in France, 1848 to 1850*. New York: International Publishers, 1964.

———. *The Eighteenth Brumaire of Louis Bonaparte*. Peking: Foreign Languages Press, 1978.

———. "Introduction." In *A Contribution to the Critique of Political Economy*. New York: International Publishers, 1970.

Marx, Karl, and Friedrich Engels. *The Communist Manifesto*. New York: Verso, 1998.

———. *The German Ideology*. Edited by C. J. Arthur. New York: International Publishers, 1981.

Meikle, Scott. *Essentialism in the Thought of Karl Marx*. Chicago: Open Court Publishing, 1985.

Milbank, John. *Theology and Social Theory: Beyond Secular Reason*. Oxford, U.K.: Blackwell, 1990.

Moore, Michael. *Stupid White Men . . . and Other Sorry Excuses for the State of the Nation!* New York: Regan Books, 2002.

Peters, F.E.. *The Harvest of Hellenism*. New York: Simon and Schuster, 1971.

Rehnquist, William. *The Supreme Court: How It Is, How It Was.* New York: William Morrow & Co., 1988.

Revolutionary Communist Party. *Draft Programme.* Chicago: RCP Publications, May 2001.

————. "Initial statement on September 11, 2001." http://www.rwor. org.

————. "On the Position on Homosexuality in the New Draft Programme," 2001. http://www.rwor.org.

————. "On the Question of Homosexuality and the Emancipation of Women." *Revolution,* Spring 1988, pp. 40–55.

Rousseau, Jean-Jacques. *Discourse on the Origin and Foundations of Inequality.* In Rousseau, *The First and Second Discourses.* Edited by Roger Masters. Translated by Roger Masters and Judith Masters. New York: St. Martin's Press, 1964.

Sartre, Jean-Paul. *Anti-Semite and Jew.* Translated by George J. Becker. New York: Schocken Books, 1965.

————. "Colonialism Is a System." In Sartre, *Colonialism and Neo-Colonialism,* translated by Azzedine Haddour, Steve Brewer, and Terry McWilliams. London: Routledge, 1964.

————. *Critique of Dialectical Reason.* Vol. 1: Theory of Practical Ensembles. Edited by Jonathan Ree. Translated by Alan Sheridan-Smith. London: Verso, 1982.

————. *Critique of Dialectical Reason.* Vol. 2: The Intelligibility of History. Translated by Quintin Hoare. London: Verso, 1991.

————. *Search for a Method.* Translated by Hazel E. Barnes. New York: Vintage Books, 1968.

Schlosser, Eric. *Fast Food Nation: The Dark Side of the All-American Meal.* New York: Perennial Press, 2002.

Skybreak, Ardea. "Working with Ideas and Searching for Truth: A Reflection on Revolutionary Leadership and the Intellectual Process." *Revolutionary Worker,* March 24, 2002.

————. "Some Ideas on the Social Role of Art." *Revolutionary Worker,* August 12, 2001 to September 7, 2001.

Spengler, Oswald. *The Decline of the West.* 2 vols. Translated by Charles Francis Atkinson. New York: Alfred A. Knopf, 1996.

Stalin, Joseph V. *Economic Problems of Socialism in the U.S.S.R.* Peking: Foreign Languages Press, 1972.

————. "Foundations of Leninism: Lectures Delivered at the Sverdlov University." In J. V. Stalin, *Problems of Leninism.* Peking: Foreign Languages Press, 1976; pp. 1–116.

Volkogonov, Dmitri. *Stalin: Triumph and Tragedy.* Edited and translated by Harold Shukman. New York: Grove Weidenfeld, 1991.

Wolin, Richard. *Heidegger's Children: Hannah Arendt, Karl Lowith, Hans Jonas, and Herbert Marcuse.* Princeton, NJ: Princeton University Press, 2003.

Index